AGING IN MINORITY GROUPS

SAGE FOCUS EDITIONS

AGING IN MINORITY GROUPS

edited by
R. L. McNeely
John L. Colen and

FOREWORD by Lennie Marie Tolliver

SAGE PUBLICATIONS
Beverly Hills / London / New Delhi

For information address:

SAGE Publications, Inc.
275 South Beverly Drive
Beverly Hills, California 90212

SAGE Publications India Pvt. Ltd.
C-236 Defence Colony
New Delhi 110 024, India

SAGE Publications Ltd
28 Banner Street
London EC1Y 8QE, England

Printed in the United States of America

Library of Congress Cataloging in Publication Data

McNeely, R. L., and Colen, John N.
Aging in minority groups.

(Sage focus editions ; v. 61)
1. Minority aged—United States—Social conditions—
Addresses, essays, lectures. 2. Minority aged—United
States—Economic conditions—Addresses, essays, lectures.
3. Minority aged—Services for—United States—
Addresses, essays, lectures. I. McNeely, R. L.
II. Colen, John . [DNLM: 1. Aged. 2. Minority groups.
WT 30 A2685]
HQ1064.U5A6344   1983   305.2'6   83-3404
ISBN 0-8039-2008-3
ISBN 0-8039-2009-1 (pbk.)

FIRST PRINTING

AGING IN MINORITY GROUPS

Contents

Acknowledgments

The editors wish to express their appreciation to the executive administrative staff of the Division of Urban Outreach, University of Wisconsin-Milwaukee. Solicitation of chapters included in this volume could not have been accomplished without the resources they supplied. In addition, the editors wish to express their appreciation to William Feyerherm of the University of Wisconsin—Milwaukee for the numerous forms of assistance he provided, and to UWM's Sharon Hong-Morten and Aris Tjendra for word processing and typing services.

Foreword

I am pleased that Drs. R. L. McNeely and John N. Colen have seized the opportunity to present the issues, problems, and concerns of minority older persons in their book, *Aging in Minority Groups*. This volume serves the important function of increasing awareness of the minority elderly's uniqueness and furthering our efforts to be responsive to them. Publication of the articles presented in this text continues the very important and recent phenomenon wherein minority persons are examined and interpreted by social scientists who are themselves members of ethnic or racial minority groups. Having undergone experiences associated with minority group status, these writers can bring a sensitivity and commitment to the concerns and issues affecting the minority elderly rarely possible by those outside the framework of minority culture. We, therefore, look to them to understand and interpret accurately the integrated effects of culture, environment, and historical circumstance on the present-day lives of America's minority elderly.

With publication and, therefore, easy access to papers such as these, we are provided a rationale for the need to consider cultural differences as a relevant variable in making policy and program decisions. We are in a period of transition; a period in which we have witnessed a change from federal responsibility to authority and autonomy at the level of government closest to the people. We have witnessed high inflation and dwindling economic resources. These conditions have caused a reevaluation of the methods and means by which older persons in our society are helped to maintain their independence in their own communities. The information reported here will help responsible officials at all levels of government to make wise decisions about the targeting of specific individuals and groups for the provision of services. Additionally, these findings provide a platform for academics, service providers, and others in the helping professions to educate and train those in the field of aging to the responsibilities they must embrace and to the rich heritages of national minority groups.

This publication is extremely timely. There are dramatic changes in the growth and composition of the older population of this country. More individuals are reaching advanced age than at any other time in the history of our country. Minority individuals 60 years of age and older are increasing at a substantially greater rate than the general population, as well as the majority elderly population. This trend is expected to continue into the first quarter of the next century. This book comes at a time when all levels of government are trying to develop the capacity to relate to the increasing numbers of minority persons they will have to service; it comes at a time when service providers are trying to determine why the old outreach methods do not work, and why the old services are not as effective or as popular with these populations; it comes at a time when community groups, families, and the elderly themselves are seeking affirmation of their right to be different without appearing to be abnormal or pathologic.

My congratulations to Drs. McNeely and Colen. Their perseverance and their commitment have brought together in one place this collection of excellent works produced by some of the brightest stars in the study of aging. The contributors, too, should be commended for the elucidating articles they have written for this important volume. Nevertheless, such efforts cannot stop here. We are focused currently on today's elderly minority persons. But we must be ready for tomorrow's elders, for they will be different from today's elders. It is through continued efforts to enhance our knowledge and understanding of minority needs and concerns, as perceived by those we seek to serve, that we shall succeed.

Lennie Marie Tolliver
Commissioner
Administration on Aging

Preface

The compilation of *Aging in Minority Groups* grew out of the need for a systematic presentation of issues pertaining to the minority elderly. Over the past decade the number of publications in social gerontology has increased markedly. Yet an equivalent increase has not occurred with respect to publications addressing issues of particular relevance to the minority aged. In fact, only one book focused exclusively on the minority elderly was in print at the time this reader was undertaken and, to our knowledge, only one other was in progress. As educators, we found the dearth of literature on minority aging to seriously hamper students and practitioners alike in their efforts to understand the cultural meanings attached by minority elders to the process of aging, and to understand the adjustments these elders make to growing old.

Several features of this book make it distinct. First, as a collection of original papers and essays, it provides perspectives on culture and race as unique visages of aging. Second, those selections that relate to a specific minority group were written by members of the particular group under discussion. This was intentional in our efforts to capture the essence of the dynamics of aging within that group. Third, it departs from much of what is available as it examines not only the decrements of minority aging, but also highlights a variety of the more favorable aspects. Another significant feature of the book is that it outlines community as well as individual intervention strategies for practitioners seeking to assist minority elders both adjust to the reality of advancing age and to ward off some of the adverse circumstances associated with aging.

Inasmuch as *Aging in Minority Groups* is intended as a relatively comprehensive description of many of the dimensions of minority aging, it should prove beneficial to several audiences. Both instructors and students of undergraduate and graduate courses in disciplines such as gerontology, sociology, psychology, social work, nursing, and related fields should find it particularly useful as a primary text in some cases, and as a supplementary text in others. Others who may find it of interest include policy makers, planners, administrators, and direct practitioners in the human services network.

The book includes four thematic sections, each beginning with a brief survey of its contents. Following an introductory review, Part II demographically profiles the aged of each minority group (Asians, Blacks, Cubans, Mexicans, and Native-Americans) and highlights many of the more important implications for policy and programming. Part III focuses on the dynamics of aging within three specific cultural groups. In Part IV, selected social problems associated with aging and the particular impact of these problems on minorities are considered. Part V concludes the book and identifies a variety of impediments to effective service delivery to the minority aged. More important, proffered in this section are potentially valuable guidelines for the development of culturally syntonic services.

The completion of any book that brings a degree of enlightenment is an accomplishment in itself. For us and the contributors, achievement of the objectives for which this volume was compiled obviously would be a much greater accomplishment. Were these objectives realized students and others would become better informed, race and culture would become a policy-relevant variable, and services affecting the quality of life experienced by minority elders would be improved.

Usage of upper and lower case letters in this text conforms to the standard practice of capitalizing proper nouns. For example, the upper case "B" in Black is used to denote reference to a racial group. The lower case "w" in white denotes reference to color, not race.

R. L. McNeely
John N. Colen

PART I

Introduction

1

Minority Aging and Knowledge in the Social Professions
Overview of a Problem

JOHN N. COLEN and R. L. McNEELY

The central premise of this book is that minority aging warrants particular attention. Although inconsistencies may be found in literature focusing upon the importance of racial differences in aging (see Jackson & Walls, 1978; Manuel, 1982), the evidence nevertheless tends to suggest that people experience aging in significantly different ways. With regard to differences between members of minority and majority-group populations, an important element emphasizing the presence of experiential dissimilarities is captured in the following definition, in which a minority group is defined as:

> a group of people who, because of their physical or cultural characteristics, are singled out from others in the society in which they live for differential and unequal treatment, and who therefore regard themselves as objects of collective discrimination [Wirth, 1945].

Contributors to this volume subscribe to the notion that aging among minority and majority populations is not a uniform experience. On the other hand, it is acknowledged that some of the observable distinguishing features amount to differences of degree rather than differences singularly peculiar to any particular group. Whether they are substantive differences of degree or features peculiar to a particular group, these distinguishing factors do not merely differentiate minority and majority-group populations. Study of the cultural context of aging suggests substantial differences *among* the various minority groups. One obvious issue is the intensity of perceived discrimination. Members of some groups are the victims of harsher forms of discrimination, resulting in more difficult life circumstances.

The collection of papers included in this volume speak to the fact of significant differences existing among and within subpopulations of the aged.

15

Several major concerns are highlighted in this overview and an attempt is made to place the content of this volume into perspective. The ensuing discussion identifies some of the methodological issues that have plagued gerontological investigations and presents concerns regarding the applicability of findings generated by these investigations to the minority aged. Thereafter, two dominant and commonly recognized theories of aging are examined in light of their limitations in explaining minority aging. We subsequently argue that there are frameworks that call attention to historical and present-day differences in life experiences other than the dominant ones that are more productive in efforts to examine minority aging.

SOCIAL RESEARCH AND THE MINORITY AGED

Shanas (1975) has pointed out that two major themes have dominated gerontological inquiries during the last decade. One set of investigations has involved lifespan studies that sought to examine changes in people as they aged. A second set has concentrated on aging and social integration. While the lifespan studies were concerned mainly with changes in the same persons as they grew older, studies on the social integration of the aged focused upon the relationship between elders and the broader society. These studies have been major catalysts in drawing attention to aging issues and have been instrumental in forging the course of gerontological endeavors.

Increasingly, research in the aging arena has come under critical scrutiny. Research conducted on minority elders has been subject to many of the same criticisms that have characterized investigations in minority communities generally. Various indictments against the research enterprise pinpoint the complexities posed by such research and persistently call attention to both conceptual and methodological issues. Burton and Bengtson (1982) suggest that there are several recurring issues with regard to research utilizing minority elders as subjects that require careful attention. Three of these include (1) value biases brought by researchers that may preclude sensitivity to the unique issues involved; (2) the comparability of the groups being examined; and (3) community concerns about the research and other contextual issues that may affect the quality of the research.

These concerns are not without support. Several authors decry the perpetuation of stereotypical views of minorities and the tendency to approach the research task from a pathological perspective. Billingsley (1970) suggests that research has mirrored the prejudice, ignorance, and arrogance endemic to larger society. He contends that investigators, 90% of whom are white, cannot be separated from their role as members of society when they engage in research activities. Thus, he maintains that research begins and concludes with a strong value bias. Likewise, Cuellar (1980) argues that most research regarding the elderly Chicano population is of limited utility due to the researchers' penchant to distort, overromanticize, and stereotype critical elements of the Hispanic life experience. In a similar vein, Kitano (1969) contends that Asian-Americans have been stereotyped as a "model minority" with no severe or immediate problems. Sue and Sue (1972) assert that dominant cultural attributes, such as the characteristic reserve of Asian people, are viewed as negative traits in the wider society. Thus, by placing a negative judgment on these characteristics, researchers subtly, and sometimes blatantly, perpetuate negative stereotypes.

Social researchers examining aged members of minority groups have relied largely on comparative methods of inquiry. This has generated two primary areas of concern. First, there is the question of the extent to which groups are distinctive. Not only is this question applicable to minorities in relation to whites, but is also crucial as one compares various minority groups with each other. Certain groups, Asian-Americans and Hispanics in particular, must be examined in the light of sensitivity to factors such as immigration status, assimilation levels, and the like (Martinez, 1979; Orleans & Kurowski, 1977; Cuellar, 1980). A second area of controversy involves the comparability question within the context of validity issues. The vast majority of research studies in which inferences are made regarding aging in minority groups proceed from the premise of homogeneity between, among, and within groups. Evidence has been presented indicating that measures developed, validated, and standardized for one group frequently are inappropriate when applied to others (Padilla, 1972; Russell, 1970; Morgan & Bengtson, 1976). This points to the need to recognize that many of the research strategies used in studying the aged white population simply will not yield the data necessary fully to understand non-white cohorts.

Another factor threatening the acquistion of an adequate data base regarding minority elders is the increased resistance of minority-group members to being the objects of research investigations. Feelings of mistrust and exploitation abound (Sue & Sue, 1972; Ragan & Cuellar, 1975). Although much of this skepticism has been leveled at white social scientists, Couchman (1973), Maykovich (1977), and others have noted that minority researchers meet with their own brand of resistance. Each author agrees that these sentiments reveal themselves in a variety of ways. Whether they are manifested by the level of cooperation in facilitating the conduct of research by influencing responses or by other means, they exert profound influence on the outcome of research attempts. Thus, each concedes that to be successful, investigators must demonstrate sensitivity to minority concerns, suspicions must be eliminated, and the research itself must contribute something to the community in return for the cooperation of community members. These issues attest to the significant challenges that research entails in minority communities.

THEORETICAL PERSPECTIVES ON AGING AND
THE MINORITY AGED

Gerontological theory is expected to explain phenomena that underlie the aging process. There appears to be rather common agreement that current theoretical frameworks remain inadequate and are of limited utility in accurately predicting adaptation to aging or explaining behavior in old age (Jackson, 1980). Nevertheless, of the fair number of these frameworks (see, for example, Atchley, 1972), several have assumed more or less universal application despite the absence of consistent empirical support. Perhaps the two most important are the disengagement and activity frameworks. Therefore, they are emphasized here. Although they include incompatible notions, deductions drawn from each are proffered as prescriptions for successful aging.

Clearly the most controversial is disengagement, and as defined by its proponents, is an inevitable process in which the individual and society make a gradual and mutual withdrawal. Viewed as a means by which society avoids major disruptions that the exit of large numbers of people might bring about, it holds that the individual is freed from the constraints of earlier life norms and is content to live with symbols of the past (Cummings & Henry, 1961; Cummings, 1976).

Conversely, activity theory holds that the norms of middle age remain consistent throughout the later years of life, and that successful aging is dependent on the extent to which roles and relationships of middle age can be sustained (Havighurst, 1963; Lemon, Bengtson, & Peterson, 1976). In short, a key assumption of activity theory is that morale and life satisfaction are a function of continued active participation in important spheres of life.

Critics have not been hesitant to question these frameworks and have labeled them theoretical orientations rather than theories in the formal sense. Atchley (1972), for example, points out a number of the concerns raised with regard to their applicability, suggesting that they do not have universal generalizability.

Gerontologists who are members of minority groups, as some of the chapters in this volume illustrate, have been quick to assert that differences in life experiences among minority and majority elderly limit the inferences that can be drawn. As Rey has noted,

While the controversy regarding activity and disengagement in the field of gerontology has concerned the consistency of empirical support for one or the other of the two theories, the central issue for minorities is the validity of both rationales. As a matter of fact, most theoretical orientations in gerontology— whether the central concept is "disengagement," "activity," "continuity," or "development"—ignore, or fail to treat sufficiently, the historically based differences between the majority culture and life in the minority communities [1982, p. 192].

He suggests that any framework that fails to incorporate a historical perspective should be viewed as suspect. The fact that rudiments of coping and adaptive styles in old age can be found at earlier stages in life is presented in the work of some of the most prominent gerontologists (see Neugarten, 1964,; Maddox, 1966; Shanas, 1975). Yet, these and other gerontologists have downplayed differences, tending much more often to emphasize similarities among the aged and, consequently, have virtually ignored the early life experiences of members of minority groups.

Other conceptual frameworks incorporate a historical perspective and perhaps are more fruitful for understanding aging in minority groups. For example, Chestang (1971) explored character development in what he termed a hostile environment, and introduced a model for understanding the interplay between Blacks and their environment, and the adjustments made to the environment. Chestang's central point is that Blacks (and other victimized minority-group members) historically have encountered three conditions that are socially determined and institutionally supported. These conditions include (1) social injustice (the denial of legal rights); (2) social inconsistency (the social immorality perpetrated on the oppressed group by the manners, morals, and traditions of the majority group, which majority-group individuals use to express group rejection of minority-group individuals); and (3) personal impotence (the sense of being powerless to influence the environment). He maintains that these three crucial conditions are of critical importance in shaping the character and societal responses of Blacks (and other oppressed minority-group members).

Several of Chestang's notions merit some elaboration. To begin with, what or how a person is, is determined in great measure by the interface between his or her family, subculture, and society. Society is expected to provide the sustaining environment including goods, services, education, and other commodities. Conversely, the family or subculture provides the nurturing environment in which feelings of belonging, self-esteem, personal identity, and similar elements of well-being are developed. For majority-group Americans, society more or less fulfills its sustaining function. By contrast, society has largely failed members of minority groups. Implicit in Chestang's argument is that when one element fails (society), another (family or subculture) must bear the brunt of its failure. This notion points to the conditions that have led to strong kinship bonds, mutual aid, and similar attributes reported to be prevalent within minority cultures. Historically, the elderly have been pivotal in maintaining these aspects of minority life.

Another interesting framework has been presented by Moore (1971). It, too, incorporates a historical perspective. The essential elements of her model focus upon a special history, the presence of discrimination, and particular coping structures involving subcultural variations. She maintains that these are common aspects of the minority experience, but notes that the content of each varies by group. Both the Chestang and Moore models provide beneficial insight into minority-group situations. However, Moore's framework is more applicable to aged minorities in that it more easily allows for within and among-group comparisons.

SELECTED HISTORICAL EVENTS

As one way to highlight further the failure of dominant aging theories to provide insight with regard to members of minority groups, a brief perusal of selected significant historical events may be instructive.

Native-Americans have had a unique history characterized by long periods of conflict, conquest, and expropriation. Moreover, because of their special relationship with the federal government, there has been a series of treaties and legislation negotiated and passed, with long-term effects. Following the landmark Northwest Ordinance of 1781, the Indian Trade and Intercourse Act of 1834 established control of Indian trade by requiring those with whom Native-Americans traded to be licensed. The Dawes Act, passed in 1887, was to allocate land to individuals, 160 acres to adults and 80 acres to children, thereby terminating tribes and converting hunters to farmers who would require less land. An underlying assumption was that it was easier to take land away from individuals than tribes. This assumption was borne out by the Indians' loss of over ninety million acres while the act was in effect (Slaughter, 1976). While this early legislation set the tone for Native-American and governmental relationships, there are other acts with which the current elderly population has had direct experience. The Indian Reorganization Act of 1934 provided the basis for most present-day reservation constitutions. While this act was purported to make Native-American tribes self-sustaining, it retained much tribalism dependency (Tyler, 1973; Grafton, Randall, & Blacksmith, 1982). Perhaps the most significant legislation of this century has been the Voluntary American Indian Relocation Program. This program provided a minimum subsidy for urban migration and employment placement. Faced with little orientation to the situation—menial jobs, deplorable housing, and other adverse conditions—most participants returned to the reservation.

Though some Indians were granted citizenship as early as 1887, it was not until 1924 that all were granted citizenship through the Citizenship Act. It was not until 1948 that all Indians were granted the right to vote and it has been shockingly recent (1953) that governmentally imposed regulations on their use of intoxicants were removed. This unique relationship with the government served to subordinate the Indian and has engendered a number of Indian myths, affected family structure and values, and fostered festering mistrust and suspicions commonly found among elderly Native-Americans (Locklear, 1972; Red Horse, 1980).

If one were to explore the histories of Asian-Americans, Blacks, and Mexican-Americans, incidents of equal import would emerge. For Asian-Americans, a group of many peoples, exclusionary immigration and natural-ization laws, hostile public opinion, mob violence, and other acts of persecu-tion have led to distinct cultural responses to mainstream society (Chen, 1971; Watanabe, 1973). Correspondingly, the ravages of slavery, the Jim Crow era, and other social forces have taken their toll on the structure of Black families, the Black psyche, and other aspects of Black life (Frazier, 1957; Gillespie, 1975). Too, Mexican-Americans have not been spared from historically traumatic experiences in this society. Migration into this country into special economic slots, mass deportation, and similar events have had profound effects (Alvarez, 1971).

When the unique histories of minority group members are evaluated, it is necessary to look beyond specific incidents and the negative circumstances that surround them. Not to do so precludes development of an appreciation for the individual and group strengths that have developed. Despite adverse circumstances, mutual aid, strong kinship bonds, and flexible family bound-aries tend to characterize minority lifestyles; thus, each group has developed its own system of in-group supports and has emerged with a remarkably stable cultural base.

CONCLUDING REMARKS

A number of problems regarding social science knowledge with respect to minority aging have been identified. Succeeding chapters provide informa-tion underscoring the different life experiences members of the various mi-nority groups have been subjected to historically and which they experience currently. Of the Hispanic groups, Cubans are noteworthy in that they have been victimized far less than members of the other groups. Nevertheless, their special circumstances, along with the fact that little has been written about them, warrant their inclusion.

As our prior discussion has suggested, frameworks that can take into ac-count the historical circumstances of minority elders, along with the differ-ential intensities of present-day discrimination suffered by the various groups, must be developed if our predictive capabilities (a key function of theory) are to be enhanced. In the meanwhile, the case needs to be made that the circumstances of minority elders are decidedly different. As noted previ-ously, viewpoints have been expressed in the literature as to whether or not minority aging is different than majority aging. Although some differences are merely matters of degree, others are not. Chapters following this discus-sion, in our view, make this point unequivocally, and several contributors offer practical guidelines about what human service practitioners and others may seek to do in addressing these differences.

REFERENCES

Alvarez, Rodolfo. The unique psycho-historical experience of the Mexican-American people. *Social Science Quarterly* 1971, 52(1), 68–77.

Atchley, Robert C. *The social forces in later life: An introduction to social gerontology.* Belmont, CA: Wadsworth, 1972.

Billingsley, Andrew. Black families and white social science. *Journal of Social Issues,* 1970, 26(3), 127–142.

Burton, Linda & Bengtson, Vern L. Research in elderly minority communities: Problems and potentials. In Ron C. Manuel (Ed.), *Minority aging: Sociological and social psychological issues.* Westport, CT: Greenwood Press, 1982.

Chen, Pei Ngor. Chinatown ferment. *Gidra,* February 1971.

Chestang, Leon. *Character development in a hostile environment.* Chicago: University of Chicago, School of Social Service Administration, 1971.

Couchman, I. S. B. Notes from a white researcher in Black society. *Journal of Social Issues,* 1973, 29(1), 45–52.

Cuellar, Jose. An expanded outline and resource guide for teaching an introduction to Hispanic aging. In George Sherman (Ed.), *Curriculum Guidelines in Minority Aging.* Washington, DC: National Center on the Black Aged, 1980.

Cummings, Elaine. Further thoughts on the theory of disengagement. In Cary S. Kart and Barbara B. Manard (Eds.), *Aging in America.* New York: Alfred, 1976.

Cummings, Elaine & Henry, William. *Growing old: The Process of disengagement.* New York: *Basic Books,* 1961.

Frazier, E. Franklin. *The negro family in the United States.* New York: Macmillan, 1957.

Gillespie, Bonnie J. The black family in the American society. *Journal of Afro-American Issues,* 1975, 3(3 & 4), 324-345.

Grafton, Patricia, Randall, Julie & Blacksmith, Kathryn. Implementation of the Indian Child Welfare Act of 1978 in Sacramento and Santa Clara Counties. Unpublished Master's thesis, Sacramento: California State University, School of Health and Human Services, Division of Social Work, 1982.

Havighurst, Robert J. Successful aging. In Richard Williams, Clark Tibbits, & Wilma Donahue (Eds.), *Processes of Aging.* New York: Atherton Press, 1963.

Jackson, Jacquelyn J. *Minorities and Aging,* Belmont, CA: Wadsworth, 1980.

Jackson, Jacquelyn & Walls, Bertram. Myths and realities about blacks. In Mollie Brown (Ed.), *Readings in Gerontology* (2nd ed. Saint Louis: C. V. Mosby, 1978.

Kitano, Harry. Japanese Americans: The evolution of the subculture. Englewood Cliffs, NJ: Prentice-Hall, 1969.

Lemon, Bruce, Bengtson, Vern & Peterson, James. An exploration of the activity theory of aging: Activity types and life satisfaction among in-movers to a retirement community. In Cary S. Kart and Barbara B. Manard (Eds.), *Aging in America.* New York: Alfred, 1976.

Locklear, Herbert H. American indian myths. *Social Work,* May 1972, 72-80.

Maddox, George L. Persistence of life among the elderly: A longitudinal study of patterns of social activity in relation to life satisfaction. In *Proceedings of the Seventh International Congress of Gerontology,* 1966.

Manuel, Ron C. *The Aged Black in America.* Washington, DC: National Urban League, 1982.

Martinez, Maria Zuniga de. Family policy for Mexican-Americans and their aged. *Urban and Social Change Review, 1979,* 12(2), 16-19.

Maykovich, Minako K. The differences of a minority researcher in minority communities. *Journal of Social Issues,* 1977, 33(4), 108-119.

Moore, Joan W. Situational factors affecting minority aging. *Gerontologist,* 1971, 11(1), 88-93.

Morgan, Leslie & Bengston, Vern L. *Measuring perceptions of aging across social strata.* Paper presented at the Twenty-Ninth Annual Meeting of the Gerontological Society, New York, 1976.

Neugarten, Bernice L. *Personality in middle age and late life: Empirical studies.* New York: Atherton Press, 1964.

Orleans, Miriam & Kurowshi, Bettina. Give up stereotypes look for differences within. Generations, 1977, 2(2), 14.

Padilla, Amado. Psychological research and the Mexican American. In M. Mangold (Ed.), *La Causa Chicana.* New York Family Service Association of America, 1972.

Red Horse, John. Family structure and value orientation in American Indians. *Social Casework,* 1980, 61, 462-467.

Regan, Pauline, & Cuellar, Jose. Response acquiescence in surveys: A study of yeasaying among Chicanos and Anglos. Paper presented at the Annual Meeting of the American Association for Public Opinion Research, Los Angeles.

Rey, Antonio B. Activity and disengagement: Theoretical orientations in social gerontology and minority aging. In Ron C. Manuel (Ed.), *Minority aging: Sociological and social psychological issues.* Westport, CT: Greenwood Press, 1982.

Russell, R. D. Black perceptions of guidance. *Personnel and Guidance Journal,* 1970, 48, 721-728.

Shanas, Ethel. Gerontology and the social sciences: Where do we go from here? *Gerontologist,* 1975, 15(6), 499-502.

Slaughter, Ellen. Indian Child Welfare: A Review of the Literature. Denver, CO: University of Denver, Denver Research Institute, 1976.

Sue, Derald & Sue, Stanley. Ethnic minorities: Resistance to being researched. Professional Psychology, 1972, 3, 11-17.

Tyler, S. Lyman. *A History of Indian Policy.* Washington, DC: Government Printing Office, 1973.

Watanabe, Colin. Self-expression and the Asian-American experience. *Personnel and Guidance Journal,* 1973, 51(6), 390-396.

Wirth, L. The problem of minority groups. In R. Linton (Ed.), *The Science of Man in the World Crisis.* New York: Columbia University Press, 1945.

PART II

The Demography of Minority Aging

Demographic data indicate that older people comprise the fastest growing segment of the population. Since 1900 there has been an eightfold increase of older persons. Current statistics show that there are over 25 million individuals in the United States who are 65 years old or older; therefore, slightly more than 11% of the population is elderly. By the year 2000, it is projected that the proportion of older people will exceed 13%.

There are a number of reasons for the steady increase. Advances in medical technology have promoted a significant decline in mortality rates at the upper end of the age spectrum. Infectious diseases, to which the young are more susceptible, largely have been controlled. Therefore, more individuals are reaching ages considered unattainable just a few decades ago. Proportionately large numbers of individuals born around the turn of the century have now survived to old age. As a result, there has been a significant increase in the actual number of persons aged 65 or older. In addition to fertility, mortality, and life expectancy factors, foreign migratory patterns have contributed to the current U.S. age structure.

The rapid growth of the aged population has forced recognition of important differences among the elderly. No longer are the aged viewed as a single homogenous group. Instead, different age groupings now are referred to by terms such as "young-old" (60 to 75 years of age), "middle-old" (75 to 85), and "very aged" (85 and older). Implicit in these references is a recognition that members of each group tend to have their own problems, needs, and desires. While the phenomenon of extended lifespans is hailed as a great advance, it also raises many questions as to the capability of the system to sustain the elderly in a manner in which they (many of whom are potentially dependent) can live their lives in dignity.

Understanding the minority aged requires simultaneous examination of sociocultural and demographic factors if ethnic strengths are to be assessed properly within the context of their underclass status within larger society. It is appropriate, therefore, that specific attention be directed to the minority aged because any informed social gerontology student should have an understanding and appreciation of the implications of those demographic and ecological factors that distinguish minority and nonminority groups.

Comparatively, members of national minority groups make up a small proportion of the aged population. In 1980, while somewhat over 83% of those 65 and over were white, only 11.7% were Black, 3% were Hispanic, less than 1.5% were Asian, and .6% were Native American. Population characteristics vary among the different groups. In illustration, about 7.9% of the Black population is 65 years of age or older, compared to about 4.9% of Hispanics, a little more than 5.3% of Native Americans, and slightly more than 6% of the Asian population; 12% of the white population is 65 years of age or older. Thus, the minority populations tend to be younger, with much smaller percentages of elders than whites. However, some subgroups within minority clusters are not consistent with this broad pattern. For example, Cubans have a much larger proportion of persons aged 65 years or older than other Hispanics or other minority groups, and a somewhat larger proportion of elders than non-Cuban whites.

These are but a few of the demographic factors that distinguish elderly minorities from their white counterparts. For too long, elderly minority groups have been treated as if they were one. It is important to recognize that culture, life experiences, and demographic factors suggest considerable variation between them that is not easily gleaned from aggregated data. This first section of the book, therefore, focuses on salient demographic trends regarding each minority group's elderly population and examines in selected cases minority and nonminority dissimilarities focusing upon life expectancy, educational achievement, economic status, regional distributions, and other differences. As discussed by each author in this section, these distinctions are suggestive of implications for policy development and other concerns.

In the first chapter, Paul Kim reports on the phenomenal increase in the Asian-Pacific population. Recognizing that "Asian" is an umbrella term encompassing a number of nationalities, he outlines many of their unique features. Kim notes how past lack of interest to treat Asians as a separate racial group in various government reports, along with the lack of consensus in defining Asian ethnicities, has created many enumeration difficulties. Nevertheless, Kim explores the impact that immigration patterns, various laws, and other factors have had in shaping the composition and subsequent life conditions of the Asian-Pacific group.

Wilbur Watson profiles the Black elderly. His essay describes the growth and current distribution older Blacks. Although the majority of Black elders live in metropolitan areas, Watson draws attention to the special plight of those living in rural pockets of poverty. He concludes with a discussion of various policy and programming implications.

Magaly Queralt chronicles the little-known experience of older Cubans in this country. A discussion of selected demographic characteristics and the most pressing problems follows her brief historical overview. Cubans have the highest proportion of elderly persons of all Spanish-origin groups in the United States, and the second largest Hispanic elderly population. Queralt provides a number of important policy-relevant recommendations.

In the next reading, Ramon Valle provides a summary of facts about the elderly Mexican-American population. There is some overlap between this chapter and the preceding one; however, Valle succinctly presents a number of issues and concerns specifically germane to elderly Mexican-Americans. Although some gains can be anticipated during the coming decade, the author projects that many of the factors adversely impacting on this group will remain as major impediments to the progress of its members.

Finally, E. Daniel Edwards highlights significant demographic features with respect to Native-American elders and provides an informative disquisition of issues related to their economic conditions, health, mental health, housing, family support, and traditional values and customs.

These five selections, if pursued as a unit of material, should enable the reader to appreciate the more detailed analysis of minority age-related issues in the remainder of the book.

2

Demography of the Asian-Pacific Elderly
Selected Problems and Implications

PAUL K. H. KIM

No one can deny the fact that America is populated by immigrants from all over the world. American immigration policies were much more liberal for the people of European countries than for Asians and Pacific Islanders until the Act (P.L. 89-236) of October 3, 1965 was legislated by the U.S. Congress (U.S. Department of Justice, 1966). Before that time, under the quota system, only 2,790 Asians were admitted to American territory by law; approximately 100 persons per country per year except for Indonesia, Japan, and other Asian areas, which had quota allocations of 200, 185, and 1,400 respectively (U.S. Department of Justice, 1966). Since 1970, the United States has been bringing in approximately 400,000 immigrants annually, and about one-third of them were from Asian countries (primarily China-Taiwan, Hong Kong, India, Indonesia, Japan, Korea, the Philippines, Pacific Oceania, and recently Thailand and Vietnam).

Nationalities or ethnicities among Asians are rather confusing in that the Department of Justice classifies Asians as being immigrants from *all* Asian countries—Pacific Islands, Far East, South East, and Near-Middle East, whereas the Bureau of the Census identifies them as being individuals with Asian/Pacific Islands' ethnicities (Japanese, Chinese, Filipino, Korean, Vietnamese, Asian Indians, Hawaiians, Guamians, and Samoans). The U.S. Commission on Civil Rights (1979), in its hearing on civil rights issues of Asian-Pacific Americans, appeared to imply that this particular minority group consisted of those who had an ethnic background of the Far East, Southeast Asia, or Pacific Islands. Social agencies designed to serve Asian-Americans (i.e., the Asian American Mental Health Research Center, the Pacific/Asian Coalition, the National Pacific/Asian Resource Center on Aging) appear to concentrate on those people who come primarily from the Pacific Islands, China (including Hong Kong and Taiwan), Japan, Korea, Vietnam, Thailand,

Cambodia, and other southeastern countries; they evidently minimize or even exclude individuals from Iran, Iraq, Israel, Jordan, Lebanon, Syria, and Turkey, who are included in the Department of Justice's Asian classification.

For this chapter, an Asian elder is defined as an older person (age sixty and older) who has come from an Asian country as classified by the Bureau of the Census. It is a rather commonly understood definition encompassing all ethnicities of the Far East, Southeast Asia, and the Pacific Islands. Interestingly enough, the 1981 Conference of the Southern Gerontological Society had a session on minority aging that included the Jewish elderly; the International Conference on Aging sponsored by the University of Hawaii School of Social Work in 1981 had representatives of Indian nationality; and the Council on Social Work Education appears to adopt the U.S. Census definition of Asians. Thus, unlike other minority elderly groups, multiple ethnicities are characteristic of Asian-Americans.

The objectives of this chapter are to enumerate and describe the current Asian-American elderly population and their specific needs, and to discuss public policy implications to better serve this particular segment of the minority elderly.

ASIAN-AMERICAN ELDERLY

It is extremely difficult even to estimate the number of Asian elderly living in this country due to the lack of research on them, to their dispersion throughout the nation, the lack of government interest in including "Asians" as a separate racial group until the 1980 census, the lack of consensus on Asian ethnicities, and to the steady increase of the number of Asian immigrants in the 1970s. According to the 1970 census, Asian-Americans amounted to 1% of the total population, or 2,089,932 individuals. The 1980 census reports Asians to be 1.5% or 3,500,636 individuals. Thus, Asians have increased by 67% during the last decade. The wave of Asian immigration has been the result of a 1965 Act (Public Law 89-236), which repealed the immigration quota and opened the doors to immigration. Implementation of the act allowed an influx of Asians which accounted for approximately one-third of the total U.S. immigrants in the 1970s; numbering, for example, 138,685 Asians in 1977 (30% of the total 462,315 immigrants). During the 1970s, approximately 1.3 million Asians came to the United States; the Chinese-Taiwanese, Koreans, and Filipinos constituted the three major Asian nationalities who immigrated into the United States in 1979 (U.S. Department of Justice, 1979). They were admitted to the country under various entitlements: (1) unmarried sons and daughters of U.S. citizens, and their children; (2) spouses, unmarried sons and daughters of resident aliens, and their children; (3) professionals; (4) married sons and daughters of U.S. citizens, their spouses and children; (5) brothers and sisters of U.S. citizens,

their spouses and children; (6) other workers; and (7) conditional entrants who may become permanent residents after two years. Under these immigration preferences, between 1965 and 1976, the number of Asian immigrants increased by over 1,000%, while the national average increase was only 34.4% and the Europeans decreased by 36.2% (U.S. Department of Justice, 1976).

Such a tide of Asian immigrants has provided many professionals needed by the United States; professionals such as natural scientists, social scientists, health workers (physicians, surgeons, dentists, nurses, pharmacists, and others), engineers, lawyers, professors, clergymen, social workers, teachers, and the like. Until the mid-1960s, America used to import these professionals primarily from Europe, North America (Canada and Mexico), and South America, but this trend has changed. Between 1970 and 1977, the median percentage of immigrating professionals from Asian countries was more than one-half of the total professional immigrants or 55.5 percent, as shown in Table 2-1.

Asia has been the most important source for various professionals needed by the country during the past fifteen years. More than one out of five Asian immigrants since 1965 were trained professionals in various scientific and human service disciplines. Many of those professionals were granted naturalized American citizenship and in turn were able to petition on behalf of their siblings and aged parents for immigration into the United States. In 1978 alone, for example, 173,535 immigrants were naturalized: 33%

**TABLE 2-1   Percentage of Immigrant Professionals:
Year by Continent**

Year	Europe	Asia*	N. America**	S. America	Africa	Oceania	Total number
1977	18	48	18	5	5	1	45,000
1976	20	55	11	4	4	1	41,068
1975	19	57	11	4	4	1	38,491
1974	18	56	11	4	4	1	35,483
1973	18	56	12	4	4	1	41,147
1972	16	58	12	3	4	1	48,887
1971	16	54	14	4	4	1	48,850
1970	22	47	13	4	7	1	46,151
1969	25	39	20	5	5	1	40,427
1968	33	24.5	29.5	5.5	2.5	1	48,753
1967	35	27	25	5	2	1	41,652
1966	40	16	29	8	2	1	30,099
1965	45	5	34	11	2	1	28,790
1964	44	8	31	12	2	1	28,756

SOURCE: U.S. Department of Justice (1964-1977).
*From countries included in the definition of Asia and Pacific Islands.
**From Canada and Mexico.

(58,065) were Asians (U.S. Department of Justice, 1978). The fact that many brought their aged parents with them exemplifies their filial duty, which has long been cherished in various Asian cultures.

With this background information, it is helpful to make two assumptions in order to estimate the number of Asian elderly people in this country: (1) that the natural increase of Asian-American population during the 1970s has been at the rate of 5.9 per 1,000 per year (a national estimate), as reported by the 1976 U.S. Vital Statistics; and (2) that the elderly immigrants who have come here since 1970 are still alive in the United States. Based on these suppositions, it can be calculated that there were approximately 444,000 Asian elderly here in 1980-1981—337,000 by natural increase, and 107,000 by immigration. Another way to estimate this particular population is to project at a conservative rate of 15% of the total Asian population of 1980, that is 525,000 elderly. Putting these two estimates together, the number of Asian elderly in the United States is assumed to be about one-half million, namely between 444,000 and 525,000. The natural increase of the Asian elderly population since 1970, and the elderly immigrants by annual cohort groups are presented in Table 2-2.

Almost one-half of the Asian elderly today were born in this country around the turn of the century, or came to the United States during the early 1900s. Most, if not all of them, were discriminated against under such laws as the Chinese Exclusion Act of 1882, the Scott Act of 1888, the Gentlemen's Agreement of 1907, the Japanese Alien Land Law of 1913, the Philippine Exclusion Act of 1934, the Impoundment of Japanese Descendents during 1941-1946, the Denial of Citizenship to First Generation Asians in 1922, the

TABLE 2-2   An Estimate of Asian-American Elderly in 1980-1981

Year	Natural Growth Total[a]	Natural Growth 60 +[b]	Elderly Immigrant Cohorts Immigrants[c]	Elderly Immigrant Cohorts Accumulative	Accumulative Total Asian Elderly
1980	2,216,564	336,918	13,394[d]	106,785	443,703
1979	2,203,563	334,942	13,394[d]	93,391	428,333
1978	2,190,638	332,977	13,394[d]	79,997	412,974
1977	2,177,789	331,024	13,394	66,603	397,627
1976	2,165,016	329,128	11,725	53,209	382,337
1975	2,152,317	327,152	9,177	41,484	368,636
1974	2,130,693	323,865	8,794	32,307	356,172
1973	2,127,142	323,326	7,594	23,513	346,839
1972	2,114,666	321,429	5,727	15,919	337,348
1971	2,102,263	319,545	4,388	10,192	329,737
1970	2,089,932	317,670	5,804	5,804	323,474

SOURCE: Department of Commerce Bureau of the Census, 1970 and 1980, Census Advanced Report
a. Estimated at the 1976 U.S. death rate of 8.9/1000 and the birth rate of 14.8/1000.
b. Estimated at the national proportion of 15.2%.
c. Department of Justice (1970-1977).
d. Estimated at the same level as 1977.

Anti-Miscegenation Statute of 1935, and more recently the Public Law 95-507 that excluded the Asian group as a protected minority under the definition of "socially and economically disadvantaged" (U.S. Commission on Civil Rights, 1979). They are still victims of social isolation resulting from earlier denial of property rights, and discrimination against them for public jobs. Thus, it is not too surprising that most of them are less educated, monolingual, more economically deprived, and more emotionally wounded than many other U.S. elderly citizens.

It is also estimated, based on the 1980 census, that 55% of the total Asian elderly are living in three western states (California, Hawaii, and Washington), 12% in two northeastern states (New York and New Jersey), and 8% in two midwestern states (Illinois and Texas). Thus, about 25% reside in the remaining states. Approximately 15% of them live in rural America, where the early settlers established their family roots as farmers, either as farm owners or migrant farm workers (Yu, 1980).

NEEDS OF THE PACIFIC/ASIAN ELDERLY

The mini-White House Conference on the Pacific/Asian Elderly, held in January 1981 under the sponsorship of the National Pacific/Asian Resource Center on Aging, identifies five areas of need: health care, income, social services, nutrition, and housing.

Health care needs. The advancement of human age brings various health problems. Functional decreases of body organs make an aged person vulnerable to viruses and their mobility is lessened. Needless to say, such physiological changes will occur among Pacific/Asians just as among all other aged persons. However, the majority of Pacific/Asian elderly, being foreign born, monolingual, economically deprived, and having fears and suspicion of government (U.S. Commission on Civil Rights, 1979), tend to practice folk medicine or to depend upon friends and family members for aid with their health problems. Many Chinese and Korean elderly people still feel comfortable with organic folk medications and distrust "chemical-synthetic" medicines. Consequently, some folk medicines are available in larger cities of the United States where Chinese, Japanese, and Korean populations concentrate. Many elderly people still order such medications from their own countries, and keep them for emergencies. This kind of approach to health problems among the Chinese ethnic elderly can be seen as a cause of underutilization of Medicare and Medicaid, though detailed health needs among them have not been documented.

Income needs. More than one out of five Pacific/Asian elders have incomes below the poverty level, which is a 33% higher proportion than the national average. The poverty figures are much worse among elderly female heads of households or unrelated females, about 31.1% to 40.4%, and at

30% among the rural elderly. Approximately 30% of the Asian elderly (age 65 and older) participate in the labor force. Nevertheless, due to limited educational attainments (about 6 years of schooling on the average, though higher among Japanese elderly with 8.5 years) and to language limitations (only 1.4% of the foreign-born Chinese elderly and 0.7% of the Japanese elderly speak English as a mother tongue), they are primarily involved in self-employment, service areas, and farming. (Almost 30% of the Filipino elderly are involved in farming.) Those elderly who have worked as migrant farmers, particularly the Filipino elderly, are not qualified for Social Security benefits. And, due to their work at cheap labor rates, most of them have no private or public pensions for their retirement.

Social service needs. Because of the insensitivity of public and private social service agencies to the cultural and language barriers of the Asian elderly, these elders underutilize all social service entitlements. Thus they are relatively unserved and kept uninformed about available services. There are few bilingual staff who can provide necessary services, and few publications that inform the elderly as to new and modified benefits, means to obtain services, and so on. Unless there exists a particular ethnic elderly program, such as ethnic senior centers, almost all of the elderly do not or cannot use social programs to which they are entitled.

The public insensitivity toward the Pacific/Asian elderly could stem from the myth that they are well cared for by their own children through their extended family system. But most of the Asians who immigrated during the early 1900s had to remain unmarried as a result of immigration laws that did not allow female immigration, though some of them married rather late in years through a "picture bride" arrangement. Many children of those who were able to marry, due in part to the stress in Western culture on the nuclear family, and to the emphasis on geographical mobility, left their foreign-born parents and established their own families in distant areas. Thus many Pacific/Asian elderly are living alone by themselves, depending perhaps more on their friends and neighbors for support than on their own children.

Nutritional needs. A diet of good food in sufficient amount is a major component of good health; the elderly person who eats well can maintain better health throughout his or her remaining life. The foreign-born elderly still wish to eat their ethnic foods at least once a day. They want it not because of its nutritional quality, but because of habit and custom.

Pacific/Asian food is not of a single type. Each Asian country has its own diet distinct in taste, style, and manner of cooking. Although some of the ingredients of ethnic foods may be available or replaced in this country, others need to be imported from countries where they originate. This implies higher costs for such imported food substances and also implies costs at unaffordable levels for the elderly who have limited and fixed incomes. Altogether, one may speculate that the elderly Asians have poor quality diets and are dissatisfied with their meals.

Housing needs. Many Pacific/Asian elderly live alone: 26.2% and 67.1% of the Chinese elderly men and women, respectively, live alone; 50% of all Japanese households outside of the West are one-person households, and 70% of these are women living alone; 28.1% of the Filipino elderly have never married. Another interesting statistic is that although the majority of the Asian elderly live in primarily urban/metropolitan larger cities, there are some older persons living in rural areas: 15% and 22.1% of the Japanese and Filipino elderly, respectively.

It is unknown as to whether the Pacific/Asian elderly own their homes or rent apartments or rooms. It may be speculated, however, due to an earlier denial of their property rights and their low wages, that most of them rent their living quarters. This means that they are experiencing housing shortages in both urban and rural areas, as all other aged persons do. Some fortunate elderly are living in subsidized apartments, although they may have to pay an increased share under the new budget cut proposal. Some unfortunate elderly, particularly in rural and colder areas outside of Hawaii and Southern California, are experiencing severe housing and energy problems. Those who have been receiving Social Security minimum payments of $122 per month may face serious problems. Even though Social Security benefits have increased by 42% since 1975, fuel oil costs have risen by 136%, natural gas is up by 126%, and electric rates have risen by 74%. In addition, the Farmers Home Administration program cut of $103 million may decrease the housing units for the rural elderly as well (Pepper, 1981).

Postfigurative role loss. This is another major concern, identified by the Mini-White House Conference on the Pacific/Asian Elderly. Mead (1970) defines the postfigurative culture as a stable one wherein children learn primarily from their forefathers. Such a system characterizes many Asian cultures with grandparents or other older persons viewed as important determinants of their descendants' survival possibilities. However, in a technological country such as the United States, the postfigurative role is less important and its loss is compounded by the empty-nest syndrome and monolingual disability. Thus, in their new country the elderly become roleless as they are increasingly victimized by deteriorating health and mental health conditions (Karl, Sidney & Brooks 1968).

POLICY IMPLICATIONS FOR
THE ASIAN-AMERICAN ELDERLY

As implied earlier, the Asian population consists of diverse ethnicities. Many ethnically distinct characteristics lose their identity when individuals are subsumed within an aggregated minority group. Each subpopulation of the Asian group, including Chinese-Americans, Japanese-Americans, Korean-Americans, Indian-Americans, and so on, has its own ethnicity (customs, values, diets). Obviously, it is useful to recognize these differences for some purposes. However, this diversity has been reinforced by public agencies in order to increase within-group competition as each subgroup pursues funding from federal and other sources for services. As a consequence, the Asian elderly population is still being underserved, and is being misused by service planners who less effectively plan for their survival.

In order to alleviate these unfortunate consequences of multiple ethnicities, the following public policies are recommended:

Unified policy and service programs for the Asian elderly: Federal funding has been available to Asian-American social agencies. Nevertheless, the problem has been that funds have been granted to one specific group; namely, through agencies primarily serving Chinese, Japanese, Korean, or other ethnic groups, or to an agency that serves several Asian ethnic groups such as the Pacific/Asian Coalition and the National Pacific/Asian Resource Center on Aging.

An Asian-oriented research agency was established, but it went out of existence after three years. Subsequently, another resource agency was established. It is an agency identified as belonging to *an* Asian group and is equipped with a staff and a board of directors. Supposedly "national" in scope, it is not national in reality: It serves selective Asian elderly populations residing in certain areas. There are, for example, three major operating organizations serving the Pacific/Asian elderly as their total or partial missions: Pacific Asian Coalition in California, the Asian American Mental Health Research Center in Illinois, and National Pacific/Asian Resource Center on Aging in the State of Washington. There also exist more than 2,865 Filipino organizations in the country (Yu, 1980). Its missions and accomplishments have not been systematically and rigorously evaluated by any funding agency. Consequently, program repetition and competition among agencies, and frustration and even hatred among the Asian elderly, prevail. A clear definition of the Asian elderly should be written into public laws and program policies, including a mandate of establishing a unified Asian representative group (such as a caucus for the Asian aged) that would relate Asian elderly issues to public agencies as does the National Caucus of the Black Aged, for example. It should act not only as an advocacy organization but also as the recipient of public fundings, which would be equitably distributed to all designated Asian ethnic groups based on a specified appropriation formula. Funding written in present laws relative to minority elderly benefit some Asians, but others are being minimally served or not helped at all.

Policy flexibility. With so many people of diverse ethnic backgrounds to be served, programs for the Asian elderly cannot and should not be standardized. The elderly, cherishing specific cultures of their own, wish to continue their own styles of life: working and living arrangements, diets, and social and cultural activities. Each Asian ethnic elderly group should be served differently to meet their needs. Nutrition programs for the Asian elderly, for example, should be supported by ethnic chefs and with foods from their native countries, where they are available, although they may cost more than regular food substances domestically produced here. Thus nutrition programs may not always be cost effective in that fewer people may be served with federal funds than through agencies under what is called an "equality" formula. Medical care is another program that should be examined from an ethnic perspective. Herbs or folk medicines are more or less well accepted by many elderly from various parts of Asia. Asians are reluctant to visit a Western physican not only because of their language problem, but also because of their cultural beliefs in their own medical treatments. For this kind of medical care, public policy should allow them the right to purchase the care of their choice. Public medical funds should be directly paid to these ethnic elderly for their health care rather than to authorized physicans or other types of vendors only.

A flexible policy is more applicable and necessary in areas where there are very few or sporadic concentrations of Asian elders. Those elderly have been left out from local planning in deference to the majority races. To provide an acceptable service to these minority people, planners require some regulatory flexibilities so that they can design and implement appropriate ethnic programs to provide the ethnic elderly with a way to get together for their cultural and social activities. Such flexibility will create innovative programs not only for the ethnic elderly but for all older persons living in rural or urban areas. Again, it may cost more, but the program cost should not dictate the quality of human life.

Support of the Asian culture. Two of the many cultural and attitudinal characteristics cherished by Asians are the configurative roles of the elderly and ethnic mutuality. The Asian elderly value their role to help their descendants to become productive members of society and to achieve positions of wealth and status. They are willing to sacrifice themselves to that end not only by taking care of their grandchildren but also by teaching all youngsters as much as they can. They set good examples of how to live under the hardships they had to overcome in their lives as immigrants. Ethnic mutuality is the attitude the Asian elderly exhibit toward their own ethnic older persons with whom they share their experiences, their understanding and the cherishing of the culture in which their descendents may be less interested. They feel comfortable with each other and try to give assistance in times of need. Unfortunatley, many Asian elderly are widely separated from their children. Consequently, elderly parents lose their active configurative roles and need to find ways to help others, such as fellow first generation older persons of similar life experiences.

As indicated earlier, the Asian elderly today, especially those who came to this country before World War II and encountered unfortunate experiences of racial discrimination, prejudice, and exploitation, are very suspicious about almost everything. Although they tend to distrust the government and others of different races, even other Asian people, many of them would like to live together and help each other. However, when they find ways to exercise their cultural values, public policy punishes them and keeps them from having a meaningful life, in that their Supplemental Security Income checks are reduced in case of cohabitation with ethnic friends or even with their own children. Although the allowance of cohabitation would save other social service funds more than SSI savings (since other supportive care they need would be provided by their friends and families), the present administration curtails such programs for the elderly rather than shifting the funds from dysfunctioning public programs to more workable, cost-effective, and meaningful services.

An Asian elderly data base. The paucity of data on the Asian elderly is almost unimaginable. The decennial census did not include the Asian population in detail until the 1980 census. Although there exists some information about the Asian elderly in this country, primarily through the San Diego State University Center on Aging, they are geographically and ethnically segmented into unbelievably small groups which have been surveyed with very limited questionnaires. Thus the Asian elderly are still widely unknown and are discussed in terms of guesses, speculations, and hypotheses.

In order to assess the reality of the Asian elderly today, it is imperative to have a law or policy that grants funds to a single Asian caucus (as suggested earlier), and to have existing laws and policies examined carefully and modified in accordance with the data. Without such research data, any nationwide planning for the Asian elderly is nothing but lip service, and the situation of the elderly will remain the same, if not worse. Asians, being rather unassertive verbally (and responding to racism by withdrawing, by accepting, by being uncomplaining) as compared to other minority groups, do not receive the share of federal "pie" they deserve, based on their percentage in the population. A data-based planning effort could become the voice of the Asian elderly, presaging a quality program for them. To begin with, a policy is needed that mandates and supports activities toward generating Asian elderly data. Piecemeal research does not substantially benefit the elderly; in fact, it often distracts attention from broad national issues of pertinence to the Asian aged.

Preventive public policy. Despite recent statistics on immigrant professionals from Asian countries, and because of language barriers and the lack of updated technological knowledge, a majority of Asian immigrants are employed for lower wages than majority-group workers. Although both parents often work, family incomes are rather meager. Thus many workers have to give up their professions and have to work at more than one job and for extended hours. If they came to the United States at middle age, their work periods are shorter than those who were born in America. Lower wage earning and shorter history of employment inadvertently result in their economic deprivation during their retirement years. Furthermore, formerly employed wives may have to collect Social Security checks at one-half of the husband's benefit level. Besides, if the minimum Social Security payment ($122 per month) is cut, many of the immigrants will have no social security check at all for their retirement since they paid little into Social Security.

A preventive policy particularly relevant to immigrants without retirement income calls for a special formula in computing Social Security checks; namely, perhaps 12 quarters rather than 40 quarters of wage earning periods prior to retirement. In the case of immigrants in low-income households with both the husband and wife working, the maximum benefit should be given to wives as well. If the wife's earnings prior to retirement were more than the husband's, which is the case in many immigrant families, the wife's social security benefit should be paid in full, rather than at 50% of the husband's.

Another measure of preventive policy is that local civil rights commissions in all 39,000 governments receiving Federal Revenue Sharing should have one or more part-time or full-time bilingual and bicultural staff, not only to see if there exists any racial discriminatory incidence against Asian and Pacific elderly living in their jurisdiction, but also to be involved in corrective activities and/or in activities that bring forth the quality of life among those elderly. The staff could be responsible for working with elderly as well as all ages of Asians at local, state, and regional levels.

SUMMARY

The Asian-American population has been steadily increasing, particularly due to the Asian immigration policy implemented since 1965–1966. Unfortunately, the Asian elderly have not been well served by governmental agencies due to the lack of a distinct identity as "Asian," to ethnic fragmentation of existing service agencies, and to the lack of knowledge about them. They share the problems facing all older persons in this country, but their experience is much more severe in all areas because of their culture, attitude toward government, value orientation, their history of low wage earnings compounded with a shorter employment record, and because of a discriminatory public policy against them.

It is suggested that public policy should mandate an Asian-American representative organization and a continuous nationwide study on Asian aging.

Flexible regulation should be assured. Recognition of Asian cultural patterns must undergird all program planning. Finally, a public policy affecting Asian immigrants should be preventive, so that their old age may be less tragic. Without such a policy mandate and provision, sooner or later this country will face yet another ghetto, inhabited by the Asian-American Elderly.

ORGANIZATIONS PUBLISHING PERTINENT PACIFIC/ASIAN ELDERLY INFORMATION

(1) International Federation on Aging, 1909 K. Street, N.W., Washington D.C. 20049
(2) National Pacific/Asian Resource Center on Aging, 618 2nd Ave., Suite 423 Alaska Building, Seattle, WA 98104.
(3) San Diego State University Center on Aging, San Diego, CA 92182.

REFERENCES

Carp, F. M. & Kataoka, E. Health care problems of the elderly of San Francisco's Chinatown. *Gerontologist*, 1976,16,30-38.

Chen, P. N. A study of Chinese-American elderly residing in hotel rooms. *Social Casework*, 1979, 60, 89-95.

Daum, M. Selected demographic characteristics of elderly Asian and Pacific Island Americans in New York City. *Fact for Action*, 1977,9(1).

Fujii, S. M. Elderly Asian Americans and use of public services. *Social Casework*, 1976, 57, 202-207.

Kalish, R. A. & Moriwaki, S. The world of the elderly Asian American. *Journal of Social Issues*, 1973, 187-209.

Karl, S. V., Sidney, C. & Brooks, G. W. Change in serum uric acid and cholesterol levels in men undergoing job loss. *Journal of American Medical Association*, 1968, 206, 2500-2507

Lewthaite, G. R., Mainzer, C. & Holland P. J. From Polynesia to California: Samoan migration and its sequel. *Journal of Pacific History*, 1973, 8, 133-157.

Mead, M. *Culture and Commitment: A Study of Generation Gap*. Garden City, NY: Natural History Press, 1970.

Morales, R. F. Philipino Americans from colony to immigration to citizen. *Civil Rights Digest*, 1976, 30-32.

Moriwaki, S. Ethnicity and aging. in I. Burnside (ed), *Nursing and the Aged*. New York, NY: McGraw-Hill, 1976.

National Pacific/Asian Resource Center on Aging. *A Grant Proposal*. Seattle, WA: Author, 1976.

National Pacific/Asian Resource Center on Aging. *Pacific/Asians: The Wisdom of Age*. 1981 Conference Report on the Pacific/Asian Elderly, Seattle. January 15-16, 1981.

Nusberg, C. & Osako, M. M. (eds.) *The Situation of the Asian/Pacific Elderly*. Washington, DC: International Federation on Aging, 1981.

Osako, M. M. Aging and family among Japanese Americans: The role of Ethnic tradition in the adjustment to old age. *Gerontologist*, 1979, 19, 448-455.

Pepper, C. *Impact of Proposed 1982 Budget on the Elderly*. A memorandum to U.S. House of Representatives Committee on Aging members from Claude Pepper, Chairman, March 13, 1981.

U.S. Bureau of the Census. *1981 Census Advanced Report*. Washington, DC: Government Printing Office, 1981.

U.S. Commission on Civil Rights. *Civil Rights Issues of Asia and Pacific Americans: Myths and Realities*. Washington, DC: Author, 1979.

U.S. Department of Justice. *Immigration and Naturalization Services Annual Report*. Washington, DC: Government Printing Office, 1964-1979.

Wu, F. Y. T. Mandarin-speaking aged Chinese in the Los Angeles area. *Gerontologist*, 1975, 15, 271-275.

Yu, E. S. H. Philippino migration and community organizations in the United States. *California Sociologist*, 1980, 3, 76-102.

3

Selected Demographic and Social Aspects of Older Blacks
An Analysis with Policy Implications

WILBUR H. WATSON

For several decades there has been steady growth in the U.S. population of persons 65 years of age or older. For example, from 1900 to 1975, the number of these individuals grew from 3 to 22 million. During the same period, the proportion of those who were 75 or older grew from 29% to 38% of the total. Moreover, the subgroup including those of the elderly population who were 85 or older doubled from 4% in 1900 to 8% by 1975 (U.S. Bureau of the Census, 1976).

From 1970 to 1980, the overall population of persons 65 or older in the United States grew from an estimated 20 million, or about 10% of the total U.S. population (U.S. Bureau of the Census, 1976), to 25.5 million or 11.3% of the total U.S. population by 1980 (U.S. Bureau of the Census, 1981). However, it is not the growth in the population of older persons that challenges the existing agencies and personnel of social and health service delivery programs in the United States, but the (1) growing proportions of frail or "functionally dependent" and homebound elderly among them; (2) the need for highly trained service delivery staff who are sensitive to ethnic differences and related needs of the elderly; and (3) the growing recognition of the importance of informal social networks, such as family members and friends as means of sustaining the health, social, and psychological functioning of older people during their remaining years of life.

Growth in the population of older Blacks since the turn of the century has paralleled closely that of the country overall. The actual increase in the proportion of Blacks who are 65 or older rose from 3% to 7% between 1910 and 1975 (U.S. Bureau of the Census, 1978a: 6). Moreover, all indications are that the growth in the population of older Blacks is going to continue for many years to come (see Table 3-1).

Data reported in Table 3-1 show that the total population of Black Americans in 1980 was 26,488,000, representing a 16% increase since 1970. By contrast, the population of Blacks who were 65 or older increased by 34% from 1,556,000 to 2,085,826 in 1980. The rate of growth among these Blacks was both more rapid than that shown in the total population of Blacks, and more rapid, as well, than the rate shown among the two subgroups of younger Blacks. Further, Table 3-1 suggests that increases can be expected to continue, although at a slightly slower rate, through the year 2000.

There have been major increases since 1970 in federal expenditures for indirect income programs, such as nutrition, transportation, Medicare, and Medicaid services. However, the high rate of price inflation during the past decade, along with the fixed income levels of many older persons (and the declining income of others), have vitiated the gains that might have been realized through the new indirect income programs of the federal and state governments. The impact on the Black elderly has been especially severe, given this group's dire economic circumstances. As a result, a growing functionally dependent and economically poor population of older Blacks has meant an increasing strain on the resources of their families, friends, and public agencies, and has made their health and psychological welfare more uncertain, especially among rural poor Blacks, most of whom reside in the southeastern United States.

TABLE 3-1   Growth in the Population of Blacks in the United States, 1970-1980, and Projections Through the Year 2000

	Black Population by Age (in thousands)			
Year	Total All Ages	Under 18 Years	18-64 Years	65 Years and Over
Estimates:				
1970	22,782	9,532	11,695	1,556
1975	24,518	9,538	13,174	1,806
1980[a]	26,488	10,082	14,320	2,086
Projections:				
1985	28,005	8,241	16,444	2,320
1990	29,799	9,406	17,788	2,607
1995	31,410	9,676	18,880	2,855
2000	32,838	9,694	20,105	3,037

SOURCE: U.S. Department of Commerce (1978b: 18).

a. The data displayed in this row of 1980 figures are based on an advanced supplementary report of the 1980 Census (U.S. Department of Commerce, 1981: 76).

THE CONCENTRATION
OF OLDER BLACKS IN
THE SOUTHEASTERN UNITED STATES

The southeastern United States is distinguished from other regions of the country by the high proportion of older Blacks who still live in the region. For example, in contrast to the white elderly, of whom 31% were still living in the South in 1980, 59% of the Black elderly were living in that region of the country (U.S. Department of Commerce, 1981). Further, an estimated 30% of the 25.5 million elderly persons in the United States still lived in rural farm and rural nonfarming regions of the country in 1980 (see Table 3-2). Rural regions, significant land areas of which are in the South, are defined as places of 2,500 or fewer inhabitants.

Table 3-2 also shows that there was a 3% increase in the population of Hispanics 65 years of age or older between 1970 and 1980. The immigration of middle-aged and older Cubans to Florida and other states of the Southeast since the mid-1980s helps to account for the increase in the Hispanic population. However, the 3% increase in the population of older whites probably is accounted for by the growing numbers who are changing their residences following retirement from the northcentral and northeastern United States to sunbelt cities located in the southern region of the country. Southern states, such as Georgia, Alabama, Mississippi, North and South Carolina, Virginia, and Tennessee are among the states with sunbelt cities and the largest proportions of rural residential areas that are populated densely by poor Black and white inhabitants.

The aging and aged, especially but not exclusively in the rural southeast-

TABLE 3-2   Change in the Regional Distribution of White, Black, and Hispanic Persons, 65 and Older, in the United States, 1970 to 1980

Region	*Population Estimates in Percentages*								
	White			*Black*			*Hispanic*		
	1970[1]	*1980*[2]	*d*[3]	*1970*[1]	*1980*[2]	*d*[3]	*1970*[1]	*1980*[2]	*d*[3]
Northeast	27%	25%	−2	16%	16%	0	8%	16%	+ 8
Northcentral	29%	27%	−2	18%	18%	0	6%	6%	0
South	28%	31%	+3	61%	59%	−2	37%	40%	+ 3
West	16%	17%	+1	5%	7%	+2	49%	38%	−11
U.S. Totals (estimates are in thousands)	18,272	22,963		1,544	2,086		383	702	

1. U.S. Department of Commerce (1978b, p. 19).
2. U.S. Department of Commerce (1982, pp. 47-59).
3. Percentage change from 1970 to 1980.

ern pockets of poverty, and in other depressed areas around the country, share many common characteristics in addition to advanced age. Younger family members have grown and moved away; health problems have sharply increased; friends and neighbors have died; and many elderly have been forced from their jobs by changes in the economic structures of their communities, by new technology, by the retirement patterns of our society, and by ill health (Bourg, 1972; Jackson, 1975). In the face of increasing personal problems and decreasing personal resources to meet them, the rural and urban elderly poor often withdraw from their few remaining personal contacts. Many feel ashamed of and hurt by their loss of important social roles in society and see themselves as powerless to affect change. They feel, and many are, in fact, left behind, discarded and rejected, and are among the most invisible of the invisible poor (Kivett & Scott, 1979).

CHANGE IN
THE ECONOMIC CONDITIONS OF
OLDER BLACKS SINCE 1970

In addition to growth in the population, there also has been change since 1970 in the proportion of Blacks aged 65 or older who live in poverty. As shown in Table 3-3, there was a 9% decline in the proportion of impoverished Blacks and whites from 1970 through 1980. While this suggests some improvement in the economic conditions of older Blacks and whites, the improvement for Blacks is minor when viewed in light of the 38% who remained below the poverty level in 1980.

TABLE 3-3   Persons 65 and Over Below Poverty, by Race: 1970 and 1980 (numbers in thousands)

	1970	1980
Blacks		
Total over 65	1,566[1]	2,083
Number below poverty	735[2]	783[4]
Percentage below poverty	47	38
Percentage change since 1970		−9
Whites		
Total over 65	18,272[2]	22,944[3]
Number below poverty	4,011[2]	3,042[4]
Percentage below poverty	22	13
Percentage change since 1970		−9

1. U.S. Department of Commerce (1978a, p. 18).
2. U.S. Department of Commerce (1978b, pp. 18, 56).
3. U.S. Department of Commerce (1981, p. 7).
4. Brotman (1982, p. 8).

The significance of these figures can be seen in several ways. First, the fact that 38% of all older Blacks were impoverished in 1980 means that the proportion of poor Black elders nearly tripled the proportion of aged whites who were poor. When compared to the Hispanic elderly, older Blacks still were disproportionately poorer. Only 30.8% of persons of Spanish origin (or Hispanic) 65 or older were in poverty in 1980 (Brotman, 1982a: 8). Moreover, while Hispanics represented only 3% of all persons aged 65 or older and 5% of the elderly poor in 1980, Blacks represented 8% of those 65 years of age or older and 20% of the 3,871,000 poor among the elderly. Further, although Hispanics and Blacks clearly are overrepresented among the poor, Blacks were more than 2.5 times as likely as their Hispanic and white American counterparts to be included among the elderly poor in 1980.

IMPLICATIONS FOR POLICY

This chapter suggests that the increasing longevity of older Blacks, as represented by the growing population of those who are 75 years of age or older, is certain to mean an increasing demand for public and private dollars and efforts in the years to come to sustain the increasing proportion of functionally dependent persons among them. The need for increases in the social security fund will mean an increasing taxation of workers in the labor force, with the incumbent risk of a taxpayers' revolt and/or pressures on Congress to find alternative means of income maintenance for the elderly poor and of meeting other needs, such as health care, for which income is needed. It is true that these needs and policy-relevant issues are not peculiar to older Blacks. However, it is also true, as indicated by Jackson and Wood (1976), Manuel (1982), and by recent findings of the U.S. Commission on Civil Rights (1982), that because of socioeconomic and racial discrimination, most older Blacks still are highly likely to be "multiply disadvantaged" by age, poverty, and race, in contrast to their nonminority counterparts. Because of these conditions and others, it has been suggested that the Black aged be provided an increased amount of financial and health security than they currently receive, such as a guaranteed minimum income that is higher than the current social security benefit, and/or increased food stamp and health service benefits to offset the disadvantages among them.

Second, the continuing concentration of older poor Blacks in the South, with significant proportions in rural residential areas, suggests the need for an intensification of social and health service planning in this region of the country. For example, recent research has shown a need for major improvements in housing, transportation, public sanitation, and water treatment facilities especially, but not exclusively, in areas where older Blacks live in the rural South (Watson, 1980). In the same study, a far greater proportion of older rural Blacks than whites expressed a need for food stamps. These findings are not surprising in light of the higher incidence of poverty among older Blacks compared to whites (Brotman, 1982b: 4). Moreover, the remoteness of many rural residential areas with their poor roads and inadequate or nonexistent public transportation has made shopping centers, health and social service offices, and other facilities inaccessible to many older poor Blacks.

It is worth noting that in the Watson (1980) study, it was the older Black females who showed the greatest need for transportation services. In addition to poor road conditions and poor health, the inability to operate a motor vehicle was included among factors that helped to account for their need for transportation services. As was the case with older Black males who showed a primary need for in-home services, such as help with meal preparations and household chores, nearly 85% of the older Black females (N=988) reported that they were most likely to depend for help on unpaid family members and friends. In this respect, policy analysts and lawmakers should give consideration to developing incentives to indigenous suppliers of transportation and other services through, for example, gasoline coupons to help cut the costs of fuel in exchange for the provision of transportation services for the poor and ambulatory-impaired elderly living in rural areas of the United States.

However, legislative enactments and economic incentives alone may not be sufficient to improve service delivery to older Blacks in the United States. For example, the 1982 report of the U.S. Commission on Civil Rights focusing on minority elderly services revealed persisting patterns of racial discrimination in service delivery to aged members of minority groups. The commission's investigation focused on Cleveland, Ohio; Bridgeport, Connecticut; Tucson, Arizona; Tulsa, Oklahoma; San Francisco, California; and Honolulu, Hawaii. Among other results, the commission found that minority involvement in service delivery and service consumption was rarely representative of their proportions in the populations of the cities where local aging agencies were located (U.S. Commission on Civil Rights, 1982: 149). The following were among the other major findings of the report:

(1) While employed by most area agencies on aging, Blacks generally were underrepresented in policy-making and supervisory positions.
(2) Although nearly all of the area agencies on aging had affirmative action plans and had specific goals for hiring minority staff, in almost no instance where goals were unmet by area agencies on aging had specific corrective actions been taken by state units or the Federal Office of the Administration on Aging.
(3) In almost none of the six cities were minority firms receiving a representative number of Title III awards, or representative amounts of Title III funds from the area agencies on aging.
(4) Despite low participation by the minority elderly in most service programs,

area agencies on aging were not engaged actively in outreach activities designed to increase minority elderly participation.

(5) In nearly all of the cities studied by the Civil Rights Commission, data collection on program activities by race and ethnicity, and program evaluation, was too inadequate and unsystematic for need assessment and planning purposes.

The conclusions of the Civil Rights Commission outlined above suggest that even though the 1978 amendments to the Older Americans Act may have called for improving services to the most economic and socially needy among the elderly, older Blacks are still at risk of not receiving services, in spite of need and changes in the law because of entrenched patterns of racial discrimination in the United States. This also means that the projected increases in the population of older Blacks in the decades ahead portend increasingly large numbers who will be among the suffering and downtrodden, so long as the patterns of discrimination found by the Civil Rights Commission persist in this society.

SUMMARY AND CONCLUSIONS

This chapter has demonstrated that the population of Blacks in this country who are 65 years of age or older has grown with each decade since 1900. Moreover, there has been a steady increase in the number of Blacks who are 75 years of age and older who tend to incur, with advancing age and more prevalent chronic illnesses, an increasing risk of functional impairment in the activities of daily living.

It was noted that in 1980, the great majority of older Blacks lived in the southern region of the United States, with a significant proportion in the depressed rural hinterlands. There is a paucity of health and social service programs in many of these hard-to-reach areas. Blacks have the highest proportion of their elderly living in impoverishment: a full 38% were poor in 1980.

These findings show clearly that much improvement is still needed in income maintenance, health care, and social service programs, in spite of the increased public and private expenditures for aging services that has occurred since 1970. Finally, as shown by the recent findings of the United States Commission on Civil Rights, the lingering problem of racial discrimination continues to plague older Black consumers who seek to avail themselves of services provided by health and social programs in efforts to enhance the quality of their lives.

REFERENCES

Bourg, Carroll J. A social profile of Black aged in a southern metropolitan area. In J. J. Jackson (Ed.), *Research conference on minority group aged in the South*. Durham, NC: Duke University Center for the Study on Aging, 1971.

Brotman, Herman B. *Supplement to Chartbook on Aging in America (Updating and Corrections by Original Chart Numbers)*. Washington, DC: 1981 White House Conference on Aging, February 1982(a).

Brotman, Herman B. *Every Ninth American*. Select Committee on Aging, House of Representatives, 97th Congress, 2nd session. Washington, DC: Government Printing Office, 1982(b).

Jackson, J. J. Aged Negroes: Their cultural departures from statistical stereotypes and rural-urban differences, In J. J. Jackson (Ed.), *Aging Black women: Selected readings for NCBA*. Washington, DC: College and University Press, 1975.

Jackson, Maurice & Wood, James L. *The Black aged: Aging in America* (No. 5). Washington, DC: National Council on the Aging, 1976.

Kivett, Vira R., & Scott, Jean P. *The rural by-passed elderly: Perspectives on status and needs*. North Carolina Agricultural Research Service. Technical Bulletin No. 260, September 1979.

Manuel, Ron C. *A re-examination of the double jeopardy hypothesis*. Paper presented at Norfolk State College, March 5, 1982.

U.S. Bureau of the Census. The percentage of the very old among the elderly is increasing. *Current population reports*, Series P-23, No. 59, May 1976.

U.S. Bureau of the Census. The social and economic status of the Black population in the United States: An historical view, 1978. *Current population reports*. Special Studies, Series P-23, No. 80, 1978(a).

U.S. Bureau of the Census. Demographic Aspects of Aging and the Older Population in the United States. *Current population reports*. Special Studies, Series P-23, No. 59, January 1978(b).

U.S. Bureau of the Census. *1980 Census of the United States Population, Supplementary Report: Age, Sex, Race and Spanish Origin of the Population by Regions, Divisions and States*. PC80-S1-1, May 1981.

U.S. Commission on Civil Rights. *Minority Elderly Services: New Programs, Old Problems, Part I*. Washington, DC: Government Printing Office, June 1982.

Watson, Wilbur H. *Older Poor Blacks and Social Services in the Southern United States*. Washington DC: Administration on Aging and the National Center on Black Aged, 1980.

Watson, Wilbur H. *Aging and Social Behavior: An Introduction to Social Gerontology*. Belmont, CA: Wadsworth Health Sciences Division, 1982.

4

The Elderly of Cuban Origin
Characteristics and Problems

MAGALY QUERALT

Although Cubans make up only about 6% of the total Spanish-origin population in the United States, their elderly constitute 12% to 16% of all aged Hispanics. Cubans have a much larger proportion of persons 65 years of age or older than Mexicans, Puerto Ricans, Central or South Americans, or other Spanish-origin groups in this country. They also have a much larger proportion of older people than American Blacks, American Indians, Chinese Americans, Filipino Americans, Korean Americans, or Japanese Americans (U.S. Bureau of the Census, 1981b; Jackson, 1980). The higher proportion of elderly people among Cubans in this country, as compared to other minority groups, doubtless stems from the selective nature of the Cuban migration described below.

While sharing some aspects of the Hispanic heritage and similar versions of the Spanish language, the various Hispanic groups in the United States belong to proud and diverse cultures and nationalities, are clustered in different geographical areas of this country, and differ in demographic characteristics and in problems. Thus, policies and programs relevant to Mexicans in the Southwest may not be applicable to Cubans in the Southeast or to Puerto Ricans in the Northeast. Indeed, it is unfortunate that social policies and programs aimed at Hispanics in this country have generally represented a single perspective that belies the diversity of the heterogeneous target populations.

Given the mature age structure of the Cuban-origin population and the large number of the elderly within their ranks, it is important that we develop a better understanding of this Hispanic group if needs associated with old age are to be met effectively. To this end, this chapter examines the situation of Cubans in the United States, with a focus on the elderly. After a brief review of the history of their migration, it covers selected demographic characteristics, identifies several pressing problems, and provides a series of recommendations aimed at meeting their special needs.

THE CUBAN EXODUS

Prior to 1959, there were approximately 50,000 Cubans in the United States (Perez, 1980). By 1982, the Cuban-origin population in this country had probably passed the 1 million mark.[1]

The Cuban exodus to the United States took place in several distinct stages. The first major migratory wave began shortly after Fidel Castro's assumption of power in 1959. As it became evident that the new Cuban government would replace the old capitalist system with a new socialist political and economic order, a large number of persons, predominantly from the upper and upper-middle classes, fled the island. Approximately 155,000 Cubans migrated to the United States between 1959 and October 1962, when commercial flights were suspended due to the missile crisis (Perez, 1980). Between October 1962 and December 1965, the exodus continued, but at a slower pace, because it was only possible to leave the island clandestinely by way of third countries (mostly Spain and Mexico) or on small boats. Even under these conditions, an additional 30,000 Cubans arrived in the United States during this period.

The second major phase of the Cuban migration started with the signing of a "memorandum of understanding" between the Johnson administration and the Castro government in December 1965. This established the Varadero-Miami airlift, which brought some 257,000 Cubans to the United States before the end of the airlift in 1973 (Prohias & Casal, 1974). The most common emigrants in the early years of these "freedom flights" were middle-class persons. Toward the later years, however, the aerial bridge brought a large number of Cuban refugees with roots in the working class. Yet, despite their lower socioeconomic, educational, and occupational levels (in comparison to previous exiles), they still overrepresented the more educated and skilled sectors of the island population. In short, they were still a select group unrepresentative of the population in Cuba.

It was during the airlift years in particular that a large number of elderly Cubans came to this country. Convinced at first that the Castro government would not survive, they had refused to leave the island when their children departed. Later, in the late 1960s and early 1970s, they gave up hope that things would change in Cuba and decided to come to join their children. The Cuban government, welcoming this exodus of elderly people dependent or soon-to-be dependent on pensions and government assistance, readily granted them permission to leave (Hernandez, 1974).

Between 1973 and the spring of 1980, Cuban immigration was once again limited to persons who could reach the United States via third countries. Suddenly, during the spring and summer of 1980, Castro opened Mariel harbor and a total of 124,779 persons made the trip to the United States (U.S. Department of State, 1980).[2] These "boat people," the Mariel entrants, were much more deprived educationally, occupationally, and economically than previous Cuban émigrés. In contrast to the airlift refugees, they were more likely to have had unskilled or manual labor jobs in Cuba and were less likely to have been in white-collar occupations. In fact, the entrants were no longer distinguishable from the island population (Office of the County Manager, 1981). Also sprinkled in this mass exodus were several thousand criminals and other institutionalized persons forced or persuaded to leave by the Cuban government.

U.S. Cubans no longer fit the old stereotype of a privileged Hispanic group: "golden exiles" (Portes, 1969). Some have undoubtedly achieved much success in their new lives in this country. Most, however, have experienced the gamut of social and economic problems that first-generation immigrants traditionally face.

CUBANS IN THE UNITED STATES: SELECTED DEMOGRAPHIC CHARACTERISTICS

According to the 1980 census, there were over 14.5 million persons of Spanish origin in this country. Slightly more than 6.3% were Cuban (U.S. Bureau of the Census, 1981a, 1981b).

Metropolitan Miami (Dade County, Florida) is the undisputed center of the Cuban community in this country, with approximately 56% of U.S. Cubans residing there.[3] Sizeable Cuban colonies also exist in New York City, Union City, Jersey City, Newark, Los Angeles, Chicago, and in the commonwealth of Puerto Rico.

With an estimated median age of 33.5 years, the Cuban-origin population is more mature than the total U.S. population or any of the other Spanish-origin populations in this country.[4] U.S. Cubans are disproportionately physiognomically white (95%), in comparison to the total U.S. population and to the population of Cuba.[5] Almost all (96.7%) reside in metropolitan areas; none of the other Spanish-origin groups in this country show such a strong urban orientation (U.S. Bureau of the Census, 1981b).

The fertility rate of Cubans is much lower than that of other U.S. Hispanic groups. In fact, it is even lower than that of the non-Hispanic white population (U.S. Bureau of the Census, 1975, p. 839).[6] Cuban families, however, although smaller than those of persons of Mexican-American or Puerto-Rican origin, are somewhat larger in average size than non-Hispanic families (U.S. Bureau of the Census, 1980), probably because a greater proportion of Cuban young adults continue to share households with their parents.

Although not as well-educated as the non-Hispanic U.S. population, Cubans in this country show considerably higher educational attainment than Mexicans or Puerto Ricans. In 1979, among those who were 25 years of age or older, 50.4% had completed four years of high school or more, and 12% had completed four years of college (U.S. Bureau of the Census, 1980).[7]

Compared to Mexicans and Puerto Ricans as well as to the total U.S. population in 1979 and 1980 respectively, Cubans showed the highest labor force participation rate and the lowest rate of unemployment (U.S. Bureau of the Census, 1980, 1981b).[8] However, their occupational status was not as advantaged as their educational attainment or employment record. Except for a higher proportion of professionals and managers, the Cuban occupational pattern, with its peak concentration in the operative category, closely resembled that of Mexicans and Puerto Ricans. In fact, Cuban-origin females appeared to be more disadvantaged occupationally than their Mexican and Puerto Rican counterparts; in 1979 they had the smallest percentage of professional, technical, and managerial workers and the greatest percentage of operatives of all three groups of females (U.S. Bureau of the Census, 1980).

Cubans are even less clearly advantaged in income than other Hispanic groups in this country. In 1978, among persons 14 years of age or older, they did have a somewhat higher average income than Mexicans or Puerto Ricans (U.S. Bureau of the Census, 1980).[9] But, given their mature age structure, they also had, proportionately, more workers who were at the peak of their earning power than either of the two other Hispanic minority groups. If Cubans were similar in age to the Mexican-origin or Puerto Rican-origin groups, their average income might be the lowest. In relation to the Cubans' income situation, it is interesting to note, for example, that in spite of the occupational advantage that having a higher percentage of professional and managerial workers might offer, proportionately fewer Cubans than Mexicans were making incomes of $15,000 or more in 1978 (U.S. Bureau of the Census, 1980).

One conclusion that may be reached from the above data is that many persons of Cuban origin are probably underemployed or underpaid, perhaps due to language barriers, inability to reestablish their professional or technical/trade credentials in this country, or some degree of discrimination. Or, some of these income discrepancies may be reflective of the geographical concentration of Cubans in areas that have traditionally afforded lower wages, such as southeast Florida.

ELDERLY CUBANS IN THE UNITED STATES

Cubans constitute the third largest Hispanic group in this country, following Mexicans and Puerto Ricans respectively; but they have the second largest Hispanic elderly population. This is because, as previously indicated, Cubans have a much larger proportion of elderly persons than any other Spanish-origin group. In 1980, it was estimated that 9.7 percent[10] of all Cuban-origin persons in the U.S. were 65 years of age or older, compared to 3.7% of the Mexicans and 2.7% of the Puerto Ricans (U.S. Bureau of the Census, 1981b). Older Cuban-origin females are overrepresented. In fact, in

1979, the percentage of the elderly among Cuban females (13.7%) exceeded that of all other groups, including non-Hispanics. There is also a sizeable number of very old persons. In 1979, 3.7% of the U.S. Cubans were 75 years of age or older, compared to 1.4% of Mexicans and 0.6% of Puerto Ricans (U.S. Bureau of the Census, 1980).

CHARACTERISTICS OF THE ELDERLY

Apart from population figures, the Bureau of the Census provides minimal information on older Cubans. Most of what is known about this group derives from two recent surveys. One survey was conducted by Clark and Mendoza who obtained information from 151 Spanish-speaking elderly persons (Cubans constituted 90% of the sample) residing in Dade County, Florida (Hernandez, 1974). The other, by far the most important source, was the first nationwide survey of older Hispanics in the United States. It was conducted by the Asociación Nacional Pro Personas Mayores (ANPPM) and employed a probability sample of 1,803 persons, including 209 elderly Cubans (ANPPM, 1980).

In 1980 there were 708,785 persons of Spanish origin 65 years of age or older in the U.S. (U.S. Bureau of the Census, 1981a). Of these, it is estimated that the Cuban elderly numbered between 85,000 and 98,500 persons.[11]

Elderly Cubans show even less geographic dispersion than the total U.S. Cuban population. They are highly concentrated in Florida, largely in Dade County, with the majority residing in Miami (particularly in the Little Havana area) and in Hialeah. These are high density, working-class, heavily Cuban sections in which elders feel comfortable because the Spanish language is widely spoken and because they are surrounded by their own people, many of similar age. The state of New York also has a relatively large proportion of elderly Cubans. However, there are few in other areas of the country (Diaz, 1981).

Most older Cubans were born in Cuba and came to the United States late in life. According to the ANPPM survey, less than 7.7% were born in this country. In contrast, 54.6% of older Mexicans were native born. Moreover, among the survey respondents, 57.4% of the Cubans reported that they came to the United States after the age of 50, compared to only 4.5% of Mexicans and 12.8% of Puerto Ricans.

Although not nearly as well-educated as their non-Hispanic counterparts, Cubans are the most educated older Hispanics in this country. In 1979, 26.9% of the Cuban aged had completed four years of high school or more, compared to 7.1% of the Mexicans. Yet, 40.7% of the non-Hispanic elderly had completed this amount of schooling (U.S. Bureau of Census, 1980).

Among elderly Hispanics, Cubans appear more likely to be full-time workers. The ANPPM survey (1980) indicated that 18.7% were employed on a full-time basis, compared to 13% of the Mexicans and 8.5% of the

Puerto Ricans. The survey also revealed that unemployment was highest among older Cubans (12%), compared to elderly Puerto Ricans (7.7%) and older Mexicans (7.6%).

A high proportion of elderly Cuban respondents (17.2%) indicated that they had been engaged in professional, technical, administrative, or managerial jobs for most of their working years. A substantially smaller percentage of Mexicans (3.6%) and Puerto Ricans (3.8%) had been similarly employed. Correspondingly, far fewer Cubans than other elderly Hispanics reported employment histories as laborers or service workers (ANPPM, 1980).

Elderly Hispanics are twice as likely to be below the poverty line. In 1979, of all Hispanics 65 years of age or older, 26.1% were poor, compared to only 13.2% of all white non-Hispanic elderly persons in this country (U.S. Bureau of the Census, 1981c). While the exact percentage of elderly Cubans living below the poverty level is not known, there is evidence that it is probably similar to that of the total Hispanic elderly population. For example, the average family income for elderly Cubans has been reported to be $4,079, compared to $3,967 for older Mexicans and $3,625 for elderly Puerto Ricans (ANPPM, 1980).

Older Cubans are predominantly (81.8%) Catholic. Yet, they apparently have the largest group of Protestants and of nonchurchgoers of all U.S. Hispanics (ANPPM, 1980).

Among the major groups of elderly Hispanics in this country, Cubans have the smallest number of children (a median of 1.94, compared to 3.64 for Mexicans and 3.16 for Puerto Ricans). As is the case with other elderly Hispanics, the Cubans maintain close ties with their children: 31.6% of those surveyed by ANPPM indicated that they resided with their children. Finally, among elderly Hispanics, Cubans reported the lowest percentage of individuals living alone (15.3%) and the largest proportion (39.2%) of persons living with their spouses only (ANPPM, 1980).

PROBLEMS OF ELDERLY CUBANS

The most pressing problems of elderly Cubans concern income, physical health, mental health/life satisfaction, language, and housing (Hernandez, 1974; ANPPM, 1980; Diaz, 1981).

Income

Income inadequacy is one of the three most serious problems confronted by older Cubans (ANPPM, 1980). Most are ineligible for social security benefits because they do not have the requisite period of covered employment in the United States. In fact, only 37.3% (mostly men) of the 65-and-over Cuban respondents to the ANPPM survey were receiving benefits. Because many of those who worked in this country have had low earnings and limited periods of coverage, they are able to qualify for minimum benefits only. Thus, President Reagan's decision to eliminate the minimum social security benefit of $122 will exact substantial hardship on many of those applying for retirement after January 1, 1982, because in many cases they will be receiving even smaller payments. This problem is exacerbated by the frequent lack of additional income from pensions. Very few older Cubans receive pensions, either because they did not hold a job long enough to qualify for a pension or because they were employed in jobs with no pension coverage at all.

Most elderly Cubans who work are employed at meager salaries within the Spanish-speaking community. Among the rest, the majority would welcome the opportunity to work (Hernandez, 1974), but language problems limit their employability.

A substantial proportion of older Cubans, particularly women, never participated in the U.S. labor force (Diaz, 1981, p. 15). Governmental assistance becomes necessary for those unable to work or to find employment whose relatives are unable to help financially. Accordingly, one quarter (25.8%) of all ANPPM elderly Cuban respondents were receiving Supplemental Security Income (SSI) benefits at the time of the survey. Recent talk of possible cutbacks in SSI benefits was causing considerable anxiety among those dependent exclusively upon this category of income for subsistence.

Physical Health

When asked to name their most serious problem, all elderly Hispanic groups ranked physical health first (ANPPM, 1980). The Cubans, in particular, suffered high levels of illness and disability. They reported the lowest incidence of wellness and the highest incidence of multiple illnesses and disability. For example, only 8.6% indicated that they had no illness, while 70% reported that they were suffering from four or more illnesses and 50% perceived themselves as highly disabled due to poor health. Ailments mentioned most frequently were, in order of importance, arthritis, high blood pressure, circulatory problems, glaucoma and other eye problems, and heart trouble. Cuban women appeared to be the most vulnerable. Possibly, problems affecting their mental well-being, to be discussed below, contribute to the physical health problems of older Cubans.

One of the most prominent health concerns of elderly Cubans is the problem of Medicare ineligibility. Few have accumulated the necessary employment credits to qualify for social security benefits and, therefore, to be entitled to Medicare. Persons aged 65 or older who have resided in the United States for a minimum of five years can purchase Medicare coverage. However, at a monthly cost of $113 for Part A plus $12.20 for Part B (effective July 1, 1982), this insurance coverage has become, for many Cubans, too expensive to purchase. Medicaid is available to those unable to receive Medicare who meet Supplemental Security Income (SSI) eligibility requirements. But, in various states, this translates into ineligibility for certain medical services, notably home health services.

Those older Cubans neither entitled to receive Medicare nor able to pay for Medicare coverage, whose near poverty-level incomes also disqualify them for Medicaid, are perhaps the most medically needy of all.

Mental Health/Life Satisfaction

Elderly Cubans ranked problems related to mental health and life satisfaction as their second most serious concern (ANPPM, 1980). Neither Mexicans nor Puerto Ricans gave nearly as much importance to these problems.

Information on the psychosocial functioning of older Cubans is very limited. What little there is suggests that they are vulnerable. For example, in a study that examined the psychosocial functioning of elderly Blacks, Cubans, and non-Hispanic whites, Cubans showed the least adjustment in terms of social participation, depression, social functioning, and life satisfaction (Linn, Hunter, & Perry, 1979).

As people age they generally suffer losses of income, family, friends, health, and social roles that can affect their overall level of functioning. In addition to those losses commonly associated with old age, many elderly Cubans have experienced other losses and separations that can cause depression. For example, losses of homeland and a familiar cultural environment; home and material possessions; familial and socioeconomic status; and separation from children, spouses, relatives, and close friends left behind in Cuba are common to the experiences of Cubans residing in the United States (Szapocznik, Faletti & Scopetta, 1979).

In the 1974 Dade County survey of elderly Hispanics, one out of five Cuban respondents said that he or she was very lonely (Hernandez, 1974). Szapocznik, Falletti, and Scopetta (1979) examined various characteristic stressors that might contribute to feelings of isolation and loneliness among the Cuban aged. These included uprootedness and forced migration, difficulties in adapting to the American culture and way of life, communication (language) barriers, and the relative weakening of family ties. One of the most important sources of familial disruption that serves to isolate Cuban elders from their children and grandchildren is the problem of differential acculturation rates. As the young acculturate more rapidly than their elders, many conflicts arise that promote distancing between generations and, consequently, a weakening of family ties. In many cases intergenerational differences become severe enough to force the elderly to move away from their children. Without a history of independence from their families, many feel neglected, isolated, and lonely. An additional contributor to the elderly's feelings of neglect, loneliness, and isolation is the hectic pace of their children's work life in this country, which restricts the time available for elders.

Language

Most elderly Cubans speak very little English. Many speak no English at all. Thus, it is not surprising that respondents to the 1974 survey rated language barriers as their second most important problem (Hernandez, 1974). Even in the more recent ANPPM survey (1980), 93.8% indicated that they spoke Spanish most of the time, and 83.3% expressed much difficulty in understanding forms written in English. Certainly, for older people who have spoken Spanish most of their lives, learning English can be a very difficult task.

Inability to communicate in English causes a great many problems. It may limit employment opportunities or result in a lack of awareness of services and benefits to which one is entitled, and it may limit utilization of social services. A language barrier also may cause feelings of isolation and loneliness by limiting assimilation of the American culture or adaptation to it, or by accentuating intrafamilial, intergenerational cultural gaps, which, as mentioned earlier, may weaken family ties. A language barrier may increase feelings of helplessness and dependency among the elderly. Also, as noted by Szapocznik, Falletti, and Scopetta (1979), it may precipitate a premature disengagement from active participation in the social environment. Finally, for the sick elderly, particularly those hospitalized, inability to communicate effectively with health providers can be anxiety-producing or even fatal.

Housing

The vast majority of older Cubans rent their housing and are thus subjected to spiraling housing costs. Only 15% own their homes, in contrast to 55% of older Mexicans, and 72% of the non-Hispanic elderly (ANPPM, 1980; U.S. Bureau of the Census,1979b). Few elderly Cubans live in public housing or receive rent subsidies (ANPPM, 1980). In view of their often meager financial resources and the prohibitive costs of housing, many must be living in substandard conditions. Accordingly, the 1974 survey identified housing as their most important problem (Hernandez, 1974).

A sizeable proportion of the Cuban aged would welcome the opportunity to live in low-cost government housing projects or to participate in rent subsidy programs, such as the Section 8 program. In fact, 66.4% of those responding to the 1974 survey indicated this preference (Hernandez, 1974). Not surprisingly, in 1982 there were thousands of elderly Cubans on waiting lists to obtain low-cost public housing. Many had been waiting for years.

RECOMMENDATIONS FOR ACTION

Various suggestions are made as a basis for the development of public policies and programs sensitive to the characteristics, special problems, and needs of elderly Cubans.

RESEARCH/STATISTICS

Little is know definitively about elderly Cubans in this country. The 1980 national needs assessment of elderly Hispanics conducted by the ANPPM filled a great void, but its findings must be viewed as tentative because of the size of the subsample (209 elderly Cubans). If we are to become better informed about older Cubans, nationwide research projects should be funded periodically. Additionally, the Bureau of the Census should collect more data on elderly Mexicans, Puerto Ricans, and Cubans as separate entities, instead of on the Hispanic elderly population as a whole. At present, census statistics available on older Cubans are minimal. Also, the Department of Health and Human Services should begin to classify the information it gathers such that the major Hispanic groups are depicted separately.

There is a special need for studies exploring the problems that keep elderly immigrants, especially recent immigrants, from full participation in programs for the elderly. At this juncture it appears that eligibility requirements bar these persons from full participation in various important services for the elderly.

REPRESENTATION

There is need for a Cuban entity at the national level (perhaps a Cuban desk at ANPPM or a division within the Cuban National Planning Council) to coordinate the collection of information on older Cubans, oversee its dissemination to various policy-making and program-planning agencies, and initiate the publication of a yearly report detailing findings and activities on behalf of this group. Similarly, the special interests and needs of older Cubans should be represented by Cuban-origin people on national councils developing aging policies and programs and, in areas of significant concentration of the Cuban elderly population, Cuban representation should extend to area agencies and state units on aging.

OUTREACH

The Cuban aged lack knowledge about the maze of federal, state, and local programs for the elderly. In fact, they show a lower median knowledge of available services than Mexicans or Puerto Ricans (ANPPM, 1980). Therefore, it is necessary to increase efforts to disseminate information in Spanish to this group, with special emphasis on the needs of the very large number of older women. Stress should be placed on mass media campaigns emphasizing personalized Spanish television public service announcements. A study by Szapocznik, Lasaga, Perry, and Solomon (1979) has underscored the effectiveness of this approach in mobilizing elderly Cubans to seek out information on aging services. All outreach efforts should utilize indigenous opinion leaders who are part of natural networks in the Cuban community.

INCOME

A minimum guaranteed income should be available to all elderly persons who have the work credits necessary to qualify for social security. The elimination of the minimum social security will hurt many elderly people, including older Cubans employed at minimal salaries during their limited work years prior to retirement in this country.

Supplemental Security Income (SSI) payments should not be reduced for the eligible elderly person sharing a household with others. On the contrary, such a living arrangement, favored by elderly Cubans, deserves encouragement as it permits a higher quality of life.

Employment would greatly help the older Cubans because many both need and want to work. Their relatively good educational backgrounds and previous occupational skills are definite assets in job placement, although their severe language barriers may be problematical. Job projects such as the Senior Community Service Employment Program and volunteer programs involving some monetary remuneration, such as the Foster Grandparents and Senior Companion Program, should be expanded. Incentives to private enterprise for hiring minority older persons also may provide needed impetus to expand work opportunities.

PHYSICAL HEALTH

As recommended in the report of the 1981 White House Mini-Conference on Hispanic Aging, Medicare should be broadened to cover preventive and health maintenance services (including dental care), as well as expanded home health care services. Medicaid should be expanded to cover home health services in all states. With a marked preference for home health care and a long tradition of preventive and health maintenance care,[12] Cubans would make very good use of all these services.

There are elderly people (including many Cubans) not entitled to Medicare whose near poverty-level salaries disqualify them for Medicaid. These medically indigent individuals should be granted Medicaid in all states. This is important particularly for aged Cubans (considering their strong preference for private medical care); with Medicaid they can go to the private health providers of their choice. (Naturally, the choice of health providers is much more limited with Medicaid than with Medicare.) In this connection, it should be mentioned that unless something is done to change the Cubans' strongly negative attitudes toward public health services, the sole provision of such services will not fulfill their medical needs because they will greatly underutilize them.

Programs for the frail elderly aimed at Cubans (and one must keep in mind that Cubans have the highest proportion of very old persons of all Hispanic groups in this country) should promote and protect the relatively strong ties that Cubans have with their elderly. They should enhance opportunities for the elderly to continue to participate in the family household. There is much need for more in-home services, such as home health care, homemaker services, and home-delivered meals, that offer support and assistance to the family unit in caring for the elderly at home. Particularly critical is the need for additional adult daycare facilities in those areas with high concentrations of Cubans, so that the frail elderly may be taken care of while relatives are at work.

Finally, the apparently very high level of health problems among elderly Cuban women deserves further exploration.

MENTAL HEALTH/LIFE SATISFACTION

Older Cubans are in serious need of mental health services, especially services sensitive to their psychological make-up and value structure, as well as to their sociocultural background (Szapocznik et al., 1978). One such treatment method is the Life Enhancement Counseling Model, which appears particularly effective in the treatment of depressed Cuban elders (Szapocznik, Santisteban, Kurtines, Hervis, & Spencer, 1982). Because of the high need for supportive services, volunteers and paraprofessionals from the community, especially older people, should be trained to assist.

The use of informal community supports merits further attention. For example, telephone reassurance and friendly visiting programs can be highly beneficial in combatting depression and loneliness. They are needed particularly by older Cubans living alone. Similarly, given the important role that religion plays in their lives, churches and other religious institutions should assume greater responsibility for the establishment of outreach and support programs. More well-publicized senior centers are needed in areas with high concentrations of Cuban elders, as the variety of social, educational, recreational, and nutritional activities they provide can be very helpful in overcoming feelings of depression and loneliness.

LANGUAGE

Bureaucratic structures must become more sensitive to the language problems of elderly Cubans because language is closely related to problems encountered in using social services as well as to degrees of satisfaction derived from services received. To require that the Spanish-speaking aged communicate their problems and needs in English is insensitive and unrealistic. Hence, there is need for more reading materials in Spanish acquainting elderly Hispanics with available services. Application forms for all elderly programs should be available in Spanish, and more Spanish-speaking staff members are still needed in public facilities located in areas of high Hispanic concentration.

HOUSING

Consideration should be given to the special housing problems of elderly Cubans and other recent elderly immigrants who have not worked in this country long enough to collect the kinds of pensions or social security benefits that would allow the renting of acceptable accommodations in safe neighborhoods. For this group, the need for more low-rent housing is critical.

Perhaps greater incentives should be given to private industry for the construction and rehabilitation of low-cost housing units to help shorten the extremely long waiting lists for subsidized housing that many elderly people must endure.

CONCLUSION

The elderly of Cuban origin differ substantially from other Hispanic elderly groups in this country. This chapter explored recent historical facts and various distinctive characteristics, problems, and needs that set this large cohort apart from other major groups of elderly Hispanics.

An effort was made to integrate the very limited knowledge that presently exists about the Cuban aged. The principal aim was to sensitize legislators, policy makers, program planners, and service deliverers to the unique circumstances of this second largest and yet little-known group of elderly Hispanics.

A good part of the information provided herein is derived from a small number of studies utilizing samples of questionable representativeness. Clearly, there is much need for an expanded data base on Cubans and especially on elderly Cubans.

NOTES

1. There were approximately 831,000 persons of Cuban origin in the United States prior to the Mariel exodus (U.S. Bureau of the Census, 1981c). Adding to that number the 124,779 Mariel entrants (U.S. Department of State, 1980) gives a total of 955,779 Cubans officially in the U.S. by the summer of 1980.

2. Castro's decision to open Mariel harbor probably was triggered by mounting discontent stemming at least partly from his decision in 1979 to allow Cuban-Americans, for the first time in twenty years, to visit relatives in residence on the island. As a result, in just a few months an estimated 100,000 persons visited their families in Cuba, taking with them much evidence of a level of prosperity and material success either unavailable or unknown to their island compatriots.

3. Through the efforts of the U.S. Cuban Refugee Program, which offered sponsors, job contacts, and temporary assistance, almost 300,000 Cubans were settled away from Miami between February 1961 and December 1972 (Perez, 1980). Understandably, however, a large number returned to South Florida, to the tropical climate to which they were accustomed and to relatives and friends of Cuban origin.

4. The median age of the Cuban-origin population thus is significantly higher than the median age of 21.4 years for Mexican-Americans, 20.7 years for Puerto Rican-Americans, and 30.1 years for the total U.S. population (U.S. Bureau of the Census, 1981b).

5. That 95% of the U.S. Cubans are physiognomically white is an instance of the selective nature of the Cuban migration pattern, since 25-28% of the population in Cuba is Black (Aguirre, 1979). Even among the Mariel entrants, Blacks constituted a somewhat lesser proportion (20%) than that observed in the island population (Office of the County Manager, 1981). Probably, Black Cubans have been less inclined to emigrate to this country because of a perception reinforced by the Castro government that the United States is oppressive and exploitive of Black people.

6. The lower fertility rate of women of Cuban origin in this country might be at least partly attributable to their labor force participation which, at 53%, is higher than that of females in the total U.S. population (U.S. Bureau of the Census, 1980).

7. In terms of educational attainment, 68.9% of non-Hispanics in the United States who were 25 years of age and older had completed four years of high school or more, and 16.9% had completed four years of college in 1979. Percentages for Mexican-Americans were 34.9% and 3.9% respectively, and for persons of Puerto Rican origin they were 38.6% and 4.1% respectively (U.S. Bureau of the Census, 1980).

8. Among males 16 years of age and older, those of Cuban origin showed in 1979 a labor force participation rate of 83% compared to 72% for Puerto Ricans, 82% for Mexicans, and 76% for all males in the total U.S. population. Similarly, among females 16 years of age and older, those of Cuban origin showed a labor force participation rate of 53%, compared to 51% for all females in the total U.S. population, 48% for Mexican-Americans, and 33% for Puerto-Rican Americans (U.S. Bureau of the Census, 1980). In relation to unemployment rates, in 1980 it was estimated that 5% of the Cuban-origin population in the United States was unemployed, compared to 6.6% of the total U.S. population, 11.7% of the Puerto Rican-origin population, and 9.4% of the Mexican-origin population (U.S. Bureau of the Census, 1981b). Although these differences may be largely a function of the more mature age structure of the Cuban-origin population (an older population is both more likely to be part of the labor force and less likely to be subject to joblessness), it is possible that they also reflect, to some extent, a strong motivation on the part of many Cuban families to regain their former status.

9. The average income figures in 1978 for those 14 years of age and older were as follows: $7,707 for persons of Cuban origin, $7,375 for persons of Mexican origin, $6,680 for persons of Puerto Rican origin, and $9,451 for the total U.S. population (U.S. Bureau of the Census, 1980).

10. This may be an underestimate because 11.3% of the total Cuban population had been previously estimated to be 65 years of age or older (U.S. Bureau of the Census, 1980).

11. At 9.7% of the Cuban-origin population (U.S. Bureau of the Census, 1981b), the estimate of the number of Cubans 65 years of age and older in the United States in 1980 is as follows: 80,607 of the 831,000 Cubans in the United States prior to the Mariel exodus (U.S. Bureau of the Census 1981c), plus 4,617 Mariel entrants 65 years of age or older (U.S. Department of State, 1980), yielding a total of 85,224. At 11.3% of the Cuban-origin population (U.S. Bureau of the Census, 1980), the estimate of the number of elderly Cubans in the U.S. in 1980 is as follows: 93, 903 of the 831,000 Cubans in the United States prior to the Mariel exodus, plus 4,617 elderly Mariel entrants, yielding a total of 98,520.

12. Home health care is important in maintaining the frail elderly at home. With good supports, most Hispanics would opt for keeping their frail elderly out of institutions. Cubans have recreated in the United States, especially in the Miami-Dade area, their old (pre-Castro) system of privately owned and operated health maintenance organizations (clinics). With emphasis on preventive and health maintenance, these clinics provide a full range of culturally sensitive, relatively low-cost outpatient and ambulatory services.

REFERENCES

Aguirre, B. E. Differential migration of Cuban races. *Latin American Research Review*, 1979, 11, 103-124.

Asociación Nacional Pro Personas Mayores *A national study to assess the service needs of the Hispanic elderly: Final report*. Los Angeles: ANPPM, December 1980 (AOA Grant 0090-A-1295).

ANPPM. *Report of the mini-conference on Hispanic aging: 1981 White House conference on aging*. Los Angeles: January 5-8, 1981.

Casal, L., & Hernandez, A. R. Cubans in the U.S.: A survey of the literature. *Cuban Studies*, 1975, 5, 25-51.

Diaz, G. M. (Ed.). *Evaluation and identification of policy issues in the Cuban community*. Miami: Cuban National Planning Council, July 1981.

Hernandez, A. R. (Ed.). *The Cuban minority in the U.S.: Final report on need identification and program evaluation*. Washington, DC: Cuban National Planning Council, 1974.

Jackson, J. Johnson. *Minorities and aging*. Belmont, CA: Wadsworth Publishing Company, 1980.

Linn, M. W., Hunter, K. I., & Perry, P. R. Differences by sex and ethnicity in the psychosocial adjustment of the elderly. *Journal of Health and Social Behavior*, 1979, 2, 273-281.

Office of the County Manager, Metropolitan Dade County, Florida. *Social and economic problems among Cuban and Haitian entrant groups in Dade County, Florida: Trends and indications*. August 1981.

Perez, L. Cubans. In S. Thernstrom (Ed.), *Harvard encyclopedia of American ethnic groups*. Cambridge, MA: Belknap Press, 1980.

Portes, A. Dilemmas of a golden exile: Integration of Cuban refugee families in Milwaukee. *American Sociological Review*, 1969, 34, 505-518.

Prohias, R. J., & Casal, L. *The Cuban minority in the U.S.: preliminary report on need identification and program evaluation*. Washington, DC: Cuban National Planning Council, 1974.

Szapocznik, J., Scopetta, M. A., Aranalde, M. A., & Kurtines, W. Cuban value structure: Treatment implications. *Journal of Consulting and Clinical Psychology*, 1978, 46, 961-970.

Szapocznik, J., Falletti, M. V., & Scopetta, M. A. Psychological-social issues of Cuban elders in Miami. In J. Szapocznik and M. C. Herrera (Eds.), *Cuban Americans: Acculturation, adjustment, and the family*. Washington, DC: COSSMHO, 1979.

Szapocznik, J., Lasaga, J., Perry, P., & Solomon, J. R. Outreach in the delivery of mental health services to Hispanic elders. *Hispanic Journal of Behavioral Sciences*, 1979, 1, 21-40.

Szapocznik, J., Santisteban, D., Kurtines, W. M., Hervis, O. E., & Spencer, F. Life enhancement counseling: A psychosocial model of services for Hispanic elders. In E. E. Jones & S. J. Korchin (Eds.), *Minority mental health*. New York: Holt, Rinehart & Winston, 1982.

U.S. Bureau of the Census. 1970 census of population. Subject reports. Final Report PC (2)-1C. *Persons of Spanish origin*. Washington, DC: Government Printing Office, June 1973.

U.S. Bureau of the Census. *Statistical abstract of the United States, 1975*. Washington, DC: Government Printing Office, 1975.

U.S. Bureau of the Census. Persons of Spanish origin in the United States: March 1978. *Current population reports*. Series P-20, No. 339, June 1979(a).

U.S Bureau of the Census. *Current housing reports*. Series H-150-78, Part A. Washington, DC: Government Printing Office, 1979(b).

U.S. Bureau of the Census. Persons of Spanish Origin in the United States: March 1979. *Current population reports*. Series P-20, No. 354. Washington, DC: Government Printing Office, October 1980.

U.S. Bureau of the Census. Supplementary reports. *1980 census of population: Age, sex, race, and Spanish origin of the population by regions, divisions, and states: 1980.* PC80-S1-1. Washington, DC: Government Printing Office, May 1981(a).

U.S. Bureau of the Census. Advance report. Persons of Spanish origin in the United States: March 1980. *Current population reports.* Series P-20, No. 361. Washington, DC: Government Printing Office, May 1981(b).

U.S. Bureau of the Census. *Current population reports. Population profile of the United States: 1980.* Series P-20, No. 363. Washington, DC: Government Printing Office, June 1981(c).

U.S. Department of State. *Memorandum from Frederick M. Bohem, Director of the Cuban/ Haitian task force, to Eugene Eidenberg, Secretary of the Cabinet and Assistant to the President for intergovernmental affairs.* Washington, DC: November 6, 1980.

5

The Demography of Mexican-American Aging

RAMON VALLE

The intent of this chapter is to present a brief review of sociodemographic issues impacting elderly Hispanics of Mexican heritage. However, several caveats need to be mentioned before proceeding with this task. First, it is important to note that the Hispanic elderly have considerable intragroup heterogeneity. Hispanics represent the convergence of many distinct national/ethnocultural heritages within one generic designation. In addition, there is considerable intragroup homogeneity within Hispanic subsets, such as within those of Mexican heritage who make up 60% or 8.76 million of the approximately 14.6 million Latino/Hispanic persons residing currently in the United States (U.S. Bureau of Census, 1981).

Too, Mexican-Americans tend to be over-identified with the southwest region of the United States. It is true that as of the mid-1960s, estimates put two-thirds of the group as residing in the area that includes California, Nevada, Arizona, New Mexico, and Texas (Galarza, Gallegos, & Samora, 1969) suggesting that 5.87 million of the current 8.76 million Mexican-heritage Hispanics reside in this region. However, a sizable concentration of Mexican-Americans and their elderly can be found in other regions of the country such as the Pacific Northwest and the Midwest; many have settled in the metropolitan centers of Seattle, Chicago, and Detroit.

Additionally, the persisting problems associated with enumeration of Hispanics in general, and the Mexican-American elderly specifically, need to be taken into account. A case in point is the continued periodic admissions of minority population undercounts despite the methodological advances of the 1980 census. As of this writing, therefore, many doubts remain about the census data base. Most often, the data obtained are not fully representative, have other problems such as noncomparability of samples, or germane data simply have not been collected. Consequently, most discussions, including this chapter, depend heavily upon information drawn from other sources. Even when more accurate Census Bureau information is released in the future, decision makers and providers may expect a natural reluctance on the part of Hispanics to accept at face value information extrapolated from this source. The reader is cautioned to keep these qualifiers in mind as the overall profile of the Mexican-American elderly is presented herein.

THE DEMOGRAPHY OF MEXICAN-AMERICAN AGING

The Hispanic elderly comprise 4.5% of the total Hispanic population (Allan & Brotman, 1981). There are approximately 657,000 Hispanics who are 65 years of age or older. As noted above, Mexican-Americans comprise about two-thirds of the total. Consequently, there are approximately 440,000 elderly Mexican-Americans. In the author's view, these estimates are very conservative. For example, as is common knowledge, the Mexican-American cohort includes a large number of undocumented persons. Second, immediate doubts arise when one looks at data obtained by other sources: The 4.5% estimate appears quite low based on mid-1970 extrapolations that placed the Mexican-American elderly at 8.4% of the total Hispanic population (U.S. Human Resources Corporation, 1976).

SOCIOECONOMIC STATUS

The 1980 census data indicate that 26% of Hispanics at or older than age 65 have incomes below the poverty line, in contrast to 12.5% of the Anglo population (Allan & Brotman, 1981). This has been a constant pattern over the years. During the 1970s, 32.7% of the total Hispanic elderly were well below the poverty line. The rate for the Mexican-American elderly was 36.7% (U.S. Human Resources Corporation, 1976). With the current era's social spending cutbacks, along with the continued placement of minorities at the bottom of the resource provision ladder, the outlook for a socioeconomic turnaround in this decade by the Hispanic elderly in general, or the Mexican-American elderly in particular, is very unlikely.

Allan and Brotman (1981) indicate that 46% of the Anglo elderly between the ages of 65 and 74 have graduated from high school, while only 18% of the Hispanic group have graduated. Among individuals in this same age group, 82% of Anglos in the general population have five years or more of formal education. Only 59% of Hispanics have had five or more years. These educational differences may have a bearing on the Hispanic elderly's access to services because information and referral processes may be pitched to the more formally educated audience of the general population's elderly.

With regard to employment, laborer was the modal occupational category for elderly Mexican-heritage males in the 1970s, and fully 40% of Mexican-heritage women were in the service worker category (U.S. Human Resources Corporation, 1976). Factory work was the second most prevalent occupational category for elderly women of Mexican heritage: About 26% were in this designation (U.S. Human Resources Corporation, 1976).

Obviously, many of the elderly under discussion are unlikely to have adequate health coverage linked to their current or prior occupations. This is supported by field studies conducted by Cuellar and Weeks (1980) which indicated that the combined economic, educational, and prior occupational status of Hispanics may act as access barriers to needed services.

HEALTH, MENTAL HEALTH, AND RELATED INDICES

Observers of elderly Latinos often have noted that Hispanics frequently fail to declare their health needs (Weeks & Cuellar, 1981). However, the Hispanic elderly in general, and the Mexican-American elderly in particular, do indeed have extensive health and mental health related problems (Valle & Mendoza, 1978; Cuellar & Weeks, 1980; Vega, 1980; Cuellar, 1981). Research conducted by Vega (1980) and Meinhart and Vega (1982) utilizing four measures of psychiatric distress identified certain subgroups of Hispanics as especially vulnerable. These subgroups include the more monolingual (Spanish-speaking only) Mexican-American middle-aged woman (40-59 years) and older males (60-69 years). These two groups were found to have unusually high levels of stress and health and mental health dysfunction. Many analysts have suggested that the Mexican-heritage population may be subject to greater health and mental health dysfunctions due to tensions and stressors related to their underclass status within the society (Karno & Edgerton, 1969; Torres-Gil, 1978; Report to the President, 1978; Roberts, 1980a, 1980b).

LIFE EXPECTANCY, MORTALITY,
AND RELATED HEALTH INDICES

Inferences drawn from recent studies indicate a trend toward improved life expectancy for the minority elderly (Bell, Kasschau, & Zellman, 1976; Brotman, 1977). While the data do not specifically sort out Hispanics, they too appear to be sharing the general improvement in life expectancy (Torres-Gil, 1982). For example, some reports indicate a decline in mortality rates among Mexican-Americans in Texas (Roberts & Askew, 1972) and the mortality rate among Mexican-American males, which in 1950 was 1.66 times greater than that of Anglos, had dropped by 1960 to approximate (1.12) the Anglo rate (Roberts & Askew, 1972). The rate for Mexican-American females, which was 2.43 times greater than the Anglo female rate in 1950, had dropped to a ratio of 1.67 by 1960.

However, inferior health has been documented extensively among Hispanic agricultural workers due to their nutritional deficiencies, working conditions, and exposure to toxic substances (California Raza Health Alliance, 1979; Morgan, 1980). Prevalent health problems include respiratory diseases and dermatological problems. Nalven (1982) has indicated the presence of similar health problems for undocumented urban workers, and Orleans (1979) for rural Mexican-Americans. Inferior dental health and hygiene also have been reported for Mexican-Americans of all social class levels (Garcia & Juarez, 1978). A recent comprehensive needs assessment survey conducted in Los Angeles among the elderly revealed that 30% of Hispanic respondents reported major health problems. In contrast, only 14% of Anglos who were 55 years of age or older reported major problems (Young, 1982).

ACCESS TO SERVICES AND ATTENDANT RESOURCES

It is important to underscore that despite the higher vulnerability of the Hispanic elderly, and the Mexican-American elderly in particular, they continue to underutilize formal care-giving services. This holds for health and mental health services (Torres-Gil, 1978) as well as for their participation in nutrition services, homemaker services, and supplemental security income programs (SSI) (Cuellar & Weeks, 1980). With regard to the SSI benefits program, for example, Cuellar and Weeks found a probable need for SSI for nearly every Hispanic respondent in their San Diego study group. Specifically, while 92% of the respondents met the SSI criteria, only 42% were receiving SSI assistance.

Meinhart and Vega (1982) have found that Mexican-heritage Hispanics of all ages (to include the elderly) are not inhibited in their use of private physicians to meet both their physical and mental health needs. They are inhibited, however, with respect to the utilization of community mental health and related human services. The list of barriers to services utilization by Hispanics is extensive and focuses upon factors such as racism and discrimination, expressed in terms of lacks in cultural and linguistic sensitivity evidenced by service providers (Valle & Mendoza, 1978; Torres-Gil, 1978; Cuellar & Weeks, 1980).

The lack of linguistic sensitivity on the part of service providers merits special attention. The 1970 census indicated Spanish as the preferred language of 71.9% of individuals in the 55 to 64 age group and 85.4% of those at or older than age 65 (U.S. Bureau of Census, 1972). Language loyalty, as reported in 1970, ran almost as high among Mexican-Americans in the 45 to 54 age group; 75% of these individuals indicated Spanish as the language preference at home (Urban Associates, 1974). More recent studies have yielded findings indicating the continued salience of language. For example, Cuellar and Weeks (1980) found 97% of their Hispanic study sample as experiencing some difficulty with English even though 43% of the respondents were identified as having some bilingual capability. It should be noted that despite the general consistency of the data base with regard to the Spanish language preference, there is no discernible move by the human services toward responding to the call for appropriate bilingual/bicultural personnel in working with the Mexican-American heritage elderly specifically, or Hispanics in general (Torres-Gil, 1982).

One additional factor, residency status, warrants attention with regard to services utilization. In any given community one can expect to fine three categories of individuals: (1) native-born United States citizens; (2) foreign-born individuals with legal residency; and (3) foreign-born undocumented persons. With regard to the latter group, an important point needs to be made. These undocumented individuals are not likely to be the new arrivals as popularly reported in the media. Rather, they are often long-time residents who were brought over as children by parents and grandparents or who fled revolutionary unrest at the earlier part of the century: All came hurriedly without documents.

Professionals in the field often attest to a key difficulty related to residency status. Specifically, although it is difficult to discern who is and who is not documented, any formal efforts to determine status may have a direct or subtle bearing on the utilization of services by many members of a population that is generally apprehensive about their relationship to the majority community's formal support systems (Valle & Mendoza, 1978; Santos, 1981). Elimination of policies requiring proof of legal residency may relieve some of this generalized apprehension.

SUMMARY

As a group, the Mexican heritage elderly have less formal education, lower lifelong income levels, and have been concentrated in lower occupational categories compared to their Anglo counterparts. While the data are not firm, their life expectancy appears to be improving. Nevertheless, this improvement is taking place within the context of continued high health and mental health risk patterns. Moreover, specific Mexican heritage subgroups such as those who are foreign-born or who are primarily monolingual (Spanish-speaking only) manifest extraordinary risk patterns in contrast to the Anglo population. As noted above, males between the ages of 60 to 69 years and females in the 40 to 59 age group are highly vulnerable.

There are many foreign-born individuals within the ranks of the Mexican elderly, an undeterminate number of whom may have difficulty in documenting their legal residency status. These individuals, as well as other elderly Mexicans, maintain a strong loyalty to Spanish as their language of communication. Finally, although the Mexican heritage elderly are concentrated in the southwestern United States with roughly two-thirds residing in the area, the remaining third is dispersed throughout a range of geographic settings with many being located in the Midwest and Pacific Northwest.

REFERENCES

Acosta, F. Barriers between mental health services and Mexican Americans: An examination of a paradox. *American Journal of Psychology*, 1979, 7(5), 503-520.

Allan, C., & Brotman, H. *Chartbook on aging in America*. 1981 White House Conference on Aging, 1981.

Atencio, T. The survival of La Raza despite social services. *Social Casework*, 1977, 52(5), 262-268.

Bell, D., Kasschau, P., & Zellman, G. *Delivery of services to elderly members of minority groups: A critical review of the literature*. Santa Monica, CA: Rand Corporation, 1976.

Boulette, T. R. Mass media and other mental health promotional strategies for low income Chicano/Mexicanos. In R. Valle & W. Vega (Eds.), *Hispanic natural support systems*. Sacramento: California State Department of Mental Health, 1980.

Burruel, G., & Chavez, N. Mental health outpatient centers: Relevant or irrelevant to Mexican Americans. In A. B. Tulepon, C. L. Attneave & J. Kingstone (Eds.), *Beyond Clinic Walls*. Tuscaloosa: University of Alabama Press, 1974.

Butler, R. *Why Survive? Being Old in America*. New York: Harper & Row, 1975.

California Raza Health Alliance. *The California Raza Health Plan: An Action Guide for the Promotion of Raza Health in California*. Unpublished report, Berkeley, 1979.

Cohen, G. D. *Gerontologist*, 1978, 18, 313-314.

Cuellar, I. Service delivery and mental health services for Chicano elders. In M. Miranda, & R. Ruiz *Chicano Aging and Mental Health*. Department of Health and Human Services Publication Adm. 81-952, 1981.

Cuellar, J., & Weeks, J. *Minority Elderly Americans: The Assessment of Needs and Equitable Receipt of Public Benefits as a Prototype in Area Agencies on Aging, Final Report*. San Diego, CA: Allied Home Health Association, Grant AOA/DHHS 90-A-1667 (01), 1980.

Galarza, E., Gallegos, H., & Samora, J. *Mexican Americans in the Southwest*. Santa Barbara, CA: McNally & Loftin, 1969.

Garcia, J., & Juarez, R. Z. Utilization of dental health services by Chicanos and Anglos. *Journal of Health and Social Behavior*, 1978, 19, 428-436.

Garcia y Griego, M. *El Volumen de la Migracion de Mexicanos No Documentados a los Estudes Unidos (Vevas Hipotesis)*. Estudios 4 Mexico, D. F. Centro Nacional de Informacion y Estudisticas del Trabajo.

Jackson, J. J. Social gerontology and the Negroes: A review. *Gerontologist*, 1967, 7, 168-178.

Jackson, J. J. Aged Negroes: Their cultural departures from statistical stereotypes and rural urban differences. *Gerontologist*, 1970, 10, 140-145.

Karno, M., & Edgerton, R. Perceptions of mental illness in a Mexican American community. *Archives of General Psychiatry*, 1969, 20(1), 233-238.

Karno, M. The enigma of ethnicity in a psychiatric clinic. *Archives of General Psychiatry*, 1966, 14(5), 516-520.

Kramer, M. The rising pandemic of mental disorders and associated chronic diseases and disabilities. *Acta. Psychiat. Scandinavia*, 1980, 62, 382-397.

Meinhart, K., & Vega, W. Health and social correlates of mental health. Unpublished paper, 1982.

Miranda, M. Mexican American dropouts in psychotherapy as related to levels of acculturation. In *Psychotherapy with the Spanish Speaking: Issues in Research and Service Delivery*. University of California at Los Angeles, 1976.

Montiel, M. Chicanos in the United States: An overview of the sociohistorical context and emerging perspectives. In M. Montiel (Ed.), *Hispanic Families*. Washington, DC: National Coalition of Hispanic Mental Health and Human Services Organizations, 1978.

Morgan, D. Morbidity and Mortality in Workers' Occupational Exposure to Pesticides. *Archives of Environmental Contamination and Toxicology*, 1980, 9, 3, 349-382.

Muñoz, R. A strategy for prevention of psychological problems in Latinos: Emphasizing accessibility and effectiveness. In R. Valle and W. Vega (Eds.), *Hispanic Natural Support Systems*. Sacramento: State of California Department of Mental Health, 1980.

Neugarten, B. L. Age groups in American society: The time of the young old. *Political Consequences of Aging Annals*, 1974, (415), 187-198.

Orleans, M. *Mexican American elderly in three Colorado communities: An assessment of needs*. Denver: University of Colorado Medical School, Grant So 2181-01, 1979.

Phillipus, M. J. Successful and unsuccessful approaches to mental health services for an urban Hispanic population. *American Journal of Public Health*, 1971, 61, 820-830.

Pitt, L. *The decline of the Californios: Social history of Spanish speaking Californians, 1846-1890*. Berkeley and Los Angeles: University of California Press, 1966.

President's Commission on Mental Health. *Report to the President, (Vol. 3) Hispanic Americans*. Washington, DC: Government Printing Office, 1978.

Roberts, R., & Askew. A consideration of mortality in three subcultures. *Health Services Reports*, 1972, 87, 262-270.

Roberts, R. The health of Mexican Americans, evidence from the population laboratory studies. *American Journal of Public Health*, 1980 70(4).

Roberts, R. Prevalence of psychological distress among Mexican Americans. *Journal of Health and Social Behavior*, 1980, 21, 134-145.

Romero, J. T. Hispanic support systems: Health, mental health promotion strategies. In R. Valle and W. Vega (Eds.), *Hispanic Natural Support Systems*. Sacramento: California Department of Mental Health, 1980.

Ruiz, R., & Miranda, M. A priority list of research questions on the mental health of Chicano Elderly. In M. Miranda & R. Ruiz *Chicano Aging and Mental Health*. Department of Health and Human Services Publication Adm. 81-952, 1981.

Ruiz, P. Culture and mental health. *Journal of Contemporary Psychotherapy*, 1977, 9(1), 24-27.

Santos, R. Aging and Chicano mental health: An economic perspective. In M. Miranda and R. Ruiz (Eds.), *Chicano Aging and Mental Health*. Department of Health and Human Services Publication Adm. 81-952, 1981.

Solomon, B. Minority group issues and benefit programs for the elderly. *Policy Issues Concerning Minority Elderly Final Report*, San Francisco: U.S. Human Resources Corporation (Grant DHEW 105-17 3004), 1978.

State of California Department of Mental Health. Ethnic and Sex Profile of Full-Time Employees by Department, Job Category, and Classification. Sacramento, CA, September 30, 1981.

Toldsfor, C. Social networker, support and coping: An exploratory study. *Family Process*, 1976, 15(4), 407-417.

Torres-Gil, F. Political behavior: A study of political attitudes and political participation among older Mexican Americans. Unpublished doctoral dissertation, Brandeis University, 1976.

Torres-Gil, F. Age, health and culture: An examination of health among Spanish-speaking elderly. In M. Montiel (Ed.), *Hispanic Families*. Washington, DC: National Coalition of Hispanic Mental Health and Human Services Organizations (OSSMHO), 1978.

Torres-Gil, F. Health and mental health issues affecting the older Hispanic. *El Centro Boletin Informativo*, 1982, 1(4), 1, 8, 1982.

U.S. Bureau of the Census. *Persons of Spanish origins in the United States*. March 1971 and 1972, Series P 20 No. 250. Washington, DC: Government Printing Office, 1973.

U.S. Bureau of the Census. *Current population reports. Population characteristics: Persons of Spanish origin in the United States*. March 1971 (Advance Report Series P 20, No. 255, Washington, DC: Government Printing Office, 1974.

U.S. Bureau of the Census. *1980 census population on housing*. Advance Report Series, PHC 80-4-1, Washington, DC, 1981.

U.S. Human Resources Corporation. *Theories of Social Gerontology for Research and Programming by the Administration on Aging, Final Report*, San Francisco: U.S. Human Resources Corporation (Grant DHEW 100-76-006) 1976.

Urban Associates, Inc. *Study of Selected Characteristics of Ethnic Minorities Based on the 1970 Census, Volume 1, Americans of Spanish Origin*. A report prepared for the Office of Special Concerns, Assistant Secretary for Planning and Evaluation, U.S. Department of Health, Education and Welfare (OS) 75-120, 1974.

Valle, R. Natural support systems, minority groups and the later life dementias: Implications for service delivery research and policy. In N. Miller, and G. D. Cohen, *Clinical Aspects of Alzheimer's Disease and Senile Dementia* (Aging, Vol. 15). New York: Raven Press, 1981.

Valle, R., & Mendoza, L. *The Elder Latino*, San Diego, CA: Campanile Press, 1978.

Vega, W. Defining Hispanic high risk groups: Targeting populations for health promotion. In R. Valle & W. Vega (Eds.), *Hispanic Natural Support Systems*. Sacramento: State of California Department of Mental Health, 1980.

Velez, C. G., Verdugo, R., & Nunez, F. Politics and mental health among elderly Mexicans. In M. Miranda, & R. Ruiz *Chicano Aging and Mental Health*. Department of Health and Human Services Publication No. Adm. 81-952, 1981.

Warheit, G., Vega, W., Shumizen, D., & Meinhart, K. Interpersonal coping networks and mental health among four race-ethnic groups. In *American Journal of Community Psychology*, 1983.

Weeks, J., & Cuellar, J. The role of family members in the helping networks of older people. *Gerontologist*, 1981, 21(4), 388-394.

Young, J. *Aging in Los Angeles County: A Needs Assessment of Service to Older Persons in Planning Service Area 19 California*. Los Angeles County Department of Senior Citizen Affairs, and Clairmont Graduate School, Center for Applied Social Research, 1982.

6

Native-American Elders
Current Issues and Social Policy Implications

E. DANIEL EDWARDS

As a group, American Indian people represent less than 1% of the population of the United States. According to statistics reported in early tabulations of the 1980 census, the population of American Indians, Eskimos, and Aleuts was 1,418,195 (U.S. Bureau of the Census, 1981). This compares with a reported population of American Indians in 1960 of 546,228 (Block, 1979, p. 186) and 763,000 in 1970 (U.S. Bureau of the Census 1978, p. 2). There are over 400 different tribal groups in the United States today. These tribal groups speak over 250 distinct languages (National Indian Council on Aging wNICAE, 1981a, p. 13). It is obvious that each tribal group and each community should be related to on an individual basis.

Slightly more than half (50.7%) of the American Indian population is concentrated in the western part of the United States. American Indians, Eskimos, and Aleuts represent 16% of the population of Alaska. They make up 4 to 8% of the populations of the states of New Mexico, South Dakota, Oklahoma, Arizona, and Montana (Bureau of the Census, 1981).

The 1980 census provides interesting data related to age distribution of American Indians in comparison with other groups as reported in Table 6-1. These data indicate that American Indians, Eskimos, and Aleuts have the

TABLE 6-1   Median Age of U.S. Citizens: 1980

Category	Median Age
United States (total population)	30.0 years
White population	31.3 years
Asian/Pacific Islanders	28.6 years
Black population	24.9 years
Spanish origin population	23.2 years
American Indians, Eskimos, Aleuts	23.0 years

TABLE 6-2 Age Composition of U.S. Citizens: 1980

Category	Percentage of Population Under 15 Years of Age	Percentage of Population 65 Years of Age and Over
White population	21.3	12.2
Black population	28.7	7.9
Spanish-origin population	32.0	4.9
American Indians, Eskimos, and Aleuts	31.8	5.3

lowest median age of all groups surveyed. However, there is considerable concern that many older American Indian people are not represented in the census survey and that more accurate information would indicate a much larger population.

The 1980 census also included information related to age distribution, with analysis of the age distribution of younger citizens (under 15 years of age) and older citizens (65 years and older). This information is reported in Table 6-2.

While the American Indian, Eskimo, and Aleut population is numerically much smaller than any of the other racial groups, the problems and concerns evidenced by this small population are demanding of serious attention. For example, the National Indian Council on Aging (1981a, p. 12) has indicated that more than 25% of Indians over 60 years of age have less than a fifth-grade education; 63% have not attended high school; and only 18% are high school graduates. More than 10% of Indian elders in a recent national survey indicated a need for job training.

INDIAN AGING ISSUES

TRADITIONAL VALUES AND CUSTOMS OF OLDER AMERICAN INDIANS

The American Indian elderly were regarded historically as an important resource to their tribal groups. Older American Indian people made significant contributions to the lifestyle and general well-being of their tribes. Traditionally, they were treated with high regard. Tribesmen and clanspeople often called elderly American Indians "grandfather" and "grandmother" without regard to blood relationship. Old age was equated with wisdom and learning; it was a period of time when honor and respect were bestowed. In addition, older American Indians were active people. They performed a variety of important and beneficial roles, including instructing the young and helping care for children. They also maintained responsibility for remembering and relating tribal philosophies, myths, traditions, and stories/events peculiar to their tribal groups. They often served as religious and political advisors to tribal leaders. In many ways, they actively supported and demonstrated the values and traditions of their tribes and promoted and encouraged feelings of cultural pride and identity in young people. Currently, older American Indians, like American Indian people generally, are facing periods of transition. Their changing cultures, lifestyles, and traditions have forced them to modify to some extent the roles and responsibilities they perform in their various tribal groups. However, Indian aged continue to manifest an interest and concern for their people and especially the youth. Tapping these resources and involving American Indian elders in worthwhile and contributing roles are important issues that should be addressed by American Indian tribes and those working with American Indian elderly.

ECONOMIC CONDITIONS OF
OLDER AMERICAN INDIANS

Several economic issues deserve attention as they relate to older American Indians. Income levels are of considerable concern. Many older American Indians live on fixed, reduced incomes in amounts of less than $3,000 that do not compensate for inflated costs of living (Judge, 1978).

In 1969, the median income of American Indians 45 years of age and older was $2,117, as compared with $3,959 for people from all races. Recent data related to poverty level figures have shown that 50.8% of American Indians 65 years of age and older received incomes below poverty levels compared to 27.3% of similarly aged individuals in other racial groups (U.S. Bureau of the Census, 1978, pp. 8-9).

Another economic issue of concern to older American Indians is employment. Employment levels of older American Indians are very low. In 1979-1980, the National Indian Council on Aging (NICA) conducted a nationwide survey of 700 Indians and Alaskan natives who were 45 years of age or older. The employment levels of these Indians are shown in Table 3 (NICA, 1981b, p. 5).

As evidenced in Table 6-3, 28.81% of all those 45 years of age or older were either out of work or working only part time. Low employment levels of

TABLE 6-3   Employment Status of American Indians and Alaska Natives by Age, 1979-80 (N = 700)

| Category | Indian/Alaska Natives by Age | | |
	45+ years	55+ years	60+ years
Employed full-time	18.5	10.7	.8
Employed part-time	9.6	8.3	7.5
Not employed, seeking work	6.3	4.7	3.9
Not employed, not seeking work	12.9	13.5	13.6
Retired	29.7	41.2	49.9
Retired on disability	14.9	16.6	16.0

this magnitude suggest the necessity of joint living arrangements among the Indian elderly, and fully 60% of Indian elderly support other family members with their inadequate incomes (NICA, 1981a). Older Indian people obviously find it an economic necessity to live with family and relatives.

Further concern is warranted by the lack of participation of older Indians in Social Security. Because many American Indians did not have employment opportunities on their reservations, social security benefits are not available to them (Chino, 1978). Older American Indians also have limited participation in private retirement programs.

Some of the policy issues that must be addressed in dealing with the economic circumstances of American Indians relate to the need for more data regarding numbers of older American Indian people in specific age categories. Attention should be given to educating American Indians regarding retirement benefits. While there is some discussion related to proposed changes in social security eligibility ages, such recommendations should not be made until a study is conducted to determine how they will affect the eligibility of ethnic populations. Income tax credits for persons who financially support older American Indian people would assist in providing more adequate care for this population. Older Indian people desire opportunities to be involved actively in their families, communities, and cultural customs. If funds were made available, older Indians could be helpful in recording Indian history, language, culture, customs, and values. They could be useful in providing education for Indian children and non-Indian children related to American Indian traditions and culture. Training for employment in aging programs could be helpful, as could work opportunities with homebound elderly people. Funding resources should be brought to the attention of Indian tribal groups who could apply for grants to provide employment opportunities for American Indian elders.

HEALTH AND MENTAL HEALTH ISSUES

Other important issues related to older American Indian people concern health and mental health care services. Data in Table 6-4 depict the four leading causes of death among American Indians and others who are 45 years of age or older (U.S. Bureau of the Census, 1978, p. 29).

As is evident in Table 6-4, accidents, cirrhosis of the liver, and influenza and pneumonia contribute highly to death rates among American Indian people. Moss (1968), in his study of excessive drinking of Ute Indians, indicated that 93 out of 102 Indian deaths over a five-year period were directly or indirectly related to excessive drinking.

Other health problems of grave concern to older American Indians include obesity, gall bladder diseases, diabetes, cataract conditions, rheumatoid arthritis, hypertension, dental problems, and liver and kidney diseases (NICA, 1978a, p. 123, 1981, p. 2).

TABLE 6-4   Four Leading Causes of Death* Among American Indians
            Compared To Persons Of All Races 45+ Years Old By Age, 1974*

Age and Cause of Death	Percentage of all deaths	
	American Indians and Alaska Natives	All Races
45 to 59 Years of Age		
Diseases of the heart	20.3	34.1
Accidents	16.9	5.3
Cirrhosis of the liver	13.7	4.9
Malignant neoplasms	13.1	27.9
60+ Years of Age		
Diseases of the heart	32.1	44.0
Malignant neoplasms	14.0	18.2
Influenza and pneumonia	5.5	3.1
Accidents	5.2	2.1
65+ Years of Age		
Diseases of the heart	32.2	44.7
Malignant neoplasms	13.5	16.9
Influenza and pneumonia	5.8	3.3
Accidents	4.5	2.0

SOURCE: Indian Health Service, unpublished data; and National Center for Health Statistics, Monthly
Vital Statistics Report, Vol. 24, No. 11, Supplement, and unpublished data.

*Diseases are listed in rank order of occurrence among American Indians and Alaska natives.

**Data for American Indians and Alaska natives are based on 24 Federal Reservation States and Alaska.

Unfortunately, data reflecting needs of urban American Indians are almost nonexistent. However, there is some published support for concerns related to loneliness and depression among urban Indian aged (NICA, 1978a).

A number of recommendations have been drafted to address the health care needs of American Indian elderly. These include development of a health policy that will adequately address the health needs and concerns of American Indian people and implement services to address these needs. Other suggestions include reviewing Indian health service facilities and services, along with subsequent provisions of adequate funding to address identified needs.

For example, one concern relates to dietary and nutrition needs of older American Indian people. An important yet unaddressed research question focuses on the contribution of diet to health problems such as diabetes, liver and kidney disease, and obesity that particularly affect American Indian people. Nutrition programs can help older American Indian people become better aware of their nutritional needs and resources. A special concern relates to the provision of non-Indian medical care in conjunction with traditional medicine. Many traditional American Indian people have confidence in and a need for traditional health care from their own tribal medicine people. Continuing to maintain and encourage cooperative relationships between traditional Indian medicine people and non-Indian medical people is particularly important. A potential problem between professional health care staff and Indian clients must also be considered. Many older American Indian people do not speak English or are bilingual with a preference for their Indian language. Provision of bilingual professional and support staff is crucial for improving the health care status of American Indian people. Another concern relates to the need for educational safety programs that focus on the Indian elderly (NICA, 1978b, pp. 187-188). Equally important is the provision of transportation for older American Indian people. Many American Indian elders do not have access to transportation on a regular basis or do not wish to impose upon others in facilitating health care treatment. Agencies must become aware of these needs and incorporate plans to address them.

HOUSING

According to a 1981 NICA report, older American Indians suffer from inadequate housing with incomes inadequate to cover their necessities of life. Overcrowding is also a condition under which many older Indian people live. Plumbing and other modern conveniences are not available to many American Indian elders. Medical and nursing care outside the home is usually costly and often looked upon with disfavor by older American Indian people. In spite of the inadequate housing situations faced by many Indian elderly, a recent study indicated that older Indian people preferred overwhelmingly to live within their own homes. Their satisfaction with themselves as individuals was positively correlated with maintaining their own residence (Manson and Pambrun, 1978).

In order to address the housing needs of older American Indians, studies should be conducted to determine the most appropriate type of housing for their use. Housing projects should, whenever possible, take into consideration the needs of the elderly people and their Indian values and customs. Nursing homes and hospitals should be utilized as a last resort, with supportive services such as homemaker services being made available to older American Indian people to allow them to remain in their homes. When nursing home care is warranted, consideration should be given to provision of tribal-owned and operated homes that make use of culturally specific building designs, with appropriate facilities for family members to sleep overnight and medicine people to provide religious services. Provisions for traditional healing practices, sweatbaths, cultural and religious ceremonies, and native foods should be considered.

FAMILY SUPPORT

As has been stated earlier, American Indians were traditionally very committed to family activities and unity. Older American Indian people have played an important role in caring for grandchildren. A recent study (NICA, 1981, p. 5) showed that 26% of Indian elderly were caring for at least one grandchild, and 67% of all older American Indians live within five miles of relatives upon whom they depend for socialization, chores, and routine obligations.

Special consideration should be given to helping American Indian people operate within the values of their particular tribal group. Specific attention should be given to ways in which families may be more responsive to the needs of older Indian people and how older Indian people can be utilized to perform meaningful roles not only with their own grandchildren, but with young American Indians generally.

For example, the NICA (1981b) has encouraged older American Indian people to become involved in the foster grandparent program and the senior companion program where volunteers may contribute tangible service and receive nontaxable stipends at the same time. They indicate that of the 62 federally funded senior companion programs in the United States, only two of these are specifically administered for American Indians. This resource should be made more available to American Indian people.

It is important that attention be given to the unique needs of older American Indian women. Over 55% of Indian women 60 years of age and older are widowed. Special problems of loneliness, inadequate transportation, and lack of resources for home maintenance and family support systems are concerns of older American Indian women (NICA, 1981a, p. 15).

A recent survey of agencies serving American Indian/Alaskan Native elderly (Edwards, Edwards, & Daines, 1981) identified many needs of older American Indian people. A number of creative aging projects were described by respondents to this survey including a variety of types of home care; health, mental, and medical services; meals on wheels and trays on sleighs; nutrition education; home improvement and home maintenance services; driver education; legal services seminars; and provision of language interpreters. An important and gratifying finding of this study was that there are many agencies and professional people who are interested in learning more about American Indian/Alaskan native elderly.

Attention should be provided by agencies while not overlooking the value and contributions of the family system. American Indian families and tribal groups must be involved in determining directions for policy implementation to meet the needs of elderly American Indians. Areas that should be addressed require attention to cultural factors, language, and American Indian religion. Feelings of belonging and tribal identity must be taken into consideration as attempts are made to address the needs of American Indian elders (Red Horse, 1981). American Indian people must be involved in planning to better meet their needs and facilitate the enjoyment of their later years. Specifically, attention should be given to addressing attitudes toward life and loneliness conditions, security conditions, health conditions, legal assistance, and transportation (Dukepoo, 1975). Grants must be made available to American Indian people with attention given to training and educating American Indian people in writing and implementing such grants (Curley, 1979).

SUMMARY

There are many needs that must be addressed if American Indian elderly are to receive the benefit of services which they deserve and from which they could prosper. The following require consideration.

(1) There is a need for more information regarding the special concerns, interests, and privations of older American Indian people. This will require well-developed research projects conducted by professionally trained people. It is hoped that these projects will involve competent researchers and that there will be efforts to train American Indian people to develop their own research and professional skills.

(2) There is a need to provide health, mental health, recreational, and daily living support systems for American Indian people.

(3) There is a need for addressing American Indian people's concerns as individuals, as members of families and communities, as members of tribal groups, and as American Indian people generally.

(4) There is a need for education of American Indian people—not only the aged but American Indian people generally—to address the needs of all American Indian people and specifically American Indian aged.

(5) There is a need to better understand American Indian people. The problems that have been identified herein must be addressed so that others may not require rehabilitative services, but may be facilitated in their personal growth through preventive measures.

REFERENCES

Block, R. F. Exiled Americans: The plight of Indian aged in the United States. In D. E. Gilfand & A. J. Kutzick (Eds.), *Ethnicity and Aging.* New York: Springer, 1979.

Chino, W. Excerpts of address. *Final report of the Second National Indian Conference on Aging.* Billings, MT, 1978.

Curley, L. Title VI of the Older American Act, Grants to Indian Tribes. In E. P. Stanford (Ed.), *Minority aging research.* San Diego: Campanile, 1979.

Dukepoo, F. Chochise in centrifuge—A brief analysis. In E. P. Stanford (Ed.), *Minority aging.* San Diego: Center on Aging, 1975.

Edwards, E. D., Edwards, M. E., & Daines, G. M. American Indians/Alaskan native elderly: A current and vital concern. *Journal of Gerontological Social Work,* Spring 1980, 2 (3), 212-224.

Judge, T. L. Welcoming remarks. *Final Report of the Second National Indian Conference on Aging.* Billings, MT, 1978.

Manson, S. M., and Pambrun, A. M. Social and Psychological Status of the Indian Elderly: Past research, current advocacy, and future inquiry, Appendix A. *Final report of the Second National Indian Conference on Aging.* Billings, MT, 1978.

Moss, F. E. *Problems resulting from excessive drinking of the Ute Indians.* Western Region Indian Alcoholism Training Center, University of Utah, 1968. (mimeo)

National Indian Council on Aging (NICA) Physical and mental health of elderly American Indians. *Final Report of the Second National Indian Conference on Aging.* Billings, MT, 1978. (a)

NICA. Data and material to support a community education and safety program to reduce accidents among the elderly Indians. *Final Report of the Second National Indian Conference on Aging.* Billings, MT, 1978. (b)

NICA. Samples of conference recommendations. *National Indian Council on Aging News,* Fall 1980, 4 (3), p. 8.

NICA. 1981 White House Conference on Aging: The Indian issues. *National Indian Council on Aging Quarterly,* Autumn 1981, 4 (1). (a)

NICA. Employment and the elderly. *National Indian Council on Aging Quarterly,* Winter 1981, 1 (1), 2-4. (b)

Red Horse, J. E. American Indian elders: Needs and aspirations in institutional and home health care. In E. P. Stanford (Ed.), *Minority aging: Policy issues for the 1980's.* San Diego, Campanile, 1981.

U.S. Bureau of the Census. *Statistical reports on older Americans: Social, economic, and health characteristics of older American Indians* (Part 2 of 2). Washington, DC: Government Printing Office, 1978.

U.S. Bureau of the Census. *1980 census of the population.* Washington, DC: Government Printing Office, 1981.

PART III

Exemplars of Aging in a
Cultural Context
Three Minority Groups

Demographic data presented in the previous section have outlined some of the quantitative aspects of minority aging. However, they do not specify either the conditions under which one grows old or how the aged and the processes of aging vary from group to group. Indeed, the decrements of aging often blur one's vision to the central role of culture and society in determining individual and group differences in aging. This suggests that knowledge of the earlier life experiences of aged individuals is crucial to an understanding of their current situations. These earlier life experiences not only help to define who the aged individual is; they also help to explain some of the variations in status, adaptive behavior, and life satisfaction.

In illustration, the three papers presented in this section identify some of the important sociocultural factors that make minority aging a unique experience. A broad range of topics is explored. However, the primary focus of each chapter is on those psychological and social forces that appear to affect the aging process most significantly. Discussed, for example, are familial support systems, self-esteem and coping patterns, racism, religiosity, and age-related prestige patterns. In the case of each group, the influences of unique historical events are taken into account.

Doman Lum highlights important features of the aging experience among Asian-Americans from the standpoint of the socioeconomic political configuration, the myth of the model minority, and traditional and changing patterns of family dynamics. In doing so, Lum identifies many of the unique characteristics that distinguish the Asian-American elderly from other aged groups.

In her discussion of the Black aging experience, Nellie Tate identifies several race-related aging discriminants. By means of a conceptual model and a survey of gerontological literature, Tate makes a comparison of Black and white elderly groups from which she derives a number of practical implications.

This section concludes with an article by Rosina Becerra examining the life experiences of elderly Mexican-Americans. Noting that the urbanization of the Mexican-American generally is perceived as being extremely disruptive in their adaptation to aging, she maintains that traditional familial structures are being modified to fit the new economic, social, and cultural conditions of urban living. In addition, Becerra suggests that these patterns, including generational acculturation, have forced the creation of other support networks, many of which are antithetical to traditional ways of meeting human needs.

7

Asian-Americans and Their Aged

DOMAN LUM

The experience of aging among Asian-Americans reflects a variety of socio-cultural factors affecting Chinese, Japanese, Filipino, Korean, and Vietnam-ese populations. Although one could assert that each Asian subgroup has its own unique history, culture, and family patterns, many Asian-Americans share the experience of having entered the United States as contract laborers at the turn of the century. Successive waves of Asian immigrants became grocery store keepers, restaurant owners, and farmers. Their children rose to become middle-class professionals and were molded in the American edu-cational system.

At present, the Asian-American elderly consist of a number of different cluster groups, including (1) retired single male elders, mainly Chinese and Filipino, who were denied marital rights due to immigration restrictions dur-ing the first half of this century: (2) elderly females, mainly Japanese, who entered this country as picture brides; (3) those who were immigrants or American-born during the early 1900s; (4) elderly family members who came with their sons and daughters during the last 20 years from China-Hong Kong, Taiwan, Korea, and the Philippines; and (5) recently arrived elderly persons who entered with their families as a result of the Vietnamese and Cambodian wars.

The purpose of this chapter is to identify some selective physiological, psychological, and social factors unique to the Asian-American sociocul-tural experience. While there are unique historical influences specific to each subgroup, the intent is to draw upon some broad themes among the Asian-American elderly without constructing artificial commonalities.

SOCIOECONOMIC-POLITICAL SITUATION FOR ASIAN AMERICAN ELDERLY

Elderly Asian Americans have experienced a series of life situations that have affected their cognitive, affective, and behavioral reaction patterns in the United States. Historically, each minority group has suffered oppression and discrimination in their interaction with the majority forces in the United States. In the case of Asian Americans, they were excluded from immigration into the United States in the early part of this century by restrictive laws. In particular, Japanese-Americans were interned in relocation centers (American concentration camps) during World War II and lost millions of dollars in property and income. More recently, the influx of Vietnamese immigrants has caused resentment and reprisals among Americans who must compete with them for welfare benefits and employment. As a result of the minority status of Asian-Americans, the elderly have known the meaning of powerlessness in the face of political, social, and economic power and control. A survival behavioral response has been to remain silent and reserved in the midst of overwhelming threat. Economic exploitation is another factor for the Asian-American elderly who do not speak English. Confined to menial jobs (e.g. dishwasher or farm laborer), these Asian elderly have experienced years of exploitation by their employers. Without adequate compensation and on meager living subsistence, many Asian elderly are angry, broken, and resentful in spirit. These feelings are often masked in order to function and cope in a society that has minimal concern for their welfare.

Perhaps these are the reasons why Asian elderly have held to culture maintenance. Turning to traditional values and customs has been a means of avoiding unpleasant realities and reaffirming cultural existence. The affirmation, protection, and commitment of cultural preservation and endorsement have remained with the elderly. The transmission of ideas, customs, skills, and the arts and language of various Asian countries from the elderly to successive generations is a major value and goal.

As a result, these life experiences have produced a cognitive mind set, affective responses, and behavioral actions for the Asian elderly. Thus a given situation that may be threatening to an Asian elderly person elicits a passive and demure response based on a conscious and deliberate choice of cognitive and affective reaction. Learned over years of dealing with authorities and institutions, the Asian elderly have set up defense barriers. However, when the same person is in a familiar ethnic community setting, the behavioral action may be altogether the opposite.

These life factors form the basis for understanding and interacting with the Asian elderly. A knowledge of the Asian community and the role and problems of the Asian elderly are the starting points for understanding them. They are reticent about sharing problems outside the immediate family.

Fujii (1976) reports that elderly Asian-Americans have very low median incomes ($1,130-$2,542 in 1970) and low service benefit utilization. Among a group of aged Issei (first-generation Japanese) in Los Angeles, it was found that while 78% were enrolled for Medicare, only 30% admitted using the benefits. Of elderly Chinese males in New York City, one-third never had contact with any public or voluntary agency (Fujii, 1976). Kim (1978) cites a number of reasons for low service utilization among Asian-American elderly: (1) language difficulty and poverty, which leads to enforced social isolation; (2) ignorance of available services; (3) and reluctance to seek existing services due to culture norms emphasizing self-reliance and denial of personal needs.

A basic awareness of these situational factors is essential for working with Asian-American elderly. Too often the majority society has extolled the success of the Asian-American at expense of minimizing the underlying racism and socioeconomic and political dilemmas. However, there is a history of social, economic, and political oppression against the Asian-American elderly, who have survived in spite of these factors.

THE MODEL MINORITY AND
SOCIAL NEEDS ISSUES

The Asian-American elderly are in "quadruple jeopardy." They are poor, minority, old, and non-English speaking. Yet, unlike other minority groups, Asian-Americans have tried to maintain their social and economic structure with a minimum of visible conflict and consciousness-raising with the host society. Historically, they have accepted much racial prejudice and economic/social discrimination without voicing strong protest. In fact, Asian-Americans frequently have been described as "the silent minority," "the quiet Americans," or "the model minority." These stereotypic labels have been the basis for assuming that Asians care for their own and do not require extensive social services; this is a variation of a racist theme for denying minorities equitable resource distribution.

The notion that Asians take care of their elderly is reinforced in several ways. One of these is the concept of the extended family in relation to the traditional Chinese family. Old age to the average Chinese marked the beginning of a lofty and respected status (Hsu, 1970). The Chinese elderly had no fear of unemployment; long before they were physically unable to work, they retired to live on the fruits of their children's labor. The attitude of young children toward the elderly is one of high respect. Chinese infants grow up in their grandparent's arms, and many children shared their elders' beds. The Chinese elderly did not admit they were old mournfully; they announced the fact proudly. As Francis L. K. Hsu states: "In Chinese families, grandparents, as originators of the parents, fill the elevated role of superparents." (Hsu, 1970, p. 319).

However, there have been major changes in traditional family patterns. In contrast to the model minority image, the thrust of Asian-American research has been to document the socioeconomic problem needs of the elderly (Kalish & Yuen, 1971; White House Conference on Aging, 1972; Kalish & Moriwaki, 1973). In recent years, as the number of elderly and immigrants have increased and as the influences of cultural norms and traditional structures diminished, the problems of older Asians have multiplied.

Inadequate income, reduced physical capabilities, and social isolation often make old age a period of degeneration and suffering. Because of cultural differences and language barriers, the usual problems of the elderly are compounded by adjustment to life stress, poverty, racial discrimination, poor health, and inadequate housing.

In the past, family or clan associations representing various provinces of China, Japan, Korea, and the Philippines or based on last names were meeting places for help. They symbolized the cohesive power of the strong family and represented places of refuge where food, shelter, employment, and protection were provided against an alien world. But these traditional social and power structures have lost influence in the last decade. They have been unable to cope with the social problems of overpopulation due to immigration, inadequate housing, unemployment, crime, and increasing health problems.

For example, Carp and Kataoka (1976) reported, based on a sample of 138 Chinese elderly in San Francisco's Chinatown, that twice as many Chinese (30%) as Caucasian (15%) elderly considered health to be their most serious problem. More than three-fourths (78%) of this sample stated that poor health was the major reason for older people's inability to function. Their particular health problems concerned serious immobility, such as trouble with walking and climbing stairs, as well as slowness and stiffness in moving. Dizziness and vision and foot problems were also prevalent in this sample.

Hurly (1970) reported that in 1970 the tuberculosis rate in San Francisco's Chinatown was three to four times that of San Francisco as a whole. A few years later, Yuen reported further that pulmonary and related illnesses were rampant among the elderly of Chinatown. He observed that the reduction in MediCal coverage of physician office visits had inhibited sufficient medical attention and had resulted in otherwise preventable deaths from influenza in the Chinese elderly population (Yuen, 1973).

There are no doubts that Asian-American elderly have multiple social needs that require specialized services. There is ample evidence, similar to studies mentioned, that refutes the model minority designation for Asian-Americans. At the same time, based on these needs, adequate social service programs in accessible facilities with bilingual staff representing major Asian-American subgroups are a primary necessity.

ASIAN-AMERICAN ELDERLY FAMILY PATTERNS

In some respects, the Asian-American family has assumed collective responsibility for its elderly in multigenerational situations. Grandparents were cared for by their children and offspring. The central role and importance of the family as an interactional and sustaining unit is recognized among those who are acquainted with Asian culture. The concept and operation of the family among Asians values a close-knit social unit from which its members derive support, security, and a sense of meaning for meeting their needs. Indeed, the family name is predominant among Asian-Americans as far as identity and honor are concerned. Traditionally, the Asian elderly were cared for by their families in multigenerational households. Respect for the aged was considered a virtue exemplified by the concept of filial piety. The elderly were consulted for each major decision because of life experience, knowledge, authority, and status. China has been described as a gerontocracy because of the position of the elderly in the family and the general veneration of the aged.

Whereas this life philosophy and structure were the basis for a natural family support system, the Western emphasis on individualism, nuclear family autonomy in a urban-industrial milieu, and economic-racial discrimination against minorities often created pressures on the children of Asian elderly. The pattern of immigration to the United States has contributed to the breakdown of traditional patterns of community and familial control. Single Asian elderly bachelors, widow/widowers, and couples often remain inside ethnic enclaves (Chinatowns, Japanese towns, Little Manilas) where their sociocultural needs can be met. Their children and American-born Asians have left the central cities and return on weekends to visit elderly parents and shop for native food items.

This change often occurs long before the family immigrates to the United States. The family structure in Hong Kong, for example, has been fluctuating throughout this century. As a result of rapid industrialization and stronger Western influence, the Chinese family's structure and function have changed in the Hong Kong socioeconomic environment. The emerging families in Hong Kong have become the nuclear units composed of parents and their own as well as adopted children (Wong, 1974). Although the elderly often settle in central city ethnic areas in this country, second and third generations leave these sections for the suburbs. These offspring feel less obligated to take care of their aged parents.

Fujii (1978) observes that veneration of the Asian elderly has been eroded by the process of acculturation. In recent years there is growing evidence of a dissolution or breakdown of customary values and practices. Adult children, for example, are less apt to take in and care for their aged parents. The elderly seem less respected in their old age than in earlier years. Likewise, Kalish and Yuen (1971) and Reynolds (1971) reiterate that traditional obligations toward elderly parents seem to have diminished because of increased lifespans, increasing social and geographic mobility, increasing reliance on public responsibility, lessening of family ties, and the lack of role models in the United States.

In a 1978 Sacramento, California study of 60 Chinese elderly in low-income housing, it was found that responsibility for care assistance fell on the elderly themselves, spouses, relatives, friends, or neighbors. Only limited assistance was provided by children because of separate living arrangements and geographic distance. Yet, children in Chinese families traditionally are taught that they are responsible for their parents, especially in health care crises and in dealing with problems of old age. Owing to geographic separation, daytime work schedules, and other lifestyle obstacles, second- or third-generation children may have to rely on ethnic-oriented public services on weekdays and fulfill their obligations to their parents on weekends or evenings. Teenage grandchildren also may be available to assist in the health maintenance of their Chinese elderly grandparents (Cheung, Cho, Lum, Tang, & Yau, 1980).

Yet it could be argued that Asian-Americans have a family support system for the elderly that has adapted to living realities and that discharges responsibilities for the elderly. Vestiges of family obligation for elderly parents remain with second- and third-generation children. Describing the various subgroups of Pacific Asians, the importance of the family as the focal point of culture, familial loyalty, filial piety, and a collective orientation predominates in the literature (Lim & Fung, 1978).

In a 1968-1973 study of 21 first generation Japanese-Americans (Issei), Kiefer (1974) reported that 16 were living with relatives, 3 with spouses, and 2 alone. In six families, Issei grandparents refused various kinds of important help proffered by their children. In several cases, the Issei refused to live with their children's families, while others rejected assistance with necessary chores or offers of financial help. A difficult and restricted autonomy was preferred to an unwanted dependency, although life-long interdependency among family members is the normal pattern for Japanese. Moreover, a comparative 1979 research project of 46 Issei and 50 second-generation Japanese (Nisei) in Chicago uncovered regular and frequent contact, intergenerational interaction, and conflict resolution when the two generations lived together. Nisei assist Issei with the provision of living space because they view the family as a corporate entity. Japanese elderly yield their authority and responsibility to the younger generation. At the same time, love and affection increase in importance in their relationships with other family members. However, rather than become dependent, Osako (1971) states that these older respondents have adequate income from Social Security, their children, rent, and interest. She explains this seeming contradiction in these terms:

> Small children and very old people are naturally less capable than adults and dependence can be interpreted as a sign of trust. Therefore, when an old Japanese American realized his dependence on the child, generally he does not feel threatened or degraded. This observation does not contradict our finding that the Japanese American elderly appreciate financial self-sufficiency. For they try to

avoid becoming dependent not because it is degrading, but because it may jeopardize their close relationship with the children [Osako, 1979, p. 453].

While there are missing gaps in family support among Asian-American elderly, Japanese-Americans tend to have cultural values of collective interdependence that create family maintenance for Issei. Yet by virtue of acculturation, urbanization, and the denial of marriage opportunities due to immigration restriction, many Asian-American elderly (particularly single elderly Chinese and Filipino males) are without family support structures.

SERVICE DELIVERY NEEDS OF
THE ASIAN-AMERICAN ELDERLY

The problems of the Asian-American elderly exceed the resources of most individuals and families and require public coordination and support through social service programs. In major urban areas, centers have appeared in the form of ethnic facilities and service projects. In the Los Angeles area and in Seattle, Keiro is a convalescent care center primarily for Japanese-Americans. Self-Help for the Elderly and On Lok Senior Health Service, both in San Francisco's Chinatown, have model programs for minority elderly services. Seattle's International Drop-In Center and Boston's Chinese Golden Age Center provide various programs for the elderly. Kuakini Home Day Care Center in Honolulu offers daycare programs, social activities, ethnic meals, and family counseling.

There are two Asian elderly social service programs that are models for other cities. Self-Help for the Elderly is an important service in San Francisco's Chinatown. It has an indigeneous philosophy of service delivery to the elderly. Information dissemination, employment, welfare, health, housing intake referral and follow-up, nutrition, and consumer advisement programs are among the numerous services offered in conjunction with other community agencies. It serves both Chinese and non-Chinese elderly and has been favorably received by the local community. According to Sam Yuen, its director: "To the recipient, it is no more than the extension of the mutual aid concept so commonly held and honored with the family-clan structure" (Yuen, p. 5). In this sense, Self-Help for the Elderly has bridged traditional Chinese family association services and public and private social services.

On Lok Center, a geriatric day health program founded in 1973, serves several community groups (primarily Chinese, Filipino, and Italian) in San Francisco. The On Lok program maintains that individuals should remain in the community as long as they wish and as long as it is medically feasible. The individual, not community service providers, should have the freedom of choice. Above all, people should be helped to help themselves. The center is a vital link in a continuum of services that includes social, financial, legal and recreational services, restorative and residential care, and referral. Toward this end, On Lok is a multiservice center within the Asian community which provides service delivery programs.

In addition to these program models, ethnic social workers, ministers, and other human service agents are needed to identify and to help clarify alternatives for Asian elderly with their families. It is also crucial to solicit from professionals and recognized community helpers who have established rapport and relationships with Asian elderly and their immediate or extended family network systems. In cases of health care problems, bilingual and bicultural public health nurses and clinical and community oriented social workers form the basis for an effort to follow through with medical and social treatment plans. In the role of physicians' social and health extenders, these nurses and social workers can make alternative care arrangements with family members, relatives, friends, and neighbors. With respect to formal support programs, Asian elderly may be referred to day care treatment programs, ethnic nutrition groups, or home health care services located in or near ethnic Asian residential areas.

In recent years, there is growing evidence of a service delivery profile that can effectively meet the needs of the Asian elderly. Public and private agencies offering health, income, housing, and counseling services should be located in or near Asian population clusters. Experience has shown, for example, that when facilities are located in the immediate neighborhood of Chinatown, utilization by the Chinese elderly, most of whom are foreign-born and Chinese-speaking, is exceptionally good (Catell, 1962). Program agencies located in or near the Chinese community should engage in extensive and active outreach programs in order to reach persons who, although in need, may be hesitant about going to agencies and anxious about their regulations and in-take procedures (Campbell & Chang, 1973). Bilingual workers should be employed in public and private agencies for service delivery to the Asian elderly. These persons often have great difficulty understanding or communicating in English when they seek public support services (Catell, 1962).

There are several instances where Asian service delivery groups have successfully presented their case before local county and city boards of supervisors for specialized Asian-American mental health programs. The Richmond Maxi Center in San Francisco, Oakland's Asian American Mental Health Center, and Stepping Stones in Sacramento incorporate the above characteristics of service delivery location, outreach, and staffing. In addition, they employ various sub-Asian bilingual staff who are fluent in Chinese, Japanese, Korean, Filipino, and Vietnamese language dialects. These service delivery principles are essential for meeting the service delivery needs of Asian-American elderly and should be applied by program administrators who oversee these population groups.

THE UNIQUENESS OF THE ASIAN-AMERICAN ELDERLY

With an overwhelming case for the need of Asian-American elderly social services, there are a number of unique ethnic characteristics of this group. From the rich tradition of Asian culture, the influence, power, and authority of the family has been a sustaining force for survival and support. The role functions of the family are reinforced by a variety of customs and beliefs ranging from holiday observances, health practices, marriage selection, and other life areas. There has been a recovery of respect for the elderly by the third and fourth generations who are in the process of rediscovering their ethnic roots. The elderly themselves are a vast storehouse of oral history. It is not unusual for Asian-American university students, enrolled in Asian-American Studies Programs, to tap the knowledge and life experiences of the elderly.

The Asian-American elderly themselves portray a unique set of behavioral characteristics: quietness, patience, hard work, a striving toward harmony, and wisdom to survive in a white majority society. In the midst of changing social values among Asian-American generations, there remains a sense of obligation to care for and support the family and the Asian-American community (friends, church). Sustaining the life and culture of the Asian-American elderly person brings him or her satisfaction and happiness. The opportunity to speak the native language with a variety of persons, to eat favorite food dishes, to practice particular holiday customs and special observances, and to interact with a circle of elderly friends are areas of life-need with this target population.

For the Asian elderly, the family association and ethnic church continue to play an important role in their ecosystem, along with nutrition and social interaction programs. Among the Asian elderly who live in public housing, there is a cadre spirit of helping and watching out for each other's safety and health, sharing favorite foods, and exchanging token gifts on special holidays.

Above all, there are Asian-American children, human service professionals, and community helpers who care about their elderly. Through family gatherings, practical living assistance, and joint community planning for elderly related projects, the Asian-American community in major cities, for example, San Francisco, New York, Los Angeles, Chicago, Seattle, San Diego, Boston, and Sacramento, have mounted ongoing social service programs for their elderly.

CONCLUSION

The intent of this chapter has been to highlight important features of the Asian-American aging experience for social service workers who may serve this population group. We have sought to identify the socioeconomic and political configuration affecting the Asian elderly. We have endeavored to shatter the myth of the model minority by citing the numerous social needs afflicting them. We have appraised the traditional and changing patterns of family dynamics. We have surveyed Asian-American elderly service delivery needs, setting forth models and program principles. Above all, we have delineated some of the unique characteristics that distinguish Asian elderly from other aging groups. We hope that these combinations of viewpoints on the Asian-American elderly life experience will be useful in a multitude of service settings.

REFERENCES

Campbell, T., & Chang, B. Health care of the Chinese in America. *Nursing Outlook*, 1973, 21, 245-249.

Carp, F. M., & Kataoka, E. Health care problems of the elderly of San Francisco's Chinatown. *Gerontologist*, 1976, 16, 34-36.

Catell, S. H. Health, welfare and social organization in Chinatown, New York City. New York: Community Service Society, 1962.

Cheung, L. Y. S., Cho, E. R., Lum, D., Tang, T. Y., & Yau, H. B. The Chinese elderly and family structure: implications for health care. *Public Health Reports*, 1980, 95, 491-495.

Fujii, S. M. Elderly Asian Americans and use of public services. *Social Casework*, 1976, 57, 202-207.

Fujii, S. M. Retirement as it relates to the Pacific-Asian elderly. In E. P. Stanford, (Ed.), *Retirement: Concepts and realities of ethnic minority elders*. San Diego: Campanile, 1978.

Hsu, F. L. K. *Americans and Chinese reflections on two cultures and their people*. New York: Doubleday, 1970.

Hurley, A. Chinatown USA, 1970. *California's Health*, 1970, 27, 2.

Kalish, R. A., & Moriwaki, S. The world of the elderly Asian American. *Journal of Social Issues*, 1973, 29, 187-209.

Kalish, R. A., & Yuen, S. Americans of East Asian ancestry: Aging and the aged. *Gerontologist*, 1971, 11, 36-47.

Kim, B. L. C., *The Asian Americans: Changing patterns, changing needs*. Montclair, NJ: Association of Korean Christian Scholars in North America, 1978.

Kiefer, C. W. Lessons from the Issei. In J. F. Gubrium (Ed.), *Late life: Communities and environmental policy*. Springfield, IL: Charles C. Thomas, 1974.

Lim, H., & Fung, V. H. *Understanding the Pan Asian client*. San Diego: Union of Pan Asian Communities, 1978.

Oskao, M. M. Aging and family among Japanese Americans: The role of ethnic tradition in the adjustment to old age. *Gerontologist*, 1971, 19, 448-455.

Reynolds, D. K. Japanese American aging: A game perspective. Paper presented at the Society for Applied Anthropology Meeting, Miami, Florida, 1971.

White House Conference on Aging. *Special concerns reports: The Asian American elderly*. Washington, DC: Government Printing Office, 1972.

Wong, F. M. *Industrialization and family structure in Hong Kong*. Hong Kong: Social Research Center, Chinese University of Hong Kong, 1974.

Yuen, S. *Planning for community services*. Chinatown's Self-Help for the Elderly Project, San Francisco, 1973.

Yuen, S. *Aging and mental health in San Francisco's Chinatown*. Unpublished manuscript, San Francisco: Self-Help for the Elderly, n.d.

8

The Black Aging Experience

NELLIE TATE

An underlying assumption of this chapter is that inequalities in American society generate differences in the ways Blacks and whites adjust to aging. These inequalities stem from the tendency of human groups to stratify themselves on some basis, whether it be by age, by sex, or by the possession of certain resources. Racial characteristics have been used to ascribe inferior status, resulting in the unequal treatment of minority-group members. With regard to Blacks, discrimination and de facto segregation have been used to maintain unequal status throughout the course of their lives.

The impact of exposure to these factors on how individuals respond to the circumstances of increasing age may be conceptualized in two cause-effect paradigms. First, empirically determined differences in life satisfaction and other sociopsychological variables may occur principally as a function of factors related to one's race, such as experience with previous or current forms of segregation and discrimination. In this paradigm, variables such as age, sex, income, and health may intervene to either mitigate or exacerbate the basic relationships posited between one's race and one's sociopsychological state in old age.

The second paradigm is similar in that exposure to widely practiced forms of discrimination and de facto segregation are conceptualized as the principal (independent) variables determining sociopsychological states. However, in addition to the sociopsychological impact, the frequency and intensity of such exposure is also viewed as a key determinant of longevity, income, health, and so on. Consequently, intervening variables in this paradigm are those that relate to the intensity of exposure to forms of discrimination common in the everyday lives of most members of national minority groups.

Although a common experience for minority individuals, members of certain groups obviously are the victims of more intensive forms of social and economic repression. Thus, minority group members may be arrayed along a continuum depicting the intensity of victimization they encounter, with those experiencing the most severe forms having to countenance substantial impairment of longevity, satisfaction, economic security, and so on.

Differences in the implications of these two paradigms amount to more than the specification of mere conceptual nuances. Those who subscribe to the first model assume minority-group individuals to have substantially greater control over their life chances than is warranted by the logic of the second model. Subscribers to this latter model are likely to characterize subscribers to the first model as victim blamers. Importantly, individuals subscribing to the first model are likely to view patterns unique to minority aging as deviant from white norms, rather than as legitimate differences.

On these points, arguments have been made recently that race is of declining significance in explaining the economic success of Blacks (Wilson, 1978). However, this argument holds only for a very small percentage of the Black population, with Blacks in the main having experienced substantial recent economic retrogression (see McNeely & Pope, 1981). I accept the validity of the second paradigm, recognizing that its predictive value is greatest for those Blacks who have been unaffected by the socioeconomic progress enjoyed by a few affluent Blacks. (In a sense, they are the exceptions to the rule that keeps the posited relationships from being correlatively perfect.) Hence, the interpretation of information presented in the succeeding pages of this article unfold from the latter point of view.

Dimensions singled out for particular scrutiny include the special history of Afro-Americans, their coping structures, and variant subculture. These are among the dimensions specified by Moore's (1971) framework as capturing the salient aspects of ethnicity, which focus on commonalities in race, national origin, history, language, and cultural values (see Gordon, 1964; Bengtson, 1979).

SPECIAL HISTORY

A special history refers to a collective experience that has placed members of a group within the American social system (Moore, 1971, p. 88). The special history of Blacks has been dominated by slavery and its aftermath, segregation. It has involved exploitation and periodic conflict. Moreover, it has mandated subordinated roles and relationships with the dominant group that persist in varying forms today.

DISCRIMINATION

Discrimination is the behavioral manifestation of prejudicial attitudes resulting in inequalities and disadvantaged status for its victims (Kitano, 1974; Newman, 1973). It is reinforced by myths and negative stereotypes about individuals and groups of people. Blatant forms of discrimination were legal-ized through the Black codes and myriad court decisions. Although gross forms have been rendered illegal, contemporary aged Blacks were not the primary beneficiaries of these changes. For them, discrimination based on race resulted in demonstratively blocked opportunities and an unequal share of this nation's economic and social resources. Statistical comparisons between aged Blacks and whites reflect the unequal starting points of each group. Quality of life indicators such as education, income, health, housing, and life expectancy underscore these disparities. Thus, as a group, today's aged Blacks are poorer, less educated, and in poorer health than their white counterparts.

PSYCHOLOGICAL CONSEQUENCES

Discrimination and segregation have their psychological correlates as well. They signify low prestige in society. They provide the mechanisms by which people can look down upon members of minority groups and make them objects of disparagement (Guterman, 1972, p. 5). Psychological studies that focus on the impact of discrimination and segregation usually measure attitudinal and adaptational dimensions such as self-concept and life satisfaction. Early on, DuBois (1903) pointed out the schizophreniclike existence of Blacks in America when he described the double consciousness of Blacks. Later, Ellison (1952) focused on the "invisibility" of Blacks, and Grier and Cobbs (1968) discussed the psychopathological forms of rage manifested by some Blacks, generated by discrimination and oppression.

Given the above, it is most surprising to find that older Blacks frequently are reported to score higher on life satisfaction than their elderly white cohorts. For example, in a study concerned with the differences between Black and white older people on the attitudinal dimensions of life satisfaction, feelings of social integration and self-conception, Messer (1968) found that Blacks were more likely than whites to show high morale. This was so even when Blacks viewed their health as poor, thought of themselves as old, and felt segregated from society. In a similar vein, in a study that examined the relationship between social interaction and life satisfaction of a group of 65 widowed Blacks, Tate (1980) found that two-thirds of these widows were satisfied with life. They, too, were in poor health, many had a number of limiting physical conditions, were confined to the inner core of a large northwestern city, and were relatively isolated. On this point, Lopata (1972) found that white widows had a more difficult time adjusting than did the Black widows in her sample.

One explanation of Lopata's findings occurs when one considers the legacy of slavery among Blacks. Slavery released the Black woman from the myth of femininity as she was wholly integrated into the productive force (Davis, 1971). And, as caretaker of the slave household, she was a central figure in the slave community and played an integral role in resisting slavery, thus ensuring the survival of Black people. It is understandable that ensuing years of segregation and discrimination have compelled Black women of every age to become self-sufficient individuals. As a consequence, adjustment to harsh social, political, and economic realities make easier the Black widow's subsequent adjustment to spousal loss and other decrements of aging.

On the other hand, some other studies have reported no significant differences (see Creecy & Wright, 1979; Jackson & Walls, 1978). Jackson and Walls concluded after an analysis of 1974 Harris survey data that "current myths about significant differences between aged Blacks and whites have little if any validity" (1978, p. 112), although they reported finding the satisfaction of low-income Blacks to be higher than that of similar status whites (1980, p. 109). Register's (1981) analysis of the Harris survey data also resulted in asymmetric findings. Even though Blacks between the ages of 18 and 64 expressed more positive attitudes toward the elderly than whites, aged Blacks reported lower levels of morale. These discrepant results suggest, in the first instance, a greater degree of accommodation by low-income Blacks to lives characterized by bitter experiences. In the second instance, while older Blacks perhaps tend to be more accepting of their status, the realities of being old and Black are not so readily accepted when selected empirical assessments of their situation are made.

Finally, high income Blacks have been found to score lower on satisfaction than high income whites (Jackson & Walls, 1978). One interpretation of this finding is that it may reflect an adverse reaction on the part of Blacks who held heightened expectations, perhaps not fully realized, and a greater unwillingness to accept subordinate status in old age. Because they are the group that is most vulnerable to institutionalized victimization (see Jackson, 1980), it may also reflect dissatisfactions associated with the inability to be sustained in an extended family network, despite expectations of support.

In sum, the question of whether or not significant racially linked differences exist for individuals aggregated across social classes remains unresolved. Of course, the conservative argument is that there are no appreciable differences. Nevertheless, even this position suggests remarkable fortitude for a people victimized by unequal access to the goods of society.

VARIANT SUBCULTURE

Exclusionary practices by a dominant group give impetus to the development of what Moore (1971) describes as a variant subculture. She emphasizes the significance of value sets and norms related to behavior in particular age groups (Moore, 1971, p. 89). Many values associated with Afro-American life are rooted in West African cultures, which tend to espouse a view of humanity living in harmony with nature (Nobles, 1974). Values associated with this philosophical perspective underscore the importance of mutual cooperation, interdependence, and the collective rather than individual good. Expressions of African-based values are reflected attitudinally and behaviorally by many older Blacks; for example, in the high degree of absorption of younger relatives into their households, in certain life-style preferences, and in the way certain phenomena are assessed subjectively.

ABSORPTION OF THE YOUNG

Absorption of the young by older Blacks represents an adherence to the norms of mutual cooperation and the collective good. Within the American context this has meant a greater receptiveness to providing sole or supplementary care and primary economic support to the children of Black school-aged, divorced, or separated females who proportionately outnumber whites by a substantial margin. To some extent this practice explains why elderly Black household heads are more likely to have young relatives living with them. For example, 22% of Black intact families (husband and wife) take in relatives under 18 years of age, compared to only 4% of the intact white elderly. In families headed by elderly Black women, 40% take in dependent children under 18 years compared to only 10% of white families (Hill, 1981, p. 4). In addition, based upon this author's prior experiences conducting gerontological research, it appears that absorbed nonindependent younger Blacks are more likely to accept their aged who become functionally impaired as a result of debilitating chronic conditions. Consequently, absorbed relatives may reciprocate important emotional and other care-giving benefits, including the subsequent provision of economic support.

This latter point is reflected in evidence suggesting that young minority-group professionals are more inclined to work with the elderly than their white counterparts. Eleanor and Merle Feldbaum (1981) found that 55% of the Black student and registered nurses, compared to only 41% of the whites in their sample, indicated a desire to work with the elderly. In their study, race was the only personal trait that correlated with plans to enter geriatric nursing. This finding suggests that younger Blacks have more interest in, and possibly more esteem for their elders. This is particularly crucial for older Blacks who may require skilled care whether in their own homes or in institutions.

LIFESTYLE PREFERENCES IN
INTERPERSONAL CONTACT

Although it is generally acknowledged that lifestyles encompass a continuum of habits (e.g., preferences in food), most gerontological literature focuses upon preferences in social participation and leisure time pursuits. Studies have shown that older Blacks interact with more extended kin (i.e., nieces, cousins, and so on) and perceive them as more significant than do older whites (Rubinstein, 1971; Hays & Mindel, 1973; Huling, 1978; Martin & Martin, 1978). Moreover, older Blacks' social interaction involves relatives and a range of "fictive" kin (Aschenbrenner, 1975; Martin & Martin, 1978); an interactional practice that is not prevalent among older whites. Fictive kin include nonbiologically related individuals who are afforded status as members of the family. Additionally, elderly Blacks are more involved in voluntary associations than their white counterparts. Clemente, Rexrod, and Hirsch (1975) found that their higher participation rates spanned involvement in social and recreational as well as church activities.

The diversity of social participation among aged Blacks suggests that many of them may be less likely to feel isolated and alone. And, in the long run, they may also form the basis for the development of self-help groups, important mechanisms for providing support.

PERCEPTIONS OF AGE

In considering perceptions of age it is interesting to note that Blacks who reach the seventh and eighth decades of life tend to live longer than whites reaching these ages (see Manton & Poss, 1977). It has been suggested that this is due to the earlier vulnerability of whites to atherosclerotic infirmities and, by implication, it suggests that the mortality crossover represents racial differences in the intrinsic rate of aging (Manton & Poss, 1977, p. 52). Other researchers, including Jackson (1980), suggest that the racial crossover phenomenon may well be related to census undercounts of Blacks in earlier years.

While scholars acknowledge the existence of a mortality crossover, its reality has had little impact on elderly Blacks' perceptions of age. For example, research studies have shown that elderly Blacks tend to view themselves as old at an earlier age than whites (see Messer, 1968; Jackson, 1970; Rubinstein, 1971). This finding may be related to a process beginning during childhood. Chestang (1971) has suggested that Black children mature more rapidly because of the adult responsibilites they are compelled to assume at a very early age. Individuals deprived of the luxury of an extended childhood may simply feel older sooner. Or, forced as they are to endure lifetimes in racially hostile environments, Blacks may react by feeling older earlier.

In a similar vein, Linn's more recent (1979) study conducted in a large Southern city found that 73% of the aged whites in his sample, compared to only 43% of the elderly Blacks, viewed themselves as younger than their actual chronological ages. This finding very possibly suggests that the stigma associated with being older is greater for whites than for Blacks. On this point, Martin and Martin (1978) have noted that the esteem accorded older Blacks precludes their hasty and inappropriate institutionalization by their young. Consequently, prestige bestowed upon Black elders may be more pronounced than that conferred upon their white counterparts. Second, when the choice is between receiving support through an extended family network, a pattern apparently more prevalent among Blacks, and institutionalization, it is logical that those approaching the latter choice would seek to view themselves as younger.

COPING:
ORGANIZATIONS AND FAMILIES

Coping structures refer to the mechanisms that provide social and/or economic support, including assistance with survival needs, opportunities for meaningful social participation, influence, prestige and power, and which engender a sense of belonging to a group (Moore, 1971, p. 89).

Discrimination and segregation fostered the development of numerous Black institutions, including fraternal organizations, self-help groups, women's clubs, and the like. These provided avenues for self-expression, the development of Black youth, and promoted the general welfare of all Blacks (Pollard, 1978).

Of all the formal organizations seeking to meet fundamental human needs, it has been the Black church that has played the most widespread and prominent role in the lives of Afro-Americans. During slavery, the church allowed worshipers a sense of freedom, recognition, and served as a vehicle to develop leadership abilities. In many instances, it was used as a fulcrum for planning efforts seeking liberation from enslavement. After slavery, it was at the vanguard of efforts to build Black educational institutions and, more recently, has provided much of the civil rights leadership and the context within which large groups of people could be mobilized into community campaigns seeking equitable treatment.

However, some of the success achieved during this period has served inadvertently to create pressures within many Black families resulting, in some cases, in a diminishment of the elder's role. For example, it was during the civil rights era that the term "Black" became accepted as evidencing a demonstratively assertive stance with regard to race and race relations. Many older Blacks reject this term, preferring instead the term "colored" (Beard, 1975). Middle-aged and younger Blacks tend to prefer the terms "Afro-American," or "Black," which reflect changing times and Blacks' changing definition of themselves. These differences in preferences are indicative of the philosophical distance separating some of the old from some of the young. Interestingly, Huling (1978) found that the aged respondents in his study were most concerned about the emergence of divergent values between themselves and their offspring. These points are important because they suggest a reduction in the ability of Black elders to occupy social roles of responsibility; for example, as role models for their grandchildren and transmitters of family history. The clash of values between young and old, implied by their differing preferences, and the rejection by some young Blacks of the pre-civil rights Afro-American experience, has been found to lead to feelings of despair among the Black elderly (Solomon, 1970).

On the other hand, just as some older Blacks have suffered, others have found the events of the civil rights and subsequent periods to result in more favorable outcomes. For example, the redefinition of the Black experience sought during the 1960s has stimulated the interest of some younger Blacks in the oral family histories that only their elders can fully recount. Alex Haley's *Roots* (1976) epitomizes this positive aspect. Older women, as the principal transmitters of family history and Black culture (Haley, 1976), have been the major beneficiaries in those families where interest has been stimulated. Consequently, their role in maintaining family life (see Frazier, 1939; Billingsley, 1968; Guttman, 1972), including the ability to forge strong extended kinships (Huling, 1978) has been enhanced.

For Blacks, the system of extended kinship (see Nobles, 1974), allowing flexibility in family boundaries and roles (Hill, 1965), has been an important coping mechanism helping family members survive hardships imposed by slavery, Jim Crow laws, and economic bust periods. That Blacks have been forced to rely on this survival system more than whites is popularly assumed, but it has also been confirmed by a number of studies (Cantor, 1975; Staples, 1972; Martin & Martin, 1978).

One benefit of extended kinships is the potential for greater assistance with daily responsibilities. For example, Cantor (1975) found in her examination of Black, Hispanic, and white families that a larger percentage (58%) of Black and Hispanic children, compared to whites (42%), assisted their elders in the chores of daily living and shopping. A very recent study has reported similar findings: 56% of Black elders received visits and instrumental support from kin, compared to 46% of their white counterparts (Tate, Greenhill, & Applegate, 1982).

As might be expected, there also is higher reciprocal involvement among Blacks than whites (Blehar, 1979). Some studies examining Black widows have reported very high kin involvement levels, assessed in terms of visits and other forms of support, although at least one study has reported minimal involvement. For example, Tate (1980) found that 87% of the Black widows in her Philadelphia study were involved with their kin, although Lopata (1972) found the kinship network among Blacks in her Chicago sample to be inoperative.

Finally, a number of studies suggest that friendships tend to boost the morale of elderly Blacks, while relationships with children have an equivocal effect (Jackson, 1972; Arling, 1976). Explanations for this paradox vary from the more cynical notion that older Blacks feel "put upon" by their children (Jackson, 1972; Lopata, 1972) to the more benign suggestion that older people prefer "intimacy at a distance" (Rosenmayr & Kockeis, 1963).

Nevertheless, a recent trend forebodes increasingly limited opportunities for direct support of the Black elderly by their young. This trend, the reverse migration of Blacks (young and old) to the South, which began as a trickle in the mid-1950s, had reached dramatic proportions by the 1970s (Farrell & Johnson, 1982). Thus, while emotional ties and economic supports can transcend geographical boundaries, the provision of instrumental help with activities of daily living is not possible when younger family members migrate southward toward jobs, leaving behind their aged. This is particularly significant when one considers that, on the whole, data indicate a pattern of higher Black involvement in the provision of assistance, both emotional and instrumental.

SUMMARY AND IMPLICATIONS

The inconsistent nature of much of the information presented suggests few unequivocally clearcut distinctions between aged Blacks and whites. However, the information raises a number of interesting questions. For example, what is important about the fact that low-income Blacks feel satisfied with life? Does it mean that they have lowered expectations; that is, it takes less for them to experience some sense of accomplishment and, therefore, are more satisfied? What about the differences in the way older Blacks perceive their ages? Is this important? If so, what does it mean? What are the implications of the increased longevity of Blacks if they reach the seventh and eighth decades of life? What are the implications of greater involvement in voluntary associations and with fictive kin? Does it mean that biological family ties are losing their importance? And, finally, what are the implications of reverse migration and emerging value divergences among the young and old in Black families?

It appears that a useful line of inquiry would be to learn all that we can about Blacks over the lifespan. Hence, factors that either enhance or inhibit life under varying conditions of racial oppression may be unearthed. As a result, bits and pieces of current knowledge (e.g., that life satisfaction and age perceptions vary both among groups of Blacks and between racial groups) may become more meaningful.

The extended longevity of Blacks at the upper end of the life span suggests questions about the possibility of a biological superiority that needs to be explored. While this has political implications that may have unintended consequences, this avenue of inquiry may lead to new discoveries that have importance for everyone.

From a social welfare point of view, the mortality crossover suggests that Black children may have exposure to grandparents, particularly those that are female, well into the children's middle-age years. What this means is that some middle-aged Blacks may be faced with juggling responsibilities to their own families, an aged parent, and an older grandparent. They truly may become a "squeezed" generation and they may well need professional help in managing family-care responsibilities and the problems they generate.

The last set of questions deals with expanded networks, migratory patterns, and value divergencies. In terms of expanded networks, the incorporation of voluntary associations and fictive kin in the life space of Blacks leads one to speculate that these avenues of expression result in greater opportunities for the continuing assumption of meaningful roles in society and, correspondingly, fewer chances of becoming isolated and lonely. While it is acknowledged that reverse migration makes this problematic for those elderly Blacks left behind in the crime-infested inner-core of large metropolitan areas, it suggests a continuing need for practitioners to take the lead in efforts to maintain these involvements, whether it be through developing groups and/or supporting efforts to make the inner city safer.

The value divergencies between the young and the old portend a questionable future for some aged Blacks. Modernization and rapid technological and social changes demand new ways of adapting, including modifications in family structures and values. Younger Blacks are no less affected than other groups. Although the preponderance of Black elderly is imbedded in a network of kin and friendship relationships, increased mobility in search of educational and work opportunities has resulted in some dissipation of roles performed by older Blacks. As Huling (1978, p. 27) suggests, "losses in interaction between current Black generations, when projected into the future, can mean the isolation of grandparents and grandchildren." That relationship, more than any other, has served to perpetuate affection and bind the generations together.

Can the expanded networks of fictive kin and friends fill the void left by highly mobile family members? Will the changing values of the young make a difference for the elderly? One cannot predict with any degree of certainty what the future will hold. However, it is important that professionals become knowledgeable about elderly Blacks, changing family patterns, and value systems. This can lead to the provision of more culturally sensitive and humane services that focus, at the microsystem level, on strengthening family ties and sharing within groups that serve as outlets for social participation and a potential for support. At the macrosystem level, this means working toward the elimination of inequalities and blocked opportunities in earlier years that manifest themselves during later years in terms of lower socioeconomic status, poorer health, and shortened life spans for the majority of Blacks. These efforts can result in improved intergenerational relationships as well as improvement in the overall quality of life for elderly Blacks.

REFERENCES

Arling, Greg. The elderly widow and her family, neighbors and friends. *Journal of Marriage and the Family*, 1976, 38, 757-768.

Aschenbrenner, J. Extended families among Black Americans. *Journal of Comparative Family Studies*, 1975, 257-268.

Beard, V. A study of a group of well-off old Blacks. Paper presented at the Annual Conference of the National Caucus on Black Aged, Washington, DC, May 1975.

Bengtson, V. L. Ethnicity and aging: Problems and issues in current social science inquiry. In D. E. Gelfand, & A. J. Kutzik (Eds.), *Ethnicity and aging: Theory, research and policy*. New York: Springer, 1979.

Billingsley, A. *Black families in white America*. Englewood Cliffs, NJ: Prentice-Hall, 1968.

Blehar, M. Family and friendship in old age. In *Families Today* NDMH Science Monographs (Vol. 1). Washington DC: Department of Health, Education and Welfare Publication (ADM) 79-815, 1979.

Brown, R. G. Family structure and social isolation of older persons. *Journal of Gerontology*, 1960, 15, 170-174.

Cantor, M. Life space and social support system of the inner city elderly of New York. *Gerontologist*, 1975, 15 (1), 23-27.

Chestang, L. *Character development in a hostile environment*. Chicago: University of Chicago, School of Social Service Administration, Occasional Paper, 1971.

Clemente, F., Rexrod, P. A., & Hirsch, C. The participation of the Black aged in voluntary associations. *Journal of Gerontology*, 1975, 30, 469-472.

Creecy, R. F., & Wright, R. Morale and informal activity with friends among Black and white elderly. *Gerontologist*, 1979, 19, 544-547.

Davis, A. Reflections on the Black woman. *Black Scholar*, January/February 1979.

DuBois, W.E.B. *The souls of Black folk*. Chicago: A. C. McClurg, 1903.

Ellison, R. *The invisible man*. New York: Random House, 1952.

Farrell, W. C., & Johnson, J. H. Implications of the Black move to the South. *Black Enterprise*, January 1982, 21.

Feldbaum, E., & Feldbaum, M. Information on aging. In *Aging Almanac*, University Center on Aging, San Diego: San Diego State University, March/April, 1982, 4.

Frazier, E. F. *The Negro family in the United States*. Chicago: University of Chicago Press, 1939.

Goode, D. A. *The Black American family: Are its strengths an untapped resource?* Unpublished substantive paper, Heller School, Brandeis University, 1964.

Gordon, M. *Assimilation in American life*. New York: Oxford University Press, 1964.

Grier, W., & Cobbs, P. *Black rage*. New York: Basic Books, 1968.

Guterman, S. S. (Ed.). *Black psyche: The model personality patterns of Black Americans*. Berkeley, CA: Glendessary Press, 1972.

Guttman, H. G. *The Black family in slavery and freedom: 1750-1925*. New York: Pantheon Press, 1976.

Haley, A. *Roots*. Garden City, NY: Doubleday, 1976.

Harris, L., & Associates. *The myth and reality of aging in America*. Washington, DC: National Council on Aging, 1975.

Hays, W. E., & Mindel, C. H. Extended kinship relationships in Black and White families. *Journal of Marriage and the Family*, 1973, 35 (1), 51-57.

Hill, R. *The strengths of Black families*. New York: National Urban League, 1965.

Hill, R. A demographic profile of the Black elderly. In *Aging*, Washington, DC: Department of Health, Education and Welfare, 1978, 2-9.

Hill, R. The economic status of Black Americans. In J. D. Williams (Ed.), *The state of Black America*. New York: National Urban League, Incorporated, 1981.

Huling, W. E. Evolving family roles for Black elderly. In *Aging*, Washington, DC: Department of Health, Education and Welfare, 1978, 21-27.

Jackson, J. J. Aged Negroes: Their cultural departures from statistical stereotypes and selected rural-urban differences. *Gerontologist*, 1970, 10, 140-145.

Jackson, J. J. Marital life among aging Blacks. *Family Coordinator*, 1972, 21, 21-27.

Jackson, J. J. *Minorities and aging*. Belmont, CA: Wadsworth, 1980.

Jackson, J. J., & Walls, B. Myths and realities about aged Blacks. In M. Brown (Ed.), *Readings in gerontology*. St. Louis: C. V. Mosby, 1978, 95-113.

Kent, D. The elderly in minority groups: Variant patterns of aging. *Gerontologist*, 1969, 9 (3), 26-29.

Kitano, H. H. L. *Race relations*. Englewood Cliffs, NJ: Prentice-Hall, 1974.

Linn, M. W., & Hunter, K. Perceptions of age in the elderly. *Journal of Gerontology*, 1979, 34 (1), 46-52.

Lopata, H. Z. The social involvement of American widows. *American Behavioral Scientist*, 1970, 41-57.

Lopata, H. Z. Social relations of Black and white widowed women in a northern metropolis. *American Journal of Sociology*, 1972, 78(4), 1003-1011.

Manton, K., & Poss, S. The Black/white mortality crossover: Possible racial differences. *Black Aging*, 1977, 3, 43-53.

Martin, E., & Martin, J. P. *The Black extended family*. Chicago: University of Chicago Press, 1978.

McNeely, R. L., & Pope, C. E. Socioeconomic and racial issues in the measurement of criminal involvement. In R. L. McNeely and C. E. Pope (Eds.), *Race, crime, and criminal justice*. Beverly Hills, CA: Sage, 1981, 31-47.

Messer, M. Race differences in selected attitudinal dimensions of the elderly. *Gerontologist*, 1968, 8, 245-249.

Moore, J. Situational factors affecting minority aging. *Gerontologist*, 1971, 11, 88-91.

Newman, W. H. *American pluralism*. New York: Harper & Row, 1973.

Nobles, W. African root and American fruit. *Journal of Social and Behavioral Sciences*, 1974, 20, 52-64.

Pollard, W. L. *A study of Black self help*. San Francisco: Research Associates, 1978.

Register, J. C. Aging and race: A Black/White comparative analysis. *Gerontologist*, 1981, 21 (4), 438-443.

Rosenmayr, L., & Kockeis, E. Propositions for a sociological theory of aging and the family. *International Social Science Journal*, 1963, 15.

Rubinstein, D. I. *The social participation of the Black elderly*. Unpublished doctoral dissertation, Brandeis University, 1971.

Solomon, B. Ethnicity, mental health and the older Black aged. In *Ethnicity, mental health and aging*. Los Angeles: University of Southern California, Gerontology Center, 1970.

Stack, C. *All our kin*. New York: Harper Colophon Books, 1974.

Stanford, E. P. Theoretical and practical relationships among aged Blacks and other minorities. *Black Scholar*, January/February 1982, 49-59.

Staples, R. (Ed.). *The Black family: Essays and studies*. Belmont, CA: Wadsworth, 1971.

Sussman, M. The helping pattern in the middle-class family. *American Sociological Review*, 1953, 18, 22-28.

Tate, N. P. *Social interaction patterns and life satisfaction of a group of elderly widowed Blacks*. Unpublished doctoral dissertation, Brandeis University, 1980.

Tate, N. P., Greenhill, D., & Applegate, W. *An assessment of the health needs and support systems of Blacks and whites*, 1981.

Wilson, W. J. *The declining significance of race*. Chicago: University of Chicago Press, 1978.

9

The Mexican-American
Aging in a Changing Culture

ROSINA M. BECERRA

The majority of the current generation of older Mexican-Americans[1] have had to adapt to two major relocations: the move from Mexico to the United States, and the shift from a rural to an urban setting. Historically, several factors encouraged movement across the border to the United States: First the dissolution of the peonage system in Mexico as a result of the success of the 1910 Revolution enabled farm laborers to leave to seek work on farms in the southwestern United States; second, the completion of railroad connections to the Mexican interior provided a means of transportation to the U.S. border for workers from densely populated, impoverished areas in central Mexico; and third, the introduction of capital and labor-intensive irrigation farming to the Southwest created a demand for seasonal wage labor (Grebler, Moore, & Gutman, 1970).

The movement from rural Mexico to the rural Southwest represented only a modest cultural shock for Mexican emigrants because they tended to work and live in ethnically homogenous settings. These communities were minimally influenced by Anglo-American culture, and provided support for maintaining traditional Mexican familial structures, which emphasized the elderly male's role as an authority in agricultural skills and the elderly female's importance in childrearing (Sanchez, 1974). This rural heritage, shared by the majority of today's elderly, came to an end, however, with the increasing mechanization of agriculture, with the *bracero* program of seasonal labor, and with the movement of rural populations to urban areas. Today, 85% of all Mexican-Americans reside in urban areas, including almost all the elderly Mexican-Americans (U.S. Bureau of the Census, 1979).

AUTHOR'S NOTE: Support for this chapter was provided through the project, "Spanish Language Research Project for Older Persons," Administration on Aging, Grant 90-AR-0003/01, Principal Investigators, Rosina M. Becerra, Ph.D. and David Shaw, M.A.

The urbanization of the Mexican-American is perceived by some Hispanic gerontologists as being the relocation that has been the most disruptive to the adaptation to aging process of the Mexican-American elder. The focus of this chapter is to examine those areas of Mexican-American life that some writers suggest are undergoing change as a result of urbanization and, hence, may present problems for the Mexican-American elder.

THE FAMILIAL STRUCTURE

The traditional structure of the Mexican family grew out of the socioeconomic needs dictated by the agrarian and craft economies of Mexico. For the traditional Mexican, the word *familia* meant an extended, multigenerational group of persons, among whom specific social roles were ascribed. By dividing functions and responsibilities among differing generations of family members, the family was able to perform all the economic and social support chores necessary for survival in the relatively spartan life-circumstances of the rural Mexican environment. Mutual support, sustenance, and interaction among family members during both work and leisure hours dominated the lives of persons in these traditional Mexican families (Miranda, 1975).

Elderly members of traditional, extended families were presumably spared many of the hazards to physical and psychological well-being usually associated with disengagement from active working roles. Adult children provided economic support and assistance with housekeeping for men and women too old to continue working. At the same time, because grandparents were given specific social roles to perform, older persons continued to be valued family members. Their expertise and importance as role models gave them status and authority highly respected by younger family members as well as playing key roles in the upkeep of the house and providing of child care (Maldonado, 1975).

There is evidence that Mexican-Americans, more than other ethnic groups continue to have this extended family orientation. Analyses of data on elderly residents of Los Angeles show that Blacks and whites generally conform to dominant Anglo-American family patterns (i.e., dominance of the nuclear family), while the Mexican-American elderly both live differently and have different expectations and opinions about familism (i.e., stronger commitment to extended family relationships, Bengtson & Burton, 1980). The variation in these indicators of familism cannot be accounted for by differences in socioeconomic status or sex (Manuel & Bengtson, 1976). Sotomayor's (1973) Denver study of Mexican-American grandparents suggests that the older cohort continue to hold traditional attitudes about intergenerational family roles and relationships. In contrast, Valle and Mendoza (1978) found the elderly Latinos in San Diego were less traditional in their attitudes toward the role of the family; they did, however, rely on support from family members in times of need.

While these findings confirm the idea that the extended Mexican family supportive of its elderly continues to operate in the United States, a second group of investigations contradicts this contention. Both Maldonado (1975) and Nunez (1975) believe rapid social change is breaking down the traditional extended family, and as a consequence older Mexican-Americans (as well as Anglos) are suffering from isolation and alienation. According to Maldonado (1975), as younger generations of Hispanics rise in social status, they become more mobile, increasing the physical distance between themselves and their kin, which also decreases familial interdependence. Urbanization, modernization, and increased acculturation among young Mexican-Americans also has tended to strengthen nuclear family ties and weaken links to extended family members. Hence, Latino elders may increasingly find themselves relatively alone in an alien culture without the type of support they value and expect.

Solis's (1975) research supports the contention that extended family structures and social support systems among Hispanics are eroding, so that today a significant number of elderly Hispanics are isolated both residentially and socially, and are vulnerable to institutionalization. As a result, positive alternatives to aging within the extended family context may be inaccessible to older Mexican-Americans. The situation is particularly acute because while Anglo elderly have been defining social roles and lifestyles that are compatible with growing old without depending upon support from family members, Miranda (1975) reports that most older Hispanics do not have the economic resources to pursue these new, independent lifestyles.

Historically, the welfare and financial support of older Mexican-American family members no longer able to work was the responsibility of the extended family. Typically, in rural areas, the primary burden fell upon older adult sons (Leonard, 1967). As the economy shifted from agrarian to industrial, functions of elderly support have been transferred to governmental institutions (Miranda, 1975). The degree to which elderly urban Hispanics have become acculturated to this Anglo-American norm of state support for the elderly is subject to debate. Carp (1968) reports that urban Mexican-Americans still prefer to care for their own elderly, and that failure to do so is seen as deviant behavior in Mexican-American communities; consequently, few elderly Mexicans are found among institutionalized populations of older persons (Newton & Ruiz, 1981).

Other authors are less convinced that the extended family in its urban form follows the tradition of assuming responsibility for the welfare of its elderly members. Penalosa (1967) reports that 61% of Mexican-American adults in a Southern California survey said the family did not have an obligation to support the elderly. A number of scholars attribute this change to the effects of acculturation, urbanization, and contemporary economics. Laurel (1976) showed in a Texas study that filial responsibilty was negatively associated with youth, urban residence, higher socioeconomic status and greater generational distance from immigrant ancestry. Neither sex nor religious affiliation of respondents was significantly associated with perceptions of filial responsibility. Rural residency was the variable most strongly associated with greater willingness to assume responsibility for the care of elderly parents. Laurel (1976) suggests this is true because stronger social pressures to conform to traditional filial patterns exist in rural areas, whereas Crouch (1972) attributes rural/urban differences to the more deprived economic circumstances of most Hispanics living in urban areas compared to their rural counterparts.

Maldonado (1975) reports that elderly Mexican-Americans are becoming more independent because they recognize it would be economically difficult for their adult children to support them. Yet 95% of the older Mexican-Americans in Sotomayor's 1973 Denver study indicated they expected relatives to take care of them, either in their own home or in the relative's home, if they could no longer care for themselves. Moreover, Bengtson and Burton (1980) found that 66% of older Mexican-Americans surveyed agreed it was the obligation of adult children to care for older parents, but only one-third expected to move in with their adult children if they no longer could live alone. Whites were only about half as likely to evince these expectations of filial support. In contrast to these findings, two-thirds of elderly Hispanics in Crouch's study (1972) felt the family was *not* obligated to care for older members.

SYSTEMS OF SOCIAL SUPPORT

Even though elderly Mexican-Americans generally have many more descendants than do individuals of other groups, this does not necessarily mean that they grow old within an extended family network. Maldonado (1975) notes that the numbers of relatives an older person has is not as important as the extent of communication and interaction between that person and his or her kin. Data show that elderly Mexican-Americans interact more frequently with family members, and are more satisfied with the frequency of that family interaction than are whites or Blacks (Bengtson & Burton, 1980). Elderly Mexican-Americans not only interacted more frequently with kin than did members of other ethnic groups, but also attributed their satisfaction with these relationships to this higher amount of interaction.

Keefe, Padilla, and Carlos (1979), in their comparative study of emotional support networks among Southern California residents, learned that Mexican-Americans are more likely than Anglos to have large numbers of relatives living close by (see also Sotomayor, 1973; Valle & Mendoza, 1978). The primary difference between Anglo and Mexican-American support networks was that Anglos were more likely than Mexicans to seek support from neighbors and friends, while Mexican-Americans were more likely than Anglos to seek help exclusively from other family members.

Both Korte (1978) and Nunez (1975) emphasize the importance of familial interaction for maintaining morale among Mexican-American elderly. Nunez shows that older Mexican-Americans have greater expectations concerning familial interaction than do elders of other ethnicities. Nunez suggests that unmet expectations of family interaction will have more deleterious effects upon older Mexican-Americans than upon older Anglos. Korte's (1978) study indicates urbanization often has negative effects upon the morale of older Hispanics because there is less kin interaction among city dwellers than among rural residents. Older rural couples showed significantly higher levels of both morale and kin interaction than did elderly Latino couples who were urban residents.

Dowd and Bengtson (1978) showed that while Anglo elderly tend to increase interaction with friends and neighbors during postretirement years, older Mexican-Americans continue to exhibit the same low levels of interaction with friends and neighbors that characterized their preretirement years, indicating that primary social interaction, in the past and in the present for older Mexican-Americans, takes place within the family.

However, friendships and mutual help from *barrio* (community) residents may take the place of family interaction for older Hispanics confronted with the dissolution of familial networks due to rapid acculturation of younger cohorts of Hispanics living in nuclear families. Sotomayor (1971) characterizes the barrio as a social arena in which people come together in order to gain a sense of security, and in which needs produced by a shared tradition of cultural customs and heritage can be fulfilled. Santisteban (1980) also believes that living in supportive ethnic communities can reduce stress caused by migration, especially if the host society displays negative prejudices that tend to add to a migrant's feelings of insecurity and anxiety. Cuellar (1978) and Korte (1978) also cite examples of adaptations to a loss of traditional forms of morale-building through social interaction among older Mexican-American barrio residents.

That the quality of neighborhood life is important to life satisfaction of older urban Chicanos also is supported by Korte's (1978) finding that the only elderly Chicanos who had high levels of morale, despite lowered levels of kin interaction, were those who had successfully substituted interaction with neighbors for interaction with kin. Cuellar (1978) links the rapid proliferation of senior citizen's clubs in the East Los Angeles barrio (a social form not found in traditional Mexican society), as proof of the need for new social settings in which elderly Chicanos can develop interpersonal relationships. Cuellar feels membership in voluntary organizations can help older Hispanics learn new social roles and relationships that will permit them to demonstrate their social competence and thereby generate prestige and self-esteem. Thus, senior citizen's clubs can help fill the psychological and social void left when traditional roles, values, and expectations associated with aging no longer exist in the urban, nontraditional setting of the host society.

SOCIAL ROLES

What is the role of the elderly in the Hispanic family? Among rural Mexican-American families, Leonard (1967) says grandparents have three primary roles: as religious advocates and teachers, as childrearers and as participants in family decision-making. While there are few studies on the topic, existing findings suggest elderly Hispanics continue to play important roles in family decision-making in urban extended families. Sotomayor (1973), for example, learned that 94% of the urban Mexican-American grandparents felt grandmothers were influential in family life, while 87% perceived grandfathers to be influential. Nearly identical proportions of respondents felt opinions of grandfathers and grandmothers were respected, and that their influential roles were due to their long history of life experience and value as role models rather than solely to the respect and love of younger family members. About four-fifths of these older Hispanics said they were satisfied with their perceived influence on their families.

Both Leonard (1967) and Sotomayor (1973) believe that the role of elderly extended family members in decision-making belies popular mythology supporting the idea that in traditional families all family authority rests in the hands of Hispanic men. The family importance attributed to grandmothers among Sotomayor's urban respondents also is shown in Leonard's (1967) research on rural Hispanic extended families. Here, he finds the woman's role in decision-making and advising increases as she grows older, deflating the popular conception of the Mexican-American family as exclusively patriarchal.

Childrearing was perceived by Sotomayor's (1973) respondents as one of the principal functions of grandparents living within the family, and older persons were more likely to consider their roles with grandchildren as instructional (53%) or caretaking (37%) rather than as affective (8%). Grandparents of both sexes see themselves as being about equally responsible for childrearing, and considered their most important tasks to be teaching grandchildren to speak Spanish and to learn traditional customs, morality, and religious behavior. In addition, one of every four older persons stressed the importance of encouraging formal education among grandchildren.

While belief in the importance of grandparents' instilling traditional customs and values among grandchildren was strong among Sotomayor's (1973) older respondents, few persons mentioned other traditional aspects of grandparenting, such as the role of the Mexican grandfather as family historian, or the grandmother's duty to pass on information concerning the preparation of native foods or use of medicinal herbs. In addition, while 86% of these older urban residents felt grandmothers had the responsibility to teach and practice religion, only 26% of the sample attended church regularly. This represents a change from Leonard's (1967) description of religious life among rural Mexican-American elderly who characteristically attended church several times per week.

THE IMPACT OF ACCULTURATION

Traditionally, older Hispanics lived in extended families where their advanced age was regarded with respect, and wherein they had specific social roles to perform. Filling these culturally determined family roles maintained their feelings of self-worth and self-confidence which had a positive effect on their mental health. But, as Szapocznik, Faletti, and Scopetta (1977) point out, these family traditions are weakened as family members become more and more acculturated into the Anglo way of life. Because younger persons acculturate more rapidly than older persons, and differences in acculturation between age groups cause interpersonal conflict, lives of older Hispanics are likely to become more and more stressful as traditional family patterns are disrupted.

While Szapocznik and associates (1977) focus on the deleterious effects of these intergenerational differences in acculturation between adolescents and their parents, their data indicate that the gap between older adults and middle-aged respondents is even more pronounced. This suggests that older adults may experience the severest amount of alienation from the cultural values and behavior of their adult offspring and from the society in which they live.

Because use of the English language is cited as a key indicator of acculturation, elderly Hispanics, many preferring to use their native Spanish, are considered to be minimally acculturated into the Anglo-American culture. A number of authors believe the continued use of the Spanish language contributes to the low level of social integration of elderly Hispanics into the Anglo-American culture. Szapocznik (1978) goes one step further when he states that language exacerbates difficulties associated with adapting to old age because Hispanics are less likely to know about and utilize health and social service programs for the elderly. Sotomayor (1971) agrees that the use of Spanish isolates Hispanic elders from the Anglo's culture, but believes it is possible this isolation has psychological benefits. By insulating older Hispanics from negative messages and discrimination coming from the broader society, the use of Spanish may protect older Mexican-Americans from psychological distress. Also, because the use of Spanish separates those who use it from members of the Anglo culture, the use of Spanish may reinforce the common bonds that unite members of Hispanic communities (Sotomayor, 1971).

DISCUSSION

It appears that the present available facts support neither those who contend that traditional familial living patterns are a thing of the past, nor those who say extended, supportive family structures still exist for a majority of U.S. Hispanics. For, on the one hand, while urbanization and modernization are making the traditional paradigm untenable for many older Mexican-Americans today, the evidence suggests that rather than disappearing completely, the extended family structure is being modified to fit changing economic, social, and cultural conditions. Moreover, the extremes of the very traditional and the very modern continue to exist alongside these changing familial patterns. While it is unclear as to how many Mexican-American elders are faced with these transitions, it does suggest that for a proportion of this aged cohort, change has many implications for life adjustment.

The majority of today's Mexican-American elderly are less acculturated than their children and grandchildren; they still maintain role expectations that more closely resemble traditional cultural roles. Thus, the interaction of modern and traditional values can present a very stressful and conflictual situation for the elderly.

But one may ask, why is this situation any different than it has been for any other emigrating group who with the passage of time has been acculturated into mainstream America? What is unique is that while change is taking place, there is also continuous interaction with first generation emigrants who are a constant reinforcement of the traditional values, so that the rate and direction of acculturative change are greatly influenced and cause some cultural values to remain unchanged. The proximity of Mexico to the United States, regardless of the amount of flow back and forth, is itself a reinforcing agent of the familial ties that span the two countries. These two factors will serve to create individuals who become accustomed to operating at several acculturative levels. The coming generation of elderly will be accustomed to this acculturation continuum, but for today's Mexican-American elder who has been exposed least to the changes as a result of recent urbanization, life in a changing culture will require new modes of adaptive behavior.

The adjustment process of the Mexican-American elder can be viewed as the interaction of a two-pronged phenomena. One dimension encompasses the phenomena of growing old with its concomitant sense of loss of occupational status, loss of perceived role as head of household, and general sense of displacement from the mainstream of societal activites. The second dimension, the general theme of this chapter, is cultural modification as a result of urbanization and the acculturative process. Because of the interaction of these two dimensions, physical as well as environmental changes, Mexican-American elders must begin to define a new role for themselves that may be in addition to or in place of the traditional role.

This may include expanding their social network outside of the extended family to encompass possibilities such as participation in senior clubs, political activity, or involvement in a variety of community-oriented tasks. This new social intercourse can be fruitful in providing them with new roles that both enhance their own independence as well as reinforcing their cultural roles as purveyors of the cultural mores to younger Chicanos and new emigrants who seek to maintain the Mexican cultural ties. Moreover, these activites can strengthen the ties to other seniors for whom they can provide social and emotional support as well as from whom they may also receive it.

With regard to economic support, many elders may have neither personal economic resources nor familial economic support and must rely upon public assistance. While many families still have a sense of economic responsibility toward their elders, the reality of low economic resources among Hispanics often prohibits meeting that responsibility. Frequently, welfare assistance and supplemental social security (SSI) allows the elder to maintain their own households, enhancing relationships with their offspring through participation in extended familial activities while minimizing intergenerational conflict that often arises from proximity in the same household.

Indeed, modified roles, expanding social networks, and living apart from offspring can create anxiety and depression among Hispanic elders, which may make them increasingly vulnerable to mental and physical disorders; however, the development of senior programs in the community especially geared to the Hispanic elder can play a large role in modifying this possibility for many. Moreover, the continuity of ethnically familiar surroundings can act as a significant buffer to the problems faced in adjustment to change. The continuing existence of such ethnically similar communities is assured because of the shared border with Mexico, which reinforces cultural ties and provides a continual flow of new emigrants also seeking the ethnically familiar until they choose to integrate into the broader host society.

The development of stronger community ties that can partially replace or enhance the ties to the family structure can be the key to creating and supporting the ethnically familiar for today's Mexican-American elder as he or she attempts to adjust to the aging process as well as to a changing culture.

NOTE

1. The terms Mexican-American, Chicano, Hispanic, and Latino will be used interchangeably. However, the focus of the chapter is only on the Mexican-American.

REFERENCES

Bengtson, V. L., & Burton, L. *Familism, ethnicity and support systems: Patterns of contrast and congruence.* Paper presented at the Western Gerontological Association, San Diego, 1980.

Carp, F. M. *Factors in the utilization of services by Mexican-American elderly.* Palo Alto, CA: American Institute for Research, 1968.

Crouch, B. M. Age and institutional support: Perceptions of older Mexican-Americans. *Journal of Gerontology*, 1972, 27 (4), 524-529.

Cuellar, J. B. The senior citizen's club: The older Mexican-American in the voluntary association. In B. G. Meyerhoff & A. Sinnic (Eds.), *Life's Career: Aging.* Beverly Hills, CA: Sage, 1978.

Dowd, J. D., & Bengtson, V. L. Aging in minority populations: An example of the double jeopardy hypothesis. *Journal of Gerontology*, 1978, 33, 427-436.

Grebler, L., Moore, J. W., & Guzman, R. C. *The Mexican-American people: The nation's second largest minority.* New York: Free Press, 1970.

Keefe, S. E., Padilla, A. M., & Carlos, M. L. The Mexican-American extended family as an emotional support system. *Human Organizations*, Summer 1979, 2.

Korte, A. O. *Social interaction and the morale of Spanish-speaking elderly.* Unpublished Ph. D. dissertation, School of Social Welfare, Denver University, 1978.

Laurel, N. *An intergenerational comparison of attitudes toward the support of aged parents: A study of Mexican Americans in two South Texas communities.* Unpublished Ph. D. dissertation, School of Social Work, University of Southern California, 1976.

Leonard, O. E. The older rural Spanish people of the Southwest. In E. G. Youmans (Ed.), *Older Rural Americans.* Lexington: University of Kentucky Press, 1967.

Maldonado, D. The Chicano aged. *Social Work*, 1975, 20, 213-216.

Manuel, R. C., & Bengtson, V. L. *Ethnicity and family patterns in mature adults: Effects of race, age, SES, and sex.* Paper presented at the Pacific Sociological Association, San Diego, 1976.

Miranda, M. Latin American culture and American society: Contrasts. In A. Hernandez & J. Mendoza (Eds.), *National Conference on the Spanish-speaking elderly.* Kansas City: National Chicano Planning Council, 1975.

Newton, F. C., & Ruiz, R. A. Chicano culture and mental health among the elderly. In M. Miranda and R. Ruiz (Eds.), Chicano aging and mental health. U.S. Department of Health and Human Services, NIMH (ADM) 81-952, 1981, 38-75.

Nunez, Francisco. *Variations in fulfillment of expectations of social interaction and morale among aging Mexican-Americans and Anglos.* Master's thesis, University of Southern California, 1975.

Penalosa, F. The changing Mexican-American in Southern California. *Sociology and Social Research*, 1967, 51, 404-417.

Sanchez, P. The Spanish heritage elderly. In E. P. Stanford (Ed.), *Minority aging.* San Diego: Campanile Press, 1974.

Santisteban, D. *Acculturation, assimilation and psychological stress: A review of the literature.* Spanish Family Guidance Center, University of Miami, 1980.

Solis, F. Cultural factors in programming of services for Spanish-speaking elderly. In A. Hernandez & J. Mendoza (Eds.), *National Conference on the Spanish-speaking elderly.* Kansas City: National Chicano Social Planning Council, 1975.

Sotomayor, M. Mexican American interaction with social systems. *Social Casework*, 1971, 52, 316-324.

Sotomayor, M. *A study of Chicano grandparents in an urban barrio*. Unpublished Ph.D. dissertation, School of Social Work, University of Denver, 1973.

Sotomayor, M. Social change and the Spanish-speaking elderly. In A. Hernandez & J. Mendoza (Eds.), *National Conference on the Spanish-speaking elderly*. Kansas City: National Chicano social Planning Council, 1975.

Szapocznik, J. *A model project for enhancing meaning of life for Hispanic elders: Implications for research, policy and practice*. Paper presented to the Gerontological Society, Dallas, November 1978.

Szapocznik, J., Faletti, M. V., & Scopetta, M. *Psychological-social issues of Cuban elders in Miami*. Spanish Family Guidance Center and Institute for the Study of Aging, University of Miami, 1977.

U.S. Bureau of the Census. *Current population reports: Persons of Spanish origin in the United States: March 1978*. Series P-20, 339, Washington DC: Government Printing Office, June 1979.

Valle, R., & Mendoza, L. *The elder Latino*. San Diego: Campanile Press, 1978.

PART IV

Selected Social Problems and the Minority Aged

Descriptions in the aging literature on the special situation of minority elders began with references to their being in double jeopardy, given their minority status and old age. Soon, this was followed by references to triple jeopardy (minority status, old, and poor) and to quadruple jeopardy (minority status, old, female, and poor). Thus it is acknowledged commonly that the lives of older minorities often are lodged in perilous circumstances. Old minority citizens have brought to their later years a lifetime of social indignities, a history of unequal educational opportunities, lifelong employment and economic inequities, years of inaccessible medical care and substandard housing, and a lifetime of second-class citizenship. Although many of the vicissitudes of aging affect the elderly population in general, their multidimensional and interrelated character frequently pose more severe complications in the lives of aged minorities. Needless to say, most of the problems of aging are not unique to minorities; more often than not, it is a matter of the degree to which they are disproportionately inherent in the minority experience.

This section of the book is not intended to be an exhaustive litany of the numerous problems that afflict the minority elderly. It is intended, however, to elucidate through detailed analysis several areas of pressing concerns as specified or alluded to in previous chapters. It is organized to focus upon five problem clusters, including: (1) housing, (2) crime, (3) health and mental health, (4) employment and income maintenance, and (5) local decision-making and political involvement. To the extent possible, each chapter covers all minority groups rather than concentrating on specific minority population subsets.

In the initial chapter, Adam W. Herbert discusses the housing needs and unique problems confronting an expanding Black elderly population. He traces the history of governmental housing programs that have been designed specifically to assure access to decent housing for the elderly in general, and observes that overall they have not adequately addressed the specific housing needs of the Black elderly. Herbert suggests possible reasons for this failure following his examination of demographic and economic factors, program priorities, and administrative rules and procedures. The chapter is concluded with recommendations as to how the housing needs of the Black elderly can be addressed more effectively.

In the second chapter, R. L. McNeely reports the most recent victimization data as obtained by the National Crime Survey. The data reveal that of all elderly population groups, minority women are most highly victimized by personal offenses, whereas minority men constitute the elderly group most highly victimized by property offenses. Victimization rates take into account land use, community size, neighborhood racial composition, family income, age, marital status, and education. John McAdoo, concerned with the effects of perceived high vulnerability to victimization, has examined fears of crime and morale by victim status. He reports the results of a study utilizing a sample of Black senior residents living in both public and private housing. McAdoo's findings indicate that subjects experienced high levels of fear regardless of residence, victim status, age, or sex. Nevertheless, morale was surprisingly high.

Selected health and mental health issues are delineated by two contributors. First, Barbara Morrison explores the health status of the minority aged from the perspective of culturally determined patterns of living and attitudes. Morrison further focuses on the role of poverty as a critical factor in the exacerbation of health problems over the life cycle and into old age. Second, Josephine Allen directs her attention to mental health concerns of older minority persons. Allen examines the concepts of mental health and mental illness from an ecological perspective and explores the viability of selected options existing for the elderly who become mentally disabled.

Focusing upon employment problems, Gaylene Perrault and Gilbert Raiford offer some historical information detailing similarities in the experiences of Black and Puerto Rican workers. Emphasis is placed on the kinds of jobs to which Blacks and Puerto Ricans traditionally have been relegated. Perrault and Raiford examine the possible impact current technological changes will bring to bear on older Black and Puerto Rican workers, arguing that the job-market survival chances of these workers has diminished significantly. Pointing out that federal programs to address these problems have been unsuccessful, the authors conclude that Black and Puerto Rican older workers face a bleak future. In the next chapter, Robert Hill provides a substantive analysis of patterns of participation by minority elders in major governmental income maintenance programs such as Social Security, Supplemental Security Income (SSI), AFDC, and federal pensions. He also assesses the extent to which members of minority groups are recipients of public in-kind benefits such as Medicare, Medicaid, food stamps, public housing, and rent subsidies.

Departing from what is considered commonly as the more substantive problems of aging, two authors focus on political involvement and influence in decision-making. Elena Bastida indicates that political autonomy and unity are of critical importance if minority group members are to have access to channels of decision-making. She draws this conclusion from a study of Blacks and Hispanics residing in rural and urban areas in which the impact of regional and structural characteristics on the control of accessibility to community resources was examined. Using a conflict theory perspective, Bastida found that the size of the minority group influenced differential control in resource allocation to the elderly. Fernando Torres-Gil's chapter follows, suggesting the nature of the political involvement required to give the minority elderly a larger voice, and sets forth a number of principles that might enhance their political organization.

10

Enhancing Housing Opportunities for the Black Elderly

ADAM W. HERBERT

INTRODUCTORY DEMOGRAPHIC OVERVIEW

Among the most significant demographic trends of the twentieth century has been the continued growth of elderly population age groups, both in absolute numbers and in relation to other segments of American society. In 1900, only 4% of the total United States population was 65 years of age or older: 3.1 million persons. By 1980, that percentage had increased to 11.3 or 16 million persons. As depicted in Figure 10-1, population projections for the United States suggest that the number of elderly will continue to increase relative to other age cohort groups, potentially up to nearly 20% of the population by 2030. These projections also suggest that there will be a substantial increase in the number of persons 75 years of age or older.

Racial breakdowns in the 1980 census indicate that a disproportionately larger number of whites comprise the 65 and older population group. In 1980, 90% of this age cohort group was white: 23 million persons. Blacks, in contrast, constituted only 8%, 2.1 million persons, while the remaining 2% were classified as Spanish origin or of other origin (U.S. Bureau of the Census, 1981). Especially significant, however, is the fact that the number of elderly Blacks is growing at a faster rate than the number of whites. Over the last decade, there was a 27.9% overall increase in the number of persons 65 or older. The rate of population increase among Blacks in that cohort group was 34% compared with 23% for whites.

As the number of elderly in our society continues to increase, particularly those who are 75 years of age or older, growing public policy and social service delivery attention must, of political and human necessity, be focused on the problems and needs of senior citizens. In making these public policy and service delivery determinations, many politicians, administrators, and some scholars previously have assumed the challenges associated with growing older in America are the same for Blacks and whites. Clearly such needs

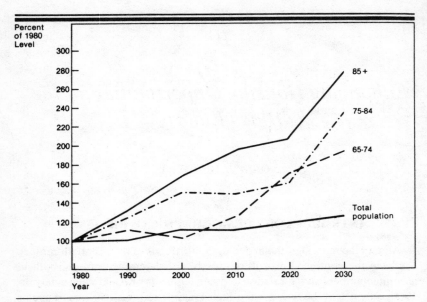

FIGURE 10-1   Projected Growth of Elderly Population Age Groups,
1980-2030

as economic security, access to essential human services, adequate housing, and personal safety exist without regard to race or ethnic background. For the rapidly growing number of Black elderly mentioned above, however, many of these needs and the related problems are more acute. The area of housing is especially illustrative of one of the more acute problems confronting the Black elderly, as well as the failure of public policy in responding adequately to them.

HOUSING PROBLEMS FOR THE ELDERLY

For the first half of this century, virtually no public policy attention was devoted either to understanding or addressing the housing problems and needs of the nation's elderly population. The first significant step in this direction occurred at the National Conference on Aging convened in 1950. That conference stressed the importance of designing housing programs responsive specifically to the needs of the elderly. Congress began to address some of these needs in a limited fashion through housing legislation enacted in 1957, and more particularly Section 202 of the Housing Act of 1959. Section 202 was designed to provide independent living opportunities for elderly and handicapped persons. It specifically authorized direct government loans to nonprofit organizations wishing to develop and operate multifamily housing projects. Although some units might receive additional rental supplements, the program was geared to those who could not afford standard private sector housing, but because of the level of their incomes could not qualify for low-income public housing. Also enacted was the Section 231 program, a mortgage insurance program designed to support unsubsidized housing for the elderly.

The decade of the 1960s was an even more active one in the area of housing for the elderly. The Housing Act of 1964 and the Housing and Urban Development Act of 1965, with its provisions for rent supplements and a rehabilitation grant program, continued the thrust of federal attention to elderly housing needs begun in the 1950s. Simultaneously, the Older American's Act of 1965 established as a matter of national policy an objective of assisting "our older citizens to secure full and free enjoyment of suitable housing, independently selected, designed and located with reference to their special needs, and available at costs they can afford." In 1968, the Section 202 housing program for the elderly was suspended and portions of it were phased into the Section 236 program. This new program also provided for rental units and added cooperative housing for lower income families. In addition, Section 235, an interest subsidy program, was also enacted to assist lower income families in acquiring home ownership. This program was not designed specifically for the elderly, although they were certainly eligible.

A few major events during the 1970s were reflective of the continuing evolution of federal housing policy for the elderly. First, the Section 236 program was curtailed in 1973 as part of a national moratorium on federally assisted housing construction. Then, in 1974, Congress reenacted Section 202 and established it as the major vehicle for financing housing for the elderly. As authorized in the Housing and Community Development Act of 1974, the Section 202/Section 8 program differed significantly from its predecessor. By combining Section 8 rental subsidies with Section 202, very few low-income persons were able to qualify for admission to 202 projects. This was an especially significant provision because the low-rent housing program has become the primary governmental vehicle designed specifically to house the poor elderly.

A historical review of the effectiveness of these federal programs in addressing the housing needs of the Black elderly is particularly disappointing. The 231 mortgage insurance program, which as stated earlier was at one point HUD's flagship program for providing unsubsidized housing for the elderly, has had very little success in attracting Black occupants. The primary reason was that the program's relatively high rents put this housing outside the economic reach of the vast majority of Black elderly.

The Section 235 program enabled a number of Black families to purchase homes, many of them for the first time. Unfortunately, the number of Black elderly making such purchases was relatively insignificant. This was not surprising, however, because the primary focus of the program was clearly not on this specific segment of the population. In contrast, the companion Section 236 rental housing program generated a slightly higher Black elderly occupancy rate because the interest subsidy on 236 mortgages allowed owners of units to charge elderly tenants reduced rents. The availability of a limited number of supplemental rental assistance subsidies in certain cases further aided the Black elderly to afford such units. Unfortunately, less than 10% of the 236 units were designed specifically for the elderly. The curtailment of the program in 1973 continued a low-income housing shortage, which for many Black elderly has still not been fully met by the Section 202/8 program.

Although Section 202 once again became the federal government's primary housing initiative for the elderly in 1974, available data suggest that from its inception racial and ethnic groups have been underrepresented among residents within funded projects (Lawton & Klassen, 1973). The one major HUD study initiated four years after the program was reenacted revealed that it was primarily serving white, elderly females who have middle socioeconomic backgrounds and incomes in the moderate to middle income range of elderly incomes (U.S. Department of Housing and Urban Development [HUD], 1978, p. 40). That study also included reports of projected minority tenant rates in all 202 projects to be in the 2.8% to 6.9% range (HUD, 1978, p. 50). Significantly, the study also revealed that most of the 202 projects in which the Black elderly reside are located in predominantly Black neighborhoods.

Without question, the most significant governmental program serving the lower income Black elderly, both historically and today, is the low-rent public housing program. Ironically, it is not a program designed specifically to address the housing needs of the elderly. In 1971, 28% of all elderly public housing tenants were Black, although Blacks constituted only 7.8% of the elderly population at the time (Lawton, 1975, p. 117). More recent data indicate that by 1976, 35% of elderly public housing tenants were Black (Struyk & Soldo, 1980, p. 201).

The reasons for the disproportionate number and percentage of elderly Blacks now living in public housing, and historically to a much greater degree than in all other federally supported housing programs, are directly linked to income, access, the absence of other programmatic alternatives, and program policies as well as administration. (These critical issues are discussed later in this essay.) The limited overall impact of these federal housing programs in addressing the housing problems and needs of a large number of Black elderly was very effectively summarized by Edward Wallace as he described the continuing housing needs of the Black elderly:

One thing is known, however, on the basis of the partial data that are available from limited surveys; except for public housing, elderly blacks have been virtually excluded from federally financed elderly housing. . . . The irony of the situation is that they are the ones who need that help most, now and in the future [Wallace, 1981, p. 59-60].

A HOUSING NEEDS PROFILE FOR
THE BLACK ELDERLY

Income and economic security. During periods of economic uncertainty, it is not surprising that economic security continues to be one of the most critical issues confronting the Black elderly. The most recent figures available for 1981 reveal that median family income for whites in 1981 was $23,517, up from $21,904 in 1980. For Black families, the median income was $13,267 in 1981, compared with $12,670 in 1980. Over this one-year period, white median income increased relative to that of Blacks by $1,020. The 1981 median household income of all persons 65 and older was $14,335, compared with $25,168 for householders 55 to 64, $29,225 for those 45 to 54, and $26,477 for householders in the 35 to 44 age range (U.S. Bureau of the Census, 1982a, p. 33, p. 12).

The 1980 census also revealed that Black elders are much more likely to be poor than their white counterparts. In 1980, the poverty rate for all elderly 65 or older dropped from 15.7% in 1980 to 15.3% in 1981. In contrast, for aged Blacks the number of persons below the poverty level increased from 38.1% in 1980 to 39% in 1981.

Even more critical is the fact that in 1980, 66.5% of Black women 65 years of age or older who lived alone were below the poverty level. Moreover, 82.5% of persons in families with female householders 65 years of age or older and with no husband present were below the poverty level in 1980 (U.S. Bureau of the Census, 1982c, p. 11, 18, 1982b). As James Manney observed in describing this situation eight years ago:

Black old age poverty is concentrated among women and those living alone. A stunning 68 percent of black women living alone subsist on less than $2,000 annually. The figure for males is only slightly lower, 54.7 percent [Manney, 1975, p. 105].

These income figures are no doubt explained in part by the fact that Blacks tend to generate comparatively lower levels of lifetime income than their white counterparts and hence are more likely to be eligible only for minimal levels of social security benefits. They are also less likely to have been able to accumulate resources for their retirement. The nature of the actual income gap implied in these statistics is reflected in Table 10-1.

The income levels listed in Table 10-1 take on added significance when one considers the realities of housing and other fixed living expenses that the elderly must pay. In 1981, the median rent for the 135,500 unfurnished

**TABLE 10-1   Income of Families and Primary Individuals in Owner and
Renter-Occupied Housing Units with Black Householder Aged
65 Years or Older: 1980**

	Median Income	
Household Composition	Owner Occupied	Renter Occupied
2 or More Person Household		
Married Couple Families,		
No Nonrelatives	$8,500	$6,700
Other Male Householder	$8,500	$5,200
Other Female Householder	$8,100	$5,900
1 Person Household		
Male Householder	$5,500	$4,200
Female Householder	$3,600	$3,900

SOURCE: Extracted from HUD (1980, Table A.4).

apartments constructed in that year was $347. Of that total, only 12,600 units
(9%) were available at monthly rental rates below $250 (U.S. Bureau of the
Census, 1982d, pp. 2-3). On an annualized basis, this represents a rental
expense of $3,000, which is only $900 less than the 1980 median income of
Black female householders living in rental units and one-half of the median
income of elderly married couples who were renters in 1980. As Struyk and
Soldo have observed in this regard:

> Those elderly with incomes below the poverty line are often spending the
> majority of their income for housing. Almost three of every five poor renters
> spend over 35 percent of income for housing, and a full 83 percent of home-
> owners with mortgage debt are in this category [1980, p. 62].

These factors suggest that even with an indexed social security system, it is
unlikely that growing numbers of lower income Black elders will be able to
afford housing that is not subsidized in some fashion.

A slightly different set of problems exists for elderly Black homeowners.
As Table 10-1 also documents, with the exception of single female householders, Black homeowners have higher median incomes (at least 30% greater)
than renters with comparable household composition characteristics. For
these Black elderly homeowners, the challenge confronting them is coping
with rapidly rising local property taxes, repairing and maintaining the physical
quality of their dwellings, paying for increasingly more expensive utilities, and
maintaining appropriate levels of insurance as home values increase (See Table 10-2 for a summary of home values by household composition).

The extent of these expenses should not be underestimated. One study has
indicated that the average elderly household spends 23% of its income for out-
of-pocket housing expenses (Struyk & Soldo, 1980, p. 68). For those elderly
homeowners who are making mortgage payments, these expenses contribute

TABLE 10-2   Median Value of Owner-Occupied Housing Units with Black Householders Aged 65 or Over, 1980

Household Composition	Median Value of Housing Units
2 or More Person Household	
Married Couple Families, no Nonrelatives	$29,900
Other Male Householder	26,000
Other Female Householder	23,800
2 Person Household	
Male Householder	$25,900
Female Householder	22,600

SOURCE: Extracted from HUD (1980, Table 4.5).

to the expanding costs of home ownership. This is especially true for one-person Black female households with their lower income levels. Thus, the major issue for Black elderly homeowners is that of assuring adequate cash flow to sustain an asset that is increasing in value and provides a level of personal security in their old age not frequently experienced by renters.

Living patterns. Over one-half of the Black population of the United States lives in central cities. Specifically, the 1980 census indicated that 58% live in central cities (U.S. Bureau of the Census, 1981). Data from the 1980 Annual Housing Survey as summarized in Table 3 indicate that 53% of Blacks 65 years or older live in central cities, 15% live inside SMSA's but not in central cities, and 32% live in nonmetropolitan areas. In differentiating between renters and homeowners, the survey reveals that Black elderly renters are more likely to reside in central cities than Black homeowners: 64% of elderly Black renters resided in central cities, compared with 46% of homeowners. Conversely, 26% of the elderly Black renters live in nonmetropolitan areas, compared with 37% of the Black homeowners.

Table 10-3 also reveals two other important living patterns among the Black elderly. First, a majority of all Black elderly (58%) live in households of two or more persons. Of that group, 51% were married to the persons with whom they were living. The remaining 49% live with either male or more frequently female relatives other than their spouses, or with nonrelatives. This reflects a growing pattern of several unrelated Black elders living together for reasons of economic survival. It also reflects a continuing, although apparently diminishing, pattern of some Black elderly individuals living with relatives in extended family settings, in spite of tax and social security program policies that discourage or penalize such practices. Second, of those Black elderly householders living alone, 69% are women. This is reflective of the longer life spans of females relative to males, and perhaps of the greater likelihood that elderly women will be more willing, and are better able to live alone and care for themselves than their male counterparts.

TABLE 10-3 **Characteristics of Housing Units with Black Householder Aged 65 Years or Older: 1980 and 1970** (Numbers in Thousands)

	Total		Inside SMSAs				Outside SMSAs	
			In Central Cities		Not in Central Cities			
	1980	1970	1980	1970	1980	1970	1980	1970
Owner Occupied								
2 or more Person Households								
Married Couples, no Nonrelatives	316	248	142	108	58	42	115	99
Other Male Householders	66	32	24	14	15	5	27	13
Other Female Householders	164	102	79	44	34	16	51	42
1 Person Households								
Male Householder	94	46	45	18	18	8	31	20
Female Householder	203	107	96	43	22	16	85	48
Renter Occupied								
2 or more Person Households								
Married Couples, no Nonrelatives	130	134	80	79	13	14	41	41
Other Male Householders	36	28	23	17	6	3	7	8
Other Female Householders	114	79	63	48	19	8	33	23
1 Person Households								
Male Householder	105	88	65	57	18	9	21	22
Female Householder	236	143	165	97	14	13	57	33

SOURCE: Derived from HUD (1980, Table 4.7).

These Black elderly household location data are consistent with the findings of Marjorie Cantor (1976), who observed in a study of the elderly in New York City that, "Increasingly, the concentration of elderly in all industrialized societies is in the largest cities—most frequently in the older central or inner-city where poverty and social and environmental blight are common conditions of life" (p. 49). This concentration appears to exist without regard to living patterns of the elderly individual or family.

This important observation by Cantor must not be minimized or overlooked as we seek to address the housing needs of the Black elderly. While their living patterns and the quality of actual housing units available to the Black elderly are important, probably of equal significance from an overall quality of life perspective are the neighborhoods in which they live. As Struyk and Soldo have appropriately observed in this regard:

> The adequacy of a dwelling unit is dependent upon not only the structural characteristics of the unit, but also how well those characteristics correspond to the needs and preferences of the inhabitant and the residential location of the unit. All three are important components of housing satisfaction, that is, adequacy as perceived by the inhabitant. Structural, personal, and environmental characteristics may be viewed as a tripod supporting housing satisfaction (Struyk & Soldo, 1980, p. 167).

From a perspective of elderly residents, I would suggest that there are at least five of these fundamental environmental characteristics that will significantly affect their assessment of housing satisfaction and impact the quality of life opportunities for them: access to human services; protection from criminal victimization; physical quality of the living unit and immediate neighborhood environment; opportunities for independent living outside of a formal institutional context; and proximity to relatives, friends, and others in the same age cohort group.

While each of these factors seems clear-cut, because of rapidly expanding national problems in the area of crime, more specific reference must be made herein to the relationship between neighborhood housing availability for the Black elderly and protection for them from criminal victimization. Six years ago, the U.S. Commission on Civil Rights conducted a study of age discrimination. Included in its findings was the following observation:

> Being black and aged frequently means the piling up of life problems associated with each characteristic. The black aged often have less education, less income, smaller or no social security income, less adequate medical services, and fewer family supports than the aged in general; their vulnerability is often heightened by their living in areas where the risk of assault and robbery is high [U.S. Commission of Civil Rights, 1977, p. 14].

There is little question but that the neighborhoods in which many Black elderly live subject them to a much greater likelihood of victimization than their white counterparts. As R. L. McNeely has documented elsewhere in this volume, the personal victimization rate for elderly Black males is twice that of elderly white males. Even more startling, however, is the fact that the rate of victimization for Black females is three times that of their white counterparts. This latter statistic takes on special significance because of the large number of elderly Black women who live alone in neighborhoods with high crime rates.

While some might argue that an easy solution to this problem is to locate more housing units for the Black elderly outside of the areas in which they have traditionally lived, this is generally unacceptable to many of the elderly who would be moved from their life-long neighborhood, friends, and their relatives. As Struyk and Soldo stress in reviewing the findings from their study,

> Eighty-six percent of elderly homeowners and 75 percent of elderly renters evaluated the overall condition of their neighborhood as being either good or excellent, although a considerable number of older persons identified specific neighborhood problems [Struyk & Soldo, 1980, pp. 167-168].

While personal safety was one of the specific problems most frequently identified by elderly respondents in this survey, it was not normally a factor that in isolation caused senior citizens to give up their roots to move to another section of the city or region. This factor carries with it significant policy implications that have generally been ignored by those who develop national housing policy.

BARRIERS
TO HOUSING THE BLACK ELDERLY

Several factors stand out as being among the major programmatic and policy barriers that have made it difficult for many Black elderly to secure decent housing. Those listed below are among the most important and must be addressed by public officials at the federal level, particularly if the low-income Black elderly are to be able to compete for units in today's housing market.

Rental rates. Perhaps the most significant barrier confronting low-income Black elderly in their effort to secure rental units is the high rental rates that can now be commanded in the housing market. The FY1983 federal budget, which has essentially eliminated new Section 8 rental subsidies and substantially reduced the number of new Section 202 units to be built with federal support, will have the effect of further reducing housing options for this vulnerable group. Simply stated, without expanded rental subsidies, lower rental rates, an increase in the number of public housing units available to them, and/or an increase in the number of new Section 202/8 units being constructed by Black sponsors (which tends to assure that Blacks will become residents) or constructed in close proximity to Black neighborhoods, the housing situation for low-income Black elderly will no doubt worsen immediately and over time.

Project location. The location of housing units appears to be a natural factor in determining the likelihood of minority occupancy of housing units. While it is difficult to establish a firm relationship between Black occupancy and the proximity of housing units to a Black neighborhood, public housing and Section 202 projects in close proximity to minority communities do tend to have high percentages of Black residents. Yet, the Department of Housing and Urban Development (HUD) historically has utilized site and neighborhood standards for housing projects that have made difficult, if not impossible, the use of federal dollars to construct housing in areas of minority concentration, or in racially mixed areas if the project would cause a significant increase in the proportion of minority to nonminority residents in the area. This policy thrust has led to a critically important observation by M. Powell Lawton:

> It seems clear that the battle to penetrate white impacted areas has to be fought relentlessly. However, it also seems very clear that there is now, and will continue to be, such a major need for housing by minority-group aged as to justify the concurrent building of projects in areas where few whites choose to apply. In addition to the need being very great, there is also strong justification for the right of a black sponsor to build in a location that will maximally serve the black community, even if there is little hope for recruiting many white tenants. Finally, as long as there is a need and some blacks prefer to live in all-black projects, it seems impossible to refuse to build them [Lawton, 1975, pp. 92-93].

It is essential that this policy struggle between the legitimate simultaneous goals of integration and neighborhood revitalization where minorities now live be addressed in a fashion that does not penalize those with both the greatest need for housing, and who are most likely to be impacted negatively by forced moves from their lifelong neighborhoods.

Marketing. Another major barrier to equal housing opportunity for the Black elderly has been inadequate and/or nonexistent marketing efforts geared to attracting Black elders to many housing projects supported by public dollars. Discrimination in housing is prohibited by Title VI of the Civil Rights Act of 1964, Title VIII of the Civil Rights Act of 1968, Executive Orders 11063 and 11246, and a number of federal agency rules, state laws and local ordinances. In spite of these requirements, however, there are too few incentives or penalties encouraging the marketing of elderly housing projects directly to the Black elderly. In the absence of a meaningful agency monitoring process and a clear commitment to enforce fair housing policies, low-income Black elderly will continue to experience difficulty in securing adequate rental housing.

Sponsoring agencies. Also impacting the availability of housing units can be the sponsoring organization or agency that constructs a project. This is particularly true with regard to the Section 202 program. The fundamental concern here centers around the fact that there are few, if any, Black elderly residents in 202 projects sponsored by predominantly white nonprofit organizations. The HUD (1978) study of the 335 projects in the original Section 202 program referenced earlier revealed that only 13 were constructed by minority group organizations. The study demonstrated that while the number of Black residents was very limited in projects constructed by white organizations, 88% of the residents in minority-sponsored projects were from minority groups.

It is essential, therefore, that this factor be given greater attention not only through the selection of more Black sponsors, but, as stated above, also through more rigorous enforcement of sponsoring agency compliance with affirmative action requirements. In short, as a matter of policy, a more vigorous multiethnic approach to enhanced housing opportunity for the elderly is essential. Such a policy must reflect the reality that given the social interaction patterns existing in our society, it may be necessary that some housing projects be targeted largely to the Black elderly *in* or in close proximity to their neighborhoods.

Availability and affordability of housing units. As stated earlier, one of the significant federal policy decisions made over the past few years has been the reduced programmatic and resource emphasis placed on construction of new housing units and/or subsidies for the elderly. Ironically, this is occurring at a time when the number and percentage of elderly within the population is increasing. The fact that more of these senior citizens are poor and increasingly will come from minority groups further illustrates the importance of expanded, rather than reduced programmatic responses to their housing needs. As has been suggested in this chapter, the joint goals of expanding the availability of more housing units and enhancing the affordability of those units specifically for the elderly must be approached with a view toward meeting the housing needs of a diverse population group.

For poor elders, more rental units must be made available at rates that can be accommodated with the lowest levels of social security derived income. Programmatic responses in this regard obviously will be reflective of political and economic reality. Within that context, a number of options are available, including more public housing units with priorities for the elderly, utilizing housing allowances for the elderly, expansion of the 202 program, greater use of Section 8 or other rental subsidy programs, and increased emphasis on housing rehabilitation with special emphasis on increasing the number of units available for the elderly. All are expensive alternatives, but the need for more units is growing and political reality will increasingly demand more effective responses.

A slightly different challenge and need exists for those elderly who can afford to purchase their own homes. As has been proposed by many students of the housing scene, including the recent President's Commission on Housing, particular attention must be given to providing opportunities for the elderly to utilize home equity to generate supplemental revenues that will better enable them to meet rising current living expenses. New opportunities for home ownership among the elderly also remain an important goal worthy of pursuit through loan guarantees and/or interest subsidies. For homeowners and renters these opportunities must be available in neighborhood settings in which they can feel psychologically comfortable and physically safe.

CONCLUSION

This chapter reflects an effort to describe the unique and expanding housing needs of the Black elderly, as well as the failure of public programs to respond adequately to those needs. In addition, the major barriers that delimit equal and adequate housing opportunity for the Black elderly have been identified. During a period of fiscal retrenchment, it is clear that there may be a reluctance among many public officials to commit the dollars necessary to overcome those barriers demanding public dollar responses. There also may exist an unwillingness to acknowledge the reality that the low-income elderly, and particularly minorities, are more vulnerable than any other segment of American society to the economic difficulties accompanying the current recessionary period. Finally, we may continue to see political and bureaucratic unwillingness to enforce vigorously the national mandate that guarantees equal access and opportunity for housing to minority group members. The demographic data presented throughout this chapter point out, however, the inappropriateness and imprudence of such continuing responses. Unfortunately, but quite clearly, without more focused public policy attention to the housing needs of the Black elderly, the problems facing them will only intensify in magnitude over time as their numbers increase and their unmet needs multiply.

REFERENCES

Cantor, Marjorie H. Effect of ethnicity on life styles of the inner city elderly. In L. M. Powell, R. J. Newcomer, & T. D. Byerts (Eds.), *Community planning for an aging society*. Stroudsburg, PA: Dowden, Hutchinson & Ross, 1976.

Dancy, Joseph R. *The Black elderly: A guide for practitioners*. Ann Arbor: University of Michigan—Wayne State University Institute of Gerontology.

Lawton, M. P., & Klassen, E. Federally subsidized housing, not for the elderly Black. *Journal of Social and Behavioral Science*, 1973, 19, 65-78.

Lawton, M. Powell. *Planning and managing housing for the elderly*. New York: John Wiley, 1975.

Manning, James D., Jr. *Aging in American society.* Ann Arbor: University of Michigan—Wayne State University Institute of Gerontology, 1975.

Struyk, Raymond J., & Soldo, Beth J. *Improving the elderly's housing.* Cambridge, MA: Ballinger, 1980.

Wallace, Edward. Housing for the Black elderly—The need remains. In M. P. Lawton & S. L. Hoover (Eds.), *Community housing choices for older Americans.* New York: Springer, 1981.

U.S. Bureau of the Census. *Population profile of the United States: 1981.* Washington, DC: Government Printing Office, 1981.

U.S. Bureau of the Census. *Money income of households, families, and persons in the United States: 1980.* Series P-60, No. 132. Washington, DC: Government Printing Office, 1982. (a)

U.S. Bureau of the Census. *Money income and poverty status of families and persons in the United States: 1981.* Washington, DC: Government Printing Office, 1982 (b)

U.S. Bureau of the Census. *Characteristics of the population below the poverty level: 1980.* Series P-60, No. 183. Washington, DC: Government Printing Office, 1982. (c)

U.S. Bureau of the Census. *Characteristics of apartments completed: 1981.* Washington, DC: Government Printing Office, 1982. (d)

U.S. Commission on Civil Rights. *The age discrimination study.* Washington, DC: Government Printing Office, 1977.

U.S. Department of Housing and Urban Development. *Annual housing survey: 1980.* Washington, DC: Government Printing Office, 1981.

U.S. Department of Housing and Urban Development. *U.S. Housing Developments for the Elderly.* Washington, DC: Special Concerns Staff, Office of Housing Programs, 1975.

U.S. Department of Housing and Urban Development. *Section 202: Housing for the elderly or handicapped.* Washington, DC: Office of Policy Development and Research, 1978.

11

Race, Sex, and Victimization of the Elderly

R. L. McNEELY

Certain facts now are well known about the victimization of elders. For example, compared to other age groups, they are not frequent victims of gratuitous violence and are least likely to be assaulted physically, although they do experience a disproportionately high amount of personal larceny with contact (Hindelang, 1976). Thus, the elderly are more prone than others to have their purses snatched or pockets picked (Hochstedler, 1980; cf. Jaycox, 1982). Neither entails the use of extreme force.

These facts have spurred a number of authors to characterize the elderly's high fear levels as excessive and unrealistic. One author, following her examination of victimization data collected for 26 U.S. cities, remarked recently that "the level of fear expressed by the elderly could safely be reduced by a considerable degree in order to relieve some of the paralyzing effects of fears that appear to be based on popular, but erroneous, beliefs" (Hochstedler, 1980, p. 1).

However, summarily dismissing the fears of elders may be a bit premature (see Jaycox, 1978). Balkin (1979) has noted that low rates of victimization may be the result of the elderly having substantially circumscribed their activities due to their acute levels of fear. He suggests that one cannot obtain a true measure of risk unless exposure is taken into account; for example, by assessing the probability of victimization per 1,000 contacts rather than per 1,000 population. Additionally, many of the pronouncements about the relative safety of older people have been made by those examining aggregate data. One result of failing to disaggregate data is the masking of rates to which different groups of the elderly population are exposed. In illustration of this point, Liang and Sengstock (1981) have reported that the risk assumed by elderly Black males may be as much as 14 times higher than that assumed by elderly white females (1981, p. 469). In addition to race, other factors Liang and Sengstock found significantly related to risk included community size, marital status, age, and sex.

This chapter presents the most recent available demographic data relevant to the victimization of American elders. These descriptive data are detailed to shed light on the prevalence of victimization with particular reference to the minority aged. Inasmuch as the objective is simply to assess differences in the most current rates of victimization experienced by the different races and genders, no presentation of victimization trends are reported.

THE DATA

The data are from the National Crime Survey (NCS) and are distributed by the University of Michigan's Inter-University Consortium for Political and Social Research (ICPSR). The NCS is an ongoing national study (see Garofalo and Hindelang, 1977). The data include victimizations subjects have reported to the police as well as those not reported; consequently, they reflect victimizations not recorded in official police statistics. Begun in 1973, the NCS is funded by the Department of Justice and is conducted by the Bureau of the Census.

The NCS employs a rotating panel with six sets of respondents. Interviewing is conducted continuously with respondents in a given set being interviewed once every six months. Respondents are asked to report about their experiences during the previous six months. Interviews are conducted covering specific reference periods, with individual responses subsequently being weighted in order to construct estimated annual rates of victimization. For example, if the objective were to estimate victimization rates for 1979, subjects reporting on a reference period that only partially included the time interval (1979) for which victimization rates are to be estimated must be taken into account. Thus, individuals interviewed in April 1979 were asked about the reference period from October 1978 through March 1979. As only the January-March period would count toward the annual rate for 1979, individual exposure during 1979 is only 3/12. In this panel set, a weight of 3/12ths would be applied to reflect the amount of exposure during the year 1979.

A somewhat different procedure was used for purposes of this report to determine estimated victimization rates. A two-year interval (July 1978-June 1980) was employed. Given the fact that yearly victimization rates may vary considerably (see Liang and Sengstock, 1981, p. 466), it was felt that a two-year period might provide more stable estimates, and this reference period is reported for each of the subjects. However, data obtained during the two-year period were annualized to reflect an estimated victimization rate of one year. This was achieved by calculating the rate of victimization for the two-year period and dividing by a factor of two. As the results are based upon two years of interviews, the rates, therefore, represent two years' worth of exposure to victimization that have been annualized for the respondents, rather than an annual rate for 1979.

Victimization rates reported in the following section have been calculated to an estimated base of approximately 26,000,000 individuals who are 65 years of age or older. They are based upon a sample of 8,456 such individuals and calculated on a weighted basis taking into account two primary factors. First, ICPSR took a 10% sample of nonvictims. Therefore, in order to achieve an appropriate base, nonvictims received a weight of 10, victims a rate of 1. Second, the Bureau of the Census, which originally collected the data, used a stratified sample with disproportionate sampling fractions and calculated an adjustment to account for nonresponse within each stratum. Both of these adjustments were supplied on the records from ICPSR.

Of the 8,456 individuals actually interviewed during July 1978-June 1980, 365 were minority males, 436 were minority females, 3,125 were white males, and 4,530 were white females. Thus, the reader should be aware that rates reported for whites are likely to be substantially more reliable than rates reported for members of national minority groups. This is due to the relatively small sample size: The actual numbers of minority males and females in the various cells reported in Tables 11-1 and 11-2 that follow often failed to exceed 100 subjects. Despite this limitation, NCS data are the best available currently.

PERSONAL VICTIMIZATION

For purposes of this chapter, personal victimizations include any offenses involving face-to-face confrontation or victim/offender contact. Robbery, assault, rape, pickpocketing and pursesnatching are common personal offenses. (Personal larceny without contact is included in property victimization data).

Vulnerability to personal victimization does vary by race and sex. Members of minority groups are at much greater risk than their elderly white counterparts. Although not reflected in Table 11-1, the combined estimated victimization rate for members of national minority groups, both male and female, is 23.1 per 1,000 population. For whites, the rate is 8.81 per 1,000 population. Thus, risk of personal victimization among members of national minority groups is approximately 162% higher.

For the entire sample, land use, community size, and age were related consistently to personal victimization. Simply put, exposure to risk declines for the elderly population as a whole as age increases, and individuals in rural locations are considerably safer than those in urbanized areas, with the highest exposure to risk occurring in cities of 100,000 residents or more. Additionally, elderly members of the overall population with the lowest family incomes are considerably more likely to be victimized than those reporting incomes of at least $5,000 per year, and risk tends to increase as the percentage of Blacks residing in an area increases.

TABLE 11-1   Estimated Personal Victimization Rates Per 1,000 Elderly Population For Selected Variables by Race and Sex (July 1978-June 1980: Annualized)

Variables	Minority Males	Minority Females	White Males	White Females	Row Totals
Land Use					
Rural Farm	**	**	<1	2.9	1.48
Rural Nonfarm	4.5	2.8	4.7	1.6	3.01
Urban	24.7	31.2	13.0	10.6	13.17
Column Totals*	20.35	25.14	9.88	8.10	10.08
Community Size					
≤24,999	9.8	4.9	4.8	3.1	4.03
25,000-99,999	14.2	7.9	12.4	6.5	8.80
≥100,000	29.7	42.3	22.5	20.2	23.79
Column Totals	20.35	24.14	9.89	8.11	10.10
Percentage Black					
<1	**	**	6.6	6.5	6.57
1-5	7.7	27.2	10.5	14.2	11.98
6-15	14.3	**	12.9	9.9	10.77
16-50	22.2	11.5	9.9	9.2	11.14
51-75	14.3	33.7	11.6	11.9	19.52
76-100	32.2	36.1	38.8	**	32.52
Column Totals	19.41	24.06	9.75	8.25	10.08
Family Income					
<$3,000	23.9	32.8	16.4	8.5	15.13
$3,000-$4,999	24.9	15.5	15.1	9.9	12.54
$5,000-$11,999	16.8	17.0	6.1	8.1	7.59
$12,000-$24,999	9.8	29.9	5.6	8.6	8.05
≥$25,000	**	**	9.4	7.6	9.18
Column Totals	19.79	24.67	9.39	7.85	9.80
Age					
65-69	19.8	34.4	11.3	8.6	11.55
70-74	35.3	16.7	9.5	8.1	9.93
75-79	10.5	22.7	9.7	8.4	9.71
80-84	12.4	7.8	6.3	7.1	6.97
85+	**	**	5.7	5.0	6.09
Column Totals	20.35	25.14	9.88	8.10	10.08
Marital Status					
Married	17.4	20.9	7.5	6.1	7.64
Widowed	8.6	21.6	7.4	8.9	9.78
Divorced	12.4	78.9	48.9	21.4	33.68
Separated	66.2	20.0	95.1	40.7	54.71
Never Married	32.7	46.4	19.7	5.9	13.98
Column Totals	20.35	25.23	9.90	8.11	10.10

(continued)

TABLE 11-1 (Continued)

Variables	Minority Males	Minority Females	White Males	White Females	Row Totals
Education					
0-6	18.2	15.5	9.6	12.2	12.47
7-12	26.4	31.0	9.0	6.9	9.05
13-16	13.5	30.3	13.9	9.5	11.84
17+	**	**	9.3	7.6	9.69
Column Totals	20.35	25.14	9.88	8.10	10.08
POPULATION TOTALS	20.35	25.14	9.88	8.10	10.08

*Column totals are not consistent by variable because of missing observations. For example, although land use and age were reported for nearly every subject, a number of subjects did not report family income.
**Too few observations to permit estimation.

The greater exposure to risk in predominantly Black neighborhoods is related to the higher concentrations of impoverishment found in those areas. For example, estimates of the extent of poverty, based on the concept of minimum adequacy rather than minimum subsistence, have shown that in the years following the 1960s, between 40 and 55% of the Black population has been either poor or nearly poor (McNeely & Pope, 1978, p. 408). These figures are put into additional perspective when one considers that the true (counting discouraged workers) unemployment rate for Blacks has been about 25% for the last several years, and the true unemployment rate for Black men in the behaviorally volatile 16- through 19-year age group has been between 60 and 65% during this same period (McNeely & Pope, 1981, p. 32).

The relationship of high impoverishment and unemployment rates to involvement in certain kinds of crimes, including personal offenses such as larceny with contact or property offenses such as burglary, is straightforward. Conceptualizing the reasons underlying involvement in other more violent offenses perhaps is not equally simple. Speaking with reference to Blacks, Curtis (1976) has suggested that blocked economic opportunities and institutional racism, along with what is described as the Black contracultural pattern of greater acceptance and justification of violence, are key explanators. Although it has been suggested that violence may be accepted and justified more often by members of lower class groups, Curtis points out that adherence to this pattern is intensified among Blacks due to their unique experiences of southern slavery and their present-day racial victimization.

Perhaps this explains why risk increases as the percentage of Blacks in residence increases, whereas risk tends to decline in areas where the proportion of Hispanics, another low SES group, increases. For example, the personal victimization rate of elders in areas where Blacks constitute 51 to 75% of the population is 19.52 per 1,000 residents. In areas with a comparable percentage of Hispanics, the rate (not reflected in Table 11-1) is only 6.92 per 1,000 residents.

On the other hand, neighborhoods where Hispanics constituted 6 to 15% and 16 to 50% of the population had respective victimization rates of 18.54 and 18.69 per 1,000 population. These rates compare to rates of 10.77 and 11.14 per 1,000 population in areas having the same proportions of Blacks in residence. Thus, areas in which Hispanics are modestly represented in the population afford higher exposure to risk than areas which have similarly modest representations of Blacks, and also afford higher risk than areas where Hispanics constitute the majority population. Too few observations in areas with the highest concentrations of Hispanics (76-100%) did not allow computation of an estimated victimization rate.

The greatest risk of victimization is suffered by elderly minority women. Majority women, in contrast, are least likely to be victimized. The personal victimization rate for minority women is 3.10 times greater than it is for white women, amounting to a risk factor that is 210% higher. Among minority women, those that are divorced experience extraordinarily high risk. Their rate, 78.9 per 1,000 population, was among the highest rates of any classification within the population subsets for which data are reported.

While divorced minority men had a much lower victimization rate (12.4 per 1,000 population) than divorced minority women, minority men who were separated from their wives registered a rate of personal victimization that approximated the high rate reported for divorced minority women. These men have an estimated victimization rate of 66.2 per 1,000 population. This compares to a rate for separated minority women of only 20 per 1,000 population. Thus, what is very high risk marital status category for members of one genderal subset is a comparatively low-risk category for their counterparts.

Never-married minority men and women had uniformly high rates of victimization. Never-married minority men were nearly twice as likely as married minority men to be victimized, and never-married minority women were more than twice as likely as married minority women to be victimized.

The victimization rates for divorced and separated white men and women were high when compared to the rates reported for their majority-group counterparts in the other marital status categories. Separated white men had the highest rate of personal victimization of any of the subgroups reported in Table 11-1. At a rate of 95.1 per 1,000 population, nearly one in ten of these men is being victimized by some form of personal transgression.

PROPERTY OFFENSES

Property offenses include crimes involving theft or damage to one's material possessions. Burglary, auto theft, and vandalism are common forms of property offenses.

Aged members of minority groups are more likely than whites to suffer property offenses. The combined estimated rate of property offenses experienced by elderly members of minority groups is 107.07 per 1,000 population. The rate for whites is 80.45. These rate discrepancies between the two populations amount to an increased risk factor among minorities of about 33%. Consequently, although minority group members experience greater risk of crime against their property than whites, the disproportionality is considerably less than that suffered with respect to personal victimization.

No consistent patterns for the entire population with regard to property offenses were observed for any variable save education; the more years of schooling the higher one's risk. However, several modest trends were observed. People in urban areas, especially those in cities with the largest populations, tended to have higher risk, as did those in the highest income categories. Individuals residing in areas where the population was 76 to 100% Black were considerably more at risk than those in areas with lesser percentages of Blacks. Although their rates are not reported in Table 11-2, areas with Hispanic populations constituting more than 75% of the population registered a rate of 152.14 property offenses per 1,000 population. This rate exceeds the rate reported for similarly constituted Black communities (124.69 per 1,000 population).

The group least victimized in communities with Blacks constituting more than 75% of all residents is minority women. Majority men and women as well as minority men all registered higher rates of victimization.

Minority men are most victimized by property offenses. Their rate of victimization, 134.89 per 1,000 population, amounts to an exposure to risk

TABLE 11-2 Estimated Property Victimization Rates Per 1,000 Elderly Population For Selected Variables by Race and Sex (July 1978-June 1980: Annualized)

Variables	Minority Males	Minority Females	White Males	White Females	Row Totals
Land Use					
Rural Farm	**	**	95.0	42.0	67.47
Rural Nonfarm	66.3	42.2	65.4	65.6	64.65
Urban	151.5	98.8	92.2	83.8	90.41
Column Totals*	134.89	86.32	84.22	77.93	82.82
Community Size					
<2,500	63.1	48.6	71.7	65.0	67.29
2,500-9,999	153.9	63.1	82.5	75.2	79.28
10,000-24,999	47.0	56.9	67.3	74.1	70.47
25,000-99,999	128.3	120.4	96.7	85.3	91.77
100,000-499,999	198.1	83.6	103.5	104.0	107.21

(continued)

TABLE 11-2   (Continued)

Variables	Minority Males	Minority Females	White Males	White Females	Row Totals
500,000-999,999	196.1	91.2	119.4	97.9	110.45
≥1,000,000	152.1	130.6	106.8	71.4	95.62
Column Totals	134.88	86.32	84.26	77.69	82.71
Percentage Black					
<1	**	**	84.2	70.3	76.13
1-5	171.4	119.9	97.0	83.8	90.80
6-15	127.2	126.9	73.9	83.3	83.90
16-50	105.6	49.3	47.9	109.2	81.13
51-75	164.1	70.3	69.7	68.2	91.02
76-100	159.8	103.0	146.5	139.1	124.69
Column Totals	136.89	86.54	83.30	78.71	83.15
Family Income					
<$3,000	134.1	80.2	90.9	88.1	90.83
$3,000-$4,999	107.1	92.7	85.9	92.3	91.51
$5,000-$7,499	186.9	143.7	79.8	72.9	81.66
$7,500-$11,999	194.5	90.5	73.4	72.6	76.07
$12,000-$19,999	167.0	44.6	91.4	77.4	84.94
$20,000-$24,999	**	**	122.6	76.0	92.88
≥$25,000	**	**	108.2	89.5	99.96
Column Totals	145.70	87.18	86.21	81.17	85.84
Age					
65-69	169.4	92.3	93.9	86.8	93.30
70-74	114.5	77.2	75.7	77.1	77.88
75-79	101.6	104.1	73.9	73.1	76.17
80-84	116.5	120.1	75.1	54.4	65.39
85+	**	**	99.1	79.3	78.98
Column Totals	134.89	86.32	84.22	77.93	82.82
Marital Status					
Married	126.7	98.9	72.6	64.9	72.39
Widowed	187.6	89.9	133.9	84.9	93.77
Divorced	142.5	98.5	194.5	180.5	176.66
Separated	109.9	59.4	204.3	116.6	120.73
Never Married	57.3	22.0	76.4	57.0	61.31
Column Totals	134.89	86.03	84.43	78.01	82.93
Education					
0-6	128.5	65.3	58.5	72.2	73.33
7-12	148.6	102.1	84.6	70.7	78.60
13-16	119.9	118.1	103.3	104.6	104.72
17+	**	**	105.0	125.0	112.92
Column Totals	134.89	86.32	84.25	77.93	82.83
POPULATION TOTALS	134.89	86.32	84.22	77.93	82.82

*Column totals are not consistent by variable because of missing observations. For example, although land use and age were reported for nearly every subject, a number of subjects did not report family income.
**Too few observations to permit estimation.

that is about 63% higher than that of all groups (82.82 per 1,000 population), and about 56% higher than the rate for minority women (86.32 per 1,000 population). In addition, they experience substantially higher risk than minority women regardless of marital status.

Just why the rate is so much higher for minority men than women is unclear, particularly given the fact that married minority men have a property offense victimization rate that is 28% higher than that of married minority women. One possible explanation that could account for this difference is sample bias. However, males and females are interviewed randomly. Thus, one would be forced to assume, if accepting this argument, that the data are reflective of a random case wherein minority women are simply less likely than minority men to report property offenses. However, though the discrepancy is less great, majority men reported higher rates than their female counterparts. Consequently, the data indicate that there are real differences in victimization with even the married males of both population groups being more highly victimized.

The author can think of only two possible explanations to account for the discrepant rates among spouses. First, in two-car households, where each car is identified specifically as belonging to one or the other spouse, males may be experiencing more car theft or vandalism than their wives. Because the NCS data do not provide good descriptions of lost property or property damage, this hypothesis could not be examined. Second, perhaps there is greater attribution of property ownership to the males among elderly couples. On this point Gans (1962, p. 52) has reported that some women have attributed the ownership of family businesses solely to their husbands. It is possible that among elderly women, attribution of ownership to husbands also is made with respect to other family possessions.

Divorced and separated whites experience the highest property victimization of any marital status group in either population. Divorced white males have an exposure to risk that is 36% higher than divorced minority males. Divorced white females have an exposure to risk that is 83% higher than minority females and separated whites of both sexes are almost twice as likely to be victimized as members of minority groups.

VICTIMIZATION OF ADULTS: BRIEF NOTES AND COMPARISONS

NCS data reported in Tables 11-3 and 11-4 for personal and property victimizations are based on a sample of 84,572 individuals and calculated to an estimated population base of 175,608,202 adult Americans (12 years of age or older). These data were collected as described previously in this chapter but, importantly, are based on much larger numbers of minority respondents than data reported for minority elders.

Data reported in these tables show clearly that elders, for the most part, are victimized at substantially lower rates than the total adult population. Minority male adults have a personal victimization rate that nearly triples (2.71 times higher) the rate reported for minority male elders, and minority female adults are victimized at a rate that is 38.2% higher than minority female elders. However, the rates reported for all adult white males and females are much more discrepant when compared to white elders' rates. For example, the rate for adult white males nearly quintuples (4.74 times higher) the rate reported for white male elders, and the rate for adult white females more than triples (3.13 times higher) that of white female elders.

TABLE 11-3   Estimated Personal Victimization Rates Per 1,000 Adult Population For Selected Variables By Race and Sex (July 1978-June 1980: Annualized)

Variables	Minority Males	Minority Females	White Males	White Females	Row Totals
Land Use					
Rural Farm	34.6	**	9.6	5.4	7.99
Rural Nonfarm	27.6	17.8	32.1	15.5	23.52
Urban	61.0	38.1	55.6	30.4	43.20
Column Totals*	55.14	34.75	46.88	25.34	36.69
Community Size					
<2,500	29.1	19.6	33.7	15.7	24.46
2,500-9,999	46.7	16.1	35.1	21.1	27.87
10,000-24,999	57.3	25.2	56.6	27.6	41.27
25,000-99,999	51.3	26.3	54.9	30.3	41.44
100,000-499,999	56.3	35.9	69.4	38.9	51.68
500,000-999,999	61.2	47.8	67.7	36.2	51.78
≥1,000,000	87.7	57.0	67.2	47.0	60.85
Column Totals	55.16	34.77	46.91	25.35	36.72
Percentage Black					
<1	57.6	42.4	43.1	21.3	32.23
1-5	69.1	33.2	46.8	28.9	38.29
6-15	35.6	33.4	47.9	26.5	36.50
16-50	49.2	26.0	42.9	23.6	33.94
51-75	55.9	39.1	60.4	42.7	47.96
76-100	62.3	39.6	104.3	59.6	51.43
Column Totals	55.12	34.57	44.94	24.57	35.57
Family Income					
<$3,000	81.2	51.4	97.2	48.6	65.30
$3,000-$4,999	68.1	36.4	54.4	32.9	42.53
$5,000-$7,499	60.3	34.2	56.8	33.7	43.93
$7,500-$11,999	53.8	34.7	50.8	27.8	39.37
$12,000-$19,999	52.2	31.2	47.7	22.8	36.03
$20,000-$24,999	34.5	19.8	37.7	19.5	28.59
≥$25,000	37.8	29.8	42.9	19.7	31.90
Column Totals	55.19	35.10	48.20	25.81	37.53

(continued)

TABLE 11-3 (Continued)

Variables	Minority Males	Minority Females	White Males	White Females	Row Totals
Marital Status					
Married	31.4	18.2	25.0	13.2	19.64
Widowed	23.6	22.4	22.1	11.2	14.09
Divorced	81.4	43.0	83.6	68.2	71.29
Separated	63.4	54.0	103.7	99.4	84.85
Never Married	77.7	48.7	84.4	43.1	64.90
Column Totals	55.04	34.75	46.80	25.34	36.65
Education					
0-6	21.6	21.5	29.9	18.5	23.61
7-12	60.8	34.4	45.5	25.4	35.84
13-16	67.3	43.9	55.5	26.2	42.55
17+	38.0	33.0	40.3	28.5	35.95
Column Totals	55.14	34.76	46.89	25.34	36.70
POPULATION TOTALS	55.14	34.75	46.88	25.34	36.69

*Column totals are not consistent by variable because of missing observations. For example, although land use was reported for nearly every subject, a number of subjects did not report family income.
**Too few observations to permit estimation.

As is evident the least discrepant rates occur for minority females. Thus, even though their rates are nearly 40% lower than all minority females, it is elderly minority females whose fears are most congruent with their actual victimization chances. For example, an elderly minority woman's chances of being victimized are almost exactly the same as that reported for all adult white females (25.14 per 1,000 population versus 25.34 per 1,000 population). If it is true that elders circumscribe their activities to reduce victimization risks, as previously cited authors have proposed, the fact that minority female elders are victimized at the same rate as younger white females (who presumably do not restrict their activities to the same degree) underscores the reality of minority female elders' fears.

Too, one should note that rates for certain locations indicate elderly minority women have an even higher risk of victimization than white female adults. For example, minority female elders residing in areas that are 76 to 100% Black have a personal victimization rate of 36.1 per 1,000 population compared to the national rate of 25.34 per 1,000 for adult white females. (At a rate of 59.6 per 1,000 population, white females in these neighborhoods have yet higher risks of victimization than minority females regardless of age). Thus, as concluded by a number of individuals conducting studies at the local level (see Jaycox, 1978; Lawton & Yaffe, 1980), there is a strong relationship between the fear of crime expressed by elders residing in certain neighborhoods and their actual chances of victimization.

Additionally, several alarming facts are masked because data reported in this chapter do not break down personal victimizations by offense types.

Although the elderly are least likely of all groups to be robbed, when they are, they are most likely to suffer physical injuries. More than half (55.8%) of elderly robbery victims sustain injuries, compared, for example, to 30.2% of individuals between 50 and 64 years and 31.1% of those 35 to 49 years (Jaycox 1982, pp. 39-41). Given their declining regenerative powers, high fear of robbery-related injury expressed by the elderly seems more than justified. Salient here is the fact that older Blacks are two and one-half times more likely to be victimized by robbery than older whites. With regard to violent crimes including robbery (rape, assault, and robbery), Black elders are victimized about twice as often as older whites. Blacks also are victimized by personal larceny with contact (pursesnatching and pocketpicking) more than any other age group, and they are victimized more than five times as often as elder whites (Jaycox, 1982, pp. 42-43).

Overall, the discrepancies in property victimization rates between elders and all adults are somewhat less pronounced than those for personal victimizations. Minority male adults have a property victimization rate that is 53.8% higher than the rate reported for minority male elders, and minority female adults are about twice as likely (2.27 times higher) as minority female elders to suffer property offenses. (Notable is the fact that minority and majority female adults have about the same rates of property victimization.) The rate for white male adults is about twice as high (2.34 times higher) as that of older white males and white female adults are about two and one-half times (2.51 times higher) more likely to be victimized than older white women.

One of the critical issues with regard to property offenses is the fact that most elderly people are living on reduced and fixed incomes. Although only about 25% have poverty or near poverty-level incomes, American elders as a group have incomes about half that of younger Americans. Aged Blacks suffer even direr circumstances; they live on incomes that are only about two-thirds that of aged whites.

The point of these income data can be simply put. Although the elderly are victimized less often than the general population, they also are less able than

TABLE 11-4 **Estimated Property Victimization Rates Per 1,000 Adult Population For Selected Variables By Race and Sex (July 1978-June 1980: Annualized)**

Variables	Minority Males	Minority Females	White Males	White Females	Row Totals
Land Use					
Rural Farm	109.6	67.3	106.8	99.5	102.8
Rural Nonfarm	110.1	118.8	143.1	146.3	142.55
Urban	228.6	210.8	226.6	220.8	222.84
Column Totals*	207.52	195.74	197.35	195.72	197.08

(continued)

TABLE 11-4   (Continued)

Variables	Minority Males	Minority Females	White Males	White Females	Row Totals
Community Size					
<2,500	146.8	146.7	153.1	155.6	153.85
2,500-9,999	164.4	133.9	184.5	164.0	171.42
10,000-24,999	172.0	168.4	207.4	210.9	205.85
25,000-99,999	249.4	230.1	230.7	229.0	230.84
100,000-499,999	243.1	220.4	275.6	273.1	265.75
500,000-999,999	243.4	222.4	286.8	286.0	271.44
≥1,000,000	223.2	212.9	222.1	197.6	211.47
Column Totals	207.59	195.85	197.51	195.87	197.22
Percentage Black					
<1	211.1	259.6	179.5	182.1	182.30
1-5	259.9	233.8	209.1	205.1	209.54
6-15	212.6	215.4	186.1	191.1	192.52
16-50	184.7	155.7	168.8	168.5	168.63
51-75	178.0	157.3	178.8	187.6	172.16
76-100	205.0	183.9	294.8	163.3	194.20
Column Totals	204.52	187.51	187.90	188.42	189.09
Family Income					
<$3,000	196.1	181.6	313.9	238.4	241.90
$3,000-$4,999	210.6	165.3	198.5	188.1	189.85
$5,000-$7,499	184.4	206.0	207.5	192.0	198.65
$7,500-$11,999	206.4	200.3	196.3	200.9	199.47
$12,000-$19,999	213.5	212.6	198.0	199.3	200.12
$20,000-$24,999	176.8	178.8	192.9	185.6	188.49
≥$25,000	233.9	233.0	205.0	213.3	210.60
Column Totals	205.46	196.67	203.01	200.49	201.57
Marital Status					
Married	187.7	198.2	156.9	186.0	173.32
Widowed	162.8	141.5	168.3	119.7	129.28
Divorced	324.0	313.4	366.0	367.0	359.19
Separated	275.3	287.3	382.4	356.7	335.52
Never Married	210.8	166.8	250.9	199.0	220.33
Column Totals	207.32	195.89	197.32	195.67	197.04
Education					
0-6	92.8	94.2	111.2	101.0	103.05
7-12	202.8	189.0	177.0	178.3	179.93
13-16	297.9	270.8	246.9	246.7	250.4
17+	260.0	231.7	240.5	300.2	260.94
Column Totals	207.41	195.79	197.25	195.67	197.01
POPULATION TOTALS	207.52	195.74	197.35	195.72	197.08

*Column totals are not consistent by variable because of missing observations. For example, although land use was reported for nearly every subject, a number of subjects did not report family income.

others to replace stolen household possessions, many of which may be psychologically more valuable than their replacement costs measured in dollars.

As mentioned previously, older minority males are the most vulnerable of all elderly population groups to property victimizations. In fact, minority male elders living in cities with more than 100,000 but less than 1,000,000 residents are victimized at about the same rate as is the general population of white adults. This is significant given the fact that elders as a group tend to be victimized by property crimes only about half as often as the total population and, given the lower incomes of minority elders, they have even less ability to replace stolen items than older whites.

Within the ranks of the elderly it is perhaps less obvious that women are especially hard hit when victimized. For example, older people who live alone tend to have less income than those living with families. Only 58% of older women live with families, whereas 81% of older men live in family settings (Jaycox, 1982, p. 18). And, the median income of older women is only about half the median income of older men (National Council on Aging [NCOA], 1978). Speaking with specific reference to elderly widows, Jaycox noted that these women tend to be

> in the worst economic positions; their income has often depended on their husband's Social Security benefits or private pension and is reduced considerably at his death. . . . It becomes obvious that vulnerable older women living alone often can neither afford the losses that victimization causes nor the time and money for crime prevention that is recommended to them [1982, p. 21].

SUMMARY AND CONCLUSIONS

Victimization rates among elders appear to warrant high levels of concern for safety despite the admonition of those who point out that the elderly, as a group, need have little to fear. While it is true that when compared to the total population, elders are victimized less often than all adults, certain segments of the elderly population have victimization rates that approximate or exceed national rates for all adults. For example, minority female elders in areas that are 76 to 100% Black have a personal victimization rate (36.1 per 1,000) that is virtually the same as the rate (36.7 approx.) for all adults. Other segments of the elderly population also have notably high victimization rates when such rates are compared to rates for the total population. Bearing in mind the diminished recuperative powers of older people and their reduced financial resources gives substance to their concerns for personal and household safety, despite their comparatively low overall victimization rates. Although they are victimized less often than others, the threat of potential victimization, given the dire consequences that may result, must be viewed with more concern. This point is quite salient for elderly women who live alone, particularly widows, because they tend to be in the poorest financial situations.

Among older people, minority elders have disproportionately high rates of personal victimization. Even more so than male minority elders, older minority women must be on guard for it is they whose exposure to risk of personal victimization is highest of all aged subgroups. Nevertheless, older minority men are more than twice as likely as white male seniors to be the objects of violence or lesser personal offenses, and therefore they, too, must remain vigilant as they strive during their later years to avoid being the victims of transgression.

Older whites who are divorced or separated are highly vulnerable to both personal and household victimizations. In fact, separated white males have the highest rates of any elderly group for personal and household victimizations. Nearly 10% of these men are the victims of personal crimes, and more than 20% experience property offenses.

Male minority elders, however, have the highest overall rates of household victimizations among the aged. As a group their rate exceeds that of all other groups and is nearly 40% higher than that of older white men.

Taken in sum these data suggest that the minority aged, both males and females, are justified in their fear of crime. The fact that their relatively high risk of exposure to personal and property offenses continues throughout a period of life in which physical and income-earning capabilities have declined legitimates their concern. Given this, one question deserving attention is whether or not awareness of risk impacts adversely on the morale of these elders. The discussion following the present chapter addresses this question among Blacks.

REFERENCES

Balkin, S. Victimization rates, safety and fear of crime. *Social Problems,* 1979, 26, 343-358.

Curtis, L. Rape, race and culture: some speculations in search of a theory. In M. J. Walker & S. L. Brodsky (Eds.), *Sexual Assault.* Lexington, MA: Lexington Books, 1976.

Gans, H. J. *The Urban Villagers.* New York: Free Press, 1962.

Garofalo, J., & Hindelang, M. *An introduction to the National Crime Survey.* U.S. Department of Justice Analytic Report SD-VAD-4. Washington, DC: Government Printing Office, 1977.

Hindelang, M. J. *Criminal victimization in eight American cities: A descriptive analysis of common theft and assault.* Cambridge, MA: Ballinger, 1976.

Hindelang, M. J., Gottfredson, M. R. & Flanagan, T. J. (Eds.) *Sourcebook of criminal justice statistics.* U.S. Department of Justice, Bureau of Justice Statistics. Washington, DC: Government Printing Office, 1981.

Hochstedler, E. *Personal victimization of the elderly: Popular opinion and the facts.* Criminal Justice Program, University of Wisconsin-Milwaukee, 1980. (mimeo)

Hochstedler, E. *Crime against the elderly in twenty-six cities.* Analytic Report SD-VAD-10, U.S. Department of Justice, Bureau of Justice Statistics, Washington, DC: Government Printing Office, 1981.

Jaycox, V. H. The elderly's fear of crime: Rational or irrational. *Victimology,* 1978, 3 (3-4), 329-334.

Jaycox, V. H. *Effective responses to the crime problem of older Americans: A handbook.* National Council of Senior Citizens, Legal Research and Services for the Elderly Criminal Justice and the Elderly Program. Supported by AOA Cooperative Agreement 90-AT-0024/ 01 and 0/2, 1982.

Lawton, M. & Yaffe, S. Victimization and fear of crime in elderly public housing tenants. *Journal of Gerontology,* 1980, 35, 768-779.

Liang, J., & Sengstock, M. C. The risk of personal victimization among the aged. *Journal of Gerontology,* 1981, 36 (4), 463-471.

McNeely, R. L., & Pope, C. E. Race and involvement in common law personal crime: A response to Hindelang. *Review of Black Political Economy,* 1978, 8 (4), 405-410.

McNeely, R. L., & Pope, C. E. Socioeconomic and racial issues in the measurement of criminal involvement. In R. L. McNeely & C. E. Pope (Eds.), *Race, crime and criminal justice.* Beverly Hills, CA: Sage, 1981.

National Council on the Aging (NCOA) Fact book on aging: A profile of America's older population. Washington, DC, 1978.

12

Fear of Crime and Victimization
Black Residents in a High-Risk Urban Environment

JOHN LEWIS McADOO

This chapter explores the differential effects of victimization and fear of crime on the morale and activity level of Black senior citizens living in a high-risk urban environment. One objective was to determine the degree to which the effects of victimization differed for those living in public as opposed to private housing.

As noted in an earlier publication (McAdoo, 1978), a review of gerontological literature revealed few studies focusing upon the consequences of crime for Blacks and members of other ethnic groups. Jackson (1979) has reported that most of the literature related to morale and life satisfaction has been based upon disengagement, activity, and personality theories. Further, the empirical studies related to these theories suffer from ethnocentric biases, as Blacks and other ethnic minorities were usually absent from the normative studies testing the theories. The present study was designed to help in filling the literature gap regarding the consequences of victimization on the morale and activity level of minority elderly.

BACKGROUND

The evidence from national surveys of criminal victimization indicates that the elderly are generally subjected to less victimization (Antunes, Cook, Cook, & Kogan, 1977; Hindelang, 1976; Hochstedler, 1977). Liang and Sengstock (1981) note that the elderly are victims of violent crimes, such as rape, robbery, and assault, at an annual rate of 9 per 1,000 population, while the rate for the general population is 32 per 1,000. However, several other authors (Sundeen & Mathieu, 1976; Gubrium, 1973; Clements & Kleiman, 1976; Lawton, 1980) suggest that while it is clear that the elderly are victimized at a lesser rate than other age groups, it is becoming equally clear that their fear of crime is high, which may cause a reduction in their social activities.

Several studies have noted that fear of crime exists to such a high degree in their older subjects that they have limited their activities, have refused to go places (Gubrium, 1973; Cunningham, 1973), and have limited their mobility and participation in community activities (Middleton, 1976). Others (Clements, 1976; Lebowitz, 1975) found an interaction between community size and fear of crime. The aged residing in communities over 50,000 were noted to have a significantly greater amount of fear of victimization than their younger counterparts or other older inhabitants of smaller towns, suburbs, or rural areas.

Several national surveys have noted that a large number of elderly respondents rate fear of crime as their most serious problem (Harris, et al., 1975; National Council on Aging [NCOA], 1975). Bild and Havighurst (1975) noted that the elderly in their Chicago study also rated fear of victimization as their most serious problem.

Among the earlier studies related to the consequences of fear of victimization, fear of victimization appears to vary in intensity according to social characteristics such as race, sex, and income level. Black women were found to have the highest degree of fear of victimization, followed by Black men, white women, and white men. Older persons of lower socioeconomic status have higher anxiety levels than those in higher socioeconomic groups (Sundeen & Mathieu, 1976; Clements & Kleiman, 1976; Lebowitz, 1975). No differences were found in central city, suburban, or retirement communities as all three communities had a higher level of fear of crime.

Sundeen and Mathieu also found that the urban elderly tended to have fewer connections with individual or community support systems, perceived that they were vulnerable to becoming victims by day as well as in the evening, had lower estimates of the likelihood of being able to depend upon informal networks of control and protection, and had a lower evaluation of the effectiveness of the police. The elderly seemed to be more concerned with their safety than with social interaction (Schooler, 1970), and this fear of victimization led to lower morale and self-imposed house arrest (Goldsmith & Tomas, 1974).

A study of the impact of crime in three New York neighborhoods by the National Institute of Justice (Victims Service Agency, 1982) found that elderly victims experienced increased psychological problems as a result of the victimization process. The study noted a decrease in feelings of well-being, joy, and contentment and an increase in anxiety, fear, guilt, and depression. The study noted that neighbors, friends, and relatives who attempt to help them also suffer increasing psychological problems.

In summary, fear of victimization appears to be an important ingredient in the older person's way of life. However, little is known about the impact of fear on the morale and social activities of the minority elderly. While information regarding victimization is available on the impact of victimization on elderly public housing tenants (Lawton & Yaffee, 1980), little is known about its differential effects on those elderly living in private housing.

METHOD

This study randomly selected 120 Black senior citizens living in the Shaw area of Washington, D.C. from a pool of 2,000 older minority residents living in the area. The residents were identified by a community survey developed by the National Caucus for the Black Aged. Efforts were made to ensure that equal numbers of older residents living in public and private dwellings were interviewed.

The subjects were interviewed by trained Black interviewers utilizing an instrument developed by the author to gain answers to questions related to fear of crime, victim status, activity level, age, sex, and marital status. In addition, the questionnaire contained the revised Philadelphia Geriatric Center Morale Scale (PGC) (Lawton, 1975). The PGC is a measure of subjective well-being that assesses the older person's sense of self-satisfaction, feelings regarding his or her place in the world, and the degree of his or her acceptance of what cannot be changed. The measure has a test-retest reliability of $r = .75$ (Larson, 1978).

The Faith In People Scale (FPS; Rosenberg, 1957) was also administered to determine general perceptions of people. The FPS assesses the degree of confidence in the trustworthiness, generosity, goodness, honesty, and general brotherliness of people.

RESULTS

Two subjects were eliminated from the study because their PCG questionnaires were incomplete; 57 (48%) had been victims of a crime. Almost 30% (36) of the sample were males, closely matching the proportion of males in the neighborhood population, and 73% (82) of the sample were females; 47% (56) of the sample were under 70 years of age, 31% were married, and 51% were separated or divorced.

There were almost equal numbers of victims living in public (49%) and private (51%) dwellings. The proportion of male (32%) and female (68%) victims, taking residence status into account, approximated the figures found for the total sample of males and females (see Table 12-1).

No significant differences were found in subjects' responses to questions related to their attitudes toward crime. Both victims (84%) and nonvictims (94%) felt that crimes should be reported. Over two-thirds of the victims and nonvictims felt that there were some crimes in the community that worried them. The overwhelming majority of the victims (97%) and nonvictims

**TABLE 12-1   Profile of the Sample by Victimization Status,
Residence, Gender, and Age**

Subsets	Victims	Nonvictims	Totals	Public Housing	Private Housing	Totals
Males	18	18	36	14	22	36
Females	39	43	82	44	38	82
Totals	57	61	118	58	60	118
69 yrs of age	28	28	56	22	34	62
70 yrs of age	29	33	62	36	26	56
Totals	57	61	118	58	60	118

(92%) felt that older people in general have changed their activities because of fear of crime, while more victims (97%) than nonvictims (89%) felt that older people in their neighborhood changed their activities because of fear of crime. None of these differences were statistically significant.

More victims (97%) than nonvictims (87%) admitted to changing their social activities because of fear of crime; 91% of the total sample admitted to changing their social activities. About two-thirds of the total sample noted that there are places in their community that they will not go to because they fear crime. More victims (93%) than nonvictims (84%) were afraid to go out at night because they feared victimization. Two-thirds of the victims (68%) as opposed to over half (56%) of the nonvictims felt that crime had increased in their neighborhood.

The residents of public housing perceived themselves as being more involved with their friends and active in community affairs than respondents living in private dwellings. Individuals living in private housing were more likely to describe themselves as loners, being less active in community group activities, and having fewer friends. This difference was statistically significant ($\chi^2 = 19.12$; $p = .0001$).

No significant residence status differences were found for subjects who perceived themselves to be loners in the types of activities they chose to be involved in. The majority of the loners spent their time visiting friends, caring for ill relatives, shopping, watching television, or listening to the radio. Very few (only about 7%) discussed participating in arts and crafts or other hobbies.

No residence differences were found in the number of friends that respondents claimed to be actively involved with in visiting back and forth, going places together with, and communicating on the telephone. Respondents living in public housing belonged to significantly more groups than those living in private housing ($\chi^2 = 4.45$; $p = .03$). However, while the public residents were involved in more groups, the intensity of their involvement (defined as the degree of activeness) was not significantly greater than that of those living in private housing.

TABLE 12-2 Respondents' Faith in People by Sex, Residence, and Victimization Status

Subjects	Mean Scores		t-values	p
	Males	Females		
Total Sample	7.36 (33)	7.04 (76)	2.28	.03
Public Housing	7.39 (13)	7.07 (41)	1.29	—
Private Housing	7.37 (20)	7.00 (35)	1.99	—
Victims	7.33 (15)	7.06 (34)	1.31	—
Nonvictims	7.39 (18)	7.02 (14)	1.84	—

For the total sample, no relationship was found between victimization, opinion about crime, and social activity variables. However, subjects who felt that crime was much more dangerous in their community scored significantly higher than other respondents on the FPS ($r = .227$; $p < .05$). In addition, those who described themselves as more sociable were more involved in their church attendance ($r = .304$; $p < .01$) and the number of church groups they belonged to ($r = .398$; $p < .05$). Obviously, one would expect those describing themselves as loners to be less involved.

Older residents in private dwellings who described themselves as loners perceived that there were higher levels of criminal activity in their neighborhoods than those who described themselves as sociable and outgoing ($r = .371$; $p < .01$). The more sociable and outgoing residents of private dwellings also were more active in church affairs ($r = .515$; $p < .001$). Similarly, subjects living in public housing describing themselves as sociable were significantly more active in church affairs ($r = .694$; $p < .001$) and in community groups ($r = .894$; $p < .001$).

There were no significant differences or interaction effects in the morale scores (PGC) of the sample by victim status, residence status, or sex for the total sample.

As indicated in Table 12-2, males, more than females, evidenced faith in people ($t = 2.28$; $p = .03$. Mean scores by sex and residence and by sex and victimization status reveal a consistent pattern of higher male faith in people. Although the only statistically significant difference was observed for the entire sample, the mean scores remain uniform for each of the subsets, indicating that lower numbers of subjects in the subsets are accounting largely for the absence of statistically significant differences. Simply put, differences observed in the mean scores for the subsets would be statistically significant if there were more subjects in these groups.

DISCUSSION

The purpose of this study was to determine the level of fear of victimization and its consequences on the activity level, morale, and well-being of Black working-class elderly residing in public and private housing in a high-crime area of metropolitan Washington, D.C. No attempt is being made to generalize these findings to the morale and well-being of other ethnic groups. However, the findings of high levels of fear of victimization (over two-thirds of both victims and nonvictims reported being worried), regardless of victim status, are consistent with other studies of older people living in communities of high crime and poor security (Lawton & Yaffee, 1980; NCOA, 1975; Victims Service Agency, 1982).

The Black subjects' fear of victimization had caused them to change their activity level, avoid going out during the day unless they had to, and to rarely go out of their residences at night. Regardless of residence and victim status, subjects took great care to minimize their risk of personal victimization (see Liang & Sengstock, 1981).

The majority of the subjects in this study felt that their friends and fellow neighborhood residents had changed their levels of community activities and activities in groups because they feared victimization. They felt that crime in their community had increased and they were worried about crime.

Subjects describing themselves as loners were, in fact, less involved in community activities and were less active visiting their friends, going to church, and participating in community organizations. The group most vulnerable, from a security standpoint, to victimization were loners living in a private residence. The loners who lived in public housing appeared to be less vulnerable but at high risk of victimization. Regardless of residence status or victim status, both loners and socializers felt very strongly that crimes should be reported to the police.

The self-reported loners were not social isolates, however, as they enjoyed visiting friends and caring for sick relatives. They appeared to prefer solitary activities with friends (movies, television, arts and crafts, and cards) more than participating in community group activities. The socializers—Black seniors who enjoyed being involved in community groups—reported a variety of solitary and community activities. The socializers living in public residences reported higher social activity and community group involvement than socializers living in private dwellings.

Even socializers felt that fear of victimization had forced them to curtail some of their community activities. However, and importantly, both the loners and the socializers appeared to be able to compartmentalize their fear of victimization. Indeed, even the loners maintained a high level of personal activity, although the socializers were more involved in a variety of activities, including a high degree of participation in church and community groups.

Consequently, one conclusion is that these subjects, despite becoming increasingly vigilant with regard to their personal safety, have not allowed their levels of fear to be overriding factors in their lives. The subjective feelings of morale and of psychological well-being were high for the total group. There were not significant residence, victim status, or sex differences found in their responses to the revised PGC (Lawton & Yaffee, 1980). The total group was also able to maintain a basically positive view of relevant others in their community. No differences were found in residence or victim status on the FPS. While both sexes' scores were generally positive, the men were found to be significantly more positive. Frankly, it is not clear why men, more than females, should evidence more faith. Perhaps the explanation lies in the high rate of personal victimization experienced by minority females coupled with their sense of vulnerability as women.

These findings suggest a need for more research focusing upon the morale and psychological well-being of the minority elderly. As Lawton and Yaffee (1980) have discovered, the minority elderly may have less fear than other ethnic groups.

The aging community would be served well by studies seeking to describe and evaluate the various coping strategies the Black aged and others have developed to control the psychological and social consequences of victimization. This new line of research activities may spawn new techniques to help older persons, either victims or nonvictims, to develop more successful strategies for handling their fear and, consequently, facilitate the efforts of elders to lead more productive lives.

REFERENCES

Antunes, G., Cook, F., Cook, T., & Kogan, S. Patterns of personal crime against the elderly: Findings from a national survey. *Gerontologist*, 1977, 17, 321-327.

Balkan, S. Victimization rates, safety, and fear of crime. *Social Problems*, 1979, 26, 343-358.

Bennett, R. Living conditions and everyday needs of the elderly with particular reference to social isolation. *International Journal of Aging and Human Development*, 1973, 4, 179-198.

Biderman, A., Johnson, L., & McIntyre, R. Report on a pilot study in the District of Columbia on victimization and attitudes towards law enforcement. Washington, DC: Government Printing Office, 1967.

Bild, B., & Havighurst, R. Senior citizens in great cities: The case of Chicago. *Gerontologist*, 1975, 16(1), 47-52.

Cantor, M. H. Effects of ethnicity on lifestyles of the inner city elderly. In M. P. Lawton, R. J. Newcomer, & T. O. Byerts (Eds.), *Community planning for an aging society*. Stroudsberg, PA: Dowden Hutchinson & Ross, 1976, 41-59

Clements, F., & Kleiman, M. B. Fear of crime among the aged. *Gerontologist*, 1976, 16(3), 207-210.

Cunningham, C. *Crimes against aging Americans, the Kansas City study*. Kansas City, MO: Midwest Research Institute, 1973.

Friedman, K. et al. Victims and helpers: Reaction to crime (Final report.) National Institute of Justice, Grant 79-N1AX 0059, 1982.

Goldsmith, J., & Tomas, E. Crimes against the elderly: A continual national crisis. *Aging*, 1974, 236-237.

Gottfredson, M. R., & Hindelang, M. J. An analysis and classification of injury and theft in personal victimization. Albany, NY: Criminal Justice Research Center, 1976.

Gubrium, J. F. Victimization in old age: Available evidence and three hypotheses. *Crime and Delinquency*, 1973, 20(3), 245-250.

Harris, L., & Associates. *The myth and reality of aging in America*. Washington, DC: National Council on Aging, 1975.

Hindelang, M. J. *Criminal victimization in eight American cities*. Boston: Ballinger, 1976.

Hochstedler, E. Personal victimization of the elderly in twenty-six cities. Criminal Justice Research Center, Albany, New York, 1977.

Jackson, J. Negro aged and social gerontology: Critical evaluation. *Journal of Social and Behavioral Sciences*, 1968, 33, 42-47.

Jackson, J., Bacon, J., & Peterson, J. Life satisfaction among Black urban elderly. *Journal of Aging and Human Development*, 1977, 12(8), 169-179.

Larson, R. Thirty years of research on the subjective well being of older Americans. *Journal of Gerontology*, 1978, 33(1), 109-125.

Lawton, M. P. The Philadelphia Geriatric Center Morale Scale: A Revision. *Journal of Gerontology*, 1975, 30(1), 85-89.

Lawton, M. P., & Yaffee, S. Victimization and fear of crime in elderly public housing tenements. *Journal of Gerontology*, 1980, 3(55), 768-779.

Lebowitz, B. D. Age and fearfulness: Personal and situational factors. *Journal of Gerontology*, 1975, 30, 696-700.

Liang, J., & Sengstock, M. The risk of personal victimization among the aged. *Journal of Gerontology*, 1981, 364, 463-471.

McAdoo, J. L. Well-being and fear of crime among the Black elderly. In D. E. Gelsand & A. Kutzik (Eds.), *Ethnicity and aging*. NY: Springer, 1978.

Middleton, F. *Analysis of statistics, senior safety and security program*. Albany, NY: Criminal Justice Research Center, 1976.

National Council on Aging. *Myths and realities of aging America*. Washington, DC: National Council on Aging, 1975.

Robinson, J., & Shaner, P. *Measures of social psychological attitudes*. Ann Arbor: Institute for Social Research, University of Michigan, 1971.

Rosenberg, M. *Society and the adolescent self image*. Princeton, NJ: Princeton University Press, 1965.

Rosenberg, M. *Occupations and values*. Glencoe: IL: Free Press, 1957.

Schooler, K. Effects on environment and morale. *Gerontologist*, 1970, 10, 194-197.

Sundeen, R. A., & Mathieu, T. The fear of crime and its consequences among the elderly in three urban communities. *Gerontologist*, 1976, 16(3), 211-219.

U.S. Department of Justice. *Criminal victimization in the United States*. Washington, DC: Government Printing Office, 1977.

Victims Service Agency. *Victims and helpers: Reaction to crime*. Washington, DC: National Institute of Justice, 1982.

13

Physical Health and the Minority Aged

BARBARA JONES MORRISON

Health among older people is usually defined in one of two ways: either by the presence or absence of disease or by the assessment of functional capacity. The former definition is more commonly used, particularly by health care providers (Shanas & Maddox, 1976). The functional capacity definition is the one used by the World Health Organization and is based on a broader view of health that encompasses all of the factors affecting an older person's ability to perform required social roles, including the tasks of daily living and vocational employment if desired. It is the latter and broader definition of health that will be used in this chapter.

By broadly defining health, one may examine the many factors that determine not only the incidence and prevalence of disease among the aged, but patterns of functional disability, utilization of health services, barriers to service utilization, and what relevant empirical research suggests for the reorganization and improvement of the health delivery system.

In this chapter the importance of race and ethnicity as factors related to health status will be explored. It should be kept in mind that the relationship between health and race often is confounded by socioeconomic status due to the proportionately higher prevalence of impoverishment among members of racial minority groups (see U.S. Bureau of the Census, 1978).

MORBIDITY AND MORTALITY

An appropriate starting point for the examination of the relationship between race or ethnicity and health status is to look at the role of poverty in determining late life morbidity (disease) and mortality (death).

The incidence and prevalence of chronic disease increases sharply with advancing age. Of people 65 years and older residing outside of institutions, 85% reported at least one chronic disease and 50% reported some limitation in functional capacity related to chronic health problems. Chronic illness among the aged is degenerative and typically involves multiple conditions with physical, psychological, and social components. The five most prevalent chronic conditions among the aged in the United States according to a 1978 study by the National Council on Aging (NCOA) are arthritis, hearing impairment, visual impairment, hypertension, and heart conditions (Shanas & Maddox, 1976). Diseases of the heart, notably ischemic heart disease, account for the largest number of deaths annually among persons 65 years and older, regardless of race or ethnicity.

Mortality (i.e., cause of death) data show that six diseases account for most deaths at all ages and claim a proportionately higher number of lives among the aged. These are (in rank order) ischemic heart disease, cardiovascular disease (e.g., stroke and generalized arteriosclerosis), malignant neoplasms (cancers), infectious diseases, and diabetes. Manton (1980) reported that among the aged, these six diseases were involved in 85% of deaths among Black males, 90% of white males, 87% of Black females, and 92% of white females.

The same patterns of chronic disability and disease were observed in a recent survey of Hispanic aged (Asociación Nacional Pro Personas Mayores [ANPPM], 1980). Arthritis was reportedly the most prevalent condition among Hispanic aged, with 48% of Mexican-Americans, 55% of Cubans, 59% of Puerto Ricans, and 56% of other Hispanics citing this problem. Hypertension ranked second with cardiovascular conditions third for Cubans, Puerto Ricans, and other Hispanics, while diabetes ranked third for Mexican-Americans. Cataracts and glaucoma (visual impairments) also ranked high, as did heart disease.

Although these conditions predominate among the aged as compared to younger people, they are not equally distributed among the aged population. There is some evidence to suggest that they are disproportionately higher among the aged in racial or ethnic minority groups. However, racial or ethnic group membership per se does not appear to be the determining factor. Rather, it is the disproportionate representation of minority aged in the lower socioeconomic strata that appears to explain much of the variance in both health status and utilization of health care services.

The lower the socioeconomic status of the individual, the higher the prevalence of disease and the higher the age-specific death rate (Cantor and Meyer, 1974; Dowd & Bengtson, 1978; Shanas & Maddox, 1976). The same relationship pertains for bed disability days and restricted activity (Shanas & Maddox, 1976). For example, using data from the National Center for Health Statistics, Soldo and DaVita (1977) reported that older Blacks tend to experience proportionately more functional disability than whites, and they experience it at earlier ages. Health-related reasons for early retirement from the labor force are more often cited by older Blacks than older whites. Frequently, early retirement due to health reasons occurs before eligibility for the maximum Social

Security benefit. Soldo and DaVita note further that while the proportion of noninstitutionalized older people who are totally bedridden is not great for either whites or Blacks, proportionately more older Blacks are completely incapacitated and are residing in community-based households.

PREVENTION AND EARLY INTERVENTION

One striking feature of morbidity patterns among the minority aged, particularly with respect to males, is the high representation of health problems amenable to early detection and early treatment. Soldo and DaVita (1977) indicate a considerable excess of older nonwhite male disease and death due to influenza, pneumonia, and respiratory conditions such as bronchitis, emphysema, and asthma. Nonwhite women show higher mortality rates for diabetes.

For many of these conditions poor personal health care, inadequate or inappropriate diet, smoking, and alcohol consumption are causal or exacerbating factors. Health education and preventive measures aimed at screening, early detection, and lifestyle modification would go a long way toward reducing illness and death due to these conditions. The same applies to hypertension and related cardiovascular conditions. Yet preventive health care measures are least available to persons who would benefit most from them. For many people the term "prevention" is typically associated with health care of the young, as if older people are "too far gone" to benefit from preventive measures and early intervention. For severely impaired older people, secondary and tertiary interventions are usually required. However, health education and lifestyle modification will often help to mitigate the severity of many health conditions that might have been initially preventable. In many ways, geriatric medicine and research on the health problems of older people provide the strongest evidence for health maintenance and prevention throughout the life cycle. The cumulative effects of inadequate health maintenance leave their most visible legacy in the old. As Futrell, Brovender, McKinnon-Mullett, and Brower note in their text *Primary Care of the Older Adult* (1980), improving the health care system is only one solution to a complex problem. Throughout their lives, individuals must be taught to practice preventive health measures and to seek early treatment for health problems in order to deter disabling effects in later life.

UTILIZATION OF HEALTH CARE SERVICES

Data from recent studies are used in this section to highlight patterns of health care services utilization by the minority aged. Utilization patterns by level of health care, that is, preventive (primary), acute (secondary), and chronic/long-term (tertiary), are discussed.

PRIMARY CARE

Physicians in private practice or ambulatory care clinics (either free-standing or attached to a large medical complex) are usual providers of primary care of reasonably healthy older adults. In their study of older Hispanics, the ANPPM (1980) reported that the doctor's office is the most usual place of medical care of Mexican-Americans, Cubans, and other Hispanics. Puerto Rican elderly, however, were more likely to receive routine care at a government or other public health facility. The highest use of the hospital emergency room as a usual source of medical care was reported by the Puerto Rican aged. Respondents in this survey were asked if they needed physicians' services but were unable to obtain them. The majority in all of the Hispanic ethnic groups studied indicated no problem in this area, with Cuban aged indicating the least unfulfilled need. The investigators note that Cubans have the highest educational level among the groups studied, as well as the highest proportion of older persons who are fully employed. They conclude that the higher socioeconomic status of Cuban aged makes them better equipped, compared to other Hispanic aged, to deal with the Anglo health system.

Cantor and Meyer (1974) conducted a random probability sample survey of New York's inner city elderly. They reported that although Medicare and Medicaid programs have narrowed the differences in utilization rates considerably, respondents with higher incomes were significantly more likely to have seen a doctor during the previous year than were those at the lowest income levels where health care needs are the greatest, regardless of race or ethnicity. They conclude that among New York inner city elderly, more affluent older persons will receive more medical attention for noncrisis ailments as well as preventive checkups than will their less affluent peers. In this same study, ethnic differences were found in the use of private physicians. Use of private doctors was most typical of white elderly who usually had long-standing relationships with their doctors, but the decline of private physicians in the inner city neighborhoods has resulted in greater use of hospital clinics as the source of primary care. In 1970, the data collection year in the Cantor and Meyer study, one-third of the inner city elderly in New York were dependent upon hospital outpatient clinics with the proportion increasing to 44% among the Black aged and almost 50% of the Hispanic (predominantly Puerto Rican) elderly.

HOSPITAL-BASED ACUTE CARE

Acute care hospitals are designed to treat short-term acute illness of an episodic nature. According to the Health Survey of 1978 (U.S. National Center for Health Statistics, 1979), 26.8% of the U.S. population over 65 years of age was hospitalized for episodic illness. The Hispanic Elderly Survey (ANPPM,

1980) indicated the utilization rates for Hispanic aged during this same period (i.e., 1978) were below established norms. Specifically, 15% of Cubans, 24% of other Hispanics, 21% of Mexican-Americans, and 24% of Puerto Ricans in their national sample reported being hospitalized during this time. These utilization rates are not necessarily reflective of need. The researchers stated that about one in five of the Mexican-American aged did not go to the hospital when recommended by a physician. This was also true for 23% of the Puerto Rican aged. Insufficient funds to pay for hospital care and fear or distrust of hospitals were the main reasons given for noncompliance.

In the Cantor and Meyer (1974) sample, inner city elderly were no more likely to have been hospitalized when compared to national norms, but they did report longer stays once admitted. The median length of stay (LOS) for the inner city elderly was 18.9 days as compared to the 1970 national median LOS of 12.7 days for patients aged 65 and over. The longer LOS for inner city elderly was attributed to poorer health and the greater probability of detecting a multiplicity of disorders requiring more complex and extended treatments. Factors found to be related to higher hospitalization rates in this study were ethnicity (i.e., being Hispanic), sex (i.e., being male), and socioeconomic status (i.e., being poor).

CHRONIC OR LONG-TERM CARE

Use of chronic or long-term care facilities by the minority aged is a topic receiving greater attention in recent years. National Nursing Home Survey data for 1973 and 1974 indicate underrepresentation of minority aged in nursing homes, especially those under proprietary (i.e., for profit) auspices. Reasons for this underutilization have been attributed to cultural values (i.e., a preference for family-based care of the aged), racial and class bias in admission criteria and referral patterns, lack of long-term care facilities in areas where minority aged reside, the high costs of nursing home care, and a lack of sophistication on the part of minority families in gaining access to the scarce number of nursing home beds.

In their study of health care services for Puerto Rican aged in New York city, Zambrana, Merino, and Santana (1979) reported that there is only one nursing home in the East Harlem area where the need for long-term care may be greater than commonly believed. In the view of these Hispanic professionals, the greatest barrier to access of needed skilled or protective chronic care is financial. They state that the Puerto Rican elderly are unable to afford nursing home care and are forced into public facilities such as psychiatric state hospitals, especially when family supports are not available. The cultural preference for family care of the aged among Hispanics is also seen as an important factor.

Dancy (1977) has made similar observations with respect to nursing home utilization by the Black aged. He notes that Black aged in need of constant care due to their mental or physical disabilities may find themselves in desperate straits. Factors, which he cites as impacting utilization, include lack of facilities in minority communities, inadequate income to pay for nursing home care, and the greater possibility that a disabled and/or demented older Black person without alternative supports will be dependent upon state resources.

To some extent the "cultural aversion" of minority aged and their families to use nursing homes may be overstated, particularly in situations of severe physical or mental impairment. The most well-intentioned and loving families have been known to be stretched to the limits of their emotional and material capacities in attempting to provide 24-hour nursing care for an incontinent, helpless parent or grandparent. In many cases, the need for skilled nursing care is an undeniable reality. Acceptability of the institutional alternative may also vary according to factors such as family composition (i.e., the availability of multiple caretakers), education, income, and degree of attachment to traditionally held ethnic or cultural values regarding filial responsibility.

FAMILIES AS CARETAKERS OF THE AGED

National studies indicate that family members are the principal caretakers of aged people during periods of illness (Shanas & Maddox, 1976; Shanas, 1962). Data from such studies indicate that for the United States, as well as most other countries, two to three times as many impaired and bed-fast older people are cared for at home as compared to institutions of all kinds. Adult children, especially daughters and daughters-in-law, are the major caretakers. A number of demographic trends, which will have an impact on the role of family members as caretakers among minority and majority aged, are now being observed. These trends include the increasing entry of women into the labor force, the decline in family size, increased urbanization with concomitant smaller living space, and the escalating cost of living. Maddox (1975) has indicated that the present ability of families to cope with impaired older members is limited and that the real costs of such caretaking in economic, physical, and psychological terms have yet to be adequately determined.

BARRIERS TO UTILIZATION OF HEALTH SERVICES

Andersen (1968) provides a theoretical framework for understanding how people use health care services. He views three sets of variables as determinants of utilization: *predisposing factors*, which include characteristics of the individual that exist prior to the illness episode that either propel him or her toward or away from seeking health care. These variables would include age, race, ethnicity, and related cultural attitudes regarding the appropriate source of medical care, sex, education, and attitudes about health.

The second set of factors are *enabling* factors, which relate to the means for acquiring needed services once the decision to seek care has been made. These variables include income, coverage, location of health facilities, and availability of services. *Need for care* factors are the third group and represent the individual's recognition that illness is imminent or existent based on self-assessment of physical symptoms.

Barriers to utilization can occur in any of these three domains. However, most of the literature reflects an attention to the enabling factors as major barriers to health care utilization by minority aged.

ACCESS ISSUES

A subanalysis of the Duke University OARS no. 1 data set, undertaken by Wright, Creecy, and Berg (1979), indicates that of several enabling variables examined, only the existence of a regular source of medical care was directly and significantly related to actual use of physicians' services. They conclude that the way in which the older Black person is linked to the health care system has important implications for determining the level and rate of utilization, and that much more consideration needs to be given to issues of access, outreach, information, referral, and follow-up services in planning effective health care programs for Black aged.

Transportation problems are frequently cited as barriers to service utilization (Cantor & Meyer, 1974; Dancy, 1977). Eve and Friedsam (1979) studied older whites, Blacks, and Mexican-Americans in Texas to identify ethnic differences in use of physicians, hospitals, and dentists. No significant differences were found in the number of hospital admissions or the number of visits to physicians, but nonwhite aged were more likely to report difficulty in obtaining needed care primarily because of transportation problems and the high cost of medical and dental care.

Many minority aged in inner city neighborhoods are relocated during periods of urban "revitalization." Some move to public housing projects, some move in with relatives while others relocate to other inner city neighborhoods. For those aged who might have had a neighborhood-based physician, the relocation will possibly create access problems. Either the elderly patient will be required to travel back to the old neighborhood for care by the familiar physician or they will have to rely on hospital outpatient clinics, private storefront clinics, or "Medicaid mills" for routine care. Distance and associated transportation costs make already expensive medical care even more costly for those aged people who can afford it the least.

COST FACTORS

Insurance coverage is a critical factor to consider when assessing cost barriers to health care utilization. A 1971 survey for the Special Committee on Aging of the U.S. Senate linked income and inadequate health insurance coverage to underutilization of health services by older people. Minority aged in particular, frequently lack the money to pay the deductibles and premiums required for the total Medicare plan (Parts A and B) (Dancy, 1977).

Cantor and Meyer (1974) reported that lower Medicare coverage among New York's inner city elderly was related to ethnicity; 88% of the white inner city elderly were covered by Medicare, as compared to 85% of Black aged and 68% of Hispanic aged. They state that this finding also pertains to Social Security, indicating that Black and Hispanic aged are less likely than their white counterparts to receive the advantages of these important entitlements. In this study, the cost of coinsurance, as well as confusion regarding the eligibility and enrollment procedures, were cited by minority aged as problems.

PARTICIPATION IN FEDERAL INSURANCE PROGRAMS

One might expect that because proportionately more minority aged are poor, they would rely more on Medicaid, which is a means-tested insurance plan. There is evidence to suggest that Medicaid is not being fully used by potentially eligible minority aged. Among the Japanese elderly in San Diego, 93% were familiar with Medicare, but less than half utilized Medicare. A little over half were familiar with MediCal (the term for Medicaid in California), but only 7% used it (Ishizuka, 1978). Similar patterns were observed by Dukepoo (1979) among the Indian aged. While there was a high level of awareness of Medicare (69%) and MediCal (68%), only 23% of rural Indian elderly used Medicare and only 17% used MediCal. Dukepoo believes the low utilization rates are related to the complex and ambiguous status of the American Indian vis-á-vis national health policy. Urban Indian aged were less knowledgeable about these programs, but among those who knew of them, utilization rates were somewhat higher, that is, 32% and 46% for Medicare and MediCal respectively.

Black and Hispanic aged in the Cantor and Meyer (1974) sample used Medicaid to a substantial degree, but many eligible persons were found to be uncovered. In an estimation based solely on reported income, these investigators found that only 71% of eligible Hispanic aged, 57% of Black aged, and 39% of white aged were on Medicaid. This was attributed to lack of knowledge about the program and its benefits, difficulties in registration and constant recertification, and the aversion to accepting any benefit with a "welfare" stigma.

Medicare and Medicaid are not panaceas for the health care problems of the aged. Essential and common necessities such as prescriptions, eyeglasses, hearing aids, and dental care, for example, are not covered by Medicare. This is significant when one considers that vision and hearing impairments were reported previously as causes of functional disability. But these programs do help to defray the ever-increasing costs of medical care, and their underutilization by poor and minority aged is an area of concern.

OTHER BARRIERS TO UTILIZATION

Other barriers to utilization cited in the literature include inability of minority aged to obtain needed services (Zambrana et al., 1979); fear of doctors and hospitals, which may be related to present or historical acts of racism by medical providers; fear of diagnosis and prognosis (ANPPM, 1980; Ishikawa, 1978); and lack of faith in the efficacy of medical professionals (Cheng, 1978; Dancy, 1977).

For some minority aged, strong beliefs in traditional cultural healers may affect utilization of the formal health care system. Zambrana and her associates describe what they term the "magic-science conflict" in the Puerto Rican culture. Puerto Ricans maintain a belief in *espiritistas*, who are indigenous folk healers. Espiritistas are the mediators between the spiritual realm and humans. Believers feel that spirits can identify the root cause of a health problem and suggest solutions to alleviate the problems. Newton (1980) made a similar observation among Mexican-American elderly, particularly those in the rural areas of Southern Texas, where *curanderos* are routinely consulted by sick people. Chinese aged have their herbalists, and many Black aged with Southern roots believe in herbal healing as prescribed by the "roots workers."

A lack of appreciation and respect for these culturally based health belief systems on the part of medical professionals may alienate minority aged from the formal health care system. As Newton (1980) notes, service providers should not consider a belief in folk medicine to obviate the need for the provision of scientifically based medical services. Recent data, he reports, indicate that folk and scientific systems are not incompatible and many ethnic aged use both systems simultaneously.

THE NEED FOR
A HUMANE HEALTH CARE SYSTEM

Minority aged have cited fragmentation of services and depersonalization as major barriers to utilization of formal health care services (Cantor & Meyer, 1974). Depersonalization results from a number of service delivery problems including long waiting hours, inconvenient hours of service, the confusing atmosphere of large busy clinics, and the insensitivity of doctors and nurses who lack the opportunity to develop an ongoing relationship with individual patients.

Zambrana and her associates (1978) believe that alternatives to the traditional health care delivery system (or perhaps, more accurately, "nonsystem") are needed both from an economic and humanistic point of view. They describe the traditional approach to health care delivery as being highly specialized, technologized, and impersonal. It is a system oriented toward diseases and emphasizes tertiary care of advanced disease states rather than prevention of disease and health maintenance. It is a system where the management needs of health care professionals receive more attention than the health care needs of consumers. The elderly poor are particularly vulnerable in such a system.

These Hispanic professionals (Zambrana et al.) have suggested two alternative approaches to the delivery of health care services that would tend to humanize health services for all people, especially the aged: (1) the *modified traditional approach* and the (2) the *intracommunity approach*.

MODIFIED TRADITIONAL APPROACH

The modified traditional approach is defined as a team approach to health service provision in which health maintenance of the patient is the goal. The team consists of a nurse, social worker, and physician who do an initial evaluative home visit during which they bring their respective expertise to the assessment of health care problems and treatment planning for each individual elderly patient. The concept of *triage* is important in this model. Patients are "worked up" and the severity of their medical problems determines the site of their medical care and the level of professional expertise required to treat health problems. Moderate medical and social problems can be managed by the geriatric nurse practitioner and the social worker, leaving more serious medical problems to the physician, whose time is most expensive.

The team would be based in a community hospital, which would serve as a backup for acute and emergency care of elderly patients routinely served by the team. With this model, more screening and early diagnosis are possible, making timely treatment more possible. Prevention, patient health education, and general health maintenance of basically healthy aged are the major tasks of the team.

Although an improvement over the traditional health delivery system, this model still relies on the use of high salaried professionals making it costly to implement. Other drawbacks may relate to the social distance between health providers and consumers.

> Regardless of how attuned to the community the team may be, it will always remain a group of professionals who invade the life of the patient, generally for the better, but who are usually distant and different in terms of age, social and economic class, place of residence, etc., even if they share the same ethnic background. For the team, the link to the community is the hospital, not the patient; they work *in* but are not part *of* the community [Zambrana, Merino, & Santana, 1978, p. 316].

INTRACOMMUNITY APPROACH

The intracommunity approach is based on two premises. The first is that already existing resources within a community can and should be used to provide health care for elderly patients under the supervision of a professional. The second is that the elderly are an integral resource in the community (e.g., the well elderly may help with the care of their sick peers). This model is viewed by its proponents as the most cost-efficient and cost-effective.

Similar to the modified traditional approach, the intracommunity approach relies on a team, but the composition of the team differs. In the intracommunity approach, the team consists of a geriatric nurse practitioner, a social worker, a community health worker, and a supervising consulting physician. It is based in a community health center as opposed to a hospital, with an emphasis on primary ambulatory care. Backup agreements with hospitals and nursing homes in the area are part of the design.

Unlike the modified traditional approach, where the physician is the head of the team, in this model the community health worker is the most important member. The community health worker would be a healthy, literate, and active older community resident who would be specially trained to: monitor the health of the patient in the patient's own home; render basic health maintenance and screening services such as assessing height and weight and taking the patient's temperature, blood pressure, pulse, and respiration; perform vision and hearing screenings; collect urine and fecal samples; perform simple lab tests such as a dip stick urine test for sugar levels; and foster patient compliance with prescribed medical regimens. The professionals on the team serve as consultants to the community health worker and provide services that require more technical skill and expertise.

These two approaches are promising alternatives to the traditional health care system, which is increasingly costly, fragmented and inhumane. As providers experiment with the implementation of these models, study data on cost-efficiency and quality of care will be available to aid forward-thinking health planners in meeting the needs of a growing elderly population.

FUTURE HEALTH CARE:
SOME CONCERNS

The 1980s will be one of decreasing public support for public health services, as President Reagan's policies clearly indicate. In an atmosphere of reactionary public fiscal policy, alternatives to the present costly health system must be found.

In 1974, several critical questions were posed in relation to the health care needs of the elderly poor. These issues are equally relevant today and satisfactory solutions are still being sought. The concerns focus upon: (1) How best to reconcile the human needs of elderly patients with the legitimate training and research needs of the medical establishment; (2) How best to bring medical services out of the hospital and into the community, thereby providing older people with easier access and more personalized service; (3) How to define the appropriate role of the hospital as backup to community-based medical programs; (4) How to find funds needed for provision of preventive medical care and health maintenance as an alternative to the episodic approach to crisis illness; and (5) How to find the best methods of locating the hidden elderly poor most in need of medical care (Cantor & Meyer, 1974).

REFERENCES

Administration on Aging. *Characteristics of the Black elderly–1980*. Statistical reports on older Americans, Washington, DC: Department of Health and Human Services, National Clearinghouse on Aging, 1980.

Andersen, R. *A behavioral model for families' use of health services*. Chicago Center for Health Administration, Research Study No. 25. Chicago: University of Chicago Press, 1968.

Andersen, R., & Newman, F.J. Societal and individual determinants of medical care utilization in the United States. *Milbank Memorial Fund Quarterly*, 1973, 51, 95-124.

Asociación Nacional Pro Personas Mayores. (ANPPM). *A national study to assess the service needs of the Hispanic elderly*. Los Angeles: Asociación Nacional Pro Personas Mayores, 1980.

Cantor, M., & Meyer, M. Health and the inner city elderly. Paper presented to the 27th Annual Meeting of the Gerontological Society, Portland, Oregon, October 1974.

Cheng, E. *The elder Chinese*. San Diego: Campanile Press, 1978.

Congressional Budget Office, U.S. Congress. *Health differentials between white and nonwhite Americans*. Washington, DC: Government Printing Office, 1977.

Dancy, J. *The Black elderly: A manual for practitioners*. Ann Arbor: Institute of Gerontology, Wayne State University, 1977.

Dowd, J.J., & Bengtson, V.L. Aging in minority populations: An examination of the double jeopardy hypothesis. *Journal of Gerontology*, 1978, 33, 427-436.

Dukepoo, F. C. *The elder American Indian*. San Diego: Campanile Press, 1979.

Eve, S., & Friedsam, H. J. Ethnic differences in the use of health care services among older Texans. *Journal of Minority Aging*, 1979, 4, 62-75.

Futrell, M., Brovender, M., McKinnon-Mullett, E., & Brower, H. T. *Primary health care of the older adult*. North Scituate, MA: Duxbury Press, 1980.

German, P. A., Shapiro, S., Chase, G. A. & Vollmar, M. H. Health care of the elderly in medically disadvantaged populations. *Gerontologist*, 1978, 18, 547-555.

Ishikawa, W. H. *The elder Guamanian*. San Diego: Campanile Press, 1978.

Ishizuka, K. C. *The elder Japanese*. San Diego: Campanile Press, 1978.

Manton, K. G. Sex and race specific mortality differentials in multiple cause of death data. *Gerontologist*, 1980, 20 480-493.

Manton, K. G., Poss, S., & Wing, S. The black/white mortality crossover: Investigation from the perspective of the components of aging. *Gerontologist*, 1979, 19, 291-300.

Newton, F. Issues in research and service delivery among Mexican-American elderly: A concise statement with recommendations. *Gerontologist*, 1980, 20, 208-212.

Nowlin, J. B. Geriatric health status: Influence of race and economic status. *Journal of Minority Aging*, 1979, 4, 93-98.

Rakowski, W., & Hickey, T. Late life health behavior. *Research on Aging*, 1980, 2, 283-308.

Shanas, E. *The health of older people: A social survey*. Cambridge, MA: Harvard University Press, 1962.

Shanas, E., & Maddox, L. Aging, health and the organization of health resources. In R. H. Binstock & E. Shanas (Eds.), *Handbook of Aging and the Social Sciences*. New York: Van Nostrand Reinhold, 1976.

Soldo, B. J., & DaVita, C. *Profiles of the Black aged*. Washington, DC: Georgetown University Center for Population Studies, 1977.

U.S. Bureau of the Census. Money income in 1977 of households in the United States. *Current Population Reports*, Series P-60, No. 117, Washington, DC: Government Printing Office, 1978.

Wright, R., Creccy R., & Berg, W. The Black elderly and their use of health care services: A causal analysis. *Journal of Gerontological Social Work*, 1979, 2, 11-23.

Zambrana, R., Marino, R., & Santana, S. Health services and the Puerto Rican elderly. In D. Gelfand, & J. Kutzik, (Eds.), *Ethnicity and Aging*. New York: Springer, 1979.

14

Mental Health, Service Delivery in Institutions, and the Minority Aged

JOSEPHINE A. ALLEN

Health, mental health, income support, nutrition programs, recreation programs, housing subsidies, transportation services, and emergency energy supports for the elderly are among those areas of the federal budget that are being reduced drastically by President Reagan and his budget advisors. The availability of health and mental health services, especially for the aged population of this country, has diminished significantly relative to existing needs. Many of these programs previously have not been effective in meeting the needs of the elderly. Thus, the threat of reducing their funding base and reorganizing their administration under the guise of implementing what the President has termed the "New Federalism" will lead to even further deficits.

This chapter explores some of the conditions affecting the vulnerable minority aged in relation to the provision of mental health and institutional services. Central themes implicit in this chapter are (1) *ageism*, defined here as the absence of uniform societal concern for providing adequate care for the elderly; (2) *racism*, which renders elderly people of color invisible and relegates their economic and mental health needs to an even lower plane; and (3) *classism*, which results in placing many poor minority and nonminority elderly persons in large, publicly funded institutions that can be described at best as custodial. In these institutions, meaningful treatment is not considered a realistic, practical, economical, or necessary course of action. Without access to care provided by family members, minority elders are likely to be overrepresented in such facilities because they experience a disproportionate share of society's poverty. This is not the case with affluent elderly citizens who have the option to apply and gain admittance to high-quality treatment-oriented, privately funded institutional settings.

An ecological perspective has been adopted as the framework for considering existing relationships with regard to mental health, institutionalization, and race. Environmental factors, including political, economic, and social influences, are key concerns. Environment is herein defined as all external factors that affect an individual's physical, psychological, and social well-being.

MENTAL HEALTH

Mental health is conceptualized very differently by various mental health professionals. There are those who advocate the use of a medical model and who more or less view mental health as the absence of illness. Subscribers to this model assert that psychiatric disorders can be traced to specific organic causes, which can in turn be diagnosed and treated (Page, 1975).

Others have adopted a psychoanalytic approach and view mental health in terms of social and psychological factors that govern the development and maintenance of problematic behavior.

The concept of competence is advanced by those scholars who view mental health in terms of an individual's ability to initiate, participate in, and complete transactions within his or her environment (White, 1971). The model, forwarded by Szasz (1961, 1970) and others, suggests that human behavior is influenced by social and cultural factors that largely determine how people cope with stress and with problems in daily living. These individuals adamantly oppose those adhering to the medical model approach to mental distress.

These models are part of a broad array of theoretical explanations of mental health and mental illness. However, the field has had little interest in recognizing the needs of the elderly or the differences that exist among the elderly members of different racial groups. As a result, elderly persons of color are at a decided disadvantage, and they are even more at risk given their disproportionate representation among the nation's economically disadvantaged.

The emphasis throughout the history of the United States on the ascribed inferiority of people of color is reflected in the field of mental health. The research of Thomas and Sillen (1972), Willie, Kramer, and Brown (1973), and Gary (1978), among others, carefully describes the perpetuation of discriminatory practices and the racist attributes of some mental health professionals, and the consequences for mentally disabled people of color. Gary calls for new concepts, techniques, and methods for dealing with the mental health of Black people, emphasizing the salience of environmental influences (Gary, 1978, p. 18).

Positive images of aging are very rare in our society. The study of gerontology and the field of geriatric practice have only recently begun to expand and to attract large numbers of health and mental health professionals. Prior to the recent proliferation of scientific information for professionals coming into the field, the existence of widely held myths and misconceptions about the aging process has meant, for example, that reversible disorders in older persons often remained undiagnosed, untreated, and subsequently led to premature debilitation or death. Treatment has all too often been thought to be of little benefit to the elderly, and their many health and mental health problems have been viewed as hopeless.

Acute brain syndrome can be caused by conditions for which effective treatments exist. Consequently, a major cause of serious behavioral problems, which would very likely result in institutionalization, can be treated. Depression in older persons has often been viewed as another condition that does not warrant treatment. Difficulties in the area of sexual functioning also have been dismissed as unworthy of treatment in the elderly population. The person

> who enters this field thus encounters a paradoxical situation: there is considerable knowledge that, if applied, will lead to substantially better mental health practice, but at the same time there are areas where much has yet to be learned about the problems of the aged [Zarit, 1980, p. 5].

Older persons generally experience a major decline in income, which causes stress and often markedly affects the quality of their lives. However, poverty-level incomes are experienced most often by elderly people of color and elderly women. Approximately 36% of the Black aged, for example, fall below the federal poverty line as compared to 30% of all Black Americans and 14% of aged white Americans (Zarit, 1980). Women of color experience the most severe income deprivation in old age. One source estimates that 96% of older Black women live in poverty (Atchley, 1977).

Several factors account for this state of affairs. First, these older persons have held the very lowest paying jobs. Individuals in these jobs either are not covered at all by Social Security or, having been compensated at very low levels, they are eligible only for the most meager benefits. Second, the Supplemental Security Income Program, which was established in 1974 in part to provide additional income to older persons whose incomes were below an established minimum level, has not reached many persons who are eligible for these benefits.

In what Miller described as the apex of full adulthood, the socially competent person has the capacity for self-management, self-regulation, purposefulness, productivity, and the creation of his or her own lifestyle (1979, p. 283). Progressive aging involves the inevitable loss of adaptive functioning capacity due to the gradual decrease in the reception of reliable sensory data in concert with deteriorating nonsensory physical functioning and enhanced loss of central nervous system efficiency, the degeneration of collagen tissue, and diminished cardiovascular pulmonary reserve, all of which significantly affect the mobility and energy level of elderly people.

In addition to physical losses, older people also may experience what one author has termed culturally determined and circumstantial losses. These include the disintegration of an individual's social and interpersonal network, economic loss resulting from retirement, vocational loss, loss of options for privacy, and loss of assigned roles due to the death of a spouse or child (Schwartz, 1974, p. 8). Obviously, changes relating to the process of aging are associated with these types of losses.

A most significant issue confronting every person is the concern for "a quality of life which translates daily experiences into a framework of self-esteem" (Schwartz, 1974, p. 6). Feelings of competence and self-esteem among the needy elderly are tied inextricably to the adequate provision of supportive services. The areas in which interventions may be required coincide with the need of every elderly person for decent, safe, and appropriately designed housing and furnishing; adequate diet and medical care; suitable clothing, economic security; appropriate stimulation and opportunities for new learning; options for privacy and for socializing; meaningful roles for work and play; and mobility via affordable and accessible transportation.

Dunn (1959) utilized the concept of high-level wellness to connote an integrated model of functioning compatible with the realization of the individual's potential within the environment in which he or she resides. Wellness is a dynamic process that encompasses change and that allows the individual to move toward a "higher level of functioning" (p. 448). Community-based supportive services are both an important and major part of the compensatory intervention process for those not afflicted with gross debilitation, profound mental disorders, or substantial retardation. Afflicted individuals require institutional services, although many nonimpaired elderly people also find themselves institutionalized simply because of a breakdown in their family support systems (Atchley, 1977). About half of all older nursing home patients are ambulatory, continent, and do not require regular assistance. When social competence can no longer be maintained by the elderly, a range of treatment and supportive service options must be explored.

INSTITUTIONALIZATION

The inevitability of substantial and irreversible mental deterioration as aging progresses is a myth perpetuated by the general citizenry as well as by a significant sector of the health and mental health professions. Early in this century, efforts to avoid the reality of their own aging and death, in addition to the belief that mental illness was a symptom of an inherent organic condition offering little hope for recovery, led these professionals to ignore totally or to give very little attention to the elderly person's need for more than custodial care. Institutionalization became the fate of many elderly people as state and county mental hospitals were being rapidly constructed during the early 1900s. The reality of the dayroom and the dormitory within these total institutions meant physical and social isolation from society.

It was after World War II that significantly more emphasis was placed on the use of treatment strategies for the mentally disabled. This trend continued for nearly two decades until the community mental health movement gained momentum in the early 1960s. The cost of institutional care, along with disclosures about very inhumane conditions in the back wards of mental institutions, precipitated this movement. Passage of legislation authorizing the development and construction of community mental health centers throughout the country was accompanied by the deinstitutionalization of persons living in state and county mental hospitals.

Although many older persons chose to remain in these settings, many others returned to community living situations. During the late 1960s, the number of older persons being admitted to state and county mental institutions declined dramatically for the first time (Kramer, Taube, & Redick, 1973). It is unlikely that the number of elderly persons residing in state and county mental hospitals will again reach the 29% level of 1969 because the community mental health movement has been successful to some degree, and because of the widespread adoption of psychotropic drug therapy. In addition, there are currently more stringent legal requirements for committing people to mental health facilities and there has been a dramatic increase in nursing home placements (Gottesman & Hutchinson, 1974).

Unfortunately, the community-based support and prevention programs promised by the community mental health legislation have not received adequate levels of funding or the requisite support from local communities that are needed in order to assure the program's success. Limited family support, minimal financial resources, and limited marketable skills further reduce the prospects for success in independent community living for this population. With the move toward reintegrating the previously institutionalized mentally disabled into more normal community and family life situations came the realization that the success of these programs would depend in large part on comprehensive and effective discharge planning, including appropriate placement, guarantees of adequate housing, the exploration of employment opportunities, and provisions for out-patient treatment. However, events of the past eight years have unfolded to reveal a very urgent situation in which the deinstitutionalized are too often having to fend for themselves. They must function in the community without the requisite continuity of care or the assistance of a system of services that would contribute to the success of those community placements.

Much of the literature points to the range of housing alternatives and the level of care that accompanies each of these alternatives including family care homes, group homes, residential hotels, and rooming houses. Unfortunately, some mentally disabled persons have been dumped into transitional neighborhoods with greatly varying levels of support. At the same time, there has been widespread agreement that the deinstitutionalized mentally disabled should be maintained in community settings with the support of nearby family and friends. Yet, many of those released from mental hospitals had no supportive family or others upon whom to rely. Despite traditions emphasizing the importance of extended families and kinship among minority groups, limitations imposed by financial realities often reduce the quality of support and care they can offer.

The attitudes of the elderly about mental health services act as further deterrents to their utilization of these services. They are often reluctant to seek assistance outside the context of their families. They wish to avoid being stigmatized and labeled as a result of their use of mental health services. In the case of people of color these attitudes often are even more pronounced.

A report of the President's Commission on Mental Health suggests that "up to 25 percent of older persons have been estimated to have significant mental health problems. Yet only 4 percent of patients seen in public outpatient mental health clinics and 2 percent of those seen in private psychiatric care are elderly" (1978, p. 7).

The placement of older former state mental hospital residents in supposedly less expensive boarding homes, where adequate medical care and other supportive services are largely unavailable, is often the plight of the low-income elderly person of color. Less than 2% of the funding for Medicare goes into mental health coverage for the elderly and the disabled. At the same time, Medicare provides disproportionately for the care of persons who are economically well-off. Community mental health centers are reimbursed only a little more than .01% of these dollars for both inpatient and ambulatory care (Krueger, 1977). The Medicaid program places emphasis on institutional care, and its provisions for outpatient mental health services are limited. In large measure these government programs have been designed in a manner that does not recognize the large and important role of the family in the provision of long-term care for the elderly. This has been done despite the widely known fact that the physical, social, and psychological needs of these persons are not best served by such institutional arrangements (Oktay & Polley, 1980). Instead, nursing home care has become a highly profitable business (Lowy, 1980).

A review of the percentage of nursing home residents who are mentally disabled suggests that older persons who were formally committed to mental institutions are being sent to nursing homes in increasing numbers. Many of these facilities offer no treatment and, in some instances, even less stimulation and fewer activities than the state hospitals (Lowy, 1980).

In a tally of existing studies, Pfeiffer (1977) reports that as many as 80% of nursing home residents may have mental health problems. The nursing home thus has become the new institution providing custodial care for the mentally impaired elderly. This development, some researchers argue, represents a definite step backward in terms of the even more limited access that older persons have to mental health professionals and treatment. Gelfand reports that the National Center for Health Statistics' 1973 Survey of Nursing Home Patients found that the largest percentage of these residents have psychiatric diagnoses. In spite of this fact, most of these older persons have had no contact with psychiatrists (Gelfand, 1980, p. 80).

Older people often view nursing homes negatively. This perspective results in part from the unfamiliar surroundings, and is influenced by an association with dependence, poverty, loneliness, death, and dying. Such attitudes are reinforced by the fact that many institutions have policies that unnecessarily segregate their residents from the outside world, stress congregate solutions to individual needs, seek inordinate control over the patient's life, and place too little emphasis on programming for the elderly. Additionally, many creative mental health professionals prefer and have access to highly verbal, well-educated, and motivated clients from other sectors of need. Thus, the best practitioners are likely to be underrepresented on the staffs of nursing homes and similar institutions, ultimately serving to compound the negative image patients in residence and others have of such facilities.

RACE AND CLASS IN THE DELIVERY OF MENTAL HEALTH SERVICES

Black Americans and other people of color tend to be diagnosed differently than whites for similar behavioral problems. Cannon and Locke (1976) cite studies suggesting that whites are more likely to be diagnosed as having depressive disorders, while Black and other nonwhite Americans are more likely to be diagnosed as schizophrenic. One of the possible explanations for this difference is the fact that minority group members are often not highly verbal and do not articulate in those communication styles preferable to white psychiatrists, psychologists, and social workers. Another explanation is suggested by Hollingshead and Redlich's (1958) early work, which found an inverse relationship between social class and the severity of mental health distress. Members of lower socioeconomic classes tend to receive more serious diagnoses (Rosen, 1974) due partly to the absence of sufficient resources with which to secure adequate services when the initial symptoms emerge, frequently resulting in the presence of more substantial disorders by the time services are secured (see Hollingshead & Redlich, 1958).

On the other hand, Sue (1977) asserts that minority group clients who seek psychotherapeutic services receive unequal and poor mental health services. Specifically, he found in an analysis of services rendered to minority clients in seventeen community health facilities that Black clients received differential treatment and had poorer treatment outcomes than whites. Outcomes were assessed by termination rates.

The research of Yamamoto, James, and Palley (1968) revealed that when compared to white patients, minority group patients (Black, Chicano, and Asian) were discharged more quickly and were more often seen for minimal supportive psychotherapy rather than individual or group therapy. The work of numerous others, including Clark (1965), Lerner (1972), Carkhuff (1972), Willie and associates (1973), Padilla, Ruiz, and Alvarez (1975), and Acosta and Sheehan (1976) all underscore the difficulties people of color experience in their search for adequate mental health care.

The literature in the mental health field supports the assertion that treatment varies in accordance with the social status of the client, with upper-class persons receiving psychological treatment and the lower-class individuals receiving custodial care. As the largest proportion of elderly mental patients are of the working class, their experience in the mental health system has been less than optimal. The stigma associated with seeking mental health services also is more pronounced for the less well-educated, lower class, and working-class citizens (Lowy, 1980).

The necessity for recognizing differences in the racial and cultural backgrounds of the elderly and for viewing these differences from a positive perspective is a focus of much of the research and writing in the field. Nevertheless, there continues to be a tendency to discuss Black, Hispanic, Native-American, or Asian elderly persons as though they constitute homogenous groups that are not subject to intragroup differences.

Many scholars in this field concur with the finding that the stress associated with a lifetime of coping with the effects of racial discrimination in both the personal and the institutional spheres has led to psychological disorders that may be found among many of these elderly persons.

Further research is needed in order to make sense of the various coping strategies that have allowed most of the older persons of color to maintain their mental health. Identifying the appropriate preventive mental health services and other mix of social services and supports for elderly persons in general and for older persons of color, in particular, continues to be an important area in which research is needed. In addition, answers are needed to such lingering questions as how much and what kind of assistance should come from the natural or informal support systems composed of family and friends, and how much should come from the formal service systems of private voluntary agencies and governmental sources (Brody, 1982).

CONCLUDING REMARKS

The mental health of the minority aged is determined by a range of social, psychological, physiological, and environmental factors. The availability of adequate and affordable health care, a decent home in a suitable living environment, a sufficient and regular income, appropriate nutritional intake, functioning family and community service support networks, and appropriate cultural and recreational opportunities are some of the factors contributing to the mental health of minority populations. Indeed, the mental health of the majority population depends on these very same factors. Preventive mental health services are not as accessible, however, to minority group members in this society, and our focus often shifts to mental illness and ways of accommodating the mentally disabled minority aged.

Much of the research in this field indicates that interpersonal racism or institutionalized discrimination against individuals solely on the basis of their cultural and phenotypical differences is a central cause of mental illness. This discrimination takes many forms, but very notably the exclusion from educational and employment opportunities results in lower total income, very minimal retirement benefits, low self-esteem, few housing options, limited access to community-based services, and a host of related needs.

When the effects of racial discrimination are combined with those of discrimination based on social class *and* with the impact of devaluing old people by an extensively youth-oriented society, the mental health of the minority elderly easily is seen to be at risk.

How then have so many of the minority aged managed to remain mentally healthy? The strength and positive energies for coping derived from immediate and extended family ties, from religion and a very strong attachment to a religious community, in addition to the support that often comes from neighbors and friends, cannot be overemphasized.

One of the difficulties that aged Black minorities often face, whether they are in nursing homes or in state psychiatric facilities, is the fact that there are few Black mental health professionals (psychiatrists, psychologists, social workers, psychiatric nurses, or mental health aides) and even fewer white staff members who have any knowledge of the life experiences, the cultural differences, or the meaningful events which these residents might wish to discuss.

The fact that therapists are most often either members of the majority group of are foreign-born and trained, that they have little knowledge of the cultural backgrounds or the real-life experiences of the minority aged, and they they tend to prefer young, verbal, and successful clients, suggests that the minority aged are at a decided disadvantage if they become mentally ill. Further, the availability of nursing homes and community group placements for these individuals is quite limited. Although institutionalization in one of the state psychiatric facilities is not the optimal alternative for most aged minority group members, it continues to be an option that is used after all other possible alternatives have been explored.

Reaganomics and the proposed New Federalism, which reflect a growing conservatism in this country, have significant implications for the future with respect to the mental health of the minority aged. The impact of the reductions in the social services on the overall quality of life for the minority aged is pronounced and quite serious. Further, the impact on families and existing community support systems that have been the mainstay of the minority elderly is and will continue to be very severe. The objective need to promote preventive mental health services and to lend more support to the families of the minority aged, who provide most of the care when those individuals become mentally ill, has not been met very effectively under existing or previous federal policies. It is not likely that state legislatures will address this growing need adequately.

REFERENCES

Acosta, F., & Sheehan, J. Preferences toward Mexican American and Anglo American psychotherapists. *Journal of Consulting and Clinical Psychology,* 1976, 14, 272-279.

Atchley, Robert C. *The social forces in later life: An introduction to social gerontology.* Belmont, CA: Wadsworth, 1977.

Bell, Duran, & Zellman, Gail. The significance of race for service delivery to the elderly. *Gerontologist*, 1976, 16, 70-75.

Brody, Elaine M. Older people, their families, and social welfare. *Social Welfare Forum, 1981*, New York: Columbia University Press, 1982.

Butler, Robert, & Lewis, Myrna. *Aging and mental health: Positive psychosocial approaches* (2nd ed.). St. Louis: C. V. Mosby, 1977.

Cannon, Mildred S., & Locke, Ben Z. *Being Black is detrimental to one's mental health: Myth or reality?* Paper presented at the W. E. B. DuBois Conference on the Health of Black Populations, Atlanta Georgia, December 14, 1976.

Carkhuff, R. R. Black and white in helping. *Professional Psychology*, 1972, 3, 18-22.

Clark, Kenneth. *Dark ghetto: Dilemmas of social power.* New York: Harper & Row, 1965.

Dunn, Halbert L. What high-level wellness means. *Canadian Journal of Public Health*, 1959, 50, 447-458.

Gary, Lawrence E. (Ed.). *Mental health: A challenge to the Black community*. Philadelphia: Dorrance, 1978.

Gelfand, Donald, & Olsen, Jody. *The aging network*. New York: Springer, 1980.

Gottesman, L., & Hutchinson, E. Long-term care in the community. In E. Brody (Ed.), *A social work guide for long-term care facilities*. Rockville, MD: National Institute of Mental Health, 1974.

Hollingshead, August, & Redlich, Frederick. *Social class and mental illness*. New York: John Wiley, 1958.

Jackson, Jacquelyne J. *Minority aging.* Belmont, CA: Wadsworth, 1979.

Kart, Cary S., & Beckman, Barry L. Black-white differentials in the institutionalization of the elderly: A temporal analysis. *Social Forces*, 1976, 54, 901-910.

Kramer, M., Taube, A., & Redick, R. N. Patterns of use of psychiatric facilities by the aged: Past, present and future. In C. Eisdorfer & M. Lawton (Eds.), *The psychology of adult development and aging*. Washington, DC: American Psychological Association, 1973.

Krueger, Gladys. *Financing of mental health care of the aged*. Paper prepared under the NIMH Contract for the Committee on Mental Health and Mental Illness of the Elderly, 1977.

Lerner, B. *Therapy in the ghetto: Political impotence and personal disintegration*. Baltimore, MD: Johns Hopkins University Press, 1972.

Lowy, Louis. *Social policies and programs on aging*. Lexington, MA: Lexington Books, 1980.

Miller, Leo. Toward a classification of aging behaviors. *Gerontologist*. 1979, 19, 283-290.

Oktay, Julianne, & Polley, Howard. A national family policy for the chronically ill elderly. In *The Social Welfare Forum, 1980*. New York: Columbia University Press, 1981.

Padilla, A. M., Ruiz, R. A., & Alvarez, R. Community mental health services for the Spanish-speaking surnamed population. *American Psychologist*, 1975, 30, 892-905.

Page, J. D. *Psychopathology: The science of understanding deviance* (2nd ed.). Chicago: Aldine, 1975.

Pfeiffer, E. Psychopathology and social pathology. In J. E. Birren & K. W. Schaie (Eds.), *Handbook of psychology and aging*. New York: Van Nostrand Reinhold, 1977.

President's Commission on Mental Health. *Report to the President* (Vol. 1). Washington, DC: Government Printing Office, 1978.

Rosen, Bernice M. *Mental health and the poor: Have the gaps between the poor and the "non poor" narrowed in the last decade?* Paper presented at the Conference on Social Sciences in Health at the 102nd Annual Meeting of the American Public Health Association, October 21, 1974.

Schwartz, Arthur A. A transactional view of the aging process. In A. Schwartz & I. Mensch (Eds.), *Professional obligations and approaches to the aged*. Springfield, IL: Charles C. Thomas, 1974.

Sue, Stanley. Community mental health services to minority groups: Some optimism, some pessimism. *American Psychologist*, 1977, 32, 616-624.

Szasz, Thomas. *The myth of mental illness: Foundations of a theory of personal conduct*. New York: Hoeber-Harper, 1961.

Szasz, Thomas. *Ideology and insanity*. New York: Doubleday, 1970.

Thomas, Alexander, & Sillen, Samuel. *Racism and psychiatry*. Secaucus, NJ: Citadel Press, 1972.

White, R. *Right to health: The evolution of an idea*. Iowa City: University of Iowa Graduate Program in Hospital and Health Administration, 1971.

Willie, C. V., Kramer, B., & Brown, B. S. *Racism and mental health: Essays*. Pittsburgh, PA: University of Pittsburgh Press, 1973.

Yamamoto, J., James, Q. C., & Palley, N. Cultural problems in psychiatric therapy. *Archives of General Psychiatry*, 1968, 19, 45-59.

Zarit, Steven. *Aging and mental disorders*. New York: Free Press, 1980.

15

Employment Problems and Prospects of Older Blacks and Puerto Ricans

GAYLENE PERRAULT
GILBERT L. RAIFORD

Never was Walter Reuther's piquant reference to the elderly as being "too young to die, too old to work" more salient than it is today. The current life expectancies for men and women who have reached the age of 65 are 14 and 18 years, respectively (U.S. Pres. Comm. 1980). While Black and Puerto Rican elderly can expect slightly shorter longevity after reaching the age of 65, Blacks, at least those who reach the age of 75, can expect to outlive whites (Brotman, 1982). Not only are persons who reach the age of 65 likely to live longer, many of the younger aged are likely to be healthy and, therefore, employable. The main significance of the trend toward a longer and healthier life for Americans is that by the year 2000, the population of those 65 and older will have increased from 26 million (the size of the current population) to 32 million. The aged, who now represent about 11.3% of the entire population, will then represent somewhat more than 12% (U.S. Pres. Comm., 1980).

The projected increase in the number of Black aged by the year 2000 is even more dramatic. The Black aged, representing only 7% of the current elderly population is expected to increase to 10% of this group (U.S. Pres. Comm., 1980).

With a significant increase in a relatively healthy elderly population, one can expect an increase in the number of persons actively seeking to participate in the labor market. Because economic growth is slow or negligible and unemployment rates are spiraling, with the 1982 rate for all Americans at (10.8%), and with even higher rates for Blacks (20.2%) and Hispanics (15.7%); Hispanic being the categorical group within which the Bureau of Labor Statistics includes Puerto Ricans, there is cause for great concern about the plight of the American aged.

Several incremental programs have been implemented to address the issue of elderly employment, such as raising the mandatory retirement age to 70; instituting job training programs for the poor in general (such as those developed under the Manpower Development and Training Act) and the elderly in particular (such as the Senior Community Service Employment Program under Title V of the Older American Act).

This chapter will examine the impact that current and projected employment problems have on the Black and Puerto Rican older workers, that is, those persons 55 years and older. This will be accomplished by presenting the following perspective: (1) a history of the Black and Puerto Rican working classes, with emphasis on the effect of racial and ethnic discrimination on the employability of individuals in these groups; (2) current trends in the labor market and the effects that these trends have on older Black and Puerto Rican workers; (3) an examination of manpower training programs and their efficaciousness in respect to ameliorating the employment problems confronting older Black and Puerto Rican workers; and (4) employment outlooks with emphasis on Blacks and Puerto Ricans in general and their older workers in particular.

EMPLOYMENT HISTORY OF
BLACKS AND PUERTO RICANS

Blacks and Puerto Ricans have been concentrated geographically in the key industrial states of the Northeast, although large numbers of Blacks are located in the industrial states of the Midwest as well. Both groups migrated to these specific areas because of increased job opportunities formerly made possible by industrial expansion. It is here that they have been segregated into low-level, unskilled occupations. The results of this segregation have meant that a disproportionately high number have spent the majority of their lives in low-wage industries, and a disproportionately low number have spent their lives in high-wage industries. This is reflected in the decreased intergenerational mobility of these groups. For example, in all major social indicants of well-being such as income, levels of education, rates of poverty, health, housing units owned, and so on, Blacks and Puerto Ricans are identical (Walters, 1982). In addition, the clustering of these groups into lower level occupations is seen consistently across all regions of this country and all age groups (Congressional Budget Office, 1978). However, the commonalities that Black and Puerto Rican older workers have shared in the industrial sectors of the Northeast will be the main focus of this chapter. Particular attention will be paid to the socioeconomic context in which the Black and Puerto Rican older workers presently find themselves. Some attention is also paid to implications this work history has for future generations of Black and Puerto Rican workers.

Blacks. Black historians have generally noted that the only periods in which anything approximating full employment occurred for Blacks were during slavery and during the Reconstruction era when the Black Codes made it illegal for Blacks in the South *not* to work. However, neither of these conditions fit the paradigm of employment under the American economic system of capitalism vis-à-vis free choices among workers to sell their labor to the highest bidders (Fusfeld, 1971). However, it is the full use of the Black labor force that provides a viable historical perspective from which one can graphically view the current plight of Black older workers.

From the outset, Black slavery became the keystone of the southern labor force, and their primary purpose was to facilitate the development of a plantation economy through enforced labor. To ensure that the slaves would be kept subdued, they were not allowed to become literate under penalty of death. It was thought that educated slaves might more quickly rebel. While some of the more courageous slaves did learn to read and write; for the most part, Blacks were an illiterate population (Sowell, 1975). This condition both limited and prescribed the type and kind of skill developments Blacks could acquire. Therefore, it did not matter very much if Blacks were to be used as slaves in the South or as menial laborers in the industrial North, as it later turned out. The die was cast for them to be at a decided disadvantage in a competitive labor market (Bennett, 1971).

It is not surprising that immediately after the Civil War the exslaves found jobs in areas familiar to them, such as domestic service, tenant farming, and sharecropping. By the turn of the century, however, the farming industry was rapidly undergoing mechanization. This process displaced many Blacks as well as white workers from traditional farm jobs, causing an enormous surplus pool of labor. Many whites, exercising their prerogative as members of the dominant socioeconomic class—that is, capitalizing on racial discrimination practices—accepted menial jobs formerly held by Blacks (Wagenheim & Wagenheim, 1973). This set the trend for Black unemployment, the rate of which has almost consistently been twice that of whites, economic conditions notwithstanding.

The negative effects of the displacement from agriculture because of technological changes and unemployment from cotton manufacturing caused Blacks to migrate to northern industrial centers, which were beginning to open up. This migration began to intensify by the 1910s, caused primarily by the negative state of the southern economy coupled with a war economy (Wilson, 1975).

Between World War I and II, the booming economy generated an increased demand for Black workers, who were generally consigned menial jobs. Frequently, they were excluded from the labor market altogether, especially as white immigrants also entered the country in sizable numbers during this time. Because Blacks were not allowed to be competitive with the aggregate group of white labor, they failed to make the economic gains of both white national and white ethnic immigrant groups (Wilson, 1975). Also, after both wars, when white males returned home, they reclaimed their former industrial jobs, further adding to the displacement of Blacks in the labor market. A disillusioned but determined Black community aborted a planned march on Washington in 1941. In 1963, however, they staged an impressive march on the nation's capital. Joined by thousands of sympathetic non-Blacks, they demanded full civil rights, including the right to prepare and compete for all employment positions.

In 1964, the Civil Rights Act was passed. Its purpose was to ban discrimination based on race and national origin. However, some observers claim that there was a move to defuse growing demands for economic equality by sending many young Black men to fight in the Vietnam War (Yette, 1971; Turner, 1977). Meanwhile, there was a 20% drop in farm employment and a further growth in the unemployment of Blacks. For example, during 1964, the aggregate unemployment rate was 5.2%, white unemployment was 4.6% and the unemployment rate of Blacks and others was almost 9.6% (U.S. Department of Labor, 1980).

In 1982, nearly 20 years after the passage of the 1964 Civil Rights Act and over 200 years after manumission, the economic plight of Black people remained dismal and certainly disproportionate to that of white Americans. Unemployment remained especially high for the Black aged who are products of a system that consigned them to restrictive employment opportunities in their younger years. As a result, seldom is there evidence in the literature that employment for the Black older worker is an issue. It seems to be taken for granted that the Black elderly should look toward resources other than employment for maintenance and well-being.

Puerto Ricans. Shortly after the institution of slavery in North America, African slaves were introduced to the island of Puerto Rico to facilitate the development of the economy. These slaves worked in the gold mines and on the plantations. Meanwhile, much intermingling of Blacks, Indians, and Spaniards occurred. This caused a hybrid population of mulattoes (Padilla, 1958).

The Spanish-American War of 1898 yielded a victory for the United States. Puerto Rico's economy at this time depended primarily on rural plantation economies. Thus, much of the employment was in agriculture, requiring only unskilled labor. In addition, there was widespread illiteracy, due to beliefs that ignorant people were easier to govern (Berbusse, 1966; Goldring, 1973).

By the end of the 1920s, Puerto Rico was in a state of economic collapse because of the damage done to crops by natural events. This created a large surplus of labor. Additionally, many of the *jubaros* (rural peasant owners) lost their lands to genetically homogeneous white, upper-class Spaniards and American businessmen willing to speculate in the Puerto Rican economy

(Berbusse, 1966). During this period, agricultural skills were no longer needed (Ghali, 1982). The combination of a surplus pool of labor displaced by local agricultural economies and an unskilled labor force meant that workers could be used quite cheaply. Labor was so cheap and there was such a good railroad infrastructure that industrialists could then ship raw material to Puerto Rico and manufacture goods for two-thirds of the production costs in the United States (Wagenheim & Wagenheim, 1973). By 1927, the first small wave of migration from Puerto Rico to the mainland began. Land in Puerto Rico was being bought up by outside investors, but little was being spent on the island's development. As crop failure was common during this time, many former farm owners and workers became displaced. Again, there was a movement to the urban areas to find work. Needlecraft industries were transported to the island because sweat shop conditions had been outlawed on the mainland. Again, the surplus pool of workers became a cheap labor supply ready for exploitation by industrialists (Wagenheim & Wagenheim, 1973).

Puerto Rico's economy closely follows the ups and downs of the U.S. economy. Consequently, the Great Depression of the 1930s also affected Puerto Rico. While there was some U.S. governmental intervention in the Puerto Rican economy during this period, it was not enough to adequately help the distressed economy and the large pools of idle workers (Hauberg, 1974). The situation changed little until the end of World War II when Puerto Ricans were lured to the mainland to fill jobs in the industrial sector. Thus, it is seen that this migratory flow was caused primarily by economic conditions, thereby placing Puerto Ricans into the same motivational categories as other immigrants.

It was, however, during the span of years between 1946 and 1960 that many Puerto Ricans were enticed to come to the United States, mainly by recruiters from the mainland. Others came by word of encouragement from families and friends who had heard about the abundance of jobs. Possibilities of employment on the mainland pulled these workers to industrial areas such as New York, New Jersey, and Pennsylvania; the lack of employment opportunities pushed them out of Puerto Rico.

What is seen in the migration of both Blacks and Puerto Ricans is the strong relationship between the inability of local economies to support a sufficient number of workers, the wholesale displacement of unskilled workers through agricultural mechanization or crop loss, and the outmigration from these areas and inmigration to industrial states where the possibility of employment seemed to be greatly enhanced (Padilla, 1958; Wilson, 1975).

Like Blacks, who had a long experience with racism, Puerto Ricans quickly found that color was a crucial barrier to finding work. Lighter Puerto Ricans who could pass as whites did so. Many others opted to call themselves Hispanics or Latinos. In so doing, they associated themselves with ethnic groups other than their own, such as Latin Americans and Spaniards, thus dodging the problems associated with being Puerto Rican and/or Black (Padilla, 1958; Levitan, Johnson & Taggert, 1975).

So, for the most part, the Puerto Rican older workers, like their Black counterparts, are products of employment displacement due mainly, but not solely, to industrial change. Purposeful efforts to keep them in low-skill positions and ignorant (Berbusse, 1966) in their younger years helped to debar their full participation in a technocratically oriented labor market. Also, because of their low numbers, (about 2% of all aged; Harbert & Ginsberg, 1975), the Puerto Rican aged are virtually ignored in the literature. This has the effect of placing them in a nonperson category when federal employment programs for the aged are proposed. The fact that their identity is often assumed or consumed in the generic Hispanic category might also mitigate against their receiving benefits from special programs.

CURRENT TRENDS IN
THE LABOR MARKET

America appears to be at the end of the industrial era (Mitchell, 1980). It can be assumed that the ratio of those permanently displaced from the industrial labor market will be disproportionately found among Blacks and Puerto Ricans, regardless of age. It certainly appears that the decline in the industries for which they have been employed in the past will not be revived any time soon, if ever. For example, declines in the rubber, tire, electronics, automotive, and related industries are due in large part to international competition. Yet, they are also due to old technologies used by these mature industries as well, thus calling for a large-scale change in fading technologies and machineries (Girifalco, 1982). Still another reason for this crisis is the former dependence on coal as a cheap source of energy and expansion (Girifalco, 1982). Since the emergence of oil as an energy supply, world suppliers have greatly increased the cost of this crucial factor of production. As oil prices increase, so will inflation and so will unemployment (National Commission for Employment Policy [NCEP], 1980).

In essence, the economy is in transition relative to the decline of heavy industry and the emergence of high technology and the service sectors (Public Welfare, 1981). The "lift the barge, tote that bale" manpower need has been replaced by the need for specialized training. For example, growth has occurred in the service sector to such an extent that in 1973, 17.3% of all jobs were in that area as compared to 12.8% in 1970. However, during the industrial era, the service sector supplied less than 10% of the jobs (Monthly Labor Review, 1975; Anderson, 1982). By 1990, it is projected this sector will command 22.9% of all jobs (Anderson, 1982). The high demand for technology has increased the need for computer literacy to such an extent that in the 1980s, 30% of all jobs will require some computer skills. By the

1990s, it is projected that this will increase to 60% (Bailey, 1982). Meanwhile, there has also been a growth in white-collar jobs. In the industrial era, for example, this sector involved from 17.6 to 36.6% of all jobs; by 1970, this figure had grown to 48.1% and by 1979, more than 71.8% of all employed workers were white collar (Monthly Labor Review, 1975; U.S. Department of Labor, 1980).

It is obvious that racial and ethnic populations historically relegated to perform in low-level agricultural and industrial jobs will not be prepared to compete in a technocratic society. Recognizing this reality, a cursory attempt has been made to address this very serious problem. The most publicized attempt is the Manpower Development Training Act (MDTA).

THE MANPOWER DEVELOPMENT TRAINING ACT: AN INSIGNIFICANT IMPACT

In a review of evaluative studies of these programs, Perrault (1980) found that they generally did not improve access to higher paying occupations, or reduce the segregation of minorities in low-level occupations. The primary benefit was to provide temporary cash assistance to the unemployed participants. Information yielded from the Congressional Budget Office (1978) also found that the net impact of these jobs was only temporary, did not affect the unemployment rate, did not improve occupational differences, and did not create the conditions for Blacks and Puerto Ricans to compete with whites for jobs at even the lowest end.

A further investigation of these programs shows that they had serious drawbacks. For example, the types of jobs for which participants were trained ran counter to dominant labor market trends in that participants were trained for low skill-level jobs. Contradictorily, the demand is for high skill-level, technologically oriented jobs. Additionally, MDTA-related jobs were generally those that paid close to the minimum wage and had little, if any, opportunities for occupational mobility (NCEP, 1980). By design, MDTA programs did not deal with the special barrier of racism that minorities had to confront in the labor market after training. There was no buffer or liaison made between the program and potential employers. Nor did MDTA stimulate the creation of jobs in the economically depressed areas where the disadvantaged lived or produce jobs in the economy as a whole (NCEP, 1980). Further, it did not disturb the lack of competitiveness between Blacks and Puerto Ricans, and white male workers in the labor market. As Galbraith, Kuh, and Thurow (1977) point out, the white, English-speaking male had/has a virtual monopoly of good jobs in commerce and industry through a virtual exclusion of these jobs from Blacks, other nonwhites, females, and Spanish-speaking populations.

In 1973, the Comprehensive Employment and Training Act (CETA) was passed. However, its focus was on the younger worker. Even so, CETA, which is currently struggling to maintain federal support, has done little to address the problem of unemployment in the elderly, either through employment or retraining (Anderson, 1982).

To address specifically the problem of elderly unemployment, Community Service Employment for Older Americans became a program under Title V of the Older American Act (1978 Amendment). Again, there is no evidence to suggest that this has been a successful program. In fact, it has been slated for elimination under the Reagan Administration's current proposal for budgetary cuts.

So, neither Black nor Puerto Rican unemployed older workers have benefited appreciatively from federal training and employment programs. Their plight seems impervious to the puny efforts of federal programs.

EMPLOYMENT OUTLOOK FOR
THE BLACK AND PUERTO RICAN AGED

It is in the 55- to 65-year-old category that lesser skilled, lower paid workers predominate. Blacks and Puerto Ricans have a disproportionate representation in this category (U.S. Department of Labor, 1972). For example, from 1954 to 1979, Black males in this category showed a decline in labor force participation by over 19.1% (i.e., a decline from 83% to 66.9%. However, even white male workers in this age category showed a decline of over 14.6%, showing that a definite trend of employing older workers less frequently has taken place. Among Black males aged 65 and older, labor force participation during this same period has declined by 21.6%. For white males of the same age, there had been a similar decline of 20.3% (U.S. Department of Labor, 1972, 1980).

About 95% of all Blacks (and a like percentage of Puerto Ricans) remain in working-class status (as opposed to being entrepreneurs). Thus, their only means of survival in a money economy is to sell labor (Jackson, 1982). Yet they continue to confront special barriers to employment in addition to the lack of jobs. Given these realities, and the state of the economy, there appears to be little or no prospects for improving the well-being of these groups. Among females during this time, Blacks in the 55 to 64 age range showed an increase in labor force participation of 3.1% as compared to an increase in white female participation of 12.5%. In the 65+ age category, among Black females, there was an increase of 1.6% as compared to an increase among white females during this same period of 1% (U.S. Department of Labor, 1980).

All in all, white workers still compete for jobs in the primary labor market, which is characterized by good benefits, high wages, and stability.

Blacks and Puerto Ricans still compete for jobs in the secondary labor market characterized by low wages, little or no benefits, and recurring displacement. Ironically, the training economy initiated by MDTA programs is itself part of the function to maintain and sustain a secondary labor market (Tussing, 1975). And, since urban unskilled workers participating in these programs had already been displaced by automation and the movement of unskilled jobs to other locations, one must question the validity of such a program as opposed to one designed for job creation.

The subsequent prolonged recession of 1969-1971, 1974-1975, and 1980 have continued to wipe out whatever gains minority workers have made (NCEP, 1980). During each recession, Blacks and Puerto Ricans have reexperienced the displacement process. Older workers, following recessionary periods, have been especially victimized by efforts to reduce inflation through the toleration of high unemployment.

CONCLUSION

The preceding discussion has suggested that the structural nature of unemployment is both historical and permanent (NCEP, 1980). It is the main contention of this chapter that Black and Puerto Rican older workers have had to contend with special barriers constructed by the historical existence of job segregation in addition to a decline of jobs in the agricultural and industrial sectors. With the increase of technological advances as an emerging source of employment, they have become a technologically obsolete class, with little or no prospect for improving their economic well-being, and little or no chance for integration into the world of work (Yette, 1971). The high level of unemployment of older Black and Puerto Rican workers is particularly grave and, at this point, seems permanent.

REFERENCES

Anderson, B. E. Economic patterns in Black America. *The State of Black America, 1982*. Washington, DC: National Urban League, 1982, 1-32

Bailey, R. The 1980 census undercount controversy: A review. *Urban Research Review*, 1982, 8 (1), 45.

Bennett, L. *Unity in the Black community*. Chicago: Third World Press, 1975.

Berbusse, C. J. The United States in Puerto Rico: 1898-1900. Chapel Hill: University of North Carolina Press, 1966.

Brotman, H. B. The aging society: A demographic view. *Aging*, January-February 1982, 5.

Congressional Budget Office, 1978.

Fusfeld, D. R. *The age of the economist*. Glenview, IL: Scott, Foresman, 1971.

Galbraith, J. K., Kuh, E., & Thruow, L. Policy and practice considerations: Toward greater minority employment. In J. Rothman (Ed.), *Issues in race and ethnic relations*. Itasca, IL: Peacock, 1977, 87-94.

Ghali, S. B. Understanding Puerto Rican traditions. *Social Work*, 1982, 27 (1), 31-37.

Girifalco, L. The dynamics of technological change. *Wharton Magazine*, 1982, 7 (1), 31-37.

Goldring, M. J. *A short history of Puerto Rico.* New York: New American Library, 1973.

Harbert, Anita, & Ginsberg, Leon. *Human services for older adults: Concepts and skills.* Belmont, CA: Wadsworth, 1973.

Hauberg, C. A. *Puerto Rico and the Puerto Rican.* New York: Twayne, 1974.

Levitan, S., Johson, W. B., & Taggert, R. *Minorities in the United States: Problems, progress and prospects.* Washington, DC: Public Affairs Press, 1975.

Mitchell, C. Afro-American equality versus Reaganite racism. *Political Affairs*, 1982, 61 (6), 15-19.

National Commission for Employment Policy (NCEP). *Hispanics and jobs: Barriers to Progress.* Washington, DC: NCEP, 1980.

Padilla, E. *Up from Puerto Rico.* New York: Columbia University Press, 1958.

Perrault, G. *The Black underclass: An evaluative analysis of manpower programs that failed.* Unpublished manuscript, Michigan State University, 1980.

Public Welfare. Book review. 1981, 39 (3), 42-43.

Sowell, R. *Race and economics.* New York: D. McKay, 1975.

Turner, T. Black American colonial economy under siege. *First World*, 1977, 1 (2), 7-10.

Tussing, D. *Poverty in a dual economy.* New York: St. Martin's Press, 1975.

Wagenheim, K., & Wagenheim, O. S. *The Puerto Rican: A documentary history.* Garden City, NY: Anchor Books, 1973.

Walters, Ronald W. Race, resources, conflict. *Social Work*, 1982, 27 (1), 24-29.

Wilson, W. J. *The declining significance of race.* Chicago: University of Chicago Press.

Yette, S. *The choice: The issue of Black survival in America.* New York: G. P. Putnam, 1971.

U.S. Bureau of the Census. *1980 census of population: Supplementary reports.* Washington, DC: Government Printing Office, 1981.

U.S. Department of Labor. *Black Americans: A decade of occupational change.* Bulletin 1760. Washington, DC: Government Printing Office, 1972.

U.S. Department of Labor. *Handbook of Labor Statistics.* Bulletin 2070. Washington, DC: Government Printing Office, 1980.

U.S. President's Commission, 1980.

16

Income Maintenance Programs and the Minority Elderly

ROBERT B. HILL

How will the minority elderly be affected by income maintenance programs during the 1980s and 1990s? Several recent developments make any expectations about increased government support for low-income and minority aged over the next decade unlikely. First, despite claims by the Reagan Administration that the elderly would be protected by a "safety net" for the "truly needy," its sweeping cutbacks in major income transfer programs for the poor (such as Aid to Families with Dependent Children [AFDC], food stamps, Medicaid, public housing, rent subsidies, and energy assistance), would significantly undermine the economic condition of the minority elderly (Hill, 1981). Second, the large-scale decentralization of social programs through block grants to states and local areas would undoubtedly reduce the targeting of funds and benefits to important subgroups of the elderly: the poor, minorities, and the handicapped. Third, with increasing speculation that the Social Security Trust Fund might be depleted in this decade, there is much anxiety and uncertainty among the elderly and non-elderly as to whether sufficient benefits will be available for their retirement years. And, fourth, if Congress enacts the recommendation of the President's Commission on Pension Policy (PCOPP) in 1981 that the age eligibility for full retirement benefits be moved from 65 to 68 years, thousands of minority workers will never receive their retirement benefits because of shorter life expectancies (PCOPP, 1981). Thus, the goal of economic security for the minority elderly appears to be much more remote for the 1980s and 1990s than it was for the 1960s and 1970s. However, in order to assess adequately the potential impact of government income maintenance programs on the minority elderly in the future, it is necessary to examine their effects on the minority aged in the past. First, we will provide an overview of the major income transfer programs that currently exist, and then describe the extent to which they have met the economic needs of the minority elderly.

The cornerstone of social welfare policies and programs in this nation for almost half a century has been the Social Security Act, which was signed into law on August 14, 1935. This broad-ranging social legislation was enacted as a result of the devastating effects of the Great Depression of the 1930s on the lives of millions of Americans. It was specifically designed to prevent or reduce economic hardships due to recession, unemployment, retirement, disability, and death.

Two kinds of income maintenance programs were established by the Social Security Act: social insurance and public assistance. Each of these two types of income transfer programs may be subdivided further into (1) those that provide direct cash assistance and (2) those that provide noncash or in-kind benefits. Social insurance programs were intended to provide economic benefits to individuals who were at risk due to unemployment, old age, and disability based largely on their own financial contribution to the insurance systems, but *not* on economic need. Benefits from social insurance programs were not intended to cover all of the basic food, shelter, and health needs of recipients and their dependents: They were considered to be supplements to income from private pensions, savings, earnings, investments, and relatives. The primary governmental social insurance programs providing cash assistance are Old Age and Survivors Insurance (OASI), Disability Insurance (DI), Unemployment Insurance (UI), Worker's Compensation, Veterans' Disability Compensation, Armed Forces Pensions and Civil Service Retirement Pensions. The only social insurance program providing in-kind benefits is Hospital Insurance (HI), which was enacted in 1965 as part of Medicare.

Public assistance (or "welfare") programs, on the other hand, were specifically designed to provide benefits to individuals based on economic need or deprivation due to old age, disability, or the unemployment or absence of a primary breadwinner. The main public assistance (or "means-tested") programs providing direct cash aid have been: Old Age Assistance (OAA), Aid to the Blind (AB), Aid to the Permanently and Totally Disabled (APTD), Supplemental Security Income (an amalgam of OAA, AB, and APTD), and AFDC. Income transfer programs that provide in-kind benefits to the poor and needy are food stamps, food commodities, Medicaid, reduced price or free school lunches, public housing, subsidized rent, low-income energy assistance, and daycare (Levitan, 1980; U.S. Joint Economic Committee, 1972, 1973).

Most Americans believe that public assistance benefits account for the overwhelming majority of government costs for social welfare programs in this nation. The fact is that about three-fourths of government expenditures for social welfare are for social insurance programs (especially Social Security, Federal Retirement, Veteran's Benefits, Unemployment Compensation, and Worker's Compensation) that primarily go to the nonpoor and nonminorities. Moreover, most of the funds for public assistance programs are not received directly by the poor, but by service providers and vendors, such as physicians, hospitals, clinics, landlords, and social welfare institutions. Nevertheless, billions of dollars are being spent to aid the poor and jobless. For example, about one-fourth of the $400 billion spent in 1980 by all levels of government for income maintenance programs went for public assistance. The aged account for the bulk of the recipients of income maintenance programs, with the nonaged poor comprising much smaller fractions. For example, five times as many households received Social Security benefits (21 million) than received public assistance (4 million) in 1979, while twice as many households were covered by Medicare (19 million) than by Medicaid (8 million). At the same time, it would be misleading to convey the impression that the elderly are the major recipients of public economic supports.

In fact, the primary beneficiaries of government income supports are affluent individuals, corporations, and other institutions. But the income maintenance programs for the rich are provided in the form of tax expenditures or subsidies. These tax subsidies, more popularly known as "loopholes," are not usually considered as income transfer programs because they do not appear as line items in the federal budget. Yet, they account for lost revenues to the treasury that are billions of dollars greater than the costs of more visible income programs for the elderly and the poor. Examples of tax subsidies for the rich include the "10-5-3" depreciation allowances (a $145 billion Treasury loss), corporate tax straddles ($1.3 billion), oil depletion allowances ($42 billion), the "Three Martini Lunch" ($3 billion), the leasing transfer of tax credits ($27 billion), and many other costly tax loopholes. Once it is clearly understood that the lion's share of the government's "welfare" dollars goes to the wealthy, our focus on programs that are targeted to more needy individuals is placed in proper perspective (Hill, 1981).

PAST RESEARCH

The biggest impediment to an adequate analysis of the impact of income maintenance programs on the minority aged is the paucity of data. In light of the widespread belief that minorities are "overdependent" on public assistance, one would expect abundant supporting data to be available. However, this is not the case. There is a surprising dearth of data and empirical studies on the extent to which different income maintenance benefits are actually received by racial minorities among the nonelderly as well as the elderly.

Most of the national data on participation in income transfer programs are based on administrative records or surveys of recipients for specific government agencies. For example, the Agriculture Department regularly provides statistics on food stamp recipients; the Department of Health and Human Services (HHS) conducts periodic surveys of the characteristics of AFDC families, and the Department of Housing and Urban Development (HUD) conducts annual surveys of beneficiaries of public housing and rent subsidies. But not one government agency regularly surveys the nature and extent of participation by minorities in the broad range of cash and in-kind income transfer programs that cut across agencies.

At present, the annual Current Population Survey (CPS) reports on income and poverty are the major source of continuing data on participation in income transfer programs. But the data in these reports are limited to the major direct cash programs (i.e., Social Security, Supplemental Security Income, and Public Assistance) and are only provided for Blacks and whites (U.S. Bureau of the Census, 1981a). In order to partly fill this void, the Census Bureau expanded its' CPS surveys in 1980 and 1981 to obtain data on participation in noncash programs (i.e., Medicare, Medicaid, school lunches, food stamps, and subsidized housing) for whites, Blacks, and Hispanics (U.S. Bureau of the Census, 1981b). One survey that would have provided the most extensive data on participation in cash and in-kind programs by racial minorities was HHS's planned Survey of Income and Program Participation (SIPP). However, budget cuts by the Reagan Administration have reduced its scope markedly. Moreover, the cutbacks have also placed continuation of the Census Bureau's expanded CPS survey of noncash program beneficiaries in serious jeopardy. Thus, it is very likely that, for most of this decade, there will be less national data on income maintenance program participation by elderly and nonelderly racial minorities than there is now.

Past empirical research on income transfer programs has been based more on simulation studies of "potential" or "categorical" program eligibility than on actual program recipiency. These simulations usually assume that all or almost all households that are categorically eligible for various income transfer benefits actually receive them. While the equation of eligibility with participation may have some dubious legitimacy for nonminority households, it is totally invalid for minorities. Contrary to conventional wisdom, empirical evidence consistently reveals that large numbers of elderly and nonelderly minorities who are eligible for income transfer benefits do not receive them (Hill, 1980).

In fact, the most significant contributions and insights about the participation of the minority aged in income transfer programs have come from needs assessment surveys conducted at the community level and not from national government surveys. These community-based surveys of the minority elderly have addressed such fundamental questions about minority participation in public benefit programs as the following:

(1) What is the extent of participation in various government benefit programs by the elderly from a broad range of racial minorities—Blacks, Puerto-Ricans,

Mexican-Americans, other Hispanics, American Indians, Chinese, Japanese, Koreans, and other Asians and Pacific Islanders?

(2) How adequate are the income maintenance benefits received by the minority elderly relative to their economic need?

(3) How equitable is the share of public benefits received by the minority aged compared to the nonminority aged?

(4) What are the major reasons for the underrepresentation of minority elderly in most government benefit programs?

(5) How sensitive are public benefit programs to the variety of cultural patterns among the minority aged in such areas as language, household composition, nutrition, health, and religious beliefs?

(6) What are the most effective means for increasing the minority aged's knowledge about the availability of government benefits and services?

Community-based surveys have been able to examine such basic issues more adequately than national surveys for a number of reasons. First, at the local level, it is easier to select communities with large concentrations of minorities, especially Hispanics, Asians, and American Indians, that are usually omitted from nationally representative surveys. Second, individuals administering community studies are usually more interested in assessing the actual needs and experiences of individuals and groups, while national surveys traditionally concentrate on opinions and attitudes. Third, community surveys tend to focus on both recipients and nonrecipients of public benefits, while national government surveys tend to focus only on program beneficiaries. And, fourth, community-based studies often consider issues about minority participation that are neglected in national surveys because of the greater involvement of minority scholars and community representatives in the planning, implementation, and analysis of research at the local level.

Two recent community-based studies funded by the Administration on Aging (AOA) that have contributed significantly to a fuller understanding of the nature of minority aged participation in governmental benefit programs are (1) the Cuellar and Weeks (1980) monograph, *Minority Elderly Americans: The Assessment of Needs and Equitable Receipts of Public Benefits as a Prototype for Area Agencies on Aging* and (2) the Guttman (1980) report, *Perspective on Equitable Share in Public Benefits by the Minority Elderly* (see Jackson, 1980). Building on Valle's pioneering cross-cultural study of minority elders, Cuellar and Weeks conducted a comprehensive survey of the extent of equity of minority aged participation in cash and in-kind government programs and services in San Diego, California. The Cuellar-Weeks study was unique, not only because 85% of the 1139 elderly respondents were minorities, but for presenting the findings separately for nine minority groups: Blacks, Hispanics, Chinese, Japanese, Filipinos, Koreans, American Indians, Guamanians, and Samoans. The study by Guttman, which was conducted in the Washington D.C. metropolitan area, attempted to determine the level of minority participation in and knowledge about 52 public benefits and services. Although sizable numbers of minority sub-groups were also surveyed by Guttman (as reflected by 60% of the 621 respondents), his findings were presented separately for only three minorities: Blacks, Hispanics, and Asians.

Another innovative community-based study of the minority aged was conducted by the University of the District of Columbia's Institute of Gerontology (UDC). On the basis of extensive household interviews, it attempted to determine the number of minority elders in the District of Columbia who might be eligible for Supplemental Security Income (SSI) benefits, but were not receiving them (UDC, 1978). This UDC survey also had an important service component because it turned over the names of potentially eligible individuals to the Social Security Administration for verification and processing. In response to a congressional mandate in Title III of the 1978 amendments to the Older Americans Act, the U.S. Commission on Civil Rights conducted studies in six communities with concentrations of Blacks, Hispanics, Asians, and American Indians to determine the extent of discrimination in the administration of public programs and services to the minority aged (U.S. Commission on Civil Rights, 1981).

One recent nongovernment study with national data on participation by minorities in income transfer programs is the National Council on the Aging (NCOA) *Aging in the Eighties: America in Transition*. This report was based on surveys that included 1,837 persons 65 years of age and older (274 of whom were Black and 190 of whom were Hispanic) conducted by Louis Harris and associates (1981). This survey was a sequel to the NCOA survey conducted by Louis Harris in 1974 (Harris et al., 1974). Moreover, the National Urban League (NUL) obtained somewhat similar data on the minority aged in its nationwide survey (Hill, 1980) of the needs and condition of 3,000 Black households conducted in 1979-1980. This NUL Black Pulse Survey secured data on the participation of over 500 Black elderly in a broad range of cash and in-kind public programs (Hill, 1980).

PAST IMPACT OF INCOME TRANSFERS

What impact have the various income maintenance programs had on the economic well-being of the minority elderly? First, we will assess the importance of four cash assistance programs: Social Security, Supplemental Security Income, AFDC, and pensions (government and private). Then we will examine their participation in four in-kind public programs: Medicare, Medicaid, Food Stamps, and Housing Assistance.

SOCIAL SECURITY (OASDI)

What is commonly called "Social Security" is really an amalgam of three social insurance programs: Old Age Insurance (OAI), which was enacted in 1935, Survivors Insurance (SI), which was established in 1939; and Disability Insurance (DI), which was set up in 1957. This is why Social Security is most often referred to as the OASDI program. Some observers refer to it as OASDHI when they wish to include the Hospital Insurance (HI) component of Medicare. In 1980, expenditures for Old Age, Survivors, and Disability Insurance totaled $115 billion, excluding $34 million paid for hospital and medical insurance.

Social Security reaches the largest number of Americans of any government income transfer program. In 1981, 36 million (or one of every seven) received cash payments from this program. Retired workers accounted for 20 million (or 56%) of OASDI recipients; disabled workers, three million (or 8%); and survivors and dependents, 13 million (or 36%); (U.S. Department of Health and Human Services [HHS], 1981b).

How have the minority aged fared under Social Security? The most obvious fact is that the overwhelming majority of the minority elderly receive and depend heavily on Social Security benefits. About four out of every five minority persons 65 years and older are Social Security beneficiaries, either as retired (41%) or disabled (12%) workers, or as dependents or survivors (47%) of retired, disabled, or deceased workers. While 89% of the white elderly are OASDI recipients, so are 83% of the Black elderly. Black elders living with spouses are more likely (90%) to receive Social Security benefits than those living without spouses (80%). But white elders living with spouses are just as likely (90%) to be OASDI beneficiaries as those without spouses (89%) (Grad & Foster, 1979; Social Security Administration [SSA], 1981). About 82% of all Hispanic elders receive Social Security (Harris, 1981).[1]

EXPANDING OASDI COVERAGE

What are some of the reasons for the high level of participation of minority aged in Social Security? The primary reason is the extensive broadening of coverage over the years. In 1945, one decade after its inception, only one-tenth of all elderly persons were OASI recipients. But as a result of the 1950 and 1954 amendments, Social Security coverage was extended to farm operators, agricultural workers, and domestic workers—occupations with heavy concentrations of minorities. Moreover, although 40 quarters (or about 10 years) in covered employment is needed to be "fully and permanently insured," one can qualify for some retirement benefits with fewer quarters as "fully, but not permanently insured." It is also possible to receive benefits as "currently insured," if one obtains at least six quarters of coverage within the three years prior to retirement. By 1981, the total number of living persons with covered employment since the inception of Social Security was about 162 million. About half of them were fully and permanently insured, one-third were fully, but not permanently insured, and only 1% were currently insured. In 1981, a worker received one quarter of coverage (up to a total of four) for each $310 of annual earnings.

Because of frequent spells of unemployment due to seasonality of work, layoffs and disability, minorities were less likely than nonminorities to be fully and permanently insured upon retirement, but were more likely to be fully, but not permanently insured or currently insured. Consequently, although these liberalized options permitted large numbers of minorities to qualify for some Social Security benefits, the amount of those benefits tended to be much lower than the amount received by permanently insured nonminorities. Furthermore, Social Security amendments in 1965 and 1966 expanded coverage to all persons 72 years of age and older who did not qualify for benefits as fully or currently insured. Thus, all uninsured persons who are not receiving any other government pensions are entitled to receive special retirement benefits upon reaching 72 years of age. Obviously, because of the relatively lower life expectancies of minorities, they tend to be underrepresented among the special age-72 beneficiaries. In fact, although minorities account for about 7% of all persons 72 years and over, they make up only 4% of the special age-72 Social Security recipients (U.S. Senate, 1971; Hill, 1972).

Yet, because of the longer life expectancies of women relative to men, minority women are more highly represented among Social Security recipients than minority men. Moreover, because of their relatively longer work histories, Black women are more likely than white women to qualify for benefits as retired workers (i.e., based on their own earning record). Among widows 62 years and over, Blacks (56%) are more likely than whites (46%) to be eligible for benefits as retired workers, while white women (70%) are more likely than Black women (59%) to qualify for benefits as (nondisabled) aged widows. However, among elderly couples on Social Security, two thirds of both white (67%) and Black (65%) women 62 years and over qualify for benefits as wives of retired workers, while half of white (46%) and Black (47%) wives are entitled to retired workers benefits based on their own past earnings (Lingg, 1982).

On the other hand, minorities tend to be overrepresented among the disabled OASDI recipients. Social Security disability benefits are only available for fully insured disabled workers who are not eligible for Medicare because they are under 65 years of age. To qualify for Disability Insurance (DI) benefits, workers must have at least 20 quarters of coverage prior to a disability that prevented gainful employment for at least 12 consecutive months. In general, Blacks are more likely to be disabled than are whites. A national survey of the disabled conducted by the SSA in 1972 revealed that, although Blacks were 10% of the U.S. population between ages 20 and 64, they made up 16% of all the severely disabled in the nation (HHS, 1981a). In 1978, Blacks accounted for 16% of the 2.9 million persons receiving Social Security disabled worker benefits. Moreover, while 13% of all white workers on Social Security in 1978 were disabled, almost twice as many (23%) Black OASDI recipients were disabled. But male retirees, among both Blacks and whites, are more likely to be disabled recipients than females; 27% of all Black male workers on Social Security in 1978 were disabled, compared to 18% of all Black female retirees. Similarly, the proportion of disabled white OASDI recipients was almost twice as large among males (15%) than females (9%) (HHS, 1982). Thus, disproportionate numbers of minority workers, especially among men, are retiring before the age of 65, not out of choice, but because of ill health and disability. Clearly, the many years of working in hazardous and physically debilitating jobs and industries are major factors in the retirement patterns of the minority aged.

SOCIAL SECURITY BENEFIT LEVELS

What are the relative levels of Social Security benefits received by minority and nonminority elderly? The amount of Social Security benefits is determined by a worker's Primary Insurance Amount (PIA), which is the monthly payment to a retired worker who begins to get benefits at age 65 or earlier for a disabled worker. The PIA is generally derived from the worker's average monthly earnings (AME) in covered employment. For most workers, monthly earnings are averaged over a period of years beginning in 1951 (or age 22, if it is later) up to the year the worker retires, becomes disabled, or dies. The five years with the lowest earnings are generally excluded from the computation of the average monthly earnings. Workers who choose to retire before 65, however, are actuarially reduced to 80% of their PIA.

But there are minimum and maximum levels of Social Security benefits. The minimum is the lowest amount (before actuarial reduction) payable to a retired or disabled worker or to a sole survivor of a deceased worker. It aids elderly persons who worked many years in covered employment at wages too low to become fully and permanently insured. The special minimum benefit is an alternative PIA that is not based on the worker's average monthly earnings, but on the number of years in covered employment. Until 1979, the minimum benefit rose at the same time as overall Social Security benefits, but recent legislation has frozen the monthly minimum benefit at $122 for elderly persons who become eligible for retirement after 1978. However, persons who retired before 1979 are entitled to minimum benefits that rise with overall OASDI benefits; thus the minimum was $134 in 1980 and $153 in 1981. Because the majority of the minority elderly spent most of their working years in lower paying jobs as domestics, farm workers, unskilled laborers, and service workers, they are overrepresented among recipients of the Social Security minimum. Conversely, minorities are underrepresented among maximum benefit recipients who held higher paying jobs most of their lives. The maximum Social Security benefit payable at retirement was $572 in 1980 and $677 in 1981.

Consequently, Social Security benefits for minorities tend to be between 80 and 90% of the amount received by nonminorities. For example, the average monthly benefits (after reduction for early retirement) for retired Black workers ($198) in 1978 were 81% of the benefits received by whites ($224) (HHS, 1982). Similarly, the average monthly benefits for disabled Black workers ($258) were 79% of the disability benefits received by white workers ($328). The gap in benefits between minorities and nonminorities is smaller among survivors and dependents however. In 1978, the monthly benefits for Black wives ($109) who were survivors or dependents of disabled, retired, or deceased workers were 84% of the benefits received by white wives ($129). But among disabled widows, who tend to have the highest survivor and dependent benefits, the benefits for Blacks ($190) were 80% of the benefits for whites ($238). Overall, the benefits for Black retired and disabled workers are about 80% of the benefits for whites, while Asian disabled workers obtain benefits that are about 90% of whites.[2] Hispanic Social Security recipients tend to generally receive benefits that are about 87% percent of those received by whites (Harris, 1981).

With the exception of disability payments, however, most Social Security benefits are below the poverty level. Among retired workers for example, the benefits received by whites, Asians, and Blacks were 90%, 85% and 75% respectively, of the poverty level for unrelated persons 65 years and over in 1978. Thus, although Social Security benefits are increased regularly to keep pace with inflation, they are still not sufficient to lift the average beneficiary, whether minority or not, above the poverty level.

At the same time, while the overwhelming majority of minority aged are Social Security recipients, it is important to underscore the fact that they are still less likely than nonminorities to be OASDI beneficiaries. For example, the Black elderly are almost twice as likely (17%) as the white elderly (11%) not to receive Social Security. The primary reason for this lower rate of participation by minorities is their greater concentration in noncovered employment. One key factor is that they are less likely to obtain sufficient quarters of coverage because of erratic employment patterns. Another is their higher representation in occupational sectors not covered by Social Security, such as in government, the military, and in the railroad industry—all of which have separate pension systems. One out of every five Black workers, for example, is employed in the public sector compared to about one out of every six white workers. Because, historically, government (especially at the federal and local levels) has been a major source of job opportunities, stability, and advancement for thousands of Blacks, they often qualify for Civil Service pensions rather than Social Security benefits upon retirement. Similarly, those who have made a career in the Armed Forces are entitled to military pensions. Furthermore, due to the traditional heavy concentration of Blacks in the railroad industry, the deductions from their payrolls over the years entitle many of them to Railroad Retirement benefits.

SUPPLEMENTAL SECURITY INCOME (SSI)

The second most important cash assistance program to the minority aged is Supplemental Security Income (SSI). On January 1, 1974, SSI replaced three state-administered means-tested programs—Old Age Assistance (OAA), Aid to the Blind (AB), and Aid to the Permanently and Totally Disabled (APTD)—which had failed to meet basic needs of the poor and disabled because of inadequate benefit levels and inequitable eligibility criteria. When Congress enacted the SSI legislation in 1972, it was convinced that a federally administered program was needed to more effectively reach the disadvantaged elderly and handicapped and to more adequately supplement their low incomes from earnings, savings, Social Security, and other pensions.

In order to qualify for SSI, one must be an economically disadvantaged person who is aged, blind, or disabled. Elderly individuals are eligible for SSI only if they are 65 years old, have minimal or no Social Security benefits, and insufficient other cash income. When first enacted, the following resources were excluded from income to determine SSI eligibility: cash resources of $1,500 for an individual and $2,250 for couples; a car valued at less than $1,200; life insurance valued at less than $1,500; household goods valued up to $1,500; and a home with an assessed value up to $25,000. But rampant inflation alone "disqualified" disproportionate numbers of low-income aged for SSI. Consequently, in 1976, the value of a home was completely eliminated as an eligibility criterion.

Interestingly, SSI penalizes elderly couples for living together. If both husband and wife are eligible for SSI and live in the same household, they are classified as a single assistance unit. Thus, because of assumed shared shelter and maintenance costs, couples receive less than two eligible persons living apart. On the other hand, SSI provides stronger incentives for recipients to supplement their income by working than either Social Security or AFDC. In computing SSI eligibility, $20 a month of Social Security payments or other income, plus $65 of earned income and half of additional earnings must be disregarded. Social Security has a ceiling on the amount of earnings that a recipient can have without any deductions in benefits. In 1982, the maximum earnings were $4,440 for persons under 65 and $6,000 for persons 65 to 71 years old. But it has no ceiling on the earnings of recipients 72 years and over. Thus, in both SSI and Social Security, the recipients with the most limited abilities to work—the blind, disabled, and the aged 72 years and over—are provided with the greatest work incentive (Levitan, 1980).

Although SSI is a federally administered program, states have the option to provide supplementary payments to recipients whose needs are not adequately met by the federal payments. Moreover, states can select to have the federal government make the state supplemental payments for them or the states can pay the SSI recipients the state supplements directly. Thus, there are two kinds of SSI payments: federally administered and state-administered.

In 1981, 4.1 million persons received SSI payments totaling $8 billion: $6 billion from the federal government and $2 billion from state supplementation. Over half (54%) of the SSI recipients were disabled, 44% were aged and only 2% were blind. Two-thirds of all SSI beneficiaries are 60 years of age and older, including 45% of the blind and 35% of the disabled recipients. And, nine out of every ten SSI recipients, regardless of whether they are aged, blind, and disabled, receive their benefits in their own households.

Minorities account for about two-fifths of all SSI recipients: Blacks (27%), Asians (4%), and Hispanics (9%) (HHS, 1982). While only 8% of all white aged are SSI recipients, so are 29% and 25% of all Black and Hispanic elderly, respectively (Harris et al., 1981). Blacks account for 25% of the aged, 28% of the blind, and 30% of the disabled who are SSI beneficiaries (HHS, 1982).

Because SSI is designed to supplement their income, its benefits for the elderly are much lower than Social Security benefits. In fact, 70% of all aged SSI recipients also have income from Social Security. In 1980, SSI provided elderly individuals with a monthly benefit of $134 and elderly couples with a monthly benefit of $205, both of which are about 50% below the poverty levels for elderly individuals and couples. Blind individuals ($217) and couples ($313) received somewhat higher benefits, as do disabled adults ($202), couples ($258), and children ($219). But, all of these categories of SSI recipients receive benefits that are between one-fourth and one-half below poverty. Nevertheless, this supplemental income is still vital to the well-being of millions of disadvantaged minority aged and handicapped across this nation. Moreover, because SSI payments are indexed to the Consumer Price Index (CPI), they are regularly increased at the same time as are Social Security benefits.

OTHER CASH AID

Only 7% of the Black elderly receive income from the AFDC program, compared to 1% of the white aged. The AFDC income received by the Black aged is primarily for the support of grandchildren, nieces, and nephews who live with them. However, the majority of these children who are informally adopted by the Black elderly do not receive welfare (Hill, 1977, 1978). In 1979, one-third of Black families headed by women 65 years of age and older reared children who were not their own, compared to one-tenth of white families headed by elderly women (Hill, 1981). Consequently, the Black elderly continue to provide vital child care functions through the extended family network as they have done for generations.

About one-tenth of all Black elderly have income from public pensions (i.e., railroad retirement, civil service, and the Armed Forces), compared to 13% of the white aged. Moreover, 7% of the Black aged receive veterans benefits, compared to 6% of the white aged. These veterans benefits include (a) Veterans' Compensation, based on service-connected death or disability; and (b) Veterans' Pensions, which are provided on the basis of economic need in circumstances where a veteran's death or disability was not related to military service (SSA, 1981).

How much do the various sources of public and private cash assistance contribute to the total income of the minority elderly? Among families headed by the Black aged, earnings account for almost half (44%) of their total aggregate income, with Social Security contributing about one-third; SSI, 5%; and public assistance, only 2%. Poor elderly Black families however, rely on three major government programs—Social Security (63%), SSI (18%) and Public Assistance (9%)—for 90% of their aggregate income (U.S. Bureau of the Census, 1981a). Elderly Blacks who live alone or with nonrelatives depend on these three government programs—Social Security (55%), SSI (11%), and Public Assistance (1%)—for two-thirds of their total income, with earnings making up (15%). But poor Black elderly unrelated individuals rely on these three income transfers for nine-tenths of their income, with earnings accounting for only 3%. Consequently, government and private pensions contribute less than one-tenth of the total income of elderly Black families and unrelated individuals (U.S. Bureau of the Census, 1981).

PAST EFFECTS AND FUTURE PROSPECTS

To what extent have these government cash assistance programs reduced poverty among the minority aged? It appears that these programs were a major factor in the sharp reduction in the official poverty rate among Black elderly families and individuals during the 1970s. While the proportion of elderly Black individuals who were poor dropped from 75 to 59% between 1969 and 1979, the proportion of elderly Black families that were poor fell from 42 to 26%. Over the same period, poverty among elderly white unrelated individuals dropped from 45 to 27%, while falling among elderly white families from 16 to 7%. Consequently, among all Black persons 65 years of age and older, the proportion that were poor fell sharply from 50 to 36%. Nevertheless, because of the disproportionate effects of spiraling inflation and periodic recessions on the minority aged, the *number* of poor Black aged increased from 689,000 to 716,000 over that decade, while the number of poor white aged fell steeply from 4.1 to 2.8 million between 1969 and 1979. In short, while the proportion of all Black elderly that were poor declined during the 1970s, the number of poor Black aged rose.

The simultaneous effects of inflation and recession also increased the need for the minority aged to supplement their cash income with in-kind government supports. Consequently, by 1979, about three-fourths of all Black aged were covered by Medicare, while one-third had Medicaid coverage. And, about one-fourth of the Black elderly received food stamps. Among Black aged who were renters, one-third lived in public housing, while one-fifth received rent subsidies (Hill, 1981).

What are the future prospects for income maintenance programs to the minority elderly? The sweeping cutbacks in income transfer programs for the poor passed by Congress in 1981 make the short-term outlook for the minority elderly rather bleak.

When the Reagan Administration launched its economic recovery plan in January 1981, it promised that programs for the elderly, most especially Social Security, would be spared from the sharp cuts in social programs. However, by the spring, President Reagan proposed reductions in Social Security that were so deep and pervasive that the public outcry forced him to withdraw some of his proposals and to establish a commission to study the problem of financing the Social Security Trust Fund.

Nevertheless, the president was successful in getting Congress to enact legislation that reduced Social Security payments sharply in a wide range of areas: parent benefits, student benefits, burial benefits, and, most important of all, in the Social Security minimum. Previously, a mother was eligible for benefits if she was caring for a child who was receiving survivor's and dependent's benefits and who was under the age of 18. But the new legislation provides that the parent benefit is available only until the child is 16 or is disabled. Formerly, students were entitled to survivor's and dependent's benefits until age 18 if they were in high school or until age 16 if they were not. Moreover, they could receive benefits until age 22 if they were full-time college students. Now, however, legislation enacted in 1981 will gradually phase out the college student benefit by April 1985 through a 25% yearly reduction that started in September 1982. Within this period, eligible students will not receive benefits during summer months and will not be eligible for any future benefit increases to which other beneficiaries are entitled. Recent legislation also eliminated the $255 lump sum death benefit for all workers who die without leaving a surviving spouse or a dependent child.

Furthermore, while existing law provided that the age at which no ceiling would be placed on the earnings of Social Security recipients would be lowered from 72 to 70 in 1982, Congress has now deferred the lowering of the age until 1983.

Yet, the most severe cut, especially for poor and minority elderly, was the elimination of the Social Security minimum. In fact, in its haste to accommodate the President's request, Congress eliminated the minimum in August 1981 for current as well as future retirees. Because of widespread public opposition, however, Congress reversed itself in December 1981 by restoring it for current retirees, but eliminating it for future retirees. This minimum, which averaged about $122 a month, was vital to the well-being of minority aged who worked most of their lives in noncovered jobs or in covered employment at low wages. Henceforth, all low-wage persons retiring after 1981 will receive only the monthly payment that their earning record indicates, regardless of how far below the minimum it falls.

During the decade of the 1980s, the minority elderly also will be affected negatively by cutbacks in programs other than Social Security. For example, Congress's increase in the Medicare deductible (from $228 to $260) automatically raises the coinsurance that a patient must pay for hospital costs, because the coinsurance is always pegged at one-fourth of the deductible. The Reagan Administration's budget for FY 1983 also has a number of reductions that will impact the poor and minority aged harshly. One proposal is that fuel aid be counted as income in determining food stamp allotments. If enacted, this law might have a devastating impact on some elderly families. For example, an elderly couple receiving $425 a month (or $5,100 a year) is now eligible for $312 in food stamps annually. This proposal would reduce the food stamp allotment to $106. But, if the couple was also receiving $32 a month in low-income energy assistance, food stamps would be eliminated entirely.

The administration also proposes to phase out the Lower-Income Rental Assistance Program, more popularly known as "Section 8," beginning in 1983. This subsidized housing program has been an important vehicle for low-income and minority aged in need of adequate and affordable housing. It is proposed that the housing vouchers averaging about $1,800 a year be alloted to low-income persons and families in the future to permit them to seek housing on their own. Because the housing subsidy covered 75% of the rental costs of low-income persons, averaging about $3,000 a year, it is clear that most poor and minority aged would not be able to obtain adequate, affordable housing with the vouchers.

The minority elderly will also be disproportionately affected by cuts in a wide range of services to the aged. The abolishing of the Community Services Administration (the successor to OEO), in conjunction with the consolidation of many social services into block grants, will reduce sharply, in a number of areas across the nation, such services as Meals-on-Wheels, transportation, senior citizen centers, homemaker services, and nutrition programs. Reductions in the budget of the Legal Services Corporations will also diminish important legal assistance to the minority aged. And, if the administration is successful in turning over responsibility for food stamps and other income transfer programs to the states, past experience with block grants clearly indicates that those funds will not be targeted adequately to those most in need: the poor, aged, handicapped, and minorities. Apparently, the significant economic gains of the minority elderly in the 1960s and 1970s will be seriously eroded during the 1980s.

NOTES

1. Because reports by the Social Security Administration do not provide data separately for Hispanics, our data on Hispanic participation in government cash assistance programs come from Harris and Associates (1981).

2. Our data on the participation of Asians in Social Security programs are based on the data for "others" in the reports. Because this group refers to "non-Black, nonwhites," who are overwhelmingly Asian-Americans with only relatively few American Indians, we refer to these "other nonwhites" as Asians. Hispanics, on the other hand, are not separated from "whites" in the Social Security Administration statistical reports.

REFERENCES

Cuellar, Jose B., & Weeks, John. *Minority elderly Americans: The assessment of needs and equitable receipts of public benefits as a prototype for area agencies on aging.* San Diego, CA: Allied Home Health Association,July 1980.

Grad, Susan, and Foster, Karen. Income of the population aged 55 and older, 1976, *Social Security Bulletin*, July 1979, 42 (7), 16-25.

Guttman, David. *Perspective on equitable share in public benefits by the minority elderly.* Washington, DC: Catholic University of America, 1980.

Harris, Louis, et al. *The myth and reality of aging in America*, Washington, DC: National Council on the Aging, 1974.

Harris, Louis, et al. *Aging in the eighties: America in transition.* Washington, DC: National Council on the Aging, 1981.

Hill, Robert B. A profile of the Black aged. In *Minority Aged in America.* Ann Arbor: Institute of Gerontology, University of Michigan—Wayne State University, Occasional Papers in Gerontology, 1972.

Hill, Robert B. *Informal adoption among Black families.* Washington, DC: National Urban League Research Department, 1977.

Hill, Robert B. A demographic profile of the Black elderly. *Aging.* September-October 1978, 287-288, 2-9.

Hill, Robert B. *The myth of income cushions for Blacks.* Washington, DC: National Urban League Research Department, 1980.

Hill, Robert B. *Economic policies and Black progress: Myths and realities.* Washington, DC: National Urban League Research Department, 1981.

Jackson, Jacquelyne. *Minorities and Aging.* Belmont, CA: Wadsworth.

Levitan, Sar A. *Programs in Aid of the Poor for the 1980's.* Baltimore, MD: Johns Hopkins University Press, 1980.

Lingg, Barbara A. Social security benefits of female retired workers and two-worker couples. *Social Security Bulletin,* 1982, 45 (2), 3-24.

President's Commission of Pension Policy (PCOPP). *Coming of age: Toward a national retirement income policy.* Washington, DC, February 26, 1981.

Social Security Administration (SSA). Income and resources of the elderly in 1978. *Social Security Bulletin,* December 1981, 44 (12).

University of the District of Columbia, Institute of Gerontology and Fund for Neighborhood Development (UDC). *Supplemental Security Income: Report on program effectiveness.* Washington, DC: UDC, 1978.

U.S. Bureau of the Census. Characteristics of the populations below the poverty level: 1979. *Current population reports,* Series P-60, No. 130, 1980. (a)

U.S. Bureau of the Census. Characteristics of households receiving noncash benefits: 1979. *Current population reports,* Series P-23, No. 110, 1980. (b)

U.S. Bureau of the Census. Money income of families and persons in the U.S.: 1979. *Current population reports,* Series P-60, No. 129, 1981. (a)

U.S. Bureau of the Census. Characteristics of households receiving noncash benefits: 1980. *Current population reports,* Series P-60, No. 128, 1981. (b)

U.S. Commission of Civil Rights. *Providing services to the minority elderly: New programs, old problems.* Washington, DC, November 1981.

U.S. Department of Health and Human Services (HHS). Disabled and nondisabled adults. *Disability survey 1972,* Washington, DC: Social Security Administration, Office of Research and Statistics, Research Report No. 56, April 1981. (a)

U.S. Department of Health and Human Services. Social Security in review. *Social Security Bulletin,* December 1981, (12). (b)

U.S. Department of Health and Human Services, Annual statistical supplement, 1980. *Social Security Bulletin,* Washington, DC, Social Security Administration, 1982.

U.S. Joint Economic Committee. Income transfer programs: How they tax the poor. *Studies in Public Welfare,* Paper No. 4, December 1972.

U.S. Joint Economic Committee. The Family, poverty and welfare programs: Household patterns and government policies. *Studies in Public Welfare,* Paper No. 12 (Part II) December 1973.

U.S. Senate, Special Committee in Aging. The multiple hazards of age and race: The situation of aged blacks in the U.S. Appendix 2, 1971.

17

Minority Decision-Making, Accessibility, and Resource Utilization in the Provision of Services
Urban-Rural Differences

ELENA M. BASTIDA

The recent near-explosion of literature on or about old age has prompted many questions about aging among minority groups, with results from these investigations pointing to the low participation of these populations in aging programs. Many of the specific problems of these groups as well as recommendations for alleviating them have been written about in depth (e.g., Bell, Kasschau, & Zellman, 1976; Colen, 1980; Gallegos, 1979; German, Shapiro, Chase, & Vollmer, 1978a, b; Jackson, 1979; 1980; Murdock & Schwartz, 1979; Newton, 1980; Stanford, 1978; Valle, 1978). It appears that what is lacking is not a new list of barriers and recommendations but a better understanding of how access to resources and privileges that come with it varies depending upon the community and the region in which aging minorities reside.

In discussing the social context in which the aging minority interacts and in which aging programs exist, it becomes important to examine how the ethnic group's level of access to resources varies with the structural characteristics of the community of residence. The community surrounding the minority elderly may be a place in which there is concern or indifference for their quality of life; a place in which decision-making boards and councils are opened to their participation or covertly discriminatory; and a place where they interact freely with the majority or are alienated. Put simply, there is a phenomenon of community context that has consequences for the status of the aged minorities. However, community and regional structures as significant analytical variables impacting on the resources available to these populations have not been systematically addressed in the gerontological literature.

AUTHOR'S NOTE: Partial support for the research reported in this chapter was provided by Administration on Aging Grant 0090-AR-2077.

In the past, research on the minority elderly has focused on individual characteristics—for example, income, health, and education (e.g., Eve & Freidsam, 1979, Faulkner, 1975; Hernandez, Estrada, & Alvirez, 1973; Hill, 1978; Jackson, 1978; Lambing, 1972a, b; Tallmer, 1977, Wu, 1975)—and on specifying distinct cultural barriers, such as language, health practices, attitudes, and normative expectations (e.g., Cantor, Rosenthal, & Wilker, 1979; Carp, 1970; Hunter, Linn, & Pratt, 1979; Jackson, 1978; Morse, 1976; Robinson, 1976; Seelbach & Sauer, 1977; Torres-Gil, 1977). Lately, emphasis has been given to the differential impact of institutionalized victimization and discrimination on the lives of these elderly (Jackson, 1980). In fact, Jackson observes that the chief social difference between minority and majority aged is that the former are subjected to and affected by institutionalized victimization. She writes:

> Thus, in the future, it would be feasible for researchers interested in differences between minority and majority aged persons to concentrate heavily upon investigations not of racial differences per se but of racism and sexism. For instance, if research findings show that aged Blacks are less likely than aged Whites to use senior citizens' centers, it would be fruitful to investigate the *environmental warmth* present in those centers as they relate to each group of different races [1980, p. 11, emphasis ours].

In this chapter we heed Jackson's recommendations and pursue those environmental factors that directly or indirectly impinge upon the community context ("environmental warmth") in which aging minorities interact.

Despite the frequency with which allusions to regional and within-group differences have been made in the gerontological literature (Moore, 1971a, b; Harbert & Ginsberg, 1979; Jackson, 1980), these distinctions usually have been based on assumed cultural variations, as one would expect to exist between the rural and urban way of life, rather than on accessibility of power resources contingent upon structural variations. Thus Moore (1971b) suggests differences between the way of life of older Mexicans living in the rural Southwest and that of their urban counterparts in Los Angeles. Within-class variations have been indicated by Lambing (1972b) and Stanford (1981) to exist between the lifestyles of older Blacks living in suburbia and of those in central cities. Jackson (1980) tactily touches upon the significance of community context when she notes the extensive involvement of elderly Blacks in the economic and social activities of Tuskegee, Alabama, where the majority of residents are Black.

It is our objective to examine the impact of regional and community structural characteristics on the control of accessibility to community resources among elderly Hispanics and Blacks residing in small towns, rural areas, and a major metropolitan area in the lower Midwest. In pursuing this line of inquiry, we have followed a conflict theory perspective in assuming that community resources are distributed as a function of power rather than as a function of individual abilities.

A test is made here of the proposition that the effect of accessibility on utilization of community resources by the minority elderly is mediated through increased control in the allocation of resources by the minority group, which is itself dependent on structural conditions. It was hypothesized that

(1) the greater the accessibility the higher the utilization of services;
(2) the higher the utilization of services, the greater the control in the allocation of resources by the minority group; and,
(3) the greater the control in the allocation of resources, the higher the concentration of the minority group within the community.

METHOD

Data were collected from two sources. Face-to-face structured interviews were conducted with 250 Blacks and Hispanics aged 60 and over residing in two metropolitan counties and three nonmetropolitan counties and from extensive participant observation. The latter consisted of attending all formally organized bodies in which decision-making activities involving the elderly minorities took place (e.g., board meetings of health agencies, Area Agencies on Aging, senior councils, community forums, and the like). A total of 26 agencies were investigated and 102 meetings attended by either the principal investigator or one of the two research assistants in the projects.

The primary sampling objective was to obtain a proportionate representation of older persons from the largest minority group within each sampling unit. No effort was made to obtain ethnic groups of comparable sizes because the research design did not require the making of across-group comparisons. The design, however, did require respondents to vary in urban-rural residence, membership to include representatives of two different minority groups, and specified degrees of minority concentration in places of residence. Based upon these requirements, the five counties selected had the following characteristics:

(1) Each county had at least 5% concentration of either Black or Hispanic residents;
(2) One county had at least a 70% concentration of rural residents;
(3) Two counties had at least a 65% concentration of urban nonmetropolitan residents;
(4) Two counties had at least a 90% concentration of metropolitan residents.

Our insistence in sampling from the largest minority group only in each county reflects the assumption that the larger the concentration of one group, the more balanced the power exchange between the group and the majority. Thus, in line with the above criteria, the five counties selected for sampling include:

(1) Two counties where Hispanics represented 15 and 13% of the population respectively, one of which was determined to be a rural county (100% rural) and the other urban nonmetropolitan county (77% urban). Herein these are referred to as the "western counties." They are located on the western perimeters of the region and are 180 miles away from the nearest metropolitan area.

(2) One county located on the eastern perimeter of the region within a 60-mile radius of three metropolitan areas is herein referred to as the "eastern county." This is an urban nonmetropolitan county (65.6% urban) with a 6% Black population.

(3) Two counties contained within a large metropolitan area of over one million people, herein referred to as the "metropolitan counties," where Blacks and Hispanics together represented 29% and 20% of the population.

Consequently, the sample included 67 Hispanics residing in the western counties, 35 Blacks from the eastern counties, and 148 Blacks and Hispanics from the metropolitan counties. The subsamples were drawn by utilizing purposive sampling techniques. Screening interviews were used to identify persons in the initial sample (i.e., matched by ethnicity and age). Two subsamples were established, a metropolitan sample consisting of 148 respondents and a rural subsample of 102 respondents. We decided to combine the rural and nonmetropolitan subsamples together, for among the latter over 50% were rural residents.

County data were abstracted from the 1977 City and County Data Book (U.S. Department of Commerce) on the demographic, economic, and political characteristics of the five counties containing the sampled population.

At the resident level, the variable of interest was utilization of community resources, indexed by the respondents' participation in service programs and utilization of other community resources (for a complete listing, the reader is referred to Appendix 17-A). Respondents were asked eight questions for each community resource listed. Utilization was first dichotomized into Yes (1) or No (0) response. If yes, frequency was measured by asking: "How frequently do you use the resource in question?" Response choices of every day, once a week, less than once a week, once every two weeks, once a month, less than once per month were offered. Scores of 5, 4, 3, 2, and 1 were assigned respectively for each of the choices. A summed score was obtained for resource utilization with a range from 22 to 0 points possible. A summed score was obtained for frequency with a range of 110 to 0 points possible. Two additional resources were included as part of the "other" category. Moreover, respondents were asked to identify what agency or program provided the service for them. This allowed researchers to compare quantitative and qualitative data during various stages for the analysis. Other items included were, "Who calls for assistance?" "Who do they go with, or who takes them, to receive assistance/support?" "How do they get there?" "How did they find out?" and finally, "How satisfied were they with the assistance/ service provided by the program or agency?"

At the community level, we examined accessibility by soliciting information from service providers, agency directors, and subjects. For example, information was sought on the extent to which the participation of the minority elderly was invited or discouraged with regard to their involvement in aging programs and decision-making activities concerning the provision and direction of services. Subjects were asked if they had been invited to participate in programs, whether or not they had been asked or elected to serve on committees and boards, whether or not they had any input in decision-making activities, and if any consideration had been given to satisfy their ethnic requests, such as for culturally syntonic foods and festivities.

At the county level, four variables were employed to represent major structural dimensions underlying the five counties under study. The variables were percentage of ethnic minorities, median income, percentage of urban population, and percentage of population voting for the Democratic party. The latter were selected to correspond to four county dimensions, identified by an earlier study to represent significant dimensions underlying the social structure of these counties (Gibbs & Hughes, 1977). The four structural dimensions and the specific variable used to represent them are heterogeneity, socioeconomic status, social differentiation, and political orientation.

Control of resources was measured by the extent to which minorities were directly employed, or served in a related capacity, in the direction, supervision, and provision of community services. Scores of 3, 2, and 1 were assigned respectively to direction, supervision, and provision for each minority person in a relevant agency/program. Summated scores were obtained for each agency or program, actual scores ranged from 0 (no minority participation in either direction, supervision, or provision) to 31. For the purposes of illustrating our method of scoring, the score of 31, for example, was obtained as follows: 4 board members (direction), 12 points; plus 4 supervisors, 8 points; and 11 providers, 11 points. Whenever dictated by analytical requirement, agency scores were summated for a given area and/or county.

FINDINGS

The data supported the first hypothesis, which specified that utilization of services is higher in communities where greater effort is made to invite the participation of elderly minorities in aging programs. This is evidenced in that residents of the metropolitan counties—where there were a greater number of programs designed to attract the elderly minorities, and where more elderly minorities served on advisory boards and special committees—had higher utilization rates than their counterparts residing in nonmetropolitan areas. As reported in Table 17-1, 45% of the metropolitan county residents had high utilization rates (utilization of two or more services at least twice a week) compared to only 11% of the small-town residents. No resident from the rural counties scored high on utilization, with metropolitan residents having the highest utilization rates.

Obviously, differences in the utilization of services could be reflective of differences in the personal characteristics of metropolitan residents rather than due to effects produced by enhanced involvement or the control of resources. Indeed, the data indicate that metropolitan residents ranked considerably higher than those in rural areas on several characteristics that have been suggested may be associated with higher utilization rates. Metropolitan residents, for example, had higher educational attainment, higher income, were retired from somewhat more prestigious occupations (e.g., twice as many had been employed as professionals) and perceived themselves to be in better health than did persons residing in rural areas.

To determine whether or not they had any significant influence, the effects of age, education, income, and perceived health status were partialled out of the relationship between accessibility to power resources and utiliza-

TABLE 17-1 Percentage Distribution of Service Utilization of Aged Minorities in Urban and Rural Communities

Utilization Scores	Metropolitan (N = 148)	Nonmetropolitan (N = 102)
Low	20	67
Medium	35	22
High	45	11*
	100	100

Differences significant at p = .05 level

*This figure indicates high utilization scores for small town residents only. No rural resident scored high on this category.

TABLE 17-2 Association Between Service Utilization and Accessibility Controlling For Age, Educational Attainment, Income and Perceived Health Status (Pearson's r)

Variables
Accessibility and Utilization

Control Variables	Partial Correlation Coefficients
Age	.42
Education	.40
Income	.43
Perceived health status	.43
Simultaneous control on all personal contacts*	.40 (beta weight)

*stepwise regression analysis

tion of services. The initial relationship between these two variables (r = .43) was slightly diminished when controlling on each of these factors. Controlling on education had the sharpest impact on the relationship, but it dropped only from r = .43 to .40. Consequently, controlling for these several variables not only did not reduce the association to statistical insignificance, it had virtually no impact on the observed relationship.

CONTROL IN THE ALLOCATION OF RESOURCES

The findings reported above on the association of accessibility to power resources and utilization of services is consistent with our hypothesis that increased effort by the community to attract minority participation contributes to higher rates in utilization of services. But the question remains as to the specific mechanism through which accessibility is mediated. A test of the second hypothesis revealed a strong association between utilization of services and control in allocation of resources by the minority group (r = .51). Indeed, three-fifths (59%) of those living in metropolitan areas indicated that they had representatives of their respective groups involved in the direction, supervision, and provision of community resources allocated to the elderly; 40% of the metropolitan residents also reported knowing of "some official in the city hall" of their own group whom they perceived as a possible source of assistance in case of special need. The need most frequently cited as necessitating requests for assistance was a reduction in funding for programs frequently used by respondents. This, they thought, was a constant source of instability (these data were collected during 1979 and 1980; therefore, it does not reflect the more severe funding conditions of the 1982 federal budget). Again, the findings may reflect a selectivity that characterizes individual rather than structural effects. Consequently, age, income, education, and perceived health status were controlled to determine

TABLE 17-3   **Association Between Control in the Allocation of Resources and Concentration of Minorities Controlling for Socioeconomic Status, Social Differentiation, and Political Orientation* (Pearson's r)**

Variables	*Correlation Coefficients*
Allocation control and minority concentration	.38
Control Variables	*Partial Correlation Coefficients*
Socioeconomic Status	.36
Social Differentiation	.35
Political Orientation	.32
Simultaneous Control on all three variables**	.30 (beta weight)

*county level data
**stepwise regression analysis

whether or not their influence was statistically significant. They were found to have minimal impact on the relationship ($r = .51$) that was obtained between utilization of services and control in the allocation of resources.

The third hypothesis, that control in the allocation of resources is associated with the concentration of minorities in the community, also was supported. While a significantly larger proportion of minorities reside in the metropolitan counties (29% and 20% respectively) as compared to the nonmetropolitan counties, again the nonmetropolitan residents had the lowest scores on resource allocation. The hypothesis was further tested by controlling on the socioeconomic, social differentiation, and political orientation of the county to determine their influence on the relationship between minority concentration and control of resources. The initial relationship between these two variables ($r = .38$) was only slightly diminished when examining each control variable individually, or on all three simultaneously. Controlling for the county's political orientation had the sharpest impact on the relationship (dropping it from $r = .38$ to $.32$), with socioeconomic status and differentiation also impacting on the association (dropping it from $r = .38$ to $.36$ and $.35$ respectively). Nevertheless, the relationship remained significant after taking into account each control variable.

SUMMARY AND DISCUSSION

The data presented here are consistent with the hypotheses in that increased control of resources by the minority group facilitates the utilization of community services by its elderly. A large proportion of respondents with high rates of utilization lived in communities where their respective minority group had a greater share in the distribution of community resources. This finding could not be explained away by differences in age, income, education, or health status of persons residing in communities with a greater share in the control of resources.

Contrary to expectation, it is not only the size of the minority group, but the joint impact of political orientation and socioeconomic status that influences the differential control in resource allocation. Here, as already noted, the degree of political autonomy and unity manifested by the group are critical. However, it is important to emphasize that access to county, state, and federal resources is based on a delicate balance of power between the minority group and representatives of other contending groups. We would like to further elaborate on this point, for it was clearly the political situation (political imbalance of power) that was significant in the nonmetropolitan counties at the time of the study.

The low utilization of services found among the nonmetropolitan respondents appears to have been affected by a gradual loss of power in the allocation of resources, incurred by the minority groups in two of the three counties examined. Indeed, it appears that the reality of minority gains in the distribution of resources is one that is constantly threatened by the delicate balance of power obtained between minority group advocates and the various majority political factions. Elderly minority residents of one of the nonmetropolitan counties were clearly affected by this critical balance of power, for during the mid-1970s they had enjoyed a greater accessibility to community resources than was available to them during the spring of 1980. During the earlier period, a minority service provider was able to obtain the cooperation of board members in designing programs to meet the special needs of elderly minorities. Although no quantifiable data were gathered, we were repeatedly told by respondents how much they had enjoyed their earlier participation in those programs. Their account was corroborated by agency personnel who claimed that "things are no longer the same and obviously we were unable to sustain their participation in our programs."

Upon a closer examination of the "utilization problem," as it was phrased by agency personnel, some critical situational antecedents surfaced. For instance, during the tenure of the minority provider, various groups of older majority persons expressed their dissatisfaction with the amount of attention the elderly minorities received. Demands were made to curtail some of their privileges, such as that of an ethnic evening once a week at the Senior Center. Eventually, upon the resignation of the provider, these programs gradually collapsed and subsequent requests by minority advocates to reinstate the ethnic evening were denied.

The above incident points to the degree that political interest groups are critical in promoting or deterring accessibility and utilization of community resources. It also reveals the rather unstable character of community power relations and how minority aging programs are directly affected by their outcomes. In fact, a very similar political atmosphere prevailed in the eastern nonmetropolitan county when a meal site catering to elderly Blacks was forced to close down upon condemnation of the building by city authorities. The request made by elderly Blacks to find another locality was denied by the planning board. Instead, they were informed that the meal site would not reopen and were invited to join the downtown site. Again, this incident marked a decrease in the utilization of services by this group of elderly who lost in the power struggle that ensued among various community interest groups.

It appears that the issue of structural effects must be approached through a consideration of the degree to which younger minority members are capable to negotiate favorable outcomes for their group. Here, structural effects are important in determining the type of selection that operates in migration to metropolitan areas. A brief examination of resources available to younger minorities in the three different types of settings studied indicates that the opportunities for well-educated younger minorities are greater in the metropolitan counties where the social differentiation is greatest. Given the very low socioeconomic status of older minorities in the rural areas studied—where not one of the elderly respondents owned land, or businesses, or had held occupations of high prestige—it was indeed difficult for the elderly parents in these areas to retain their achievement-oriented children. Although, in general, the outmigration of young people from the midwestern states is high, the latter appears to affect disproportionately the minority population by selectively depriving it of its better educated and more politically active youth, who, in turn, are the ones most likely to advocate successfully on behalf of the elderly.

In contrast, the metropolitan counties studied revealed a relatively large proportion of younger minorities, who not only served as providers and in advisory capacities, but who were skillful in negotiating a better allocation of community resources for their elders. This is a major mediating factor on the utilization of services by the target population, for presently this is, generally speaking, a population with low educational and economic attainments. Therefore, the better educated younger members are a most important human capital resource. Older minority persons in the metropolitan areas are the ones most likely to benefit from the power leverage exercised by the more politically active younger members. Through their advocacy, community resources usually are more equitably distributed among the older minorities. Hence, in studying their accessibility to community resources and services utilization, it becomes important to explore further the differential impact of structural effects on the distribution of resources affecting the quality of life of elderly minorities. These findings point to the significant contribution of younger cohorts to a more equitable allocation of resources. It also indicates that the presence or absence of younger, better educated, and politically active minorities depends to a large extent on the structural differentiation of the community of residence.

While there are important social policy implications to be drawn from our analysis, extensive review of our qualitative data indicate that a critical issue undermining a more equitable distribution of resources for the minority elderly is political behavior especially as it relates to grassroots politics. Whether it is a group or individual behavior, the primary objective of political action is to maintain or attain some degree of control over one's life and that of the collectivity. To the extent that existing community politics remain unavailable and/or incongruent with needs of this population, we can expect a growing feeling of powerlessness among them. This prospect seems entirely negative in its dimensions, if no modifications in the present formal and informal political systems are forthcoming. We will briefly address some possible modifications that could lead to greater community involvement by the elderly.

Given our present political concern with the national deficit and the concurrent trimming of the federal budget, the informal mechanisms of political control generated by the younger cohorts may become less viable as their efforts become either more dispersed or more concentrated on maintaining earlier political gains. Such a condition may become especially acute since in this particular climate any political action that seeks to attain rather than to maintain control may be considered unrealistic. Thus the elderly may stand to lose if younger advocates find it necessary to divert their attention to other issues.

While there are certainly massive pressures that could change traditional relationships within minority communities, historically these institutional arrangements have shown a remarkable adaptive capacity to social change. An important aspect of political behavior within the community is the continuity of roles, relationships, and mutual cooperation. Thus it may be to the collective's advantage, if the younger more politically active cohorts were to begin delegating more political responsibilities on the elderly.

Our data indicate that in the metropolitan counties where the younger cohorts had become more involved in all aspects of resource allocations to the elderly, the latter were eager to be given the opportunity to participate in decision-making activities, but found the younger providers reluctant in accepting their involvement. Generally speaking, there is a tendency among middle-aged and younger advocates and providers to perceive the minority elderly as politically unresponsive. While, indeed, this population tends to have low rates of electoral behavior and unwillingness to join large formal associations, many, if given the opportunity, are eager to participate at the grassroots level. Most of our metropolitan respondents were anxious to take part in decision-making processes whose outcomes would have impinged upon the quality of their lives, and they resented the now powerful younger providers and/or decision makers for adopting a caring but nonetheless paternalistic attitude toward them.

In short, while not seeking statewide and national political involvement, most minority elderly would welcome the opportunity to become active on educational and housing committees and various service-oriented, church-related, and recreational associations within the community. As a result of the traditional modes of behavior into which most were socialized, they tend to be nonaggressive and softspoken in their demands, patiently waiting to receive opportunities rather than to fight for them. This attitude should not be interpreted erroneously as unawareness, lack of interest, or unwillingness to change. Thus, it remains for the more engaging advocates to find alternative modes of political behavior that will assist in broadening the base of this population's political functions.

We suggest the creation and recruitment of elderly minorities to formally organized bodies such as police relations boards, and other committees concerned with high crime rates, housing issues, and the like. However, it is important to realize that for this recruitment to be successful, arrangements must be made in advance in order to secure their attendance (e.g., transportation and so on).

Beyond grassroots activities, structural conditions have strong implications for the control and allocation of community resources. Elderly minorities who reside in communities where the size of their group is small and the geographic mobility of the young is high are most likely to be adversely affected in the allocation of resources. These structural conditions are usually indicative of operant economic pressure that again may handicap the political mobilization of the old; it is usually when resources are limited that competition among groups intensifies. Many of our older respondents felt threatened by such conditions and would not contend for power, thus heightening their sense of political powerlessness.

In situations such as the above, mandates that include wide community participation in such organizations as health agencies, legal services, and mental health boards are usually overlooked or manipulated by more powerful groups by selecting last-minute members as token representation, scheduling meetings in remote areas, or by same-day notices announcing meetings. While it is usually difficult to deal with such unscrupulous behavior, the minority elderly will stand to gain if they become politically alert about these practices and openly articulate their illegality. In such incidents, younger advocates and providers can indeed contribute to their political development by assisting the elderly in articulating their problems and demands. We emphasize the difference between providing assistance in dealing with social and political issues and paternalization.

In short, as communities experience greater limitations in the amount of social resources at their disposal and as more groups vie for fewer resources, the older minorities may find younger cohorts engaged in other political actions and thus unable to advocate on their behalf. As federal and state budgets are trimmed, older minorities may find that only through organized political action of their own can they maintain resources already allocated to them and attain access to others needed. Younger cohorts of advocates and providers can facilitate this process by aiding in the creation of grassroots political organizations, learning to delegate political responsibilities on the elderly, providing greater accessibility to decision-making processes, and in engaging the elderly at all levels of community politics.

APPENDIX 17-A

Visiting Nurse
Information and Referral
Reduced Taxes
Senior Center

Meals-on-wheels
Congregate Meals
Public Housing
Personal Care
Health Care
   (a) Medical Screening
   (b) Visits to Physicians
   (c) Visits to Clinics
   (d) Therapy
Prescription Plan
Tax Preparation
Special Adult Education
Transportation (Title III)
Public Transportation
Discounts (Movies, Public Function, Others)
Housekeeping
Home Repairs
Counseling
Recreational
Library
Other Community Resources (e.g., Use of Facilities)

REFERENCES

Bell, Duran, Kasschau, Patricia, & Zellman, Gail. *Delivering services to the elderly members of minority groups: A critical review of the literature.* Santa Monica, CA: Rand, 1976.

Cantor, Marjorie H., Rosenthal, Karen, & Wilker, Louis. Social and family relationships of Black aged women in New York City. *Journal of Minority Aging,* 1979, 4, 50-61.

Carp, Frances M. Communicating with elderly Mexican-Americans. *Gerontologist,* 1970, 10, 126-34.

Colen, John. Social service research and the minority aged: An old issue, a new approach. Paper presented at the 33rd Annual Meeting of the Gerontological Society of America, San Diego, 1980.

Eve, Susan B., & Friedsam, Hiram. Ethnic differences in the use of health care services among older Texans. *Journal of Minority Aging,* 1979, 4, 62-75.

Faulkner, Audrey O. Life strengths and life stresses: Explorations in the measurement of the mental health of the Black aged. *American Journal of Orthopsychiatry,* 1975, 45, 102-10.

Gallegos, Daniel. To Integrate or not to integrate? Elderly minority participation in community programs. Paper presented at the 32nd Annual meeting of the Gerontological Society of America, Washington, DC, 1979.

German, Pearl S., Shapiro, Sam, Chase, Gary A., & Vollmer, Mary. Health care of the elderly in a changing inner city community. *Black Aging,* 1978, 3, 143-46. (a)

German, Pearl S., Shapiro, Sam, Chase, Gary A. & Vollmer, Mary. Health care of the elderly in medically disadvantaged populations. *Gerontologist,* 1978, 18, 547-55. (b)

Harbert, Anita J. & Ginsberg, Leon H. *Human services for older adults: Concepts and skills.* Belmont, CA: Wadsworth, 1979.

Hernandez, Jose, Estrada, L., & Alvirez, D. Census data and the problem of conceptually defining the Mexican-American population. *Social Science Quarterly,* 1973, 53, 671-87.

Hill, Robert B. A demographic profile of the Black elderly. *Aging Numbers,* 1978, 287-288, 2-9.

Hunter, K., Linn, M. W., & Pratt, T. C. Minority women's attitudes about aging. *Experimental Aging Research,* 1979, 5, 95-108.

Jackson, Jacquelyne J. Special health problems of aged blacks. *Aging Numbers,* 1978, 287-288, 15-20.

Jackson, Jacquelyne J. *Minorities and aging.* Belmont, CA: Wadsworth, 1980.

Jackson, Jacquelyne J., & Walls, Bertram E. Aging patterns in Black families. In A. J. Lichtman & J. R. Challinor (Eds.), *Kin and communities, families in America.* Washington, DC: Smithsonian Institution Press, 1979.

Lambing, Mary L. Social class living patterns of retired Negroes. *Gerontologist,* 1972, 12, 285-88. (a)

Lambing, Mary L. Leisure-time pursuits among retired Blacks by social status. *Gerontologist,* 1972, 12, 363-67. (b)

Moore, Joan W. Situational factors affecting minority aging. *Gerontologist,* 1971, 6, (1, part 2): 88-93a. (a)

Moore, Joan W. Mexican Americans. *Gerontologist,* 1971, 11 (1, part 2), 30-35. (b)

Morse, Dean W. Aging in the ghetto: Themes expressed by older Black men and women living in a northern industrial city. *Industrial Gerontology,* 1976, 3, 1-10.

Murdock. Steve H., & Schwartz, Donald F. Family structure and the use of agency services: An examination of patterns among elderly Native Americans. *Gerontologist,* 1978, 18, 475-481.

Newton, Frank Cota-Robles. Issues in research and service delivery among Mexican American elderly: A concise statement with recommendations. *Gerontologist,* 1980, 20 (2), 208-214.

Robinson, James H. Migrant labor and minority communities: Class, ethnicity, age, and gender as social barriers to health care. *Journal of Health, Politics and Law,* 1976-1977, 514-522.

Seelbach, Wayne C., & Sauer, William J. Filial responsibility expectations and morale among aged parents. *Gerontologist,* 1977, 17, 492-499.

Stanford, E. P. *The Elder Black.* San Diego: Campanile Press, 1978.

Stanford, E. P. Paper presented to the Mid America Congress on Aging, Kansas City, 1981.

Tallmer, Margot. Some factors in the education of older members of minority groups. *Journal of Geriatric Psychiatry,* 1977, 10, 890-98.

Torres-Gil, Fernando, & Becerra, Rosina M. The political behavior of the Mexican-American elderly. *Gerontologist,* 1977, 17, 392-399.

U.S. Department of Commerce. *City and county data book.* Washington, DC: Government Printing Office, 1977.

Valle, Ramon, & Mendoza, Lydia. *The Elder Latino.* San Diego: Campanile Press, 1978.

Wu, Frances Y. Mandarin-speaking aged Chinese in the Los Angeles area. *Gerontologist,* 1975, 15, 271-275.

18

Political Involvement Among Older Members of National Minority Groups
Problems and Prospects

FERNANDO TORRES-GIL

The development of social policies for older persons in the United States is a highly politicized process involving advocacy, special interest groups, lobbying, and money, all leading toward influence with elected and appointed officials. In the past decade there has been a growing awareness of the problems confronting elderly Americans. Some of these problems are being addressed by organizations that advocate and lobby for legislation specific to age-related issues, such as the American Association of Retired Persons/National Retired Teachers Association (AARP/NRTA), National Council of Aging, and the Grey Panthers. These groups have not only created increased public knowledge of the circumstances facing the elderly, but have also promoted interest in the study of the political behavior of the aged. With increasing frequency, political scientists and sociologists are turning their attention to the study of the political attitudes and participation of older persons, as well as to such questions as the social and cultural factors influencing political behavior and the role of senior citizen's organizations within the political process.

The involvement of older persons in political activities is an evolving process that has resulted in major gains. Individuals associated with the Townsend Movement in 1933 and the McClain movement of 1948 respectively fought for old age pensions and the revision and liberalization of programs of public assistance for the aged. Through the years the elderly have developed considerable political leverage to influence legislation, funding of programs, and public attitudes related to their concerns (Puttnam, 1970; Cottrell, 1960; Holtzman, 1954; Pratt, 1974). However, the older population is changing demographically and this may significantly affect the political directions they take in the future.

Recent data (1980) indicate that an increasingly high percentage of the elderly population will consist of members of the various minority groups (U.S. Department of Health and Human Services [HHS], 1981). As minority groups become a larger portion of the overall elderly population, it can be expected that directions and issues previously pursued will change, given that minorities in the United States face some unique and relatively severe problems and circumstances (HHS, 1979). Unfortunately, existing studies of the political behavior of the elderly generally are limited to samples of white middle-class senior citizens. This research cannot be generalized to a minority elderly population. Consequently, it is of limited usefulness as a description of the political behavior of minority elders and provides little empirical basis by which future trends and patterns may be forecast accurately.

Nevertheless, it seems clear that minority elders currently are not as politically active or organized as their nonminority counterparts, although they may be more involved in other forms of community activities (see McClure, 1972). Obviously, they would have much to gain from increased political involvement. Studies have shown that minority elders are more likely to face inadequate transportation, low income, insufficient education, poor health, and substandard housing (San Diego State University, 1978; Newquist, Berger, Kahn, Martinez, & Burton, 1979). Older minorities also face barriers to the utilization of services, a lack of bilingually and biculturally sensitive services, the prohibitive location of facilities, and the lack of financial resources with which to obtain needed services (Guttman, 1980; Cuellar & Weeks, 1980). As indicated, population statistics suggest a growing potential for these individuals to become a viable political constituency. The extent to which this potential is translated into political power will depend upon key factors that influence political behavior, including these elderly's perceptions regarding the efficacy of political activism and the barriers they encounter.

INVOLVEMENT

There are a variety of political activities an older person can participate in. Involvement may range from passive to increasingly active forms. Milbrath (1965) has presented a hierarchy of political involvement that includes spectator activities (voting, discussion and opinion leadership, using buttons or stickers), transitional activities (petitioning political leaders, monetary contributions, attending political meetings), and gladiatorial participation (campaigning, active party membership, soliciting political funds, protesting, demonstrating, and office seeking and holding).

Research generally indicates that the elderly maintain a high level of political activity across the spectrum of involvement possibilities. For example, Campbell (1971) has shown that in the years 1960, 1964, and 1968, people aged 65 or over were at least as active as those 21 to 29 years of age in voting, financing parties, attending political meetings, and working in political campaigns. Other studies (Hausknecht, 1962; Riley, Johnson, & Foner, 1973; Hudson & Binstock, 1976) suggest that older people are more likely than younger individuals to volunteer time and money, to vote in elections and to follow political events through the media. Although Nie, Verba, and Kim (1974) initially found political participation to be lower among the young and old, with the highest participation rates in the middle years, when their data were corrected for educational background, it was determined that the elderly participate at the same rate as the average population. Nie's analysis revealed young people to be the true underparticipants in political activity. More recently, Brotman (1977) has found that a greater percentage of elderly voted in the 1976 presidential election than the general population. Those over 65 represented 16% of the votes in the 1976 election, about one out of every six votes. Thus, as an aggregated group, older people are active participants.

On the other hand, little is known about the active political involvement of older minority members. Observation indicates that minority elders often get involved in church activities and senior citizen clubs, and at times attempt to influence local government through active forms of participation such as demonstrating against the elimination of bus discounts and traveling to state legislatures to lobby representatives on other matters (Cuellar, 1978). However, the extent to which this activity is characteristic is largely unknown.

One study (Torres-Gil, 1976) examined participation among elderly Mexican-Americans by hypothesizing that their level of political activity would be low due to negative experiences with the American political system, the influence of Mexican political culture (which does not stress civic involvement), and exclusion by younger Hispanic activists who do not consider older persons as viable political allies. The level of political activity and sense of political efficacy was found to be generally low. Factors adversely affecting participation included fear, lack of communication, and low socioeconomic status. However, and importantly, the potential for involvement was present. Many of the older persons surveyed had been involved in political activities during their younger years as participants in strikes, protests, and picketing. They were no longer involved partly because they had not been encouraged to remain involved. Yet they remained interested and discussed political issues frequently. Torres-Gil and Becerra (1977) refer to these individuals as spectators who need only encouragement to become more involved in gladiatorial activities. Principles to guide activities designed to foster greater minority involvement will be discussed.

NATIONAL ORGANIZATIONS

On a national level, the 1971 White House Conference on Aging represented a historical watershed in the development of minority aging advocacy despite initial underrepresentation of minority groups at the conference. Prior to 1971, minority aging advocates had remained virtually unorganized and, hence, lacked visibility and influence in the formulation of national policies on aging. Owens, Torres-Gil, and Wolf (1973) and Bechill (1979) describe criticism about the "over politicizing" of this White House conference by the Nixon Administration and the apparent exclusion of groups that did not match a political "litmus" test. Black advocates for the elderly who felt they had been excluded staged a counter conference to protest the lack of attention given to minority concerns. The result was the formal creation of the National Caucus on Black Aged organized to advocate and represent the Black elderly. Subsequently, pressure exerted by Hispanics, Asians, and Native Americans led to the creation of nationally based organizations, including the National Indian Council on Aging, the National Hispanic Council on Aging, the Asociación Nacional Pro Personas Mayores, and the National Pacific/Asian Resource Center on Aging. These organizations have been effective in promoting the recruitment and training of minorities in the field of aging, increasing the number of minorities on governmental peer review panels, influencing the development of legislation and regulations affecting minorities, and generally representing the needs of the minority elderly.

MOTIVATION IN PARTICIPATION

Motivation is the impetus for engagement in political activities, spurring the individual to make the necessary commitment and expend the energy required to participate. Three important factors largely shape a person's level of motivation. These factors provide a framework for assessing barriers to participation affecting the minority elderly.

First, a person must feel that he or she is a member of society with a personal stake in the political system; only then do the rituals, forms, rules, and content become meaningful to him or her. Second, a person must have a sense of efficacy. He or she must feel that his or her actions will make a difference. Without a sense of efficacy a person will feel that his or her actions are not worthwhile. Consequently, he or she will be less likely to participate. Third, an individual must have access to the political system he or she wishes to participate in. Hence, he or she must be physically capable, competent, and legally qualified to vote. Access includes physical, environmental, socioeconomic, and legal factors that affect a person's ability to participate. If he or she is sick, lacks transportation, cannot read or write the language, or is not a citizen, then he or she will be incapable of participating. A sense of involvement in the political system, a sense of efficacy, and access to the political system are important if an individual is to be motivated to participate. If any or all of these factors are missing, an individual probably will remain politically inactive.

PARTICIPATION BARRIERS

For the elderly Black, Hispanic, Asian, and American Indian, these three factors take on special significance. If older minority people feel they do not belong in this country or have no right to be here, they will not feel they have a right to participate in the political system. If they feel they are not a part of the political activities of their respective ethnic group, they will not be motivated to participate in ethnic or age-related politics. In addition, if they feel that participation will bring no personal benefits, or if they are physically incapable of participating, they will be less likely to be politically active.

Estrangement is particularly severe for some older Blacks, Hispanics, and Asians. Many have been deliberately excluded and forcibly prevented from participating. Past repression and lynchings by the Ku Klux Klan in the South, harassment and vigilante activism against Black participation in the North, internment of Japanese during World War II, and forced deportations of Mexican-Americans in the Southwest, have created a climate of fear among many older minorities who were victimized by these events when young. Consequently, these experiences have made it more difficult for them to feel that they can effectively and safely participate in political activities. That these feelings can be changed is evident in cities such as Atlanta, Detroit, and San Antonio, where members of minority groups have succeeded in acquiring political power and creating a climate of participation despite prior exclusion.

Older minority members are unique in that they represent that segment of the ethnic population closest to the values and traditions of their respective cultures and countries of origin, although there are younger Blacks and Hispanics attempting to rediscover their roots and live by traditional values. Among elderly members of the ethnic populations, assimilation, acculturation, and the effects of generation-specific cohort experiences become important in understanding political participation and the factors that inhibit it among minority elders (Trela & Sokolovsky, 1979).

Assimilation implies that the members of the host society completely accept an immigrant in primary face-to-face relationships. Acculturation implies that immigrants adopt basic values and patterns of behavior of the host society that enable them to function effectively in society (Gordon, 1964). An individual may be politically acculturated and not fully assimilated. Examples of this can be seen in places such as New Mexico and Hawaii where national minority groups dominate politically, yet maintain their cultural identities.

Cohort analysis attempts to explain the political behavior of an elderly group as resulting from specific historical experiences shared by members of that generation. The influence of certain experiences can be detected many years later in the shared political behavior among members of that generation. For example, major events affecting today's Black elders during adolescence and early adulthood include large-scale migration from the rural South to the Midwest and West Coast. Hispanics, in turn, were greatly influenced by the aftermath of the Mexican Revolution of 1910. Asians, particularly Filipino, Chinese, and Japanese were affected by restrictive immigration laws, that, in some cases, did not allow them to intermarry with non-Asians or to immigrate with their family members, resulting in a disproportionate number of elders without close kinship ties.

The aggregate political behavior of this generation of ethnic minority elders is to a large extent shaped by the interplay of these factors: social assimilation, political acculturation, and cohort experiences. Characteristically, these vary among older persons of different ethnic backgrounds. For example, many older Mexican-Americans maintain Spanish as their primary language, live in segregated neighborhoods, lack formal education, and maintain close contacts with relatives in Mexico. Fear of deportation, founded in their experiences of large scale "repatriation" programs effected at various times during their lives, coupled with a respect for authority originating in the Mexican political culture, can result in an approach to politics marked by extreme caution. Mexican-American elders may be unaware of politics, or even mystified by the complexity of the political process, further hampering their motivation to participate. The resulting sense of low political efficacy is often reinforced by lack of access to the political system, for example, due to linguistic or literacy barriers, fear, or to transportation problems.

Torres-Gil (1976) refers to this as the "politics of deference", an overriding respect and fear of authority figures (e.g., courts, police, welfare institutions) that lead toward a cautious and conservative approach to political involvement. Other minority elderly exhibit many of the same tendencies in varying degrees. Black elders, remembering segregation and violent repression, are often careful not to create antagonistic situations that may affect their security. The politics of deference is a generalized description of a style of political involvement. It does not negate political activism per se, but, in examining the level of political motivation among minority elders in this country, it remains a useful tool for understanding the factors that inhibit or encourage minority elders to participate.

PHASING, ACTION GUIDELINES, AND PRINCIPLES FOR PROGRESS

One notable feature is paramount in examining the participation of older minorities in age-related politics: They have not provided the leadership. While advocacy organizations for the minority elderly are the most visible indication of the political activity of older minority members, it is not, in general, the minority senior citizen who provides the leadership or staffing of advocacy efforts on a national level. The prerequisites of successful political advocacy on a national level—political sophistication, tightly structured organizations, and educated staff—have resulted in advocacy organizations staffed primarily by middle-aged professionals. The politics of minority aging can thus be viewed as a process composed of two phases: the professional phase and the senior activist phase. The first phase includes involvement by professionals in age-based organizations and in leadership of age-related issues. The second phase consists of direct involvement and leadership by the seniors, themselves. The first phase predominates currently in the politics of minority aging. The second phase occurs to a limited extent, but is not visible to most professionals and scholars in the field. It includes involvement of minority elders in senior clubs, local issues, church-related activities, and community-based politics.

In time it can be expected that the second phase will ascend with older minorities assuming leadership in age-specific activities, both ethnic and nonethnic related. Evidence that this is occurring can be seen in the 1981 White House Conference on Aging. Partly due to the efforts of the minority organizations, the conference insured that proportional representation of older persons from the four minority groups would occur. This served as a major catalyst for encouraging older minorities to become interested in age-specific issues and to become active in campaigning for selection as delegates to the 1981 White House Conference on Aging. For example, in Los Angeles, among the 20 delegates alloted for the City and County of Los Angeles, approximately half were minority seniors.

The numerous meetings, caucuses, and strategy sessions by minority elders bore striking testimony to the motivation that results when they feel their participation will have an impact, access is provided, and they are encouraged to be involved. Much of the organizing and leadership was provided by the established senior citizen clubs and organizations with the active assistance of minority professionals. This cooperative effort is an example that the second phase is beginning to occur.

Political events may hasten the development of the second phase. The decentralization of services and programs by the federal government through block grants, leading to greater local control, will put a premium on participation by groups and locally based individuals. Given that seniors become more active on a local level and become better organized, they may have greater opportunities to influence the allocation of funds and resources previously administered by federal agencies. Therefore, to the extent minority elders can use their networks of senior clubs and organizations, the greater probability that they will influence politics on a local level. In turn, it will require minority professionals who had predominated on a national level to become more involved and aware of local issues affecting minority elderly.

As we enter inevitably into the second phase, certain principles for progress may be exploited to gain a greater minority voice in policy formulation.

Hanhardt and Wyden (1976) have offered several suggestions to assist those seeking to organize the elderly. These also are useful for minority elderly. Advocates are encouraged to:

(1) Meet weekly and divide the work of political organization equally, with members reinforcing each other;

(2) Use the media to reach the elderly and to dramatize the likelihood of success due to political organizing efforts;

(3) Work closely with the elders to bring out the best advocacy skills each member has to offer;

(4) Provide a politically-skilled coordinator available and active on a near full-time basis.

In addition, several other suggestions for involving minority elders may prove useful. For example:

(1) Identify the existing groups, service clubs, and organizations and individuals who work with seniors. In every community there are existing organizations and individuals who have developed credibility and provide leadership based on long years of association with minority seniors. Generally, the church, senior citizen clubs, and local grass-roots organizations are best suited for this role;

(2) Identify the established politicians and organizations, not necessarily part of the local community, who can contribute to the needs of the communities. Again, every local area, whether a city, county, or region, will have politicians and organizations who can bring in money, resources, and legislation beneficial to seniors. It will be important, particularly in certain states, to involve state and congressional legislators, city councilmen and county officials if substantive accomplishments are to occur for minority seniors;

(3) Link the existing groups in the local communities with established politicians and organizations. By linking these two entities it becomes possible to identify specific areas around which seniors can mobilize and around which established politicians can develop constituencies. Many local politicians will have already garnered their senior citizen support. However, this does not always guarantee that they will have provided actual resources or support to the seniors which can be measured in increased funds, better legislation or programs. Often, it takes a "broker," possibly a professional, practitioner, or local organizer, to bring them together and continually prod, monitor, and otherwise assure that followup and continuity occurs;

(4) Stay with these efforts for extended periods of time. It is critical that individuals not mobilize and generate enthusiasm and then leave quickly. This will generate ill will and a feeling of being used, which in turn will make it more difficult to organize later. Individuals and organizations who seek to mobilize seniors must be prepared to immerse themselves in these communities and stay for extended periods;

(5) Concentrate on visible and substantive short-term gains while working on long-run issues. In most communities, few if any minority seniors are present on local

boards, commissions, and advisory groups. These positions, while ceremonial at times, can become important and effective if filled by articulate seniors from the local community. They provide positions of leadership and visibility for the local communities and can be accomplished quickly, thus providing concrete accomplishments from which long-term efforts can follow;

(6) Create linkages with nonminority aging organizations. Many local communities will have important and politically powerful senior organizations which, in all likelihood, will not contain minority seniors. To the extent these groups (generally middle-class white retirees) are willing to be supportive, important allies will be formed. Create opportunities such as forums, receptions, and meetings whereby minority and nonminority senior leaders will interact and develop mutual trust;

(7) Conduct workshops and sessions which provide training and orientation for seniors who may not be fully aware of the issues important to the larger community. Often, minority seniors who are leaders in their communities will not have had the opportunity to understand the large issues affecting the entire community. In order for them to be knowledgeable, competent, and effective in larger nonminority settings, it is important to conduct training and orientation sessions.

SOME QUESTIONS

A final issue in future minority aging politics concerns the changes occurring in ethnic age-cohorts. Today's minority youth are, in general, better educated and more assimilated than their grandparents. As they grow old, they may focus their attention on age-specific, nonethnic issues, creating a tremendous resource for aging advocacy organizations in the future. How will they be affected by their experiences? Will their ethnicity significantly influence their political behavior and attitudes? Or will they be more likely to become involved in non-age related and non-ethnic specific issues? These questions are important and deserve attention.

On the other hand, many young Blacks and Hispanics are currently affected by poor quality education, an extensive welfare system, and isolation from mainstream society. They could constitute an age cohort that conceivably might carry feelings of political inefficacy and alienation into their old age. If, as many media commentators and sociologists point out, we have an underclass (see Wilson, 1978), younger population that is ill-prepared for a technological society and dependent on a welfare system, they may be less able to cope with aging than their grandparents, most of whom lived harsh lives but expected to rely solely on themselves and their families. This issue must be explored.

Changes in the politics of minority aging will depend on the extent of political activity, the motivation for involvement by older persons, the parameters of concern, the techniques used in organizing, and the changes in future cohorts. Each of these factors must be empirically examined to obtain a better image of the implications of an increasingly growing population of older minority persons.

In summary, minority elders may become an increasingly critical link in the political maturation of ethnic groups in the United States, and in the development of age-based politics. The political interaction of age, ethnicity, and politics will present tremendous challenges in the coming years.

REFERENCES

Bechill, William. Politics of aging and ethnicity. In D. Gelfand & A. Kutzik (Eds.), *Ethnicity and aging*. New York: Springer, 1979

Brotman, Herman B. Voter participation in November 1976. *Gerontologist*, 1977, 17, (2), 157-159.

Campbell, Alan. Politics through the life cycle. *Gerontologist*, 1971, 2, (1), 112-117.

Cheng, Eva. *The elder Chinese: A cross-cultural study of minority aging*. San Diego: Campanile Press, 1978.

Cottrell, W. Fred. Government functions and the politics of age. In C. Tibbetts (Ed.), *Handbook of social gerontology*. Chicago: University of Chicago Press, 1960.

Cuellar, Jose. El senior citizen club: The older Mexican-American in the voluntary association. In A. Simic & B. Myerhoff (Eds.), *Life's career–Aging*. Beverly Hills, CA: Sage, 1978.

Cuellar, Jose & Weeks, John, *Minority elderly Americans: The assessment of needs and equitable receipt of public benefits as a prototype for area agencies on aging*. A Final Report. Allied Home Health Association, San Diego, October 1980.

Cutler, Stephen J. Age differences in voluntary association memberships. *Social Forces*, 1976, 55, 43-58.

Cutler, Stephen J. Aging and voluntary association participation. *Journal of Gerontology*, 1977, 32, 470-479.

Dukepoo, Frank. *The elder American Indian: A cross-cultural study of minority aging*. San Diego: Campanile Press, 1978.

Gordon, Milton. *Assimilation in American life*. New York: Oxford University Press, 1964.

Guttman, David. *Perspective on equitable share in public benefits by minority elderly*. Washington, DC: Catholic University of America, March 1980.

Hanhardt, Arthur M., Jr., & Wyden, Ron. Senior lobby: A model for senior/student action. *Perspectives on Aging*, September 1976, 5, 8-10.

Hausknecht, M. *The joiners*. New York: Bedminster Press, 1962.

Holtzman, Abraham. Analysis of old age politics in the United States. *Journal of Gerontology*, 1954, 9, 56-66.

Hudson, Robert, & Binstock, Robert. Political systems and aging. In R. Binstock & E. Shanas (Eds.), *Handbook of Aging and the Social Sciences*. New York: Van Nostrand Reinhold.

Ishikawa, Karen C. *The elder Japanese: A cross-cultural study of minority aging*. San Diego: Campanile Press, 1978.

Ishikawa, Wesley H. *The elder Guamanian: A cross-cultural study of minority aging*. San Diego: Campanile Press, 1978.

Ishikawa, Wesley H. *The elder Samoan: A cross-cultural study of minority aging*. San Diego: Campanile Press, 1978.

McClure, Jesse. The utilization of individual and neighborhood characteristics to analyze participation in voluntary associations. Unpublished Ph.D. dissertation, Heller School, Brandeis University, 1972.

Milbrath, Lester. *Political participation*. Chicago: Rand McNally, 1965.

Newquist, Deborah, Berger, M., Kahn, Karen, Martinez, Charles, & Burton, Linda. *Prescription for neglect: Experiences of older blacks and Mexican-Americans with the American health system*. Andrus Gerontology Center, University of Southern California, 1979.

Nie, Norman H., Verba, Sidney, & Kim, Jae-on. Political participation and the life cycle. *Comparative Politics*, April, 1974, 6, 319-340.

Owens, Yolanda, Torres-Gil, Fernando, & Wolf, Rosalie. *The 1971 White House Conference on aging: An overview of the conference activities*. Heller School, Brandeis University, 1973.

Peterson, Roberta. *The elder Filipino: A cross-cultural study of minority aging*. San Diego: Campanile Press, 1978.

Pratt, Henry J. Old age association in national politics. *Annals of the American Academy of Political and Social Science*, 1974, 106-119.

Puttnam, Jackson K. *Old age politics in California*. Palo Alto, CA: Stanford University Press, 1970.

Riley, Matilda, Johnson, W., & Foner, A. *Aging and society*. New York: Russell Sage, 1973.

Stanford, E. P. *The elder Black: A cross-cultural study of minority aging*. San Diego: Campanile Press, 1978.

Torres-Gil, Fernando, M. *Political behavior: A study of political attitudes and political participation among older Mexican-Americans*. Unpublished dissertation, Heller School, Brandeis University, 1976.

Torres-Gil, Fernando, M., & Becerra, Rosina M. The political behavior of the Mexican-American elderly. *Gerontologist*, 1977, (5), 392-399.

Trela, James, & Sokolovsky, Jay. Culture, ethnicity, and policy for the aged. In D. Gelfard & A. Kutzik (Eds.), *Ethnicity and aging*, New York: Springer, 1979.

U.S. Department of Health and Human Services (HHS), Federal Council on Aging. *Policy issues concerning the elderly minorities*. Washington, DC: Government Printing Office, 1979.

U.S. Department of Health and Human Services, Human Development Services, Administration on Aging. Characteristics of the Hispanic elderly. *Statistical reports on older Americans*. Washington, DC: Government Printing Office, 1981.

Valle, Ramon, & Mendoza, Lydia. The elderly Latino: A cross-cultural study of minority aging. San Diego: Campanile Press, 1978.

Wilson, W. J. *The declining significance of race*. Chicago: University of Chicago Press, 1978.

PART V

Guidelines for Service Delivery

A number of problems particular to minority elders were delineated in the preceding section. Not only do these problems reflect conditions that characterize the lives of many aged minority persons, but also reflect the miscarriage of society to fulfill its obligations to meet their unique needs. Inasmuch as members of minority groups bear a disproportionate share of aging problems, one might reasonably expect, or at least hope, that the human service system would function to reduce significantly the jeopardies associated with the dual status of being minority and old. However, apologists for present human services programming often stress the fact that human services, both health and social services, are legislated, planned, and delivered largely without regard to the cultural diversity of the target populations. Moreover, they contend that all older people should be treated "equally." Of course, this point denies the reality that minority elders differ from whites in the degree to which they are afflicted by problems related to underclass status and other factors. Given this greater burden, one could assert that older minority people receive less than an equitable share of public benefits.

In this section of the book, several deficiencies of the current service network are brought into focus. These chapters include topics related to service utilization, program innovations and adaptations in delivery methods, prescriptions for effective direct practice, as well as evaluation models for programs delivering services.

In the first chapter, Shirley W. King examines current trends in service utilization by elderly minority persons. She also provides a synopsis of selected literature pertaining to factors that affect utilization behavior. She observes that prevailing discriminatory practices have alienated a large number of the minority elderly from services. King advances the notion that this exclusion has resulted in members of minority groups having developed a worldview spawning coping mechanisms focused at a hostile environment. She suggests that this worldview influences their services utilization behavior.

In the next chapter, John Colen extends the discussion of the service utilization issue but focuses attention largely on identifying program elements that enhance program success in meeting needs and serving minority elders. His discussion provides a conspectus of current thinking and centers upon aspects of (1) program planning, design, and operations; (2) specialized activities used as vehicles to attract and engage minority elders; and (3) staffing patterns and provider-client relationships. Colen de-emphasizes clients as the objects of change in improving service delivery and details organizational deficits requiring program modifications as mechanisms to achieve program success. While he outlines a number of proposals to overcome limitations to service use, he recognizes the need for additional research to validate more firmly the solutions presented.

The next two contributors direct their attention to "micro" practice issues in serving elderly minority persons. Maria Zuniga-Martinez concentrates on individuals and families and explores a number of critical dimensions to selecting intervention strategies and options. She maintains that workers involved in human service intervention with the minority elderly must consider the role and impact of familial, cultural, and discriminatory factors in the life experiences of each client. She continues her discussion by outlining exigent practice issues in each of these respective areas. Martinez concludes her chapter by underscoring the importance of employing a humanistic intervention style in working with elder minorities that stresses the individualization of clients.

Hisashi Hirayama, on the other hand, provides an informative essay on the use of and issues pertaining to group work with older minority elders. He pinpoints a number of salient psychosocial dynamics of minority cultures to which workers must be aware if they are to be effective. Further, he lists and expounds on the responsibilities of group leaders. As a matter of summary, Hirayama highlights the potential of group work as an instrument by which to reach aged members of minority groups.

The discussion of service delivery is brought full course in the final article by Robert Washington. The central theme of this article is that the two important approaches to evaluating human services programs that serve minority elderly should be (1) to measure the extent to which programs and services are organized, structured, and administered to reach effectively those for whom they are intended; and (2) to measure the extent to which these programs and services afford minority elderly an opportunity to improve their lifestyles, life chances, and, consequently, gain mastery over their environments. An underlying premise is that other program evaluation techniques—for example, cost benefits analysis, and the like—do not adequately take into account sociocultural factors that influence client satisfaction and culturally defined measures of effectiveness and efficiency. Washington points out that there are basic tools and designs for any comprehensive evaluation and that program evaluation strategies employed to assess minority programs must incorporate some of these essential technologies.

19

Service Utilization and the Minority Elderly
A Review

SHIRLEY WESLEY-KING

Those in the greatest need, yet possessing the least power and means of improving their quality of life, tend to get the most ineffective responses from society. For the general elderly population, these practices have been documented since the colonial period (Kutzik, 1979). During that time, response to the elderly's needs was so inadequate and misguided that service constituted the placement of elders in institutions along with the mentally impaired, criminals, and orphans. While some would suggest that at least a response to the elderly's needs was made, the minority elderly obviously were excluded from even these meager services. Social provisions that seek to improve the welfare of the elderly, especially those who are of minority status, still leave much to be desired.

Sociodemographic data reveal that a number of the elderly struggle through their last years in circumstances characterized by inadequate income, dilapidated housing, inferior and often inaccessible medical care, as well as many other unmet areas of need. As has been the case in the past, these conditions are merely compounded for the elderly of minority groups. For them, atrocities suffered throughout life are simply amplified in old age.

Concern about the welfare of the minority elderly has demanded that legislators develop responsive policies and effective programs that will begin to address the multitude of problems existing among these groups. Although these demands have resulted in amendments to the Older Americans Act requiring that priority be given to those elderly with the greatest economic and social needs, the measured results have found these to be relatively ineffective. In addition, a most significant and conceivably deleterious change has occurred recently at the policy level. In 1978, amendments to the Older Americans Act diluted the authority that gave primacy to these very needy groups of older people. Specifically, the Act's language made the mandate that human service agencies give priority to poor and minority elderly less potent. Unless legislative policy designates that those with the greatest need (and who are most vulnerable) be given priority, their needs are not likely to be met effectively.

Complex organizational procedures pose another problem for the minority elderly. For example, it is clearly documented that those with highest educational and social awareness tend to be best equipped to negotiate formal systems of services, particularly those with complex organizational procedures (Wan, 1977; Watson, 1981). Thus, the poor and minority elderly will be at a greater disadvantage in having their needs met than their more affluent Anglo counterparts.

This chapter seeks to provide a selective and up-to-date literature review on service utilization by the minority elderly. It will include an examination of factors that affect service utilization, a report of service use levels by the minority elderly, and a discussion of several implications.

FACTORS THAT AFFECT SERVICE UTILIZATION

An examination of factors that affect service utilization raises concern about what elements or combination of elements inhibit or facilitate service utilization. Earlier studies on health services utilization produced frameworks to guide this area of inquiry. Two of the most recognized frameworks were those generated by Suchman (1964, 1965) and Anderson and Newman (1973).

Suchman's hypothesis was that the selection of the course of care reflects the knowledge, availability, and convenience of such services, and that social group influence plays a key role in how these different elements are acted upon. As described by Suchman, his hypothesis was based on a number of assumptions:

> Lower socio-economic and minority groups are more socially isolated or ethnocentric than are upper socio-economic groups and majority ethnic groups, and this ethnocentrism is highly related to lower levels of disease knowledge, unfavorable attitudes toward medical care and dependency upon lay support during illness . . . the more ethnocentric and socially cohesive the group of a community, friendship, or family level, the more likely are its members to display low knowledge about disease and skepticism toward professional medical care, and dependency during illness [Suchman, 1965, p. 322].

Anderson and Newman (1973) developed a medical model that was comprised of three broad categories (1) *predisposing variables* (individual characteristics such as age, sex, race, education); (2) *enabling variables* (factors influencing the availability of services such as income, distance to the service facility, knowledge of service, and the like); and (3) *medical care needs of patients and clients*. The enhanced utility of this model is due to its consideration of the influence individual characteristics may have on the elder in seeking assistance along with the extent to which one is able to get services and the patient's need state (whether physical, mental or social). In their framework, race and/or ethnicity would be classified as a predisposing variable.

RACE AND ETHNICITY

In 1969, a study conducted by Richardson on health service utilization revealed that use of services increased significantly for the poor and Blacks when third party payments were available. Similarly, Bice, Eichorn, and Fox (1972) found that a number of factors—health status of the group, race, and educational level—all affected utilization. Race and educational level were positively associated with health service use. More specifically, although Blacks showed a higher incidence of illness (for the Black elderly this incidence rate is higher due to their lower level of health education), they were found to use physician services at a much lower rate than whites.

Wan's (1977) research results corroborated those reported by Richardson (1969) and Bice and associates (1972). His findings revealed that access to physical health care is governed to a large extent by insurance coverage and income level. Wan suggested that where income levels were higher or insurance coverage in use, access to health care was greatly enhanced. These factors meant the burden of costs was either defrayed or eliminated for the client/patient, which enabled him or her to meet service expenses.

Another study in this area, conducted by Eve and Friedsam (1978), queried 8,065 elderly Texans and found that among minorities, the conditions of lack of transportation and absence of insurance coverage, along with rurality and low income, were primary inhibitors to health service utilization. Furthermore, these researchers reported that neither age, sex, ethnic identity (predisposing factors), nor perceived level of disability (an enabling factor) covaried with utilization.

Other studies have focused on factors of a more interpersonal nature. For example, Trinidad and Borg (1976) examined a sample of Puerto Ricans and found the existence of a trusting relationship between service providers and clients to be of primary importance in utilization. Demko's (1977) study of high and low users of senior centers revealed differences in perceived life space, club affiliation, number of friends, and living arrangements. Moreover, the researcher noted that utilization seemed to be related to social losses and gains, indicating the significance of need states among the elderly.

In a study conducted by Watson, Well, Hargett, & King (1981), which included the solicitation of information from area aging office directors regarding minority elders use of social services, it was found that the Black elderly reportedly feared the loss of their social security if they participated in agency services. Also reported in this study was the fact that many elderly members of minority groups refused social security benefits. Presenting similar findings, Bell, Kasschau, & Zellman, (1976) reported that people sometimes fail to apply for services because of fears that the government may impose on their personal lives, although this pattern appears to be lessening with time.

Combined, these factors reflect the multifaceted nature of elements that affect service utilization. Utilization of services is unquestionably affected by a combination of predisposing, enabling, and need-state factors. The enabling factors include characteristics peculiar to the individual (e.g., knowledge of services and income levels) as well as factors such as availability of transportation services and the degree of bureaucratic sensitivity to a culturally diverse clientele. In addition, some minority elderly use alternative systems in the form of effective, yet informal kinship-based supplementary support networks (Manuel, 1979; Jackson, 1972b).

One of the more recent and comprehensive studies of minority elderly utilization of public services was conducted by Guttman (1980). It was funded by the Administration on Aging to determine whether or not the minority elderly had an equitable share of public benefits as compared to nonminority elderly. The investigation focused upon (1) the needs of minority elderly; (2) their knowledge of and information about public benefits; (3) their use of and reliance on government programs; and (4) their perception of public benefits, including the barriers that prevent the seeking of aid and/or use of available benefits.

The study sample consisted of 621 Black, Hispanic, Asian, and nonminority male and female elders ranging in age from 55 to 97 years. One of the most significant findings regarding the minority elderly's use of health and social services was the fact that 20% of the population had unmet needs but did not seek publicly sponsored assistance. The five most serious problems identified were (1) lack of income (26.1%), (2) health care (19.3%), (3) transportation (15.5%), (4) housing (14.5%), and (5) crime (11.4%). Moreover, the study revealed that (1) minority group membership is a significant factor in under- and nonutilization of public benefits (fewer minority elderly both knew about and used public benefits than did nonminority elderly); (2) eligibility requirements and difficulties with procedures were the leading reasons for problems in applying for and in receiving public benefits; and (3) among those minority elderly who stated having no knowledge of a particular public benefit, such as senior nutrition programs, Asians evidenced the least knowledge, followed by Hispanics.

In the past, one of the most pervasive barriers to improving services to the minority elderly has been the failure of providers to recognize race as a critical factor in the provision of services. Jackson has noted that:

Race is a reality and we should not deny it. . . . Insofar as (minority) old people are concerned, I think that we should not now begin to treat them as white old people. They are not. Racism has adversely affected their preparation for old age [1972a, p. 38].

Any effective system of service delivery that will appeal to minority elderly must be based on a concerted effort to create culturally responsive programs sensitive to the uniqueness of diverse groups. Researchers have documented the facts that members of racial minority groups tend to respond more favorably to (1) systems with staffs that reflect the racial and cultural backgrounds of the clients, or staffs that are bilingual/bicultural; (2) programs with meals that meet the participants customary dietary preferences; and (3) programs that are located in areas permitting reasonable access (Bell et al., 1976; Watson et al., 1981).

Although it is imperative for practitioners to be sensitive to the significance of race and culture in serving the minority elderly, it is important that these clients not be viewed as a homogeneous collective group. In short, it is the responsibility of human service professionals to acquire the knowledge, skills, and sensitivity that will enable them to create systems that effectively respond to the pluralistic nature of target populations.

It has been the combination of predisposing, enabling, and need-state variables that have served as barriers to minority elderly in the past. To date, a great deal of research has identified what these factors are and to some extent how they work in tandem to inhibit use by minority elderly. The next section of this chapter will examine levels of service utilization by minority elderly.

LEVELS OF UTILIZATION

Authors of recently published literature have gone beyond merely cataloging factors that inhibit services utilization, focusing instead on the establishment of more precise determinations of the extent to which the minority elderly are using the existing service systems.

One such study was conducted by McCaslin and Calvert (1975). These researchers secured a random sample of 51 subjects from the first 1,000 individuals who contacted the referral service of a comprehensive program for the elderly. Their primary focus was that of determining in what way race affected utilization behavior. With a sample of Blacks (44%) and whites (56%), they concluded that Blacks, in contrast to whites, utilized services in greater proportion to their numbers in the general population. These researchers reasoned that elderly Blacks are in greater need of services than are their white counterparts. This line of reasoning is consistent with Manuel's (1979) remarks that minority group members' documented higher levels of need should result in higher utilization patterns. In short, although aged Blacks utilize services at a disproportionate rate compared to elderly whites, they continue to underutilize services given their higher levels of need.

Mindel and Wright (1982) examined the role of formal and informal support systems in explaining social service utilization among the minority elderly. While most service utilization research has focused on individual characteristics of clients and organizational variables as barriers to minority elderly utilization behavior, and assertions have been made that minority elderly are under-utilizers of service because of their reliance on a functional informal support system, little is known about the roles of informal support networks as determinants of service use among the elderly. These researchers used path-analytic procedures to test an explanatory model of utilization by a national area probability sample of 2,026 noninstitutionalized elderly persons who were 65 years of age or older.

Using the Anderson and Newman (1973) model (discussed previously in this chapter) Mindel and Wright conceptualized utilization as the end product of a complex pattern of interactions among predisposing, enabling, and need-for-care factors. They suggest that some individuals have a higher propensity to use services than do others, and that this propensity can be viewed as the outcome of certain background characteristics of the individual.

Predisposing factors, such as sex, age, race, education, marital status, morale, beliefs, and attitudes were assumed to determine the propensity of an individual to seek assistance. However, actual service utilization will only occur when the individual has the means for acquiring the needed services.

In the Anderson and Newman model, means of acquisition are described as enabling factors, including variables such as income, insurance coverage, transportation, service availability, and accessibility. A third critical element is the degree to which the individual is aware of a need for care. Obviously, awareness of need must precede solicitation and receipt of services. In sum, service utilization involves a number of causal relationships described by Mindel and Wright: Enabling factors may be caused by the predisposing factors; the need-for-care factors may be caused by both the predisposing and enabling factors; and the utilization variable may be caused by the predisposing, enabling, and need-for-care factors.

The researchers used the National Senior Citizens Survey, a data set collected in 1968. An interview schedule consisting of 154 questions was administered in face-to-face interviews with the sample population. Enabling variables included income, population size, access to public transportation, perceived availability of services, family aid, family contact, and informal nonfamily support. The need-for-care variables were comprised of perceived need for services and self-rated health status. The criterion or dependent variable was utilization of social welfare services.

Results from this study indicated that only two of the variables directly predict the number of services utilized. The number of services needed and the number of services perceived available accounted for 67% of the variance in service utilization. The other variables explained insignificant amounts of variance in utilization, suggesting no direct effect on use.

Number of services needed was affected directly by six variables. Respondents needed more services if they were in poor health, did not have access to public transportation, were female, had low morale, and received assistance from kin.

With respect to race, the researchers divided the sample into Black and white racial groups to examine the potentially different utilization patterns of the two races. Their analysis revealed that race was a significant indirect predictor of social service utilization. A most significant difference between the races was found with respect to the role of the informal family support system. For whites, family support appeared to be of minor importance, whereas for Blacks, it played a more pronounced role. Among the Black elderly, those who were oldest (75 and older) visited and were visited by kin less often than those who were younger (less than 75). More important, the Black elderly who tended to receive aid from family members were also the ones who needed and used the greatest number of social services. Mindel and Wright found that those who received family support were most likely to be lower income females. And, rather than serving as an alternative support system, the family appeared to be providing supplementary aid to those in greatest need.

SUMMARY AND IMPLICATIONS

Research findings from studies conducted on factors that affect service utilization and rates or levels of service utilization among minority elders yield relevant practice implications. Service utilization patterns can be attributed to an array of factors.

Specifically, service utilization patterns for the minority elderly are influenced by a combination of need-for-care variables, predisposing and enabling factors. As discussed in this and other chapters, the minority elderly do face barriers to service utilization due to the influence of their racial status and/or cultural uniqueness, and due to organizational and individual biases of agency staff. It is the interaction of these factors that make the minority elderly's circumstances worthy of special response. For example, as research findings have documented repeatedly, minority elders, compared to their white counterparts, are two to three times more likely to have lower incomes and educational levels. They are also more likely to have poorer health and to live in substandard housing.

Policy makers must examine critically the realities facing minority families, and practitioners at all levels of the service network must be educated and sensitized to the needs and strengths of the minority elderly. The service delivery system itself must undergo modifications that will enable it to establish supportive alliances with members of existing informal support systems within minority communities so that the needs of the minority elderly can be met more effectively.

REFERENCES

Anderson, R., & Newman, J. F. Societal and individual determinants of medical care utilization in the United States. *Milbank Memorial Fund Quarterly*, 1973, 51, 95-124.

Bell, D., Kasschau, P., & Zellman, G. *Delivering services to elderly members of minority groups: A critical review of the literature*. Santa Monica, CA: Rand, 1976.

Bice, T. W., Eichorn, R. L., and Fox, P. D. Socioeconomic status and use of physician services: A reconsideration. *Medical Care*, March-June 1972, 10, 261.

Bice, T. W., Rabin, D., Starfield, B., & White, K. Economic class and use of physician services. *Medical Care*, 1973, 2, 287-296.

Demko, D. *Utilization attrition and the senior center*. Paper presented at the 30th Annual Meeting of the Gerontological Society, San Francisco, November 1977.

Eve, S. B., & Friedsam, H. J. Multi-variate analysis of health services utilization among elderly Texans. *Gerontologist*, October 1978, 18 (5), 70.

Guttman, D. *Perspective in equitable share in public benefits by minority elderly: Executive summary*. Washington, DC: March 1980, Grant 90-A-1671DHHS/AOA.

Jackson, J. Black aged in quest of the phoenix. In *Triple jeopardy–myth or reality*. Washington, DC: National Council on Aging, 1972. (a)

Jackson, J. Social imports of housing relocation upon urban low-income Black aged. *Gerontologist*, 1972, 12, 323-377. (b)

King, S. W., & McNeil, J. S. *Agency-based planning and programming for effective service delivery to minority elderly*. Proceedings of the First Annual Symposium on the Black/Chicano Elderly, University of Texas at Arlington, Graduate School of Social Work, Arlington, Texas, Aril 1980, 39-46.

Kitano, H. H. L. *Japanese Americans. The evaluation of a subculture*. Englewood Cliffs: Prentice-Hall, 1969.

Luck, E., & Berman, J. T. Patient's ethnic backgrounds affect utilization. *Journal of American Hospital Association*, 1971, 45, 64-68.

Manuel, R. *Minority aged clients in the aging network: A study of utilization behavior in region III*. Unpublished paper, Washington, DC, 1979.

McCaslin, R., & Calvert, W. R. Social indicators in Black and white: Some ethnic considerations in delivery of services to the elderly. *Journal of Gerontology*, 1975, 30, 60-66.

Mindel, C., & Wright, R. The use of health and social services by the minority elderly: The role of social support systems. *Journal of Gerontological Social Work*, 1982, 4, 3-4.

Richardson, W. C. Poverty, illness and use of health services in the United States. *Hospitals*, 1969, 34-40.

Rubenstein, D. An examination of social participation found among a national sample of Black and white elderly. *Aging and Human Development*, 1971, 2, 172-178.

Suchman, E. A. Social patterns of illness and medical care. *Journal of Health and Human Behaviors*, 1964, 6, 2-16.

Suchman, E. A. Sociomedical variations among ethnic groups. *American Journal of Sociology*, 1965, 70, 319-331.

Trinidad, L. L., & Borg, S. K. *Facilitating utilization of services by Puerto Rican elderly*. Paper presented at the 29th Annual Meeting of the Gerontological Society, New York, October 1976.

Wan, T. T. H. The differential use of health services: A minority perspective. *Urban Health*, 1977, 16, 47-49.

Watson, W., Well, R., Hargett, S., & King, S. W. *Study of minority elderly utilization of social services in the commonwealth of Pennsylvania*. Washington, DC: National Caucus on Black Aging, 1981.

Wu, F. Y. T. Mandarin-speaking aged Chinese in the Los Angeles area. *Gerontologist*, 1975, 15 (5), 271-275.

20

Facilitating Service Delivery to the Minority Aged

JOHN N. COLEN

The passage of the Older Americans Act in 1965 signalled an acknowledgement by Congress of the physical and social transitions of the aging process, and the problems attendant to those transitions. Its enactment and subsequent amendments ushered in a formidable array of programs and services to accommodate the unique needs of the aged population. Given the extensive services currently available, it seems reasonable to assert that the basic issue is no longer the lack of services. To a considerable degree, the elderly have available to them nutritious meals, housing assistance, medical care, in-home and other services, although the extent to which they are available varies by locale.

The availability of services notwithstanding, access to them by minority elders is problematic at best. In part, this situation is attributed to the lack of an adequate data base regarding aged minorities at the time the vast majority of these programs began. Early gerontological studies relied almost exclusively on data collected from white subjects, and at best, studies focusing on minority elderly were ancillary or sporadic (Hendricks & Hendricks, 1980). In fact, it was not until the 1970s that Congress acceded to evidence that there are indeed "multiple hazards of age and race" (U.S. Senate, 1971).

The lack of support for the special circumstances of the minority aged, coupled with the paucity of data, fostered a number of important activities. In an attempt to assure that their unique needs received attention, initial efforts concentrated on bringing audience to the plight of minority elders and evoking public support for their cause. Subsequently, numerous research investigations ensued and were aimed at understanding aging within a cultural context. These studies and reports have been instructive in that they represent major strides in demographically defining elderly minority populations, delineating the shortcomings of public policy, and illuminating many of the inadequacies of the human services system (Jackson, 1971; Hernandez, Estrada, & Alvirez, 1973; Golden, 1976).

More specifically, these and other studies have illustrated that service utilization patterns among the minority aged are neither consistent with those of whites, nor in many cases are their rates of service use commensurate with their own levels of need. Moreover, they have indentified many obstacles that continue to obfuscate successful service delivery to the minority aged (McCaslin & Calvert, 1975; Mindel & Wright, 1980, Watson, 1981).

Since issues related to service utilization were explored extensively by Dr. King in the preceding chapter, detailed discussion of them will not be undertaken here. Suffice it to say, insensitive policies, inappropriate service structures, and unacceptable staff practices have engendered a series of negative encounters by aged minority persons with the human service system. Simpson and Yinger (1972) report that faced with these experiences, older minorities react to the service network largely in terms of aggression, avoidance, or acceptance, with most responses confined to the latter two categories. Hence, the situation is exacerbated by an estrangement between the older minority client and the service delivery system (Slaughter and Batey, 1982).

Increasingly, investigators, and especially minority gerontologists, have shifted their focus and have sought to identify means by which program participation of aged minorities might be improved. Furthermore, they have approached this task from the perspective that institutions and programs should be the primary targets of change rather than the individuals in need. Based on this premise, a number of propositions have been proffered as potential solutions to the service utilization question of elderly minorities.

The primary purpose of this chapter therefore is to reemphasize the need for modifications in the current service system in order to more effectively meet the needs of the minority aged. More specifically, it is intended as a compilation of existing proposals rather than as a presentation of strikingly new information regarding service delivery to elderly members of minority groups. In addition to some general considerations, it is organized around those themes most consistently identified in the literature as areas of particular concern. They include (1) program planning, design, and operation; (2) specialized activities used to attract and engage minority elders; and (3) staffing patterns and provider-client relationships.

GUIDELINES OF SERVICE DELIVERY TO THE MINORITY AGED

Examination of the literature readily produces some general guidelines viewed as essential if programs are to achieve any meaningful degree of success in reaching minority elders. McCaslin and Calvert (1980), for example, suggest that ethnic considerations enter into the design and delivery of services to the elderly at two different but equally important levels. First, and more commonly recognized, is the need for preferential consideration of minority elderly in response to their "double jeopardy" situation. Equally important, and less often discussed, is the need for differential consideration of the various ethnic groups being served.

Murase (1980) emphasizes the need for changes in public policy. Murase calls for stricter monitoring of programs and better enforcement of compliance with nondiscrimination legislation. Similarly, Stanford (1977) sees the need for stricter accountability in programming. Both authors support an expansion in the scope of programs for broader inclusion of the minority aged and a need for increased governmental support for those that implement culturally relevant services.

Informal networks have received significant attention for their importance in the lives of minority persons. More extensive use of these systems is commonly considered both desirable and necessary (Gallego, 1980; Barber, Cook, and Ackerman, 1980; Colen, 1982). Other studies (see Erickson, 1975; Staples, 1976; Safier & Pfouts, 1979) have shown that these informal systems can be key factors in identifying persons at risk, determining help-seeking behavior, and can be tremendous resources in the actual provision of services.

Many authors have stressed the importance of sensitivity to the lifestyles and cultures of minorities. For example, White (1977) and Stanford (1977) note the need for services to be delivered through means that preserve the personal dignity of the recipient. Sensitivity, as defined by Bello (1976), includes the feeling of respect for ethnic people of color as individuals; the recognition that minority groups have unique cultural beliefs and patterns; the practice of incorporating their beliefs and practices into the provision of services; and the ability and willingness to act on behalf of ethnic clients who are being denied program access or quality services.

While this list of guidelines is not exhaustive, it is representative of the more general concerns raised about the existing service system. Others have focused on specific elements of service delivery and will be considered in the discussion to follow.

PROGRAM DESIGN AND OPERATION

In this section, various aspects of program planning, structure, and operation will be considered. The importance of these programmatic elements cannot be overemphasized as they determine the parameters within which services are delivered. While the planning process covers a broad range of activities, those most often cited as having direct impact on the level of minority participation in programs are discussed.

The extent to which there is congruence in perception of need between clients and providers is regarded as one of the most salient dimensions to alleviating service barriers. Speaking to this issue, Warren (1977) notes that the organizational arrangements through which services are delivered are determined to a large degree by the way problems and needs are defined. Moreover, he suggests that what gets defined as a problem is controlled in the main by experts, or, as he puts it, the "knowledge definers." These experts, he maintains, not only define reality but also have the ear of those who generate and pass legislation and those who design, implement, and administer programs. In a similar vein, Berger and Luckmann (1967) suggest that these experts' view of the world is shaped by the social and cultural milieu in which they grow and develop, a social and cultural context that all too often is incongruent with that of those for whom they plan.

This point of view has been validated through a number of studies. For example, Riesenfeld et al. (1972) showed through their data that the consensus of opinion from agency personnel differed markedly from responses of their elderly sample, both in terms of service needs and problem remedies. Similarly, Bley and her associates (1973), in a comparison of client and program staff perceptions, revealed a disparity in views regarding the elderly's incentives for service utilization. Corresponding conclusions were reached by McConnell and Davis (1977), who uncovered vastly different perceptions of problems and needs between major decision makers and elderly recipients of services. Recognizing that services frequently are based on inadequate premises such as these studies illustrate, Piliavin (1968) warns that once programs are implemented, their appropriateness comes to be taken for granted. They become institutionalized, and their institutionalization is dysfunctional because it engenders an atmosphere within which it is difficult to recognize the need for change.

Explicitly, these findings illustrate the need to involve appropriate individuals in the early stages of planning service delivery programs. Sainer, Schwartz, and Jackson (1973) found that when the Black elderly took an active role in establishing their own social services, utilization improved because the elderly were able to establish those programs they felt were needed most. Corroborating findings are reported by Colen and Soto (1979) not only in relation to Blacks but also to Asians, Mexicans, and Native Americans. In their study, the level of consumer input into major decisions was one of the most striking findings in distinguishing programs successful in reaching minority elders from those that were not. Additionally, Colen and Soto found that program success increased when program planning included the establishment of minimal standards of minority participation, the provision of transportation either directly or by arrangement through other sources, and the placement of sites in minority communities and near complementary vital services. Similar findings have been reported by Regnier (1975), Guttman (1980), and Cuellar and Weeks (1980).

Several researchers have pinpointed operational procedures as impediments to service utilization. Solomon (1970) contends that governmental agencies and institutions do not reflect the minority experience and therefore are less appealing to them. Likewise, Sears and McConahay (1973) maintain that agencies' routine procedures generally are designed by middle-class Anglos with their own values foremost in mind and not with consideration of minority consumers. The resulting organizational climate is highly rational and equally as rigid, a climate often antithetical to behavioral patterns of minorities. Implicit in these arguments is the need for involvement of persons familiar with the behavioral patterns exhibited by elderly minorities. More important, however, is that rules, regulations, and operational procedures must be interpreted in a flexible manner because rules made for the older Anglo do not fit the minority aged.

ALTERNATIVE METHODS TO
ATTRACT AND ENGAGE MINORITY CLIENTS

An area that has received notable interest is the identification of particularized techniques that might be used to secure the participation of elderly minorities in programs. Traditional approaches employed to attract and engage program participants have fared poorly with potential minority clients. Consequently, it is commonly acknowledged that alternative modes are imperative. These methods are the subject of this section and are broadly defined to encompass vehicles to achieve these goals.

Publicity about services should be a component of continuing educational efforts to convey the right of the elderly to lead a comfortable and decent life. Two reports (Wesley-King & McNeil, 1980; Colen, 1980) are particularly revealing as to the effectiveness of program advertisement specifically targeted to minority audiences. Minority-oriented television and radio shows appear to be particularly effective. The broadcast format used by such programs focuses on the affairs of the minority community; thus they not only are an important means of informing elderly clients themselves of the availability of services, but also other family members who might find it necessary to serve as brokers in connecting elderly relatives with the social service network. Because this type of publicity frequently affords the agency representative an opportunity for discussion, program content, eligibility criteria, if any, and other important aspects of the service will be better understood by the age minority client prior to program contact. Similarly, minority newspapers, natural community centers such as churches, neighborhood organizations, and civic and social club announcements have proven to be beneficial sources in informing minority clients of the availability of services.

Outreach activities can be of tremendous value in engaging minority clients with service programs. The success of various methods has been observed to be highly dependent on the extent to which naturalistic systems are recognized and used and the degree to which approaches are personalized (Kushler & Davidson, 1978; Manuel, 1980).

Valle and Mendoza (1978), from the standpoint of integrating formal and informal systems, were able to describe a critical path from a person in need to services and identified certain levels of helpers. The first contact was the local link person (often a neighbor), not necessarily more knowledgeable about services, but who generally knew the second contact, the community service broker. These brokers not only were more aware of potential assistance, but were in touch with the third level of helper, the agency link person. While the community service broker aided agency staff in understanding the client and served as a buffer, the agency link person generally had established contacts in other agencies who were disposed to extending services to the community through culturally syntonic modes.

Other methods of reaching the minority elderly can be gleaned from the work of Litwak and Meyer (1966). Included among these are indigenous workers, natural opinion leaders, common messengers (individuals who are regularly members of both formal organizations and informal groups), and, in a more formal sense, detached experts (professional persons who act with relative autonomy and by direct participation in the primary group), such as a public health nurse who frequently was in touch with community members.

Other alternatives also have been suggested. Both formal and informal arrangements with minority oriented service agencies and information and referral centers are seen as beneficial. Due to the important position these centers generally occupy within the network of support services and the trust placed in them by aged minority clients, they frequently prove to be the critical link between client and programs. In each case, these exchanges should be complementary, rather than competitive situations in which one agency attempts to replace the services of the other (Colen & Soto, 1979).

Having achieved the goals of attracting and engaging minority clients, retention is problematical. Since retention is largely a function of the manner in which personnel interact with clients and the approach that they use in serving them, this issue will be covered in some detail in the next section of this chapter.

STAFFING PATTERNS AND
CLIENT-PROVIDER RELATIONSHIPS

Staffing patterns and staff performance cannot be overemphasized as key elements in the successful delivery of services to minority elders. Staffing is a multidimensional issue that affects both service access and use. One approach to this issue is from the position of the proportion of individuals who represent a particular racial or ethnic group. This stance appropriately assumes that racial and cultural consistency between client and provider has greater potential in fostering an atmosphere conducive to client retention. As perceived, not only is the composition of internal program staff crucial, but so is representation on boards, project councils, and within the ranks of volunteers. Given the diversity found among elderly minority groups in terms of language, lifestyles, preferences, and other cultural characteristics, the necessity of bilingual-bicultural staff seems obvious. Yet, proponents of improved service delivery to the minority aged continue to decry their lack of involvement in decision-making and service arenas (Fujii, 1976; Moriwaki, 1980; Cuellar & Weeks, 1980).

In view of the fact that program personnel are largely in place, radical changes are unlikely in the near future. Perhaps most important at this time is that providers, regardless of racial group, demonstrate a sensitivity to elderly minorities and adopt service approaches that reflect this sensitivity. Merton (1957), as a result of his study, has cautioned that success comes not merely from granting aid, but from the manner in which aid is provided. Heisel and Moore (1973), Levy (1978), and others commonly agree that programs whose services are delivered in a more personalized manner are more attractive to and effective with elderly minorities.

Several authors note the lack of this sensitivity, while others suggest ways in which services can be made more personal. For example, White (1977) studied provider-client interactions in health settings. She found that clients of color were often treated in a dehumanizing way or ignored, an accusation lodged against the service system generally. As a consequence of this treatment, minority clients are less likely to return.

Perceptions of staff by minority clients are generated by their experiences in larger society. Therefore, Sue, McKinney, Allen, and Hall (1974) stress the need to establish trust and rapport with minority clients and note the difficulties often encountered in doing so. Nonetheless, unless this trust and rapport are engendered, minority elders' perceptions of staff are likely to be reinforced.

Various practitioners have provided some clues as to how trust can be fostered. Aguilar (1972), addressing the Mexican-American family, stresses the importance of initial contacts. This author indicates that when Mexican-Americans meet to negotiate or arrange affairs, the first step is to set the climate or *ambiente*. As an expansion of this theme, Vontress (1976) sets forth some general areas that must receive particular attention if rapport and trust are to be forthcoming. He includes communication, both verbal and nonverbal, the cultural roles of various family members who might be present in the interaction, patience, and tolerance. In all cases, practitioners would do well to demonstrate sincerity, empathy, and respect.

SUMMARY

As is evident from the foregoing discussion, effective service delivery to the minority aged eludes the human service system in its current arrangement. Persistently, evidence shows that minority elders bear a disproportionate share of the jeopardies associated with old age. Services expected to mitigate the problems of aging continue to be beyond the reach of elderly minorities for numerous reasons. Paramount among them is the resistance of those charged with the design and implementation of programs to acknowledge race as a policy and program relevant variable.

By virtue of the choice of modes of service, location, staffing patterns, or inherent value premises in the small details of how services are carried out, programs might tend to favor one class or group to the disadvantage of the others (Kahn, 1970). With current low levels of input into decisions concerning policy, design, and operation of the existing array of services by advocates of aged minorities, it is reasonable to speculate that the disadvantage will continue to be borne by the minority elderly. It is disappointing that key actors in the system have at their disposal tremendous resources such as naturalistic helping networks, yet they have chosen largely to ignore them.

Clearly, to achieve any meaningful degree of success in reaching the minority aged, the structure and operation of the human service system must be altered. Minimally, requisite modifications include (1) increased sensitivity to minority cultural differences, needs, and potential remedies; (2) the use of alternative and more effective methods to inform, engage, and retain minority clients; and (3) the creation of better provider-client relationships. While many of the propositions contained herein are research based, others are speculative. Thus additional investigation is appropriate for validation and to further delineate the circumstances under which they are most effective.

REFERENCES

Aguilar, Ignacio. Initial contacts with Mexican-American families. *Social Work*, May 1972, 66-70.

Barber, Clifton, Cook, Alica, & Ackerman, Alan. *Attitudes of Navajo youth toward supporting aged parents*. Paper presented at the Annual Scientific Meeting of the Gerontological Society, San Diego, 1980.

Bellow, Teresa A. The third dimension: Cultural sensitivity in nursing practice. *Imprint*, 1976, 23, 36-38, 45.

Berger, Peter L., & Luckmann, Thomas. *The social construction of reality*. Garden City, New York: Doubleday, 1967.

Bley, Nina, et al. Client's perceptions: A key variable in evaluating leisure activities for the elderly. *Gerontologist*, 1973, 13 (3), 365-367.

Colen, John N. *Social service research and the minority aged: An old issue a new approach*.

Paper presented at the Annual Scientific Meeting of the Gerontological Society, San Diego, 1980.

Colen, John N. Using natural helping networks in social service delivery systems. In R.C. Manuel (Ed.), *Minority aging: Sociological and social psychological issues*. Westport, CT: Greenwood Press, 1982.

Colen, John N., & Soto, David. *Service delivery to aged minorities: Techniques of successful programs*. Sacramento: California State University, 1979.

Cuellar, Jose, & Weeks, John R. *Minority elderly Americans: A prototype for area agencies on aging*. Executive Summary, Administration on Aging, Grant 90-A-1667 (01). San Diego: Allied Home Health Association, 1980.

Erickson, Gerald. The concept of personal network in clinical practice. *Family Process*, 1975, 14(4), 487-498.

Fujii, Sharon. Elderly Asian-Americans and the use of public services. *Social Casework*, 1976, 57, 202-207.

Gallego, Daniel T. *The Mexican-American elderly: Familial and friendship support system . . . fact or fiction?* Paper presented at the Annual Scientific Meeting of the Gerontological Society, San Diego, 1980.

Golden, Herbert M. Black ageism. *Social Policy*, 1976, 7(3), 40-42.

Guttman, David. *Strategies for increased utilization of public benefits by minority elderly*. Paper presented at the Conference on Provision of Services to Minority Elderly, Lake Tahoe, California, 1980.

Heisel, Marsel, & Moore, Margaret E. Social interaction and isolation of elderly blacks. *Gerontologist*, 1973, 13 (3), 100.

Hendricks, Jon, & Hendricks, C. Davis. *Aging in a mass society: Myths and realities*. Cambridge, MA: Winthrop, 1980.

Hernandez, Jose, Estrada, L., & Alvirez, R. Census data and the problem of conceptually defining the Mexican-American population. *Social Science Quarterly*, 1973, 53, 671-87.

Jackson, Jacquelyn J. The blacklands of gerontology. *Aging and Human Development*, 1971, 2 (3), 156-171.

Kahn, Alfred. Perspectives on access to social services. *Social Work*, 1970.

King, S. W., & McNeil, J. S. *Agency based planning and programming for effective service delivery to minority elderly*. Proceedings of the First Annual Symposium on Black/Chicano Elderly. The University of Texas at Arlington, Graduate School of Social Work, Arlington, Texas, April 1980, 39-46.

Kushler, Martin, & Davidson, William S. Alternative modes of outreach: An experimental comparison. *Gerontologist*, 1978, 18 (4), 355-362.

Levy, Valerie. Self-reported needs of urban elderly Black persons. *Gerontologist*, 1978, 18 (5, Part 2), 94.

Litwak, Eugene, & Meyer, Henry. A balance theory of coordination between bureaucratic organizations and community primary groups. *Administrative Science Quarterly*, 1966, 11 (1), 31-38.

Manuel, Ron C. Leadership factors in service delivery and minority elderly utilization. *Journal of Minority Aging*, 1980, 5 (2), 218-232.

McCaslin, R., & Calvert, W. R. Social indicators in Black and white: Some ethnic considerations in delivery of services to the elderly. *Journal of Gerontology*, 1975, 30, 60-66.

McConnell, Stephen, & Davis, William. *Social and cultural contexts of aging: Decisionmaker survey report*. Los Angeles: University of Southern California, Andrus Gerontology Center, 1977.

Merton, Robert. *Social theory and social structure*. (rev. ed.). New York: Free Press, 1957.

Mindel, C. & Wright, R. The use of health and social services by minority elderly: The role of social support systems. *Journal of Gerontological Social Work*, 4, 3-4.

Moriwaki, Sharon. *Implementing culturally relevant programs for Asian/Pacific elderly: A conceptual paper*. Paper presented at the Conference on Provision of Services to Minority Elderly, Lake Tahoe, California, 1980.

Murase, Kenji. *Implementing culturally relevant programs for Asian/Pacific American elderly*. Paper presented at the Conference on Provision of Services to Minority Elderly, Lake Tahoe, California, 1980.

Piliavin, Irving. Restructuring the provision of social services. *Social Work*, January 1968, 34-41.

Regnier, Victor. Neighborhood planning for the urban elderly. In D. Woodruff and J. Birren (Eds.), *Aging: Scientific perspectives and social issues*. New York: Van Nostrand Company, 1975.

Riesenfeld, Mark, et al. Perceptions of public service needs: The urban elderly and the public agency. *Gerontologist*, 1972, 12 (2, Part I), 185-190.

Safier, Ellen, & Pfouts, Jane. *Social network analysis: A new tool for understanding individual and family functioning*. Paper presented at the Annual Program Meeting of the Council on Social Work Education, Boston.

Sainer, Janet, Schwartz, Louise, & Jackson, Theodore. Steps in the development of a comprehensive service delivery system for the elderly. *Gerontologist*, 1973, 13 (3), 98.

Sears, D.D., & McConahay, J.B. *The politics of violence*. Boston: Houghton-Mifflin, 1973.

Simpson, George, & Yinger, J. Milton. *Racial and cultural minorities: An analysis of prejudice and discrimination*. New York: Harper & Row, 1972.

Slaughter, Oliver, & Batey, Mignon O. Service delivery and black aged: Identifying barriers to utilization of mental health services. In R.C. Manuel (Ed.), *Minority aging: Sociological and social psychological issues*. Westport, CT: Greenwood Press, 1982.

Solomon, Barbara. *Ethnicity, mental health and older black aged*. In Proceedings of Workshop on Ethnicity, Mental Health and Aging. University of Southern California Gerontology Center, April 13-14, 1970.

Stanford, E. *Comprehensive service delivery systems for the minority aged*. San Diego State University, University Center on Aging, 1977.

Staples, Robert. *Introduction to Black sociology*. New York: McGraw-Hill, 1976.

Sue, Stanley, McKinney, Herman, Allen, David, & Hall, Juanita. Delivery of community mental health services to Black and white clients. *Journal of Consulting and Clinical Psychology*, 1974, 42 (6), 794-801.

U.S. Senate, Special Committee on Aging. *The multiple hazards of age and race: The situation of aged Blacks in the United States*. 92nd Congress, 1st Session, 1971.

Valle, Ramon, & Mendoza, Lydia. *The elder Latino*. San Diego State University, University Center on Aging, 1978.

Vontress, Clemmont E. Counseling middle-aged and aging cultural minorities. *Personnel and Guidance Journal*, November 1976, 132-135.

Warren, Roland. *Lecture on the sociology of knowledge*. Brandeis University, 1977.

Watson, H., Well, R., Hargett, S., & King, S. W. Study of minority elderly utilization of social services in the commonwealth of Pennsylvania. Washington, DC: National Center on the Black Aged, 1981.

Wesley-King, S. W., & McNeil, J. S. *Agency based planning and programming for effective service delivery for minority elderly*. Proceedings of the First Annual Symposium on the Black/Chicano Elderly, University of Texas at Arlington, April 1980, 39-46.

White, Earnestine H. Giving care to minority patients. *Nursing Clinics of North America*, 1977, 12(1), 27-40.

21

Social Treatment with the Minority Elderly

MARIA ZUNIGA-MARTINEZ

Recognition must be given to the fact that culturally based supports providing nurturance act as a buffer to hostile institutions such as unresponsive welfare departments, discriminatory housing authorities, or other negatively perceived institutions that are supposed to foster social well-being (see Chestang, 1976). Thus, attention must be given to the natural support systems that have been developed within one's cultural base. In particular, attention must be given to the role of the family in the support of its minority aged, and to natural systems such as the Black elderly's *kith* (Langston, 1981) and the Latino elderly's *servidores* (Valle & Mendoza, 1978). Also, organizations such as Chinese benevolent societies and minority churches have been found to offer their members meaningful support activities.

When any of these systems break down, the elderly may find themselves unprepared, in the absence of anticipated culturally linked support, to deal efficaciously with the bureaucratic institutions that presumably provide care. For example, many Asian aged have been socialized to expect filial support and reverence in old age from both their family and community systems. Often these expectations are not met due to the changing values of younger family members, mobility factors that may undercut mixed generational households, and traditional community settings (Lum, Cheung, Cho, Tang, & Yao, 1980). Obviously, responsible human service workers must be sensitive to disparities that exist between the cultural roles and status expectations the elderly minority may have, and the ability of their family and community to meet these expectations. This point is important given the fact that family life in minority cultures tends to be of more significance in determining the emotional and physical well-being of elders—due to the respect, nurturance, and material support traditionally afforded them—that they continue to expect. Uneven acculturation across generations can contribute to intra- and interfamilial conflict.

The emphasis in some minority groups on shared decision-making further illustrates the importance of familial factors. For example, in the area of health care, decisions about surgery or hospitalization are viewed frequently as a familial decision, often including extended family members in the consultation process. In Anglo culture, such decision-making may include some family members, but more likely tends to be an individual decision (Brownlee, 1978). In view of this orientation, the inclusion of the family in working with the minority elderly must be considered so that group involvement is supported and family linkages may be maintained as well as strengthened.

Another task of the worker involves the assessment of defenses and behavior that are reactive-adaptive responses to a racially hostile environment. This will steer the worker away from problem conceptualizations that view minority behavior as pathological or deviant. Conversely, it should force the worker to assess behavior in relation to the external social environment. For example, many minority aged who have experienced racism react by refusing to accept help from nonminority agencies or to participate in nutrition programs where they would have to interact with whites (Gallego, 1981). Senate hearing testimony has underscored this type of behavior in relation to elderly Mexican-Americans:

> In the past, part of the defense against the economic political and social isolation imposed upon our people has been self-insulation . . . This is particularly true of the elderly Mexican American . . . because he has been rudely and crudely used by the larger society. The elderly Mexican American has withdrawn behind walls of self-protection. He deliberately uses the differences in language and culture to provide and emphasize the gap between him and what he sees as a menacing larger society [U.S. Senate Hearing, 1969, p. 340].

At these hearings, Henry Santiestevan of the Southwest Council of La Raza recommended the following: "If we are to help them we must do so on their own terms and approach them with their own people" (1969, p. 430).

This recommendation has been supported by research on minority aged services indicating that the most effective programs for aged minorities are those staffed by minority personnel (Colen & Soto, 1979). In view of the fact that this idea is not always feasible, workers must heed the other aspect of Santiestevan's testimonial and apply it not only to Mexican-American aged but to all minority aged: Help them on their own terms.

HUMANIZING INTERVENTION

Helping the minority aged on their own terms requires the worker to respect the elder's interactional style. For instance, practitioners should expect

to spend more time at initial interviews so that the minority client has sufficient time to look them over. Jim Goodtracks (1973) stresses the importance
of learning "Indian time" in working with Native Americans. This requires
the worker to wait patiently for acceptance from a Native-American client,
and to recognize that these elders may not ascribe the same importance to
punctuality as the worker has been socialized to value.

Workers must also concern themselves with the protocols of authority and
power at this initial critical phase. The manner in which workers present themselves during initial contacts will be examined within the context of elders'
prior experience with racial discrimination and oppression. This is particularly
noteworthy for Anglo practitioners formerly in positions of authority or other
roles that involved the use of power. Workers' behavior must reflect a sincere
respect for prospective clients. Thus, workers should present themselves as
individual human beings and interact with minority elders as individual clients, while taking into account the broad cultural factors associated with their
clients' racial backgrounds. Specifically, bureaucratic coolness in interpersonal exchange is likely to antagonize minority elders, who prefer interaction
manifestly respectful of their age. A warm yet formal approach may be most
advantageous. For example, workers should avoid, unless requested, addressing elders by their first names (see McNeely and Badami, 1983). At the same
time, workers should respond positively to client requests for personal information. Typical requests involve questions about workers' age, marital status,
number of children, and place of residence.

RECIPROCITY

Reciprocity refers to the recognition by the worker that the client, too, has
expertise to offer. This process is similar to the "transactional teaching-
learning process" outlined by Harriet Trader (1979) as an effective practice
model for social work with Blacks. This writer views transactional teaching-
learning as an equally viable framework for work with all minority clients,
but particularly with the minority aged. It undercuts the power roles many
helpers use in working with clients, especially minorities. It offers tribute to
the elders' seniority in living as well as respect for culturally based knowledge from which practitioners can benefit.

Consequently, this approach not only balances the power relationship that
is an important aspect of work with minorities (Solomon, 1976) but institutes
reciprocity wherein minority aged can also offer some important service in the
transaction, thereby protecting their sense of pride (Zuniga-Martinez, 1981).
In short, this approach is sensitive to the expectations often held by the minority aged regarding their age-related status and corresponding prestige.

For the practitioner, this teaching-learning exchange serves another valuable goal. It is a mechanism for learning about the past history of the minor-

ity elder, especially that aspect related to experiences with discrimination. In addition, it is an avenue for receiving data on the philosophy of life of the client and his or her cultural framework. This sharpens the worker's ability to be effective because it also provides information on the effects of racism that may be vital in understanding a minority client. Furthermore, the worker's probes and questions about a client's culture and experiences are suggestive of the worth ascribed to the culture and client. Resultingly, the humanistic exchange is enhanced.

REMINISCING

Reminiscence is a technique that denotes a humanistic approach while serving to assess the behavior and needs of the client more extensively. As noted by Kaminsky (1978), reminiscing by the elderly was often viewed in the past as indicative of approaching senility. However, Butler (1963) has shown that reminiscence can be a positive coping mechanism for the elderly, serving a variety of purposes, and Pincus (1970) has depicted how an elderly client's reminiscence offers important assessment clues to the worker. The goals of treatment can be more clearly specified "after an accurate assessment of the psychosocial problems which are revealed in and through an individual client's particular use of reminiscence" (Kaminsky, 1978, p. 26). Other recent work on the Mexican-American aged and the use of reminiscence delineates its effectiveness in surfacing painful or unresolved experiences with racial discrimination (Zuniga-Martinez, 1982).

Moreover, it strengthens the client/worker relationship, as it allows the worker to obtain insights on how clients perceive themselves, relative to their past experiences, sense of satisfaction, and accomplishments. It also offers the opportunity for life review that elucidates how effectively the client is striving for closure (Kaminsky, 1978).

TASK GENERALIZATION

Intervention with minority elders requires flexibility of workers because their responsibilities might need to be generalized as individual circumstances dictate. In illustration, administrators of the Apache Tribal Guidance Center, a mental health agency in Arizona, initiated a visitation program for elderly Apaches residing in predominantly white nursing homes (Cooley, Ostendorf & Bickerton, 1979). The center sponsored transportation on a monthly basis because of the extensive distance relatives had to travel. As a result, displaced Apace elders were assured of a meaningful bridge between themselves and their culture. Workers took on transporting, facilitating, and linking responsibilities to provide needed cultural and familial inputs to these aged: They performed nontraditional treatment tasks to meet Apache elders' cultural needs within the predominantly Anglo nursing·home.

CASE MANAGEMENT AND PATERNALISM

Workers employing the case management approach must also wear a variety of hats. Monk describes case managers as individuals who act as permanent consultants or facilitators in behalf of their clients.

> Case management individualizes the client. The relationship between the case manager and his or her client is a unique and personal one, and the process of case management itself is based on a proactive and holistic view of the elderly client (1981, p. 63).

The case management approach involves the worker's intervention at differing levels of need, often simultaneously, while performing roles in a flexible manner dictated by the client situation (Compton & Galaway, 1979).

Monk (1981) describes the importance of case management being a process that supports a client's goal-oriented behavior and personal responsibility. As with any approach, case management embodies certain shortcomings or dangers: Workers may easily become paternalistic, especially with clients who are more dependent or who require protective services.

I believe that paternalistic practice with minority elders often stems from expectations that unduly anticipate greater dependency on the part of these clients. Such expectations may be racist in character or, in contrast, may result from the worker's efforts to prove he or she is not racist and can like or help a minority person. Although this latter form may be more well meaning, it also is intolerable. Paternalism is incompatible with humanistic intervention, whatever its form or source.

COMMUNICATION

Because the initial contact must reveal one's humanism, the interaction should begin by following the ritual expected in each respective culture. However, certain rules of thumb are common. As previously indicated, one shows respect by addressing the client with a title (Mr. or Mrs.) and last name, rather than attempting to be folksy by using first names. For Mexican-American elderly, the use of first names by a stranger, especially one that is younger, denotes disrespect. Nakao and Lum (1977) have reported similar findings in their study of Chinese clients. Traditionally, Anglos have had accessibility to minority persons' first names, but have expected to be addressed by their last names as a sign of respect or deference (McNeely & Badami, 1983). The use of formal names demonstrates to the minority aged that one is according them respect.

In research done on Mexican-American elderly in San Jose (Torres-Gil, 1976) and San Diego (Zuniga-Martinez, 1980), the experience of sharing information about one's self and family was found to inspire client trust, with the result of enhancing cooperation.

Particularly if the worker is a minority person, clients are likely to be interested in information about one's parents, why they came to this country, if they were immigrants, and so on. Conversely, the practitioner may obtain information, utilizing a comfortable conversational style, by discussing pictures or objects in the room in regard to children, relatives, and circumstances. In short, the critical factor is to humanize the relationship. Impersonal businesslike styles are unlikely to enhance cooperation.

This orientation is similar to the "Platica" research method (Valle, 1974) used in the cross-cultural study of minority aged in San Diego, California. Dukepoo (1980) describes its use with Native-American elders whose mistrust and emphasis on noninterference (Goodtracks, 1973) might result in their being characterized as more difficult to reach. Attributes of the Platica method are embodied in the statement below:

> First, the interview is seen as an interaction which has all the trappings of a beginning interpersonal relationship. . . . Second, the strategy builds upon an open discussion approach, a format that allows development of trust and confidence on a conversational and mutual exchange basis. Third, within this kind of interviewing, the research focus is first of all on the human exchange aspects and secondarily on the information to be obtained. Fourth, the maintenance of the relationship-oriented conversational approach is seen as continuous throughout the total interview. Fifth, the strategy includes the incorporation of observational techniques . . . wherein the interviewer observes the living surroundings and environmental interactions of the interviewee. . . . Sixth, at all points of the interview, the interviewer secures the consent of the interviewee to obtain information on an ongoing basis as appropriate throughout the interview process (Dukepoo, 1980, p. 9).

Finally, the importance of working with minority aged within their own homes cannot be stressed enough. This is another leveling factor in the relationship because the worker must follow the ground rules of the home in which he or she is a guest. Home visitation is also very helpful during the assessment period for determining if and how observable environmental and familial variables affect the client.

Other aspects of communication that are relevant focus on the issues of eye contact, nonverbal cues, and touch. First, attempt to be seated in a manner that is comfortable for conversation. This might entail using space to ensure that the client is not overwhelmed by the practitioner's presence by sitting too close, sitting in a threatening position, or hovering over them if they are bedridden.

Second, use of eye contact and nonverbal cues should be sensitive to clients' culturally linked preferences. For example, some minority aged perceive a direct eye-contact style to be confrontive, disrespectful, and aggressive. Levine and Padilla (1980) recommend that workers should not attempt to maintain eye contact with a Hispanic who tries to avoid it. McNeely and Badami (1983) point out that very direct eye contact may be interpreted by Blacks as a confrontation cue. Brownlee (1978) notes that on the Papago reservation, the practice of averting one's eyes is the accepted norm, while continuous direct eye contact might be viewed as a rude form of staring. Puerto Ricans tend to avert their eyes from a speaker to show respect (Lewis, 1966). Japanese-Americans tend to prefer similar patterns of eye contact and evidence concern for status-oriented conversational interaction. Self-effacing behavior that underpins some communicative traits for Japanese-Americans is based on norms that are related to modesty, a disavowal of power or personal aggrandizement (Johnson, Marsella, & Johnson, 1974).

Some of these distinct communication styles might be misinterpreted by Anglos to evidence boredom or slyness, thus confusing their efforts to intervene across racial lines.

One must evaluate the use of touch with the minority elderly carefully. Touching appears to be a common phenomena among Hispanics (Levine & Padilla, 1980). For example, when pairs of Anglos, Blacks, and Mexican-Americans were examined, it was found that Mexican Americans touched one another at significantly higher levels than either Blacks or Anglos (Baxter, 1970). Thus, another important task for the worker is to determine when body contact or physical closeness between individuals is allowed, prohibited, or expected amongst the different cultural groups (Brownlee, 1978). However, there may be occasions when the human denominator of pain may override cultural differences and an outreached hand, a touch on the arm, or an actual embrace may be the only appropriate human response.

ACCULTURATION FACTORS

Acculturation is defined as "the process of selective diffusion of traits customs, beliefs, values, and behavior that occurs when two previously autonomous cultural traditions come into continuous first hand contact and with sufficient intensity to promote extensive change in one or both" (Woods, 1975, p. 28). Practitioners cannot ignore assessing the extent to which minority elders have become acculturated to Western values and preferences. While Blacks may not have a distinct language that is commonly used, and are the products of a variety of African and other heritages, they do manifest different levels of adherence to within-group values that contrast sharply with Anglo cultural preferences. The assessment of acculturation is, therefore, as appropriate for this population group as it is for those who retain their native language.

Assessment of acculturation is important because it offers the worker some notion of the extent traditional values are of importance to the client and thus gears interpersonal interaction to that cultural level. For example, one may need to be more formal and concerned with cultural cues with a less acculturated client. In addition, when considering practice options, knowledge of acculturation also allows one to identify resources that are suitable to the client. For instance, someone who is not proficient in English may need to receive services in their native language. Or someone who does speak English, but still adheres to a traditional style, may be more comfortable with culturally senstive services.

In assessing acculturation, one uses common sense along with an awareness of factors identified in the literature on acculturation. Obviously, the preference not to speak English is likely to be a strong indicator of other native cultural preferences. Other factors identified as predictors of traditional values among Mexicans include contact with the native country, preference for ethnic food and music, education in Mexico, foreign-born status, Mexican ethnicity of friends, and Mexican name preference (Zuniga-Martinez, 1980). Significant indicators for Native Americans include the preference for reservation versus urban living, and the identification of self based on tribal affiliation rather than race (Dukepoo, 1980).

With regard to Japanese-Americans, a general assessment may be based on the way generations are classified. The immigrant first generation are the Issei, who would be the most traditional. The second generation are the Nisei, or children of the Issei. The third generation are the Sansei, or grandchildren of the Issei. The term *Kibei* refers to the Nisei who were sent to Japan to be educated. Kibei tend to be more culturally conservative than their Nisei counterparts, and more often maintain fluency in the Japanese language. However, the loss of language facility among the Japanese does not imply loss of traditional values (Green, 1982).

In a similar vein, changed cultural values via acculturation can be earmarked for second-, third-, and fourth-generation American-born Chinese. Thus acculturation measurement for this group would include the delineation of generational status, and whether or not the individual is native or foreign-born (Green, 1982).

For Blacks, who may be more assimilated, factors such as income, education, occupation, length of residence in a neighborhood or city are also important variables for consideration. Higher occupational status, income, and education could imply greater resources as well as deepened acculturation.

Finally, information on the length of U.S. residency or length of time in a neighborhood (Zuniga-Martinez, 1980) may be directly related to the elders' ability to utilize such support systems as neighbors, friends, church, or social organizations.

Workers need to be sensitive to these factors in identifying acculturation levels. Assessments should include observation, indirect questioning, and possibly some direct questions to clarify cultural preferences. Awareness of acculturation levels helps to insure implementation of culturally syntonic interventive choices.

SUMMARY

This practice section has attempted to delineate the importance of family systems, cultural factors, and racism in working with the minority elderly. Humanistic practice methods such as the use of reciprocity and reminiscence were depicted as undercutting these elders' fear, distrust, and resistance resulting from their experience with racial victimization. Although the case management intervention approach was viewed as useful, certain caveats were offered for consideration. Emphasis was placed on cultural factors, particularly as they relate to communication preferences in effecting relationship building, and their relevance in determining intervention options. The objective has been to make services for aged minorities more meaningful and to address their needs more fully.

REFERENCES

Baxter, J. Interpersonal spacing in natural settings. *Sociometry*, 1970, 33, 444-456.

Brownlee, A. *Community, culture, and care*. St. Louis: C. V. Mosby, 1978.

Butler, R. The life review: An interpretation of reminiscence in the aged. *Psychiatry*, 1963, 20, 65-76.

Chen, P. Continuing satisfying life patterns among aging minorities. *Journal of Gerontological Social Work*, Spring 1980, 2.

Chestang, L. Environment influences on social functioning: The Black experience. In P. Cafferty & L. Chestang (Eds.), *The diverse society*. Washington, DC: NASW, 1976.

Clark, M. *Health in the Mexican American culture*. Berkeley: University of California Press, 1959.

Colen, J., & Soto, D. *Service delivery to aged minorities: Techniques of successful programs*. Washington, DC: Agency on Aging, 1979.

Compton, B., & Galaway, B. *Social work processes*. Homewood, IL: Dorsey Press, 1979.

Cooley, R., Ostendorf, D., & Bickerton, D. Outreach services for elderly Native Americans. *Social Work*, March 1979.

Dukepoo, F. *The elder American Indian*. San Diego: Campanile Press, 1980.

Fromm, E. *The sane society*. New York: Rinehart, 1955.

Gallego, D. To provide or not to provide services for minority elderly. In E. P. Stanford (Ed.), *Minority aging: Policy issues for the 80's*. San Diego: Campanile Press, 1981.

Gil, D. *Unraveling social policy*. Cambridge, MA: Schenkman, 1973.

Goodtracks, J. Native American non-interference. *Social Work*, November 1973, 30-34.

Green, J. W. (ed). *Cultural awareness in the human services*. Englewood Cliffs, NJ: Prentice-Hall, 1982.

Hall, C., & Lindsey, G. *Theories of personality*. New York: John Wiley, 1979.

Jackson, J. J. *Minorities and aging*. Belmont, CA: Wadsworth, 1980.

Johnson, F., Marsella, A., & Johnson, C. Social and psychological aspects of verbal behavior in Japanese-Americans. *American Journal of Psychiatry*, May 1974, 131,5.

Kaminsky, M. Pictures from the past: The use of reminiscence in casework with the elderly. *Journal of Gerontological Social Work*, Fall 1978, 1, 19-32.

Langston, E. Kith and kin: Natural support systems; Their implications for policies and programs for the Black aged. In P. Stanford (Ed.), *Minority aging: Policy issues for the 80's*. San Diego: Campanile Press, 1981.

Levine, E., & Padilla, A. *Crossing cultures in therapy*. Monterey, CA: Brooks/Cole, 1980.

Lewis, O. *La vida*. New York: Random House, 1966.

Lowy, L. *Social work with the aging*. New York: Harper & Row, 1979.

Lum, D., Cheung, L., Cho, E., Tang, T., Yau, H. The psychosocial needs of the Chinese elderly. *Social Casework*, February 1980, 100-106.

McNeely, R. L., & Badami, M. K. Race and communication in school social work. *Social Work*, (in press).

Mendoza, Lydia. *The servidor system*. San Diego: Campanile Press, 1981.

Monk, A. Social work with the aged: Principles of practice. *Social Work*, January 1981.

Nakao, S., & Lum, G. *Yellow is not White and White is not right: Counseling techniques for Japanese and Chinese clients*. Unpublished Master's thesis, University of California, Los Angeles, 1977.

Pincus, A. Reminiscence in aging and its implications for social work practice. *Social Work*, 1970, 15 (3), 47-53.

Solomon, B. *Black empowerment: Social work in oppressed communities*. New York: Columbia University Press, 1976.

Torres-Gil, F. *Political behavior: A study of political attitudes and political participation among older Mexican Americans*. Unpublished Ph.D. dissertation, Brandeis University, 1976.

Trader, H. Survival strategies for oppressed minorities. In B. Compton & B. Galaway, *Social work processes*. Homewood, IL: Dorsey Press, 1979.

U.S. Senate Hearing. *Availability and usefulness of federal programs and services to elderly Mexican Americans* (Part 4). Washington, DC: Government Printing Office, 1969.

Valle, R. Amistad. *Compadrazgo as an indigenous network compared with the urban mental health network*. Unpublished Ph.D. dissertation, University of Southern California, 1974.

Valle, R., & Mendoza, L. *The elder Latino*. San Diego: Campanile Press, 1978.

Woods, Clyde. *Culture Change*. Los Angeles: W. C. Brown, 1975.

Zuniga-Martinez, M. *Los ancianos: A study of the attitudes of Mexican Americans regarding support of the elderly*. Unpublished Ph.D. dissertation, Brandeis University, 1980.

Zuniga-Martinez, M. The Mexican American family: A weakened support system? In E. P. Stanford (Ed.), *Minority aging: Policy issues for the 80's*. San Diego: Campanile Press, 1981.

Zuniga-Martinez, M. Reminiscence theory and Mexican American aged: Practice issues. Paper presented at the 28th Annual Western Gerontological Society Conference, San Diego, 1982.

22

Group Services for the Minority Aged

HISASHI HIRAYAMA

Groups appear to be a particularly useful tool for work with the minority aged for several reasons. First, similar to other elderly persons, the minority aged have needs to associate and share their thoughts, feelings, and past and present experiences with people of similar backgrounds. Second, they have needs to share their ethnic and cultural heritages with their cohorts as well as with younger generations. Third, their ethnic identity and natural consensus-seeking group behaviors may lend themselves to the formation and operation of groups.

It is not sufficient for social workers to work with the elderly solely in formally organized groups. It is particularly important to extend interventions and working relationships to the elderly's microenvironments, strengthening support systems at home and in the neighborhood. To do so, workers must develop an understanding of the particular minority community in question, including its values, patterns of interpersonal relationships, problem-solving mechanisms, and how support systems operate. Without this knowledge, the worker may act contrary to the interests of clients by unintentionally disrupting, rather than strengthening, whatever informal support systems exist. Numerous opportunities to use existing natural groups, such as families, extended families, or informal neighborhood groups of the elderly, tend to be overlooked as valuable mediums for service delivery. Thus it is important for workers to learn to use various techniques of working with intergenerational groups of grandparents, grandchildren, extended family groups, and others.

GROUP SERVICES FOR CLIENT NEEDS

The minority elderly may be classified into three different groups based on their patterns of service utilization:

(1) The first group is comprised of those who can benefit from group services at neighborhood centers, health clinics, social clubs, congregate dining programs, and various other forms of day programs. These individuals tend to be physically, mentally, and socially capable of taking advantage of the available services and can enjoy new relationships and developmental group programs.

(2) The second group is comprised of those who are prevented from benefitting from the available programs because of access factors. Lack of transportation, a language barrier, a physical handicap, poor health, illegal immigration status, or cultural traits all are factors that may discourage participation. This group's activities and support systems are pretty much centered on their neighborhood, for example, visiting friends, neighbors, family members, and nearby stores.

(3) The third group involves those who are institutionalized in such places as nursing homes, mental institutions, and boarding homes. The contrast between a home environment and that of a nursing home unquestionably poses problems for all who must stay in a home, but to the minority aged it usually poses special problems because of cultural and/or language barriers. Residents often become isolated and withdrawn as they are unable to cope with a variety of unfamiliar institutional and interpersonal demands.

For the elderly who are physically, mentally, and socially capable of taking advantage of various programs, group services make significant contributions. At present, numerous group activities are being run under different organizational auspices. The objectives of these groups are to provide opportunities for socialization, development, education, and support. One example is senior citizens' centers which have been established throughout the nation. The centers provide a balanced program of social group work, recreation, physical education, and adult education. The emphasis has been, by and large, on human relationships whereby the elderly are helped to preserve their ability to function in the community and their horizons are broadened through virtually every conceivable form of activity. Most programs provide opportunities for passive and active participation, self-government, and continuing nourishment of special interest groups and club activities (Euster, 1977).

In recent years, agencies have begun to provide more comprehensive programs and services. Some have been designed as multipurpose senior centers. These centers frequently offer low-cost meals, individual counseling, health screening, and health maintenance. It is possible to develop objectives other than socialization and recreation. One example is a problem-solving group whose function is the development of better health care. The program includes physical excercise, nutrition, cooking, discussions with physicians and nurses, and improving the use of health care facilities (Hirayama & Vaughn, 1980).

A variety of innovative and experimental approaches have been tried in order to remove barriers to service utilization experienced by the second group and increase their participation in social and health care services. One very common approach is to bring services closer to the elderly by establishing ethnically oriented centers in the heart of minority residential areas. This approach has shown considerable success in improving service delivery and has helped to increase participation by the elderly.

In community-based settings, groups may play a prominent role as a natural medium for service delivery, and offer several advantages. For example, information related to the availability of services and how and what to do to obtain them may be dispensed in groups. Misconceptions about eligibilities and value conflicts and resistance to approaching agencies may be resolved in group processes. Importantly, facilitation of a mutual aid system among members encourages their individual self-determination.

Much has been written about the use of groups in institutional facilities (see Burnside, 1971; Katz, 1976). Many reports are concerned about the use of groups to stimulate residents' participation in interpersonal activities (see Hulicka, 1963; Unger & Kramer, 1968; Katz, 1976). Various writers have indicated that participation in activities and general interaction with the environment constitute appropriate therapy for these aged (Hoyer et al., 1974; McClannahan, 1973). McClannahan and Risley (1974) discuss the importance of engagement with the environment and list consequences resulting from a lack of activity, such as a slowing down of bodily processes, muscular atrophy, and the permanent loss of social relationships. A variety of stimulative techniques have been demonstrated (Burnside, 1971; Saul & Saul, 1974; Linsk, Howe, & Pinkston, 1975). However, although the infusion of culturally relevant programming is of particular importance, most studies have not differentiated between clients' backgrounds, have assumed that the needs of the elderly are homogeneous, and that individuals respond equally to certain methods, regardless of racial and cultural backgrounds.

One exception is reported by Cooley, Ostendorf, and Bickerton in their discussion of Apache elderly placed in nursing homes located hundreds of miles from their reservation homes. They point out that:

> Most Apaches are bilingual but use Apache as their primary language. Many elderly Apache rely heavily or exclusively on the use of Apache and, when confronted by an all English-speaking environment, predictably become withdrawn because they feel isolated. The physical environment likewise contrasts sharply with the relatively simple laissez-faire atmosphere of the reservation. Mass institutional feeding, grooming, and toileting schedules, and other forms of regimentation are especially foreign. The foods are strikingly different and unappealing in contrast to the traditional diet. In short, the elderly Apaches are displaced from their lifelong homes into an alien environment with foreign demands and expectations and without a usable language [1979, p. 151].

In order to bridge the deep cultural gap between the institutional environment and Apache home environment, the Apache Tribal Center initiated a visitation project for Apaches housed in Phoenix-area nursing homes. Initially, the project involved transporting relatives to and from Phoenix for a two-day visit a month. Subsequently, the project was expanded to include regular scheduled visitation by Apache-speaking mental health workers. These workers bring the latest gossip from the reservation and answer questions about friends or events from the home community. Finally, the project was expanded to include group gatherings that included a number of cultural activities for Apache residents.

SELECTED GUIDELINES
FOR THE GROUP WORKER

CULTURE-SPECIFIC BEHAVIOR

There are certain unique psychosocial and cultural traits of the minority aged that the worker must be aware of when he or she attempts to work with the elderly in groups. By and large, the effectiveness of group work depends upon the amount of sensitive attention the worker is capable of giving in group process to these unique traits. Consequently, the success of the worker's influences and activities is related directly to his or her knowledge and acceptance of a given culture, its formal and informal systems, and its norms. For example, Lewis and Ho (1975) report that using the group to pressure American Indian members who are late or silent will not only jeopardize and shorten the group's existence, but increase alienation and withdrawal from future activities.

Solomon has divided the activities of the helping process into four categories: (1) establishing rapport, (2) establishing the practitioner's expertise, (3) assessing accurately the client's strengths, and (4) establishing the client as a causal agent in achieving a solution to the presenting problem. She states that rapport is extremely difficult to achieve among Blacks and whites because it requires willingness to let people know what you think, feel, or want. Specifically:

Self-disclosure is likely to occur only in the context of trust and blacks have had little reason to trust whites as a consequence of the racism which has effectively poisoned their relationships (Solomon, 1976, p. 316).

Difficulty in establishing rapport is likely to occur with members of other minority groups. At one time or another during their lifetimes, elderly minority persons have experienced a bitter and antagonistic relationship with whites. They generally have little reason to trust whites. For example:

The historical treatment of American Indians provides some basis for their suspiciousness of Anglo people in "authority roles." On occasion, Indian clients have been "promised" results that were not obtained, or they have misunderstood the procedures, "promises," or role of the professional person. These misunderstandings may lead to suspiciousness, mistrust, and reluctance to become involved with other professionals [Edwards & Edwards, 1980, p. 449-450].

Establishing rapport with clients is crucial in group work. However, the difficulty may be more pronounced in certain regions where racism and remnants of racial segregation still exist. For example, a group of Black elderly with chronic illnesses was organized and led by two young social work students, one Black and one white, in a southern city. In the meetings, group members called the Black worker by her first name and the white worker by his last name, as Mr. So and So. Despite that worker's repeatedly asking them to call him by his first name, they simply refused to do so throughout the six weeks of group sessions. In general, the group members approached him with polite friendliness, but definitely kept social distance from him.

The social worker should not expect Asian-American elderly group members to express their deep emotions and feelings. At best, it will take a long time until they really feel comfortable doing so in a group. Thus it is very important for the worker to approach a group of clients with the utmost sensitivity and respect.

Expressing one's strong emotions and feelings, particularly negative ones, is not one of the cultural traits passed on by Asian tradition. The worker should not pressure them to express such feelings and should avoid using confrontation techniques in group process. Furthermore, openly asking for help from strangers, including the social worker, is not socially acceptable behavior for many elders.

Group consensus and cooperation are very important for many Asian-Americans. This writer's observation of one case of decision-making by elderly Japanese group members is illustrative. Initially, the members were asked to choose a chairperson who would facilitate group discussion. It took 30 minutes to achieve consensus in choosing a discussion leader! Members of other ethnic groups might be able to arrive at consensus sooner. However, going through all the rituals of polite status recognition, role definition, and representation is extremely important for Japanese elders. There was no way the group could have shortened the process.

In addition, the image held by Japanese of the term "group leader" is different from the concept often held by Westernized individuals. For example, the development of group cohesion based on group consensus is far more important than an individual's outstanding performance in the group. The group leader plays the role of a spokesperson who articulates the will and consensus opinions of the group members without trying to influence formation of that will.

Shared decision-making has also been emphasized among members of many American Indian tribes.

Group consensus was valued by most Indian tribes. Many meetings, discussions, and "powwows" were lengthy because American Indians strove for group consensus, not majority rule, in the decision-making processes that would affect the majority of Indian people [Edwards & Edwards, 1980, p. 498].

Consequently, the value that many American Indians continue to place on consensus can be used readily in forming the basis of sound group work practice.

Newton (1980) emphasizes the importance of *personalismo* among Mexican-American elders. They prefer patterns of social intervention wherein individuals relate to each other as whole persons. Vital concepts include *orgullo* (pride), *dignidad* (dignity), and *respecto* (respect). Polite conduct is the norm, with each person honoring the other's *dignidad* by demonstrating *respecto*. Purely impersonal or contractually based interaction is unlikely to be well received.

GETTING STARTED

When working with the minority aged in groups, the worker must assume major responsibility for organizing, convening, and guiding the members, the group process, the discussion, the activities, and the flow of ideas and emotions (Hartford, 1976). The notion that it is enough to get old persons together in a group and that something good will happen with little guidance is erroneous. The social worker must be clear as to the purpose he or she intends to achieve through the group and should remember that he or she is trying to form and develop a group with people who are fearful, skeptical, suspicious, and reluctant about participating in a group. Particularly during the developmental stage of groups, members need a good deal of direction, encouragement, and stimulation from the worker.

Obviously, there are certain criteria for the composition of any group, based on the group and its purpose. Mayadas and Hink state,

Prior to deciding whether a person should be in a group, the worker must determine the level of attraction of the person for groups per se and specifically for the group (in terms of interpersonal relationships and group goals) he is being invited to join [1974, p. 441].

There are groups with informal and open membership that meet for indefinite times, such as activity or program-centered groups at senior citizens centers; on the other hand, others are more formal, time-limited, closed membership groups, whose focus may be on certain problem-solving activities. The type of group to which one belongs should be fitted to the nature of one's individual preferences.

ETHNIC AND RACIAL COMPOSITION

If the group is going to be mixed ethnically and racially, workers should consider a balance of membership. Davis (1979), for example, has suggested after his study on the racial composition of groups that Blacks as well as whites exhibit resistance to being "greatly outnumbered," that members of both races are more inclined to share intimate information with persons of their own race, that the number of members from a single racial group should not exceed 60% of the total, and that the use of biracial leadership must be considered. Davis also supports Hartford's (1976) suggestion that racially integrated groups are best kept task focused, because the potential for racial conflict is lessened when biracial group members are attempting to complete a task. It is heightened during personalized examinations of one another. Decisions concerning what language may be used in group meetings, for example, English, Korean, or Spanish, must be made prior to the initial group meeting. The worker should remember that for many minority elders, use of their own ethnic language becomes a decisive factor in the formation and participation in groups (Sotomayor, 1977).

TRANSPORTATION

The availability of transportation to and from homes and meeting places often plays a crucial role in the success of any group meeting. Because of slowed physical and mental reactions, intolerance to long waiting on street corners, bad weather, or lack of car fare, the elderly will not and often cannot use public transportation to attend weekly meetings regularly. In addition, if the worker wishes to reach out to the elderly who have physical handicaps or who reside in seclusion, door-to-door pick up service is facilitative.

ATTENDANCE

A degree of dropping-out and absenteeism should be anticipated. Some members are bound to become ill, hospitalized, or even die. Unless they are prepared and flexible, workers may have trouble in handling these kinds of losses in their group, and it is usually harder for younger workers to appreciate the sense of loss experienced by older persons.

Working with elderly individuals who are ill, physically handicapped, or poor, demands far more active participation of the worker in many areas of the group members's life. Continuing participation of group members obviously requires a good deal of effort on their part. The worker must give close attention to meeting the individual needs in and out of the group in order to help group members fulfill their contract to attend the group meetings regularly, thereby maintaining group cohesion (Hirayama & Vaughn, 1980).

DEPENDENCY VERSUS EMPOWERMENT

Workers must be aware of risks associated with creating excessive client dependency. The elderly, particularly those who live alone, tend to develop a stronger dependency on the worker once they believe that the worker cares and is willing to help. The worker must keep in mind that creating excessive dependency not only defeats the purpose of the group but can be very damaging if service is terminated. One way to prevent this is for the worker to keep his or her attention on the tasks that the members are to perform by encouraging individual members to assume responsibility within the group. The worker tries to facilitate decision-making and problem-solving abilities in both the individual and the group as a whole.

Dancy (1977) is critical of social workers who show a crippling over solicitude of the black elderly. He attributes some of this behavior to historically paternalistic attitudes or guilt feelings. An overprotective practitioner will contribute to any existing feelings of dependency and helplessness.

Solomon proposes empowerment as a goal of social work practice with minority persons. Empowerment is "a process whereby persons who belong to a stigmatized social category throughout their lives can be assisted to develop and increase skills in the exercise of interpersonal influence and the performance of valued social roles" (Solomon, 1976, p. 6). Empowerment in group process enables members to maintain or enhance their self-esteem. It motivates use of their skills, individual resources, and group resources in the effort to achieve self- as well as group-determined goals. She identifies two roles for practitioners that are consistent with self-determination and, consequently, enhancement of self-esteem. These are the "resource consultant" and "sensitizer" roles.

The resource consultant role is defined as one who links clients to resources in a manner that improves their problem-solving capacities. This role is considered to be much broader than that of a resource dispenser who merely delivers tangible resources to clients. Workers may seek to justify their exclusive use of resource dispensation when they work with the very poor, ill, or frail elderly because it is less time-consuming. Solomon cautions that the provision of resources may be least helpful in achieving the goal of empowerment if such provision only serves to reinforce a sense of powerlessness and dependency.

The sensitizer is defined as one whose "role behaviors are designed to assist the client gain self-knowledge necessary for him to solve his problem or problems" (Solomon, 1976, p. 348). Many problems brought to agencies by the elderly cannot be solved by material resources alone. Thus the development of knowledge necessary for them to solve their presenting problems is an important ingredient in the helping process. Solomon elucidates this role by differentiating teacher/trainer functions assumed by the social worker from those of the traditional teacher. The teacher is concerned with the management of a learning process whose goal is the acquisition of knowledge related to growth and maturation or the development of special skills. The social worker, on the other hand, manages a learning process with much more specific aims, including the completion of tasks or the resolution of problems related to social living. In short, resource attainment requiring enhancement of clients' problem-solving capacities must be the workers' ultimate goal.

Groups can be particularly effective in providing opportunities for the worker to take on the consultant and sensitizer roles in attaining resources because the group provides opportunities for members to share ideas, information, and experiences, develop a sense of power and, concomitantly, self-esteem. Workers should seek to promote a sense of belonging among members, promote a sense of cooperation among the elderly, and encourage a feeling of achievement (see Mayadas & Hink, 1974). Gratification from task accomplishment is important and the worker should help select realistic goals where gratification is immediate and perceptible.

SUMMARY AND CONCLUSIONS

Working with the aged presents a challenge to social workers. Indeed, it is not easy for social workers to work with the elderly, regardless of race. A source of difficulty for social workers seeking to intervene across racial lines is the fact that minority elders are in double jeopardy, suffering from ageism and racism in American society. A large number of minority aged are both materially poor and poorly educated. Thus, social workers face not only generation gaps but also social class and educational gaps that become barriers to the development of relationships and communication. Another source of difficulty for social workers is the diversity of racial and cultural backgrounds presented by the minority aged. Problems and needs of the minority aged are not alike. Thus social workers are compelled to develop an understanding of the unique psychosocial and cultural traits of each ethnic group.

Service needs of the minority aged continue to be greater than any other population group. Hence, social workers must continue to search for new and innovative ways to provide more and better services to the minority aged. Reaching out to thousands of the elderly who are desperately in need of services, but have not yet been a part of the service system, is particularly important. Groups may certainly play a valuable role as a medium for service delivery.

REFERENCES

Ackley, H. Group meetings with men on old age security. In N. Fenton & K. Wiltse (Eds.), *Group methods in the public welfare programs*. Palo Alto, CA: Pacific Books, 1963.

Ackley , V. Group meetings in a home for the aged. In N. Fenton & K. Wiltse (Eds.), *Group methods in the public welfare program*. Palo Alto, CA: Pacific Books, 1963.

Burnside, I. M. Group work with the aged: Selected literature. *Gerontologist*, 1970, 10, 241-246.

Burnside, I. M. Long-term group work with hospitalized aged. *Gerontologist*, 1971, 11, 213-218.

Cooley, R., Ostendorf, D., & Bickerton, D. Outreach services for elderly Native Americans. *Social Work*, 1979, 24, 151-152.

Dancy, J. *The Black elderly: A guide for practitioners*. Ann Arbor: University of Michigan, 1977.

Davis, L. Racial composition of groups. *Social Work*, 1979, 24, 208-213.

Edwards, E., & Edwards, M. American Indians: Working with individuals and groups. *Social Casework*, 1980, 61, 498-506.

Euster, G. Direct services to the aged. In L. Baumhover & J. Jones (Eds.), *Handbook of American aging programs*. Westport, CT: Greenwood Press, 1977.

Hartford, M. Group methods and generic practice. In R. Roberts & H. Northern (Eds.), *Theories of social work with groups*. New York: Columbia University Press, 1976.

Hirayama, H., & Vaughn, H. *Reaching out to alienated chronically ill Black elderly through groups at inner city primary health care centers*. Paper presented at 1980 Symposium on Social Work with Groups, Arlington, Texas, November 20-22, 1980.

Hoyer, W. et al. Reinstatement of verbal behavior in elderly mental patients using operant procedures. *Gerontologist*, 1974, 14, 149-152.

Hulicka, I. Participation in group conferences by geriatric patients. *Gerontologist*, 1963, 3, 10-14.

Katz, M. Behavioral change in the chronicity pattern of dementia in the institutional geriatric resident. *Journal of the American Geriatric Society*, 1976, 24, 522-527.

Lewis, R., & Ho, M. Social work with Native Americans. *Social Work*, 1975, 20, 379-382.

Linsk, N., Howe, M., & Pinkston, E. Behavioral group work in a home for the aged. *Social Work*, 1975, 20, 454-463.

Mayadas, N., & Hink, P. Group work with the aging. *Gerontologist*, 1974, 14, 440-445.

McClannahan, L. Therapeutic and prothetic living environments for nursing home residents. *Gerontologist*, 1973, 13, 425-428.

McClannahan, L., & Risley, T. Design of living environments for nursing residents: Recruiting attendance of activities. *Gerontologist*, 1974, 14, 236-240.

Monk, A. Social work with the aged: Principles of practice. *Social Work*, 1981, 26, 61-68.

Newton, F. Issues in research and service delivery among Mexican American elderly: A concise statement with recommendations. *Gerontologist*, 1980, 20, 208-213.

Saul, S., & Saul, S. S. Group psychotherapy in a proprietary nursing home. *Gerontologist*, 1974, 14, 446-450.

Solomon, G. *Black empowerment: Social work in oppressed communities*. New York: Columbia University Press, 1976.

Sotomayor, M. Language, culture, and ethnicity in developing self-concept. *Social Casework*, 1977, 58, 195-203.

Unger, J., & Kramer, E. Applying frames of reference in group work with the aged. *Gerontologist*, 1968, 8, 51-53.

23

Evaluating Programs Serving the Minority Aged

ROBERT O. WASHINGTON

Human services programs designed to meet the needs of the minority aged have failed largely because they do not respond to the culture and lifestyles of minority recipients (Rogers & Gallion, 1978). As a result, the myriad programs, public and private, operated to serve minority elderly are used less frequently by the minority aged than the elderly population in general (Bell, 1975; Davis, 1975; Fujii, 1976; Torres-Gil, 1977). The consequence of this situation is that the extended family and its network among minority groups tend to provide most of the care and services to its aging kin (Simpson, 1981; Martin & Martin, 1978; Stack, 1974; Eribes & Bradley-Rawls, 1978).

Most community-oriented aging programs are administered by middle-class-oriented whites. The minority elderly are often alienated by the middle-class-oriented activities, particularly leisure-time activities conducted by these programs (McCarley, 1981; Lawton, 1978; Jackson, 1973). In the sense that these programs do not attract the clients for whom they are designed, they have failed. The National Advisory Council on Aging noted,

> Examination of public and private programs aimed at human betterment has shown that many of them fail because they do not understand recipients' culturally determined attitudes, beliefs, and values. Programs designed for married, affluent, white, urban Americans are sometimes barely workable; when the same programs are applied, unchanged, to the poor, the widowed, members of minority groups, residents of rural areas, or citizens of other countries, outcomes are predictably disappointing [Haber, 1978, p. 1].

The report also noted that program planners should not ignore cultural factors in designing programs for the aged because (1) aged populations are extremely heterogeneous (in terms of education, class, race, income, health, and so on), and (2) aging itself is a cultural, as well as biological, process. "Culture invests the aging process with particular meanings and defines the appropriate relationship of the aged to themselves, to others, to social institutions, and to their environment" (Haber, 1978, p. 2).

Other reports suggest that the manifest differences in class and lifestyles between the minority and nonminority elderly that in turn frequently reflect the differences of tastes and interests also account for low utilization of out-of-home human services.

Perhaps the most important reason why minority elderly do not use services is because they do not know that they exist.

Simpson notes, "Information about the programs is usually featured in local newspapers, but illiteracy is high among older Blacks, particularly in rural areas, where half of the elderly Blacks live" (1981, p. 46). This situation, coupled with the fact that older persons rarely travel outside of their own neighborhoods (Carp & Kataoka, 1976; Kalish, 1975), offer persuasive evidence as to why services are underutilized.

A STRATEGY OF EVALUATION

The proposition to be derived from the foregoing is that an essential goal in evaluating programs serving minority elderly should be to measure the extent to which these programs and services are organized, structured, and administered in such a way as to effectively reach those for whom they are intended. This measure may be designed in the form of an adequacy of performance index. A second goal should be to measure the extent to which such programs and services afford the minority elderly an opportunity to improve their lifestyles and life chances, in other words, to gain mastery over their respective environments. Such a measure may be constructed using an evaluation paradigm that defines a state-change relationship. Such a paradigm is built upon a design in which (1) the target for change[1] is identified, (2) there is a measurement of its state before introduction of the program, and (3) there is a measurement of the state (measures of change) after completion of the program.

These two themes will be developed as the major approaches to evaluating programs and services to the minority elderly. However, before proceeding, I would like to establish some basic definitions and decision rules common to any systematic evaluation process.

EVALUATION DEFINED

Evaluation is defined as a systematic process of determining the significance or amount of success a particular intervention had in terms of costs, benefits, and goal attainment. It is also a process that assesses adequacy of performance, the appropriateness of the stated goal, the feasibility of attaining it, as well as the value or impact of unintended outcomes.

This concept of evaluation is used because it emphasizes the state-change relationship between the intervention and the outcome and the assumption that human services programs are goal directed and respond to validated needs. Through program evaluation, the decision maker seeks to determine, first, whether or not the program was carried out in accordance with the prescriptions set forth in the planning and development stages, and, second, whether or not it worked. As the definition implies, evaluation also helps the program administrator to ascertain whether the expenditure of resources has been efficient in comparison with alternative means of achieving the same goal and the extent to which the need has been reduced by the introduction of the intervention.

PURPOSE OF EVALUATION

Using this line of thinking, the primary purpose of evaluating is to collect data in order to make decisions about (1) planning and policy development, (2) management and administration, (3) fiscal and performance accountability, and (4) effective service provision.

(A) PLANNING AND POLICY DEVELOPMENT

A major function of evaluation is to help decision makers decide whether to continue, modify, expand, or eliminate programs or program services. Therefore, five major evaluation questions related to planning and policy-making ought to be as follows: (1) Are comprehensive services available to those who need them? (2) Are they organized in such a way as to reach effectively those for whom they are intended? (3) Are there needs that are not being served? (4) How can service delivery systems be modified to be as comprehensive, accessible, and responsive as required? (5) Is there a continuum of services adequate to meet the requirements of a particular category of need or problem?

An illustration of evaluative data used for planning and policy development is the 1977 Report to the Congress by the Comptroller General on home care services compared to institutionalization. The report concluded,

Until older people become greatly or extremely impaired, the cost of nursing home care exceeds the cost of home care including the value of the general support services provided by family and friends. However, for the greatly or extremely impaired, the value of services provided by family and friends becomes a dominant factor in their care and well-being. Thus, those greatly or extremely impaired elderly who live alone are the most likely to become institutionalized. The Congress should consider focusing on jobs to be created to assist the sick and elderly under the President's welfare reform proposal to those elderly who live alone and are without family support.

Planning and policy development are sometimes referred to as *strategic planning*, which includes the process of policy formulation, goal setting, and resource allocation. It generally includes some form of needs assessment and determines the operational goals of the organization and the policies and strategies that will govern the acquistion, use, and disposition of resources to achieve these goals. When evaluation is used for this purpose, it includes the formulation of a mission statement that describes or prescribes the ideal or reason for existence of the organization. It also expresses the value frame of reference as well as the philosophy of the organization. The mission statement provides the parameters within which policies and priorities for operation are established and may include specifications of practice, physical facilities, fiscal arrangements, legislative proposals, and so on. It may also include specifications of resources to be allocated to each target group and their expected effectiveness. Allocation is achieved by taking into account at least three criteria: the size of the respective target group, the needs of the group, and the estimated cost-effectiveness of the best services for helping each type of recipient.

Existing statements of policy and goals should be examined by the evaluator not only because they reflect the organization's mission, but also because they set forth the conditions under which the acquisition, use, and disposition of resources to achieve program goals will be carried out. A review of organizational policies will also give the evaluator a better understanding of requisite staff competencies and personnel needs.

(B) MANAGEMENT AND ADMINISTRATIVE DECISIONS

Evaluations are also undertaken in order to assess the adequacy of staff, site, and facilities; to judge the appropriateness of program goals; to identify ways to improve the delivery of services; and to measure compliance.

In the case of compliance, evaluators are concerned with financial integrity as well as legislative compliance. They are particularly concerned with (1) whether financial operations are properly conducted, (2) whether the financial reports of the program are presented properly, and (3) whether the program has complied with applicable laws and regulations or with the guidelines or mandates of the sponsoring organization. The evaluator also collects data about whether the program is carried out in accordance with the prescriptions set forth in the planning and development stage.

Some people refer to this form of evaluation as program monitoring. Program monitoring may be distinguished from evaluation in a strict sense in that monitoring rarely questions the relevance or the rationale of the program. It begins with a predetermined model that describes how the program should be administered. It is usually conducted on an ongoing basis while the program is still in operation. It seeks to respond to questions about the extent to which procedures and practices need to be modified in order to conform to an original plan or to operate more efficiently. It involves on-site visits and focuses upon whether the staff measures up to predetermined qualifications. Monitoring also seeks to determine if the administrative hierarchy and table of organization as planned are operative, if proper reporting forms and procedures are being used as planned, and if services are being provided as originally conceived. It should be remembered that, while on-site monitoring can generally be implemented immediately, it is sometimes difficult to develop objective standards to use in assessing program operations.

In the case of measuring adequacy of staff, site, and facilities (organizational competence), the evaluation seeks to determine (1) whether the program is managing or using its resources (personnel, property, space, and so on) in an economical and efficient manner, and (2) the causes of any inefficiencies or uneconomical practices, including inadequacies in management information systems, administrative procedures, or organizational structure. The basic questions to be answered here are, Do the benefits justify the costs, and are there more efficient means of achieving the same goals? Assessing program efficiency is related to measuring how economically the program accomplishes its goal. The efficiency criterion is usually applied when there is need to make some changes in the allocation of resources. This may include changes in the amount allocated, the combinations of resources allocated, and purposes for which resources are allocated, and timetables for allocation, procedures of allocation, and the criteria for allocation.

Garnett, Goldberg, & Lowenthal (1981), in their report of the evaluation of a drug therapy facility, illustrate the use of evaluation data for management and administrative decisions. The objectives of this study were to establish a model for the implementation of clinical pharmacy services in extended care facilities, set guidelines to determine the priority of selecting residents for evaluation, develop procedures for the evaluation of residents and for presentation of recommendations to physicians, and document the effect of consultant pharmacy services on drug therapy.

Using guidelines generated for geriatric patients, a clinical pharmacist made 138 recommendations in a two-month evaluation of 48 long-term residents. Of the 80 recommendations submitted to the attending physician, 17.5% were drug related, 50% were disease-management related, and 32.5% were dispensing related; 11 recommendations were considered significant to resident care.

This is a specific illustration of an evaluation study focused upon administrative decisions. However, since most evaluation studies focus upon measurement of organizational competence, the reader should be able to find others in any text on program evaluation.

(C) FISCAL AND PERFORMANCE ACCOUNTABILITY

Accountability evolves from a relationship in which some one or group in authority delegates to another the responsibility for providing certain services in exchange for certain compensation, benefits, or incentives. For most human services focused toward the minority aged, authority rests in some legislative body, legislative mandate, or governing group. Accountability assumes the existence of an agreement that the authority has been designated and accepted by one party to perform certain activities on behalf of another; for example, a contract agency providing chore services under Title XX. It assumes consensus as to the criteria by which performance will be measured, and expectations are stated in the form of some contract or compact.

Program evaluation focused upon performance accountability ought to answer the questions: (1) What did you do and how well did you do it? (2) What difference did the intervention make? and (3) How accountable is the program to its constituents? In other words, decision questions relative to performance seek to determine whether the program worked. This aspect of evaluation requires data about the recipient of services, service delivery structure, process flow, and measures of effectiveness.

Measures of fiscal accountability seek to determine the fiscal soundness of the program. Traditionally, evaluations of human services programs have not given adequate attention to fiscal operations. The scandals relative to mismanagement of funds and poor fiscal procedures among human service programs during the War on Poverty era are well known. This author has been involved in the evaluation of certain programs in which record keeping was so poor that it was impossible to conduct a fiscal audit. In some cases this condition was premeditated; in others it occurred out of sheer ineptness.

With the growing scarcity of resources, program evaluators are required more and more to address issues of productivity and accountability. An important contribution the evaluator can make is to suggest steps that would provide assurance that transactions are properly authorized and accurately recorded, and that an appropriate accounting is made of funds.

The federal government frequently sponsors evaluation studies that measure the fiscal soundness and effectiveness (plan versus performance evaluation) of aging programs. During the 1960s, cost-benefit analysis was an often-used technique for evaluating health care programs. Cost-benefit analysis later lost some of its glamour because of its inability to quantify psychic and consumption benefits.

(D) EFFECTIVE SERVICE PROVISION

The bottom line for most human services programs for the minority aged is effective services. Indicators of effectiveness are improved social well-being, individuation, and responsiveness and availability of services.

When we talk about human service provision and human services planning, we frequently use the term human resources development. This term is important in program evaluation because it implies a capital investment in people. We define human resources in terms of people. Our social values dictate that human resources should be maximized and conserved. Therefore, the ultimate goal of effective human services provision is to conserve and maximize human resources. This concept is very important to the evaluator because very often the *worthwhileness* or the *effectiveness* of a given program is measured in terms of the extent to which social well-being is improved.

The focal point of effective service provision must be the individual in need. This means that the way in which services are organized and delivered must be congruent with the social and cultural ethos of the recipients. Therefore, the service provider and the evaluator must know something about the history and ethos of the minority group. The administrator must know in order to make the service individualized and responsive to the minority aged's lifestyle. Evaluators must know for the same reason; in addition, they must know in order to judge what constitutes satisfaction and social well-being for the minority aged. They must also know in order to assess the extent to which services respond to *validated needs* among the minority aged.

This is a very important principle in evaluating services to the minority aged because needs differ among minority and ethnic groups, and they change over time and with changing aspirations. The evaluator cannot assume that the needs of the general aging population are identical to the needs of a specific minority group at any given time.

The longitudinal study carried out by the Andrus Gerontology Center of the University of Southern California and the Westat study, both conducted in 1974, are examples of studies focused upon measures of service effectiveness. Both studies funded by the Administration of Aging (AOA) focused upon the effectiveness of local area agencies on aging and their ability to improve service delivery.

BASIC TOOLS OF EVALUATION

Any evaluation paradigm seeks to answer questions related to at least the following: (1) *Effectiveness*—Did any change occur? Was the change the one intended? Here emphasis is upon measuring results. (2) *Significance*—Here concern is upon impact and the meaningfulness of the outcome. It relates to such questions as: Will the achievement of the goals contribute to the economic development or social well-being of the people served? Does the achievement of program goals contribute to the stated mission and to what extent? Are goals soundly conceived or appropriate in terms of needs? What are the program's advantages over possible alternatives? And what are the spillover effects? (3) *Efficiency*—Is the cost reasonable, and do the benefits justify the costs? To answer these questions, Evaluators have the entire arsenal of social research techniques and tools available to them. These include survey methodology, the use of questionnaires and interview techniques, observation, ratings and scales, statistics, content analysis of documents and existing records, research designs, and so on.[2]

AN EVALUATION MODEL

This brings us back to the central theme of this chapter. That is, the two important approaches to evaluating human services programs serving minority elderly should be (1) to measure the extent to which these programs and services are organized, structured, and administered in such a way as to effectively reach those for whom they are intended; and (2) to measure the extent to which these programs and services afford minority elderly an opportunity to improve their life styles and life chances—gain mastery over their respective environments.

An underlying premise is that other program evaluation techniques—for example, cost-benefit analysis, and the like—do not adequately take into account sociocultural factors that influence client satisfaction and culturally defined measures of effectiveness and efficiency.[3] Also implicit in these two models is the assumption that program evaluation strategies should give equal attention to input, process, and outcome evaluation techniques and should not give greater weight to one over the other. Another assumption is that input and process data are both essential to measures of adequacy of performance and that outcome evaluation provides information for measuring the state-change phenomenon.

In summary then, the evaluation strategy proposed for assessing programs serving the minority aged is one which may be depicted as in Figure 23-1.

The paradigm is built upon a three-stage evaluation of input, process, and outcome. Evaluators must incorporate measures of input into their strategy. While logically these constitute measures of the independent variables or intervention, they may at times obviate the need for any measure of the dependent variables or outcome, since a program with little or no input cannot, by definition, be producing results. They also clarify subsequent findings of changes in the dependent variables and provide an index of the efficiency of a program, which might be defined as the effect per unit of expenditure. For example, a program that produces a moderate effect for a small input may be better than a program that produces greater effects but at a prohibitive cost.

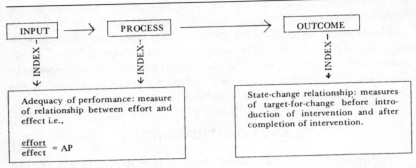

These are essentially qualitative measures which seek to answer the following questions:

1) How adequate is intervention in relationship to universe of need?

2) Is the program reaching right persons?

3) What is the impact of predisposing conditions upon process and outcomes?

4) How adequate is staff, site and facilities?

These are essentially quantitative measures which include a range of designs — from the highly rigorous classical experiment to the less rigorous correlational models. They seek to answer the following general questions:

1) What difference did the intervention make?

2) What is the amount, rate, nature, and direction of change?

3) Did intervention produce intended effect (outcome)?

SOURCE: U.S. Department of Health and Human Services, Health Care Financing Administration, "Long-Term Care: Background and Future Directions" (January 1981, p. 11).

FIGURE 23-1

Process evaluation is concerned with how and why an outcome was achieved, and it can have both administrative and scientific significance, particularly where the noted effects indicate that the program is not working as expected. Outcome evaluation focuses upon the terminal behavior of the recipient of services once the intervention has been made and therefore seeks to identify results.

The proposed evaluation strategy superimposes adequacy of performance and state-change criteria upon these three stages because the evaluator cannot always attribute outcome to a specific set of input variables without an understanding of process.

Following is a brief discussion of the three stages of evaluation and how they relate to the two sets of measures.

INPUT EVALUATION

The measurement of input focuses upon the degree to which the actual program resembles the proposed program, and the degree to which the program is organized to meet the needs of those for whom it was intended. This process also identifies program goals and independent variables (the ways in which goals are being implemented) and permits the comparison of baseline (before intervention) and postintervention data.

Input variables include such factors as the identifying characteristics of those receiving the intervention or service, administrative resources, the amount of effort staff exert toward the achievement of program goals, the nature and demands of the program components, the inherent characteristics of staff that affect their ability to carry out certain goals, recipient demands and aspirations, and the debilitating and facilitating features of the social environment in which the program is operating. All of these factors are important indicators of whether a program will reach the group toward whom it is intended.

The rationale for the use of input measures is that program impact cannot be measured unless program compliance is measured first. Since the two fundamental tasks of evaluation are to measure the extent to which the program has achieved its predetermined goals and to demonstrate that program outcomes can be attributed to the implementation of program inputs, an evaluation strategy that does not include measures of input should be considered methodologically inadequate.

Input evaluation makes an important contribution to decisions about how resources should be used to attain program goals. It does so by (1) identifying and appraising the potential of agencies and staffs, (2) comparing and analyzing possible strategies for achieving goals, (3) formulating designs for implementation, and (4) estimating immediate staff and other resource requirements and costs, as well as possible difficulties.

PROCESS EVALUATION

Process evaluation is an essential step in evaluating minority aging programs because outcomes cannot be measured unless the process of implementation is understood. Process variables include physical facilities; services offered; staff attitudes and characteristics, including occupational training; demographic aspects and behavior; administrative practices and policies; social norms; cultural ethos and other community attitudes and behavior that may affect the outcomes.

Measures of process seek to answer the question: What factors brought about change? They also provide data on the attributes of the program, the population exposed to it, the situational context within which the program takes place, and the effects the program produces.

Process evaluation allows program managers to review and possibly alter earlier decisions. It (1) detects malfunctioning in procedures or their implementation, (2) identifies the sources of difficulty, (3) provides information for program revision and improvements, (4) appraises adequacy of resources, (5) appraises site and facilities, and (6) projects additional resource requirements not originally anticipated.

OUTCOME EVALUATION

Outcome (or output) evaluation is a measure of dependent variables representing the behavior the client is expected to demonstrate at the completion of the intervention, improved life chances, and the extent to which the recipients of services have gained mastery over their environments. Outcome measurement also involves (1) identifying the correspondence of and the discrepancies between goals and attainments; and (2) identifying unintended results and suggesting possible causal factors.

Outcome evaluation seeks to measure change—that is, progress in the direction of a social ideal—and the relationship between input and outcome. It also provides data for (1) determining whether to change previous planning, input, and process decisions; (2) providing quality control through recycling the program to attain unmet goals; and (3) deciding whether to continue, modify, or terminate the program.

By way of summary, the important rule to remember from the foregoing is that a systematic evaluation requires measures of input, process, and outcomes. Expressed in terms of a set of linked evaluation hypotheses:

(1) If *inputs* then *process*.
(2) If *process* then *outcomes*.
(3) If *outcomes* then *purpose*.
(4) If *purpose* then *goal-attainment*.

A research design that expresses these hypotheses is depicted in Figure 23-2. It should be remembered however that the questions to be answered, funds available for the evaluation and how the evaluation findings will be used will determine the research design. Rossi (1972, pp. 47-48) suggests that there is a hierarchy of evaluation research designs that ranges from the most desired—the classical Fisherian experiments, to the least desirable—project and program administrators' narrative reports. When it is not feasible to employ the experimental design, softer techniques such as quasi-experimental models and correlational designs with statistical controls should be used.

Four principles guide us as to how high in the hierarchy of designs one should go in a particular evaluation study. First of all, when the evaluator wishes to measure massive effects of a particular program, softer techniques are just as good as subtle and precise ones. Second, if there is no noted effect when the program is evaluated by a soft method, then the program is not likely to show any noted effects when evaluated by harder, more precise methods. Third, when a soft method produces positive findings, a problem of interpretation occurs. In other words, soft methods require either follow-up using a controlled experiment or a sufficient number of replications that eliminate all doubts.

What is proposed here is a strategy of evaluation in which soft methods are used to eliminate ineffective projects and to detect potentially effective

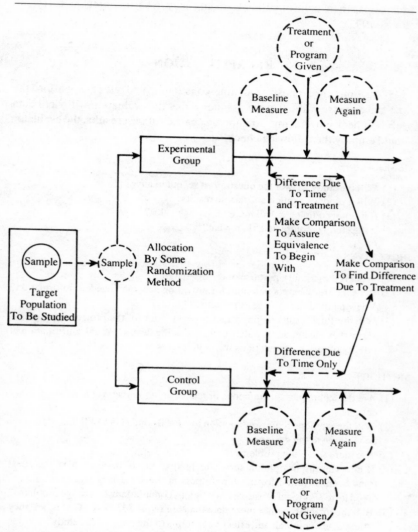

SOURCE: Reprinted from *Evaluation Handbook,* second edition, Office of Program Evaluation, USAID, MC 1026.1 Supplement II, Washington, D.C. 20523.

FIGURE 23-2

ones. Those found to be potentially effective then require further and more precise evaluation through controlled experiments or close approximations to such designs. Fourth, there are certain circumstances in which only correlational designs will yield information of use to decision makers. For example, if the desired effects are ones postulated to be the result of long-acting treatments, then controlled experiments may take too long to carry out (Rossi, 1972).

RECAPITULATION

Evaluations are expensive and time-consuming, and one cannot afford the time and expense without some assurance that the evaluation will yield data useful for decision-making. To improve chances of best results, the evaluator should employ the following checklist:

GENERAL

(1) Will the study answer the questions it set out to answer?
(2) Will it produce explicit and usable results?
(3) If it is not completed, will there be salvage value?
(4) If the study is completed, then what?

OBJECTIVES

(1) What is the primary purpose of the evaluation?
(2) Does the study have a potential for providing new (and needed) information? A new method? Technique? Procedure? Policy?
(3) Will the final results be important or significant for the project or program? Might they change some policy or way of doing things? Would confirmation of validity of earlier expectations warrant the cost of the study?

METHODS

(1) Are the techniques, instruments, or modes of inquiry appropriate to the study design?
(2) Will the methods require adaptation to a local condition? Will this adaptation do violence to the design?
(3) Are there sampling problems?
(4) If interviewing or opinion-survey techniques are to be used, have the questions been reviewed for meaningfulness in the local language and culture? Good taste? Political sensitivity? Religious connotation? Language problems?
(5) Will the methods gather more data than are required? Less? That is, are they efficient, economical, and effective in terms of the goals of the study?

DATA PROCESSING

(1) Are the procedures for the statistical manipulation of the data stated clearly? Is there a clearly conceived plan for the analysis that will be done once the data have been collected?
(2) Have statisticians or data processing experts been consulted regarding the program to be used?
(3) Are the analytical procedures likely to produce meaningful statements?

ANALYSIS AND INTERPRETATION

(1) Have a wide variety of potential findings been considered?

(2) Does the logic or design of the study permit clearly stated generalizations?

COSTS

(1) Are the dollar costs for the evaluation study reasonable for the various categories (personnel, travel, supplies, overhead, and so on)?

(2) Are there luxury or unnecessary items in the budget?

(3) Has the budget estimate omitted consideration of some item?

(4) Are the total costs proportional to the scope or importance of the study? Is the study worth the investment? Will the study cost more than its result might save?

CONCLUSION

This article has attempted to present an evaluation paradigm for evaluating programs directed toward the minority aged that is built upon two concepts. First, an approach that focuses upon measures of adequacy of performance and, second, one that measures changes in behavior and conditions of clients affected by the intervention.

The article assumes that all human services evaluations address one or more of the following four areas: (1) planning and policy development, (2) management and administration, (3) fiscal and performance accountability, and (4) effective service provision, and that the methodological tools and concepts available to the evaluator are essentially the tools and concepts of the social researcher. A major point of the article is also that certain tools and concepts are more useful than others because some are more sensitive to the sociocultural perceptions of minority clients regarding social well-being, effectiveness, and responsiveness of services. In other words, certain evaluation tools tend to lead to conclusions that define program benefits more in relation to the government and society than to the individual. Implicit throughout the article is the proposition that the evaluation of aging programs in general and those that focus upon needs of the minority aged specifically should focus less upon how the program outcomes contribute to an increase in the GNP but more upon how such programs improve individual social well-being and assist recipients in gaining mastery over their respective environments. In this instance, emphasis is far greater upon qualitative measures.

NOTES

1. The concept of targets for change is used to designate the target population or condition toward which a social intervention is directed. Targets for change are operationally defined as

(1) persons or groups who are regarded as either deviants or problem individuals or persons affected by problems or persons who are objects of undesirable activities or conditions; (2) professionals or other individuals who are functionaries of service delivery systems; and (3) physical objects or territorial units such as housing conditions, recreational facilities, or neighborhoods that are to be changed by the social intervention.

2. The reader may refer to any basis social research text for an elaboration of these tools and technology. For an extensive discussion of how selected research tools are used for program evaluation, see Washington (1980).

3. The author is a strong advocate of the position that most program evaluation designs used to assess aging programs and services do not give adequate attention to culturally determined indices of client satisfaction and program effectiveness. While any evaluation strategy implies measures of cost-efficiency, the primary focus of the evaluation of some aging programs and services such as nutrition, transportation chore services and others should be upon their *worth-whileness* rather than their efficiency of operation. For example, a Meals-on-Wheels program in which the service provider delivers only 20 meals a day, but spends time chatting and visiting with recipients may be considered inefficient when compared with another that delivers 50 meals at the same cost. But, since a secondary goal of the program is to reduce social isolation, the former program may be more worthwhile than the latter, and, in a sense, more effective.

REFERENCES

Bell, B. D. Mobile medical care to the elderly: An evaluation. *Gerontologist*, 1975, 15, 100-103.

Carp, F. M., & Kataoka, E. Health care problems of the elderly of San Francisco's Chinatown. *Gerontologist*, 1976, 16, 30-38.

Davis, K. Equal treatment and unequal benefits: The Medicare program. *Milbank Memorial Fund Quarterly*, 1975, 53, 449-488.

Eribes, R. A., & Bradley-Rawls, M. The underutilization of nursing home facilities by Mexican-American elderly in the southwest. *Gerontologist*, 1978, 18, 363-371.

Fujii, S. M. Elderly Asian Americans and use of public services. *Social Casework*, 1976, 57, 202-207.

Garnett, W. R., Goldberg, J. A., & Lowenthal, W. Implementation and evaluation of clinical pharmacy services in an extended care facility. *Gerontologist*, 1981, 21, 151-157.

Haber, P. A. L. (Chair). *Our future selves: A research plan toward understanding aging.* (Report of the Panel on Research on Human Services and Delivery Systems National Advisory Council on Aging, DHEW Publication No. NIH-78-1443). Washington, DC: Government Printing Office, 1978.

Kalish, R., Lurie, E., Wexler, R., & Zawadski, D. *On-Lok senior health services.* Final report, November 1975.

Jackson, J. J. *Proceedings of Black aged in the future.* Durham, NC: Center for the Study of Aging and Human Development, Duke University, 1973.

Lawton, M. P. Leisure activities for the aged. *Annals*, 1978.

Martin, E. and Martin, J. M. *The Black extended family.* Chicago: University of Chicago Press, 1978.

McCarley, L. *Differential perceptions of needs of the elderly upon organizational structures and administration of multipurpose senior centers.* Unpublished Ph.D. dissertation, Ohio State University, 1981.

Report to the Congress by the Comptroller General of the United States. *Home health—The need for a national policy to better provide for the elderly.* December 30, 1977. (HRD-78-19)

Rogers, C. J. & Gallion, T. E. Characteristics of elderly Pueblo Indians in New Mexico. *Gerontologist*, 1978, 18, 482-487.

Rossi, P. H. Testing for success and failure in social action. In P. H. Rossi & W. Williams (Eds.), *Evaluating social programs*. New York: Seminar Press, 1972.

Simpson, J. C. Prisoners of our silver ghettos. *Black Enterprise*, September 1981.

Stack, C. *All our kin*. New York: Harper & Row, 1974.

Torres-Gil, F. *Age, health and culture: An examination of health among Spanish-speaking elderly*. Paper presented at the Research Utilization Project/The Generation Connection, State Department of Public Welfare Conference, McAllan, TX, January 1977.

Washington, R. O. *Program evaluation in the human services*. Washington, DC: University Press of America, 1980.

About the Authors

Josephine A. Allen earned her Ph.D. in political science and social welfare administration and policy from the University of Michigan. She is Assistant Professor of Human Service Studies, Cornell University. Dr. Allen's current research focuses upon identification of the essential service needs of mentally disabled adults in nonmetropolitan communities. Her scholarly interests also include policy analysis in the areas of housing, income maintenance, and comparative welfare policy.

Elena M. Bastida earned her Ph.D. in sociology from the University of Kansas, Lawrence. She is Assistant Professor of Sociology at Wichita State University. Her major teaching areas include sociology of aging, sociological theory, and ethnic and race relations. Dr. Bastida's present research examines women's issues, focusing upon sociocultural definitions of illness and functionality among the ethnic aged.

Rosina M. Becerra earned her Ph.D. from the Florence Heller School for Advanced Studies in Social Welfare, Brandeis University. She is Associate Professor of Social Welfare, University of California, Los Angeles. Dr. Becerra is coauthor of the books, *Defining Child Abuse*, and *Mental Health and Hispanic Americans*, and a forthcoming reference volume entitled *The Hispanic Elderly: A Research Guide*.

John N. Colen earned his Ph.D. from the Florence Heller School for Advanced Studies in Social Welfare, Brandeis University. He is Dean and Professor, School of Health and Human Services, California State University, Sacramento. Dr. Colen's present research interests focus upon the identification of factors that enhance service delivery to the minority aged, and determination of factors that enhance the academic performance of minority pupils in public schools.

E. Daniel Edwards earned his D.S.W. from the University of Utah. He is Associate Professor of Social Work and Director of the American Indian Social Work Program at the University of Utah. His principal teaching areas are in social policy, institutional racism, and American Indian culture and life. He is a Yurok Indian from Northern California and the author of numerous articles in several areas related to American Indians, aging, and education.

Adam W. Herbert earned his Ph.D. from the Graduate School of Public and International Affairs at the University of Pittsburgh. He is currently Professor of Public Administration and Dean of the School of Public Affairs and Services at Florida International University. Dr. Herbert has held a variety of governmental service assignments, including appointments as a White House Fellow, Special Assistant to the Secretary of the U.S. Department of Health, Education and Welfare, and Special Assistant to the Under Secretary of the U.S. Department of Housing and Urban Development. He has held academic and administrative appointments at Virginia Polytechnic Institute and State University and at the University of Southern California. He was also director of research at the

Joint Center for Political Studies in Washington, D.C. His primary areas of research have been minority group political and administrative participation, applied management techniques, urban management, housing policy, and public policy analysis.

Robert B. Hill earned his Ph.D. in Sociology from Columbia University. He is Senior Research Associate at the Bureau of Social Science Research, which he joined in 1981. During the 1970s he served as the National Urban League's Director of Research. Dr. Hill authored numerous works on the social and economic status of Blacks. Two of his monographs that highlight the important role of the Black aged in extended families are: *The Strengths of Black Families* (1971) and *Informal Adoption Among Black Families* (1977).

Hisashi Hirayama earned his D.S.W. from the University of Pennsylvania. He is Associate Professor of Social Work at the University of Tennessee, Memphis. Dr. Hirayama has published papers in the areas of aging, human sexuality, and mental retardation in both American and Japanese journals.

Barbara Jones Morrison earned her D.S.W. from Columbia University. She is Codirector of the Murray M. Rosenberg Applied Social Work Research Center of the Mount Sinai Medical Center in New York City and Instructor of Community Medicine (Division of Social Work) in the Mount Sinai School of Medicine. Dr. Morrison has published articles and monographs on ethnic factors in service delivery to minority children and minority aged, particularly those in long-term institutional care settings.

Paul K. H. Kim earned his D.S.W. in social welfare from Tulane University. He is Professor of Social Welfare and serves as Chairman of the M.S.W. graduate specialization in social gerontology, Florida International University. Dr. Kim is the author of numerous articles on social work and aging. He recently published a coedited book on the rural elderly.

Doman Lum earned his Ph.D. from the School of Applied Social Sciences, Case Western Reserve University. He is Professor of Social Work, California State University, Sacramento. He is the author of numerous articles on health maintenance organizations, ethnic minorities, suicide prevention, lay counseling and religion, and mental health. Dr. Lum recently published his second book on social work and health care policy.

John Lewis McAdoo earned his Ph.D. from the University of Michigan. He is Associate Professor of Social Work, University of Maryland at College Park. He has completed doctoral-level training in mental health epidemiology at Johns Hopkins University and also finished postdoctoral work undertaken at Harvard University. He has published several articles in the areas of aging and crime, parent-child interaction, and racial attitudes and self-esteem of Black children. Dr. McAdoo is involved currently in an examination of the morale and well-being of the aged.

R. L. McNeely earned his Ph.D. from the Florence Heller School for Advanced Studies in Social Welfare, Brandeis University. He is currently Visiting Professor and Director, Department of Social Work, Florida International University. He is on leave from the University of Wisconsin-Milwaukee where he is Professor of Social Welfare, School of Social Welfare, and Director of the UWM Center for Adult Development. Dr. McNeely is the author of numerous articles published in social welfare, sociology, and education journals focusing upon a variety of social development and other concerns. His book, *Race, Crime and Criminal Justice*, was published by Sage in 1981.

Gaylene Perrault earned her Ph.D. in ecological psychology from Michigan State University, and did postdoctoral research at Yale University. She has written articles on unemployment and various social policy issues. She serves currently as Director of Planning Research and Evaluation at Miami Mental Health Center.

Magaly Queralt earned her Ph.D. in education from the University of Miami. A Danforth Foundation Associate, she is Associate Professor and Coordinator, Human Behavior and Social Environment Sequence, Department of Social Work, Florida International University. Dr. Queralt's current research interests focus upon the role of mentorship in career development.

Gilbert L. Raiford earned his Ph.D. from the Florence Heller School for Advanced Studies in Social Welfare, Brandeis University. He is Associate Professor of Social Work at Barry University. He has had extensive experience as the director of several programs serving the elderly.

Nellie Tate earned her Ph.D. from the Florence Heller School for Advanced Studies in Social Welfare, Brandeis University. She is Associate Professor of Social Work, University of Tennessee, Memphis Branch. Dr. Tate is director of an interdisciplinary research project as part of her work with the University of Tennessee Health Sciences Gerontology Center.

Fernando Torres-Gil earned his Ph.D. from the Florence Heller School for Advanced Studies in Social Welfare, Brandeis University. He is Assistant Professor of Gerontology and Public Administration, Leonard Davis School of Gerontology, and a policy associate with the National Policy Center on Employment and Retirement, both at the University of Southern California. He was formerly a White House fellow and has worked as a special assistant to past Secretary Patricia Harris, Department of Health and Human Services. Dr. Torres-Gil is a founder of the National Hispanic Council on Aging. He has published in the areas of politics and aging, ethnicity and aging, and human services planning for the aged.

Ramon Valle earned his Ph.D. in urban studies from the University of Southern California. He is Professor of Social Work, School of Social Work, San Diego State University. Dr. Valle has published in several areas, including health, mental health, and minority aging. His current research interests focus upon examining the utility of social networks for the elderly.

Robert O. Washington earned his Ph.D. from the Florence Heller School for Advanced Studies in Social Welfare, Brandeis University. He is currently Dean and Professor, School of Social Work, University of Illinois, Champaign—Urbana. He is the author of numerous articles focusing upon evaluation research concerns and social development issues. Dr. Washington recently published his fifth book in the area of social policy.

Wilbur H. Watson earned his Ph.D. in medical sociology from the University of Pennsylvania. He is Edmund A. Ware Professor of Sociology, Chairman of the Department of Sociology and Anthropology, Editor of *Phylon*, and Director of the Center on Aging of Atlanta University. His most recent publications are *Aging and Social Behavior* (1982) and *Stress and Old Age* (1980). He is engaged currently in research on elder abuse and neglect, folk medicine and older women, and the need for body contact in human groups.

Shirley Wesley-King earned her D.S.W. from the George Warren Brown School of Social Work, Washington University. She is Assistant Professor of Social Work, University of Texas at

Arlington. She has published several articles and monographs in the area of minority aging that focus upon social service utilization and self-help groups. Dr. King is currently conducting two aging-related studies focusing upon elderly substance abuse and community linkages.

Maria Zuniga-Martinez earned her Ph.D. from the Florence Heller School for Advanced Studies in Social Welfare, Brandeis University. She is Professor of Social Work, California State University, Sacramento. Dr. Zuniga-Martinez has authored articles on the Mexican American aged and currently is coediting a book focusing upon social work practice with minority clients.